A DESPERATE FIGHT

A DESPERATE FIGHT

---◆---

THE LIVES OF
LOUISIANA'S
CONFEDERATE SOLDIERS

---◆---

HENRY B. MOTTY

LOUISIANA STATE UNIVERSITY PRESS
Baton Rouge

Published by Louisiana State University Press
lsupress.org

Designer: Kaelin Chappell Broaddus
Typefaces: Bulmer MT Std, text; MPI Gothic, display.

Cover photograph: Unidentified soldier in Confederate uniform and
Louisiana state seal belt buckle with musket. Liljenquist Family Collection,
Prints and Photographs Division of the Library of Congress.

Chapter 1 first appeared as "'The Trumpet of War Is Sounding': Louisiana's
Secession and State Loyalty," *Louisiana History* 61 (2025): 329-48.

Library of Congress Cataloging-in-Publication Data

Names: Motty, Henry B. author
Title: A desperate fight : the lives of Louisiana's Confederate soldiers /
    Henry B. Motty.
Description: Baton Rouge : Louisiana State University Press, [2026] |
    Includes bibliographical references and index.
Identifiers: LCCN 2025045768 (print) | LCCN 2025045769 (ebook) | ISBN
    978-0-8071-8615-2 (cloth) | ISBN 978-0-8071-8662-6
    (epub) | ISBN 978-0-8071-8663-3 (pdf)
Subjects: LCSH: Soldiers—Louisiana—History—19th century | Civilians in
    war—Louisiana—History—19th century | Louisiana—History—Civil War,
    1861–1865 | Louisiana—Social conditions—19th century | United
    States—History—Civil War, 1861–1865—Social aspects
Classification: LCC E565 .M68 2026 (print) | LCC E565 (ebook) | DDC
    976.3/061—dc23/eng/20251114
LC record available at https://lccn.loc.gov/2025045768
LC ebook record available at https://lccn.loc.gov/2025045769

for S., B., & J.

CONTENTS

Illustrations follow page 130.

ACKNOWLEDGMENTS

Special thanks are in order to the archival staffs at the following universities who assisted me in locating the manuscript collections central to this book: Louisiana State University, Baton Rouge; the University of Louisiana at Lafayette; Northwestern State University, Natchitoches; Southeastern Louisiana University, Hammond; and the University of North Carolina at Chapel Hill. I would also like to thank Raymond Allain Sr. for sharing a copy of his ancestor Alexander Pierre Allain's diary.

Rand Dotson at Louisiana State University Press was extremely helpful in answering my many questions and assisting me with getting this book published—I truly appreciate all the help. Several individuals had a hand in offering valuable critiques and constructive criticism. I would like to thank Gaines Foster and John Bardes for their help, insight, and valuable feedback with this project. Aaron Sheehan-Dean not only read and critiqued several versions of this work, but also kindly guided and mentored me in the historian's craft. I truly appreciate your patience, time, and valuable advice you offered me throughout all the stages of this work. Thank you.

My fascination with Louisiana history was first sparked by my eighth-grade Louisiana history teacher, Mrs. Trula Minvielle. Though she has passed away, I am forever grateful to her for being an outstanding educator who, several years ago, instilled in me a passion for wanting to know more about our great state's history (both good and bad)—and the value of learning from the past. I remember well her stories about Iberville and Bienville, Henri de Tonti, "Bloody" O'Reilly, Bernardo de Gálvez, Andrew Jackson's forces who defended New Orleans, and Louisiana's Civil War soldiers. My grandparents, especially my Pawpaw, who was a Korean War veteran, and my Mère, also had a hand in cultivating my fascination with the past through their many stories of their lives and experiences. They will never know the impact and impression they have left on me. My mom and dad have always been encouraging and believed in me in all my endeavors. Likewise, my wife and children continuously support me with their love and encouragement. Though they often tolerate the countless history stories I feel compelled to bestow upon them, they always remind me of what's most important.

A DESPERATE FIGHT

INTRODUCTION

Civil War soldiers and civilians lived intertwined and interdependent lives during the conflict. Gen. Robert E. Lee recognized the vital connection between soldiers on the front lines and civilians on the home front when he wrote in 1864, "They are one in reality & all for the Country."[1] Historians have conducted extensive research on the lives of Civil War soldiers, including their motivations for fighting, their wartime experiences, their perspectives on the conflict, and their transition back to civilian life. A second body of literature has explored civilians' roles and involvement, many of whom were women on the home front, and the various issues these individuals faced during the war. The distinction that some participants and many later historians drew between the battle front and home front often blurred as soldiers and civilians interacted in both realms. While historians debate the role and impact political ideology and Confederate nationalism and identity had on soldiers' motivation to go to war, it was their family and community ties that remained central to their wartime experiences. Confederate soldiers depended on civilian support and cooperation.

A soldier's defense of (and loyalty to) his community, which included his home and family, along with feeling a part of that community, sustained him through the war.[2] Indeed, nationalism and state loyalty existed and were intertwined with home defense; however, family and communal bonds, which centered on the Southern home, proved most powerful to motivating and sustaining a soldier to fight.[3] And civilians, too, remained committed to their sense of family and community as their relatives-turned-soldiers marched off to war. In *General Lee's Army: From Victory to Collapse,* Joseph T. Glatthaar argues that the local ties to the Confederacy's new military units "generated a powerful communal interest." Many Southerners who opposed secession eventually supported the Confederacy "simply because their children, relatives, and neighbors were suddenly in harm's way. With loved ones at risk, they could not turn their back on Confederate independence or the war."[4] This cooperative network between soldiers and civilians remained integral to a soldier's wartime experience, which both motivated—and more importantly—sustained him to fight.

Much of the present scholarship of Louisiana's soldiers focuses on unit histories, their actions in major engagements, or famous wartime commanders.[5] *A Desperate Fight* presents Civil War Louisiana through the lens of its soldiers and their experiences—and interdependence—with civilians. The vast majority of the state's defense forces came straight from civilian life, making their connections to and interactions with civilians so important. While separation between loved ones was common, soldiers and civilians did not endure the war in isolation, and the importance of the social bonds that developed between soldiers and civilians cannot be understated. Without civilian support and interaction, Confederate soldiers would not have been able to defend their new nation effectively.

Once in the army, Southerners retained many aspects of their civilian lives, especially as regimental companies often consisted of men from the same neighborhoods and parishes. Another relic of civilian life—electioneering—remained a fixed feature in the newly formed Confederate army, as many soldiers voted for their leadership at the company and regimental level. The military campaigning and the engagements that ensued shaped the world soldiers operated in, but it also affected civilians who had to deal with the destruction caused by such actions. Property damage or loss, the injury or death of a loved one, shortages of goods or trade items, which were confiscated or unavailable because of the loss of a territory or denied access to markets, were all issues civilians and soldiers alike contended with—their wartime experiences were inseparable.[6]

Indeed, soldiers fought battles near populated areas, which bear the names of a nearby town or city, such as Manassas, Gettysburg, Vicksburg, Franklin,

Baton Rouge, Mansfield, and thousands of others. Caught in the fray of active campaigning, civilians engaged in support roles by aiding wounded soldiers, burying the dead, and rebuilding communities. The fluid boundaries between the home front and battle front impacted and shaped the wartime relationships between soldiers and civilians. Suffering, both physical and psychological, equally plagued both groups, regardless of their proximity to the chaos of a battlefield. Mark A. Weitz notes that "In many cases battlefield and home front were the same place . . . even if the battlefield was not in one's own backyard, it was never far from home."[7]

Though I discuss wartime motivations, this is not a study of why soldiers fought the conflict. My work centers on the importance of soldiers' and civilians' relationships and interactions with one another and how these communal attachments and solidarity powered soldiers through the war. Personal and emotional relationships also lay at the heart of the conflict. Soldiers, the majority of whom intended to be *citizen* (not professional) soldiers, required civilian support, and many civilians who sympathized with the Confederacy expected their soldiers to protect and defend them. While the ideology of patriotism and nationalism motivated men to enlist, their civilian relationships provided a meaningful connection to their sacrifices—soldiers believed they fought to protect and defend their loved ones, along with their conceptions of civilian freedom, something they expected to enjoy after the war.

Based on the surviving military service records, Louisiana fielded between 56,000 to 65,000 men for the Confederacy, equaling nearly 16 to 18.5 percent of the state's White population. Overall, Confederate authorities organized at least 982 companies for military service, which included local home-guard units composed of old men and boys. Though a Louisiana soldier's wartime experience and duty station varied, nearly one-fifth of them died while in the service.[8] Of the state's parishes that fielded soldiers, Orleans Parish raised the most companies, with at least 208, followed by East Baton Rouge Parish, with at least 28. About 301 companies were raised in the parishes bordering the Mississippi River (over two-thirds came from Orleans Parish alone), and 86 companies came from the parishes bordering the Red River. Louisiana's Florida Parishes above Lakes Pontchartrain and Maurepas and east of the Mississippi raised at least 102 companies, and the state's Acadiana region (the southern part of the state west of the Mississippi River) raised nearly 111. Overall, north Louisiana's parishes fielded at least 217 companies, while southern Louisiana raised well over 400 (Note that some of these parishes fall into more than one category mentioned above and are counted in each estimation. For example, the Florida Parishes, while counted as a separate region, are also southern Louisiana Parishes, and the region also contains parishes that border the Mississippi River).[9]

Louisiana unit rosters reflect soldier diversity, sometimes displaying their prewar occupations and nationalities. For example, of the nearly thirteen thousand Louisiana infantry troops who served in Virginia, their backgrounds included clerks, planters, farmers, laborers, students, teachers, sailors, and Mississippi River boatmen. The number of foreign-born soldiers, who came from at least thirty different countries or territories, including a few men who claimed they were born at sea, was almost equal to those who originally hailed from Louisiana. Of these Louisiana companies heading to Virginia, over eighty came from New Orleans alone. Several parishes statewide were composed of the other companies, which included five raised from Catahoula, four from Rapides, and three from Pointe Coupee, St. Landry, and Jackson Parishes, respectively. The nearly other thirty parishes or cities that fielded troops for the Virginia theater contributed between one and two companies apiece.[10] However, Louisiana's residents' support for the Confederacy was never unanimous, and by the war's second year authorities pressed men into the ranks. John M. Sacher notes that based on existing records, the Confederacy conscripted at least 81,993 men into the army, which "admittedly is an undercount." Louisiana's conscription records also vary, but Sacher claims that "by the end of 1862 . . . 8,690 of the approximately 40,000 Louisianans in the armed service were conscripts."[11]

Though Louisiana's sons served the Confederacy in various theaters and capacities, they retained their Louisiana—and civilian—connections and identities. Even the famed Louisiana troops serving in the Army of Northern Virginia under Gen. Robert E. Lee remained *Louisiana's* Tigers. Military service did not erode their civilian connections—it strengthened them and often acted as a unifier. Even as many men came from different ethnicities or cultural backgrounds, soldier and civilian wartime encounters linked the men to a sense of community, which was not only representative of their home communities, but also of the new communities that formed (which often revolved around a camp) as Louisiana soldiers interacted with people far from home. Retaining meaningful contact with civilians and receiving aid from them not only proved vital to operations, but helped soldiers remain connected with individuals outside of the army.

Soldiers' interactions with African Americans—both enslaved and free—constitute another often overlooked aspect of Confederate military history. The political turmoil over the expansion of slavery into the nation's western territories brought on the Civil War. A desire to defend the "peculiar institution" from perceived threats from the Republican Party and the Lincoln administration inspired secession. By the time of the Civil War, Louisiana's enslaved population exceeded 331,000 individuals, which was nearly half of the state's population. But not all of Louisiana's Black population was enslaved, and the state's African American experience was unique compared with the rest of the nation. The war's onset in Louisiana saw a wave of Free Black volunteers for the state's militia, drawing on a military legacy dating back to the eighteenth century. Once Federal forces arrived in Louisiana, eventually establishing African American regiments, nearly twenty-four thousand Black Louisianians would find themselves serving as Union soldiers.

However, the largest contribution Louisiana's African Americans made to the Confederacy was through their forced labor—especially since enslaved laborers freed the South's White males for military service. For the plantations that remained intact during the war, their produce immediately became vital for the Confederacy. But enslaved people were also common sights in Confederate camps and fortifications as many Louisiana soldiers noted their presence and contributions. Like soldier records, precise numbers of enslaved people who labored for the Confederacy are scant, but across the South thousands of enslaved laborers contributed to the Confederate war effort.[12] Union statistics offer a better analysis, as one historian estimates that by the war's end between half a million to one million enslaved people reached Union lines, where "some 200,000–300,000 of whom would serve as noncombatant laborers." Contending with unwilling planters who disliked providing Confederate commanders with laborers also harbored problems for authorities, along with the fact that laboring near Union lines presented enslaved workers with opportunities to escape.[13] Some Louisiana soldiers, specifically enlisted men subjected to the discipline of military life, compared their wartime experiences to the bondage of slavery—especially since the institution remained visible within the army. The African American wartime experience in the context of their relation to Confederate White society was yet another thread linking soldiers and civilians.[14]

A Desperate Fight is divided into eight chapters. Moving thematically, each chapter discusses the Louisiana soldiers' experiences, specifically in relation to civilians (both at home and in their vicinity of operation), and how maintaining communal and familial ties remained an integral part of their military service. However, relationships between soldiers and civilians sometimes remained contested and enigmatic throughout the conflict, especially when contending with unpopular measures placed on residents by the Confederate government.[15] Though opinions and attitudes varied, soldiers quickly realized the importance of the civilian population to their military success. They also understood that civilian interaction would fulfill their human desires to connect physically and emotionally with others, especially those of the opposite sex. For individuals who remained on the home front, their support and encouragement to the men fighting the war proved invaluable.

Chapter 1 examines Louisiana's residents' debates and reactions to secession. Louisiana's withdrawal from the Union remained a lukewarm affair. This chapter highlights how residents negotiated secession (which was not unanimously supported) through their correspondence, personal records, and public dialogue. This social process (and debate) eventually produced a unifying factor for the men who eventually became Confederate soldiers. Since the overwhelming majority of Louisiana's soldiers arose from the home front, their connections to their home communities cannot be understated. Despite hailing from different regions within the state or having different cultural backgrounds, this communal—and familial—connection became vital to their wartime experiences.

Chapter 2 explores Louisiana's military organization, volunteerism, and recruitment within the early wave of patriotism that prevailed after the war began. Communal connections remained highly visible—and strong—as Louisiana's residents mobilized, especially when recruits hailed from the same neighborhoods and parishes. Though Louisiana's ranks reflected the state's diverse population, these men would soon experience and endure soldier life together. Their wartime experiences became a unifier as these diverse men retained their family, communal, and *Louisiana* connection. Civilian organizations did their part to foster familial and communal ties as they provided soldiers with the necessities needed to sustain them in the field. Wealthy planters, who often bankrolled and led newly formed regiments, also funded the unit and financed supplies for it. These civilian-made or donated items highlighted the cooperative bonds that existed between civilians and soldiers who deployed from or operated in their local communities.

Chapter 3 discusses the contested topic of conscription from the lens of how both soldiers and civilians viewed this coerced service. But communal and family ties—within the context of home defense—also remained visible amidst the draft, especially since many soldiers wanted to ensure their families and property remained protected in their absence. Women played a major role in home-front operations as conscription fostered a restructuring of Southern society.

Chapter 4 explores soldier and civilian camp experiences and the communal ties that remained vibrant within them. Camps, while often harboring what many onlookers and participants considered sinful activities and spreading disease and insect infestations, quickly became spaces for interaction and a middle ground for cooperation between soldiers and civilians. The camp experience also retained civilian elements, as soldiers attempted to incorporate civilian comforts to their new settings. Sometimes these encounters created problematic situations for both groups as the question of patriotic duty versus overreaching and confiscating private property and provisions by Confederate authorities caused some civilians to distrust or dislike the soldiers stationed near them. Despite officers' best intentions, Confederate camps remained somewhat porous, which helped cultivate communal ties between soldiers and civilians.

Chapter 5 offers insight into the physical interaction between soldiers and civilians, especially women, in a variety of settings, which included visits in camps and hospitals. Soldiers frequently visited hospitals; as one Louisianian told his mother, "I am a man of much experience, in all things pertaining to Hospitals, having been in them so often."[16] But hospitals did not just spring up once bullets and cannon balls started flying, and many soldiers found themselves in private homes receiving civilian care while battling illnesses or injuries. These types of encounters brought with them reminders of home and perhaps some hope of returning home. Keeping relatives informed of a wounded or sick soldier also formed relational bonds between soldiers and civilians. These physical encounters not only reminded soldiers of why they fought, but also reminded them of what they left behind. Soldiers also developed new relationships with the people who lived in their vicinity of operation. As one Louisiana soldier wrote his cousin from Mississippi, "I always want as many friends as I can gain and have neaver [*sic*] failed to gain them where ever I go."[17] For soldiers stationed far from home, the local population who lived near them became a source for companionship, encouragement, intelligence, and trade and commerce. Even campaigning soldiers on detached service found themselves in contact with sympathetic civilians, who sometimes offered them an invitation for a meal or shelter. And many civilians, both Black and White, performed numerous domestic services for the soldiers stationed near them.

Chapter 6 examines the importance of civilian contributions to supplying soldiers with military necessities—especially clothing and provisions. After New Orleans—the South's largest and wealthiest city—fell into Union hands early in 1862, Louisiana remained a front for conquest and trade. The rise in illicit trade, which caused problems for Confederate authorities, also displayed soldier and civilian cooperation (and dissent) as both groups participated in enemy trading to obtain needed (and sometimes luxury) goods. Familial and community ties remained visible between soldiers and civilians, and their engagement in wartime trading as these actions remained both contested and supported—especially in the name of survival. However, their actions in obtaining supplies, whether legal or illegal, benefited the Confederate war effort and allowed family members separated by war the ability to survive the conflict's economic woes. The sacrifices made by civilians linked them to the hardships their kin in uniform faced, especially the women whose husbands were off fighting. These women played a major role in physically and psychologically supporting their state's soldiers and bore much of the brunt of caring for their families—especially young children—without the aid or protection of a husband. They also managed their families' property and their interactions through physical encounters and correspondence provide evidence of how the conflict shaped their lives.

As many men marched off to war, Louisiana soldiers (at least literate ones) remained connected to their relatives and friends by relying heavily on correspondence for communication. Chapter 7 displays the psychological connection soldiers and civilians maintained in times of separation. Writing letters not only offered soldiers and civilians the ability to transmit information and news, but it also kept their social bonds tight as they expressed their private thoughts and emotions. But the written word sometimes proved a double-edged sword as it could offer both peace and solace or anxiety and fear about the well-being of a relative or friend.

The final chapter explores soldier and civilian interaction within the context of wartime violence. Civilians sometimes found themselves witnesses to, or participants in, the war's carnage—or its aftermath. The large-scale campaigning in Virginia and Tennessee is well documented, and the South's destruction throughout the war, which included parts of Louisiana, is also well known. Perhaps one of the most notable events of soldier and civilian interaction was Gen. William Tecumseh Sherman's march through Georgia and South Carolina aimed at destroying Confederate civilians' will to continue supporting the conflict—what one historian terms a "domestic war." The Union's strategy, which eventually shifted and developed into a "hard war" policy, aimed to disrupt Southern civilian abilities—and willingness—to support the rebellion.[18] But Louisiana, too, remained a contested region. Confederate forces also took and destroyed civilian resources, while government policies often placed the Confederacy's survival above individual rights. The longer armies operated in the field the more personal freedoms eroded for Confederate civilians and the more destruction occurred.[19] Even after General Lee's surrender at Appomattox, Union and Confederate troops remained in the state poised for (though not necessarily engaged in) action. It was not until several weeks later that the Confederate forces stationed here finally surrendered.[20] And, just like the war, the conflict's aftermath remained complicated—and a social experience.

Quotations by soldiers and civilians are left as they were found in the sources, even the spelling and grammatical errors. Occasionally some mistakes will be labeled using [*sic*] or corrected using [brackets] to signify misspelled or missing words or letters, but not always. Their words and punctuation, whether incorrect by modern standards, deserve to be shown as they described their opinions, their actions, and their experiences in their own way. Of the numerous individuals quoted throughout this work, the voices of five Louisiana soldiers who hailed from different regions within the state are frequently cited because of their keen observations of soldier life in relation to their fellow comrades and civilians. Though they were all educated (and some came from means or wealthy families), these men differed in marital status, prewar occupations, and social experiences.

From southwest Louisiana, Frank L. Richardson, an unmarried son of a St. Mary Parish planter and politician, served in three different Louisiana regiments in Tennessee, Kentucky, Mississippi, Alabama, and Louisiana. His personal correspondence to his relatives provides detailed insight into the common soldier's experiences. Richardson also gives an honest description about the role enslaved body servants had in Confederate camps, along with offering his opinions and feelings toward the cultural differences between Confederates who hailed from different states.[21] W. H. King, an Alabama (and Texas) transplant who served in the 28th Louisiana Infantry, kept a journal of his Trans-Mississippi theater wartime experiences, which were largely related to his time in camp. He critically unveils numerous topics relating to the soldier's life, such as camp discipline, conscripts and the draft laws, along with providing valuable insight to soldiers' experiences interacting with local civilians, including women.[22]

New Orleans militiaman H. A. Snyder offers an early look at the martial air that initially engulfed the South's largest city, along with his interaction with the wealthy and perhaps less committed citizen-soldiers of his militia unit, the Confederate Guards. Snyder, a New York native and married New Orleans grocer, also expresses the economic concerns he and other like-minded businessmen had over soaring prices and shortages. He turns down the opportunity for active Confederate service and eventually abandons Confederate militia duty and Louisiana.[23] Northwestern Louisianian John Coleman Sibley served in the 2nd Louisiana Cavalry and provides a detailed account of his military service in relation to his fellow Louisianians, both soldiers and civilians, Black and White. Sibley also records his wartime experiences through the lens of a concerned and loving husband and father. His diary and letters are both warm and heart-wrenching, as he honestly expresses his opinions and emotions about what he witnesses in camp and on the battlefield.[24] A young and single southeastern Louisianian, E. John Ellis, was a university student when he became an officer with the 16th Louisiana Infantry. Though largely recalling his wartime experiences from the confines of a Union prison camp, Ellis provides a descriptive account of soldier life, his interaction with fellow soldiers and civilians, and his gruesome recollection of his participation in the fighting in Tennessee.[25] Together, the importance of the wartime experiences and the communal bonds that developed between soldiers and civilians is what these Louisianians—and numerous others—aim to convey.

CHAPTER I

―――◦◇◦―――

LEAVING THE UNION

―――◦◇◦―――

In December 1859, Louisiana State Seminary of Learning and Military Academy's superintendent, William Tecumseh Sherman, took note of the nation's growing political tension and sectional crisis. "As long as the abolitionists and the Republicans seem to threaten the safety of slave property," he wrote, "so long will this excitement last, and no one can foresee its result; but all here talk as if a dissolution of the Union were not only a possibility but a probability of easy execution."[1] Within a year of Sherman's warning, Louisiana's secession convention organized and met in December of 1860. Many of these Louisiana politicians had little doubt as to their next move. In national politics, Louisiana Sen. Judah P. Benjamin defended secession to the US Senate on December 31, 1860. "We desire, we beseech you, let this parting be in peace," he exclaimed. As he spoke, he foretold his fellow Northern senators that "you may carry desolation into our peaceful land . . . but you can never subjugate us. An enslaved and servile race you can never make of us—Never! Never!"[2]

But not all Louisianians were enthusiastic about secession, nor did they all openly support it. As the Deep South followed South Carolina out of the Union, it was not with the support of an overwhelming majority of Southerners. Historians have documented these Southerners' reluctance to embrace secession, which included many Louisianians.[3] Chester G. Hearn notes that, out of Louisiana's free population of 376,280, only 20,448 votes went for the secessionists, while 17,296 went for Union candidates. He questions the plausibility of Louisiana's support for leaving the Union, claiming many of the pro-Union delegates "were obviously persuaded by their peers to repudiate those who had sent them to the convention."[4] Charles Dew also argues that Louisiana's secessionists' slim popular vote majority indicates that many Louisianians harbored serious doubts about the wisdom of secession as some state officials (and newspapers) questioned the election's narrow results. Serious consequences, especially the state's economic prosperity, could follow Louisiana's withdrawal.[5]

Many Louisianians who disapproved of secession did not publicly make their opinions known. Several residents discussed their true feelings about withdrawing from the Union through their conversations, personal correspondence or diaries, and public dialogue. It was this social process, which was not necessarily unconditional and involved numerous Louisianians' efforts, that produced a central unifying factor for these future Confederates. The sectional crisis was a local affair that unfolded at home. These residents were not oblivious or naive about secession's consequences, nor did they blindly follow their state's fire-eater politicians. Several Louisianians recognized the disastrous economic effects secession could produce, and many military-aged males understood the likelihood of an armed—and bloody—conflict in the wake of secession. But once Louisiana's politicians cast the secessionist die, many Louisianians, perhaps reluctantly, supported their state. Immediately following secession, many young men anticipated military glory; however, as the war continued and enthusiasm waned, Confederate Louisiana later demanded her sons' services.[6] The state's soldier population literally rose from the home front, reinforcing the familial and community ties that remained vibrant between these citizen-soldiers and civilians. It was this commitment and connection to their homes and communities that proved vital for their wartime success. For all Louisianians who became involved, the conflict proved to be— and remained—a social experience.

THE GATHERING STORM

As the excitement over secession intensified throughout 1860, unionist sentiment existed, as many Louisianians contemplated the rash and potentially dangerous action. Writing to a friend in New Orleans, Livingston Parish resident W. H. Pearce disapproved of the secession rumor, which "threatens the destruction of all that is valuable to us as citizens." Grieved over the political turmoil, Pearce injected his religious faith into the equation, stating that the secession crisis could be God's punishment for harboring rebellious spirits. "Can it be," he wrote, "that an Offended God has given us over to anarchy & confusion, that we may feel the consequences of our own folly?" Although he feared the Lord's judgment, Pearce also believed in God's mercy. The United States, he claimed, was "in a most remarkable degree a child of Divine Providence . . . that we have yet fulfilled our mission as a Political Power. I trust therefore, that God will again interpose in our behalf, & cause wise consuls to prevail." He further hoped that wisdom and discernment would guide the nation's political leaders to "stand in the breach till the People—both North & South—have time to reflect. It would be strange indeed, if after calmly & fairly estimating the cost, such a money-loving and pleasure-loving people should be willing to make the sacrifice."[7] He earnestly believed—and hoped—the Union would hold fast.

As Pearce soon learned, the nation's political leaders failed to compromise. Some people believed that the crisis emerged from the extremists on both sides; as one Northerner wrote to his cousin in Louisiana, "If there are fanatics among us, there as many with you. Those peppery leaders in S. Carolina, Calhounites, are as conceited, self-willed, unreasonable & ultra as the most violent of the Abolishionists." But, at least for this Northerner, the failure to compromise politically apparently originated from a greater intellectual force that was sweeping across other parts of the world. The brewing troubles between the North and South represented "the spirit of the age working out its fruits in all nations," he wrote, "in some by blood-shedding, in others it is done by legislation; it is seeking to Educate, & Elevate the masses; to Equalize & ameliorate the condition of mankind." This "progressive spirit" was steaming ahead throughout Europe and parts of Asia as "serfdom & involuntary labor in whatever form & name are gradually giving way," and "no where so fast as in our own country," specifically in the North.[8]

Henry Slack, a Northerner writing from New York to a relative in Louisiana, claimed, "The disasterous Effects of disunion to both sections of the country can not be Estimated." Though many Southern elites might have feared the demise of slavery, Slack stated that in his "mind the safety of the South and his peculiar institution is undoubtedly in the Union." He argued that abolitionists were the minority, and much of the hype over the Republican Party's growing power should not overshadow most Northerners, who were "friendly to the

South and its interests," he wrote. Further labeling "Every northerner as an abolitionist, will have the Effect to Estrange many who have stood up manfully . . . against the Republican party."[9] Despite these level-headed viewpoints, the country's political scene was polarized.[10]

Lincoln's ascension to the presidency alarmed many White Louisianians, who saw his administration as a threat to Southern liberties and slavery. One Jewish New Orleanian, Abraham Jonas, who had personal ties to Lincoln, wrote to the newly elected president to remain on guard as rumors circulated of extremists willing to take matters into their own hands. "You perhaps are aware that I have a very large family connection in the South, and that in New Orleans I have six children and a host of other near relatives" who kept him well informed. One correspondent notified Jonas of a plot conceived in New Orleans to assassinate the president.[11] Such extremism highlighted the great lengths at least a handful of would-be conspirators were willing to go based on fearful perceptions. Even Lincoln felt the national crisis was only led by a few radicals who had persuaded many of their neighbors to act irrationally. But to the fire-eater secessionists, the sectional tension over slavery and the perceived threat that the Lincoln administration aimed to meddle with it stirred fear and anxiety. Some Southern planters argued that Northern prosperity was possible because of the South's slave labor system. One merchant claimed it was the planters who bore the "enduring toils and privations of a backwoods life . . . bearing the odium of being slaveholders," while Northerners reaped "the lion's share of their labors, living in ease and luxury." To the planters who favored separation, secession would ensure that the wealth and prosperity created by their plantation system "with all the horrors of slavery upon it," would continue unmolested.[12]

Louisiana's plantation economy and the importance of slavery played a major role in the secessionist debate. Limiting the institution's expansion and existence threatened the White South's—and Louisiana's—economic prosperity, and the state's fate remained in the hands of the affluent (and slaveholding) Louisianians who aimed to protect their wealth. J. Matthew Ward notes that, to many of these secessionist elites, secession was both socially and politically motivated, which to them "reflected the divinely orchestrated order of society."[13] Within Louisiana's political arena, the "co-operationists" and "immediate secessionists" political factions held the state's future in the balance and drowned out many of the private concerns of residents. Though both factions supported secession, the co-operationists included many conservatives who sought compromises—and specifically constitutional amendments—for slavery's protection. Many of the co-operationists' protests about rushing to disunion had to do with fears of disrupting Louisiana's "material interests."[14]

One concerned citizen, Haller Nutt, a planter with large landholdings in both Louisiana and Mississippi, urged Judge Alonzo Snyder, a cotton planter and state senator from northeastern Louisiana, to attend the secessionist convention. "My object in writing you this is to say you must be a candidate—you must go to the convention. . . . I do not know your particular views in regard to the objects of the convention—but I know you so well." Trusting Judge Snyder's good sense and judgment, Nutt explained, "Disunion is inevitable—We can only differ in regard to point of time to decide. The commercial interests of N. Orleans are too important to take hasty steps without due reflection." Fearing suspensions of shipping and cotton sales, Nutt further urged Snyder's attendance and stated that if secession was Louisiana's only alternative, it could "join others at the last hour," but the state should "hold on as long as advisable."[15]

Because Louisiana's pro-secessionists remained a minority, some residents still hoped for a compromise. H. Safford wrote to his sister from Natchitoches, claiming, "Disunion sentiment passed through the country like an epidemic; the policy of the leaders was to press the election before the people had time to think; & . . . to bully all who were inclined to be moderate, & repress any expression of contrary sentiment." Despite Safford's claims of political intimidation, he noted that "there were some who saw the danger & acted; & it is wonderful how great a reaction took place throughout the State during the ten days preceeding the election." He hoped enough moderates would "serve as something of a check" and became active in promoting an anti-secession stance in his parish. "I wrote & rode & talked (not speechifying but reasoning with the people quietly, at their own firesides, & everywhere else where I met them)," claiming his actions were not unnoticed. The opposing camp "did not believe we had the audacity to oppose them."[16] Other Louisianians echoed Safford's desire to keep Louisiana in the Union. Iberville Parish planter Edward J. Gay explained that he and fellow residents "made a strong effort in our Parish to elect safe conservative men who would restrain hasty action in the Convention . . . and who would nurture every possible hope to preserve the Union."[17]

The only co-operationist delegate at the Louisiana secession convention who openly defied and protested the convention was James G. Taliaferro from

Catahoula Parish. He asserted that secession would not guarantee a lasting confederation—or cooperation—between the seceding states and would leave the South powerless with a weak government. He even stated his sincere belief that "secession will defeat the purpose it is intended to accomplish, and that its certain results will be to impair instead of strengthening the security of Southern institutions." As his protest continued, he argued that Louisiana's interests would best be served by aligning itself with the border states, "which nature has connected her by the majestic river which flows through her limits; and because an alliance in a weak government with the Gulf State east of her, is unnatural and antagonistic to her obvious interests and destiny." Although Taliaferro had sympathizers, no fellow delegates championed his stance.[18]

Unlike Taliaferro, several White Louisianians did not feel strong bonds holding them to the Union.[19] Though hopeful about remaining in the Union, Sarah L. Wadley, whose father and ancestors originally hailed from New England, wrote in the fall of 1859 that "the Union is but a name, there is no concord, no real heart Union any longer." According to Wadley, "The Abolitionists have sowed the seeds of dissension and insurrection among us . . . they would take away our freedom and give it to the negro. . . . We can no longer claim them as brothers." Her strong feelings were somewhat tempered, as she noted that "the North is not all filled with Abolitionists, there are some true hearts left."[20] In contrast to the co-operationists, immediate secessionists "pledged to act without co-operation or consultation."[21] One Plaquemines Parish sugar planter, Effingham Lawrence, proclaimed to a pro-secessionist group, "The duty of Louisiana and every citizen . . . is to stand and defend Louisiana through fire and blood if necessary."[22] Another sugar planter, A. Franklin Pugh, defended his and other fellow secessionists' views as he explained, "All honor to the men, who had the courage to take this first step, to prosperity which will be as permanent as earthly things may be."[23]

Some preachers also carried the immediate secessionists' banner; W. H. Pearce wrote, "I was sorry to see in Sunday's Delta a strong commendation of the of the Sermons of Drs. Leacock & Palmer on Thanksgiving-day on the ground that they advocate secession—The influence of such men when they became Partisans—and especially in such a case as this must be patent for evil." Though disgusted with the pulpit being used to further political division, Pearce hoped these preachers were "misrepresented" by the newspaper, claiming that "the Delta . . . misrepresents most things of a Political Character."[24]

Misrepresentation was all a matter of opinion, and many fire-eater preachers, such as Leacock and Palmer, spewed themed sermons that attacked abolitionism and defended slavery.[25]

In 1860, Louisiana's voters elected Thomas Overton Moore as governor. Moore stated in his inaugural address that "loyal as Louisiana is known to be to the Federal Union, it must not be forgotten that she is something more than a mere State of the Union," noting that Louisiana's position as a slaveholding state allowed it to take action against any hostilities toward the institution that were "guaranteed by the Constitution and protected by acts of Congress."[26] He initially used caution when dealing with disunion, but with Lincoln's political victory he sided with the secessionists. On the day the tally came in for the secession vote, the convention returns showed 113 to 17 in favor.[27]

Louisiana's withdrawal from the Union, which residents met with mixed emotions, sent shock waves across the state. Now the question of loyalty—to Louisiana, the newly formed Confederacy, or to the Union—was in the balance. "Our State was declared out of the Union yesterday at 2 oclock," wrote Louisiana planter Isaac Erwin. Secession was "a very important Matter for us all[.] now the questun is will we have sivil ware [sic] or Not[.]"[28] "I think it is too bad that you have seceded," wrote one Northern relative to her Louisiana cousin. Not fully knowing what was to transpire with secession, she asked, "Do you think we shall have a war?"[29] John Foster wrote to his grandmother about the unfolding events, explaining, "We are out of the Union. . . . I can not immagine what is to come next. Probably war."[30] Several Louisianians wasted little time amid the growing excitement to prepare a military response—even before secession had transpired. In an earlier report to the governor dated December 4, 1860, Louisiana's adjutant general, Maurice Grivot, noted that in "New Orleans and various parishes" the presidential election had set "a strong desire for the forming of volunteer corps, to protect their homes, their families, and their property." Unable to meet the volunteers' "urgent and daily demands" for arms and supplies, he "felt deep regret."[31]

By mid-January 1861, wartime preparations were in full swing. Governor Moore issued orders that "all Government property" be surrendered to the state, which included the Baton Rouge arsenal.[32] Other federal posts, such as Forts Pike, Jackson, and St. Philip, met similar fates, even forcing the hand of Louisiana State Seminary of Learning and Military Academy's superintendent, William T. Sherman, to comply with state officials' demands, as he claimed,

"Thus I was made the receiver of stolen goods."[33] This initial confiscation of US property by Louisiana troops provided the state's residents with a martial spectacle, which, to some individuals, reflected strength and a growing desire to become independent. However, these actions also highlight the polarization and coerciveness Louisiana's pro-secessionists embraced to keep up the momentum of support.[34]

Noting the air of unity, one New Orleanian wrote, "There is no division among the people here. There is but one mind, one heart, one action. . . . Mr. Lincoln and his cabinet have made them of one mind."[35] Perhaps this individual's inner circle of friends and acquaintances had similar viewpoints, but many divisions existed among Louisianians, sometimes between families and friends. On one plantation, the "exuberance of spirit" of secession was so high that James McHatton's wife flew a homemade Confederate flag on the estate's levee, much to his dismay. McHatton had been a delegate at the secession convention in Charleston and disapproved of Louisiana's withdrawal. He "had his impulsive wife haul down the flag," ending her short-lived celebration.[36] Wartime diarist Kate Stone recorded "a warm discussion" with her plantation's tutor as she and her family disagreed with his political stance against secession.[37] Another Louisiana woman held similar views, claiming it was the South which "held fast to the Constitution. The Yankees have no right to it; they have been the persecutors and meddlers even from the witch-burning time until now."[38] Lisa Tendrich Frank notes how some pro-secession Southern women, especially from the slaveholding class, engaged with the political crisis shaping its outcome. These ladies helped sway their husbands to support secession, linking it to a "sense of familial duty and honor."[39] But while many Southern men heeded to the calls (and pressures) of duty and honor, one Louisiana diarist wrote that "whatever comes, it is woman's lot to wait and pray . . . a woman should submit."[40]

Newspapers captured (and sometimes influenced) Louisianians' mixed feelings about secession. One north Louisiana newspaper reported, "As Louisiana is no longer a member of the federal government, we this day, as orderly citizens, lower the 'stars and stripes' from our masthead! It is with heart-felt emotions, better imagined than portrayed, that we fold the saucy looking 'star spangled banner' that we have always loved, and place the precious memento under our pillow."[41] But for some Louisianians, the political excitement surrounding secession shifted public opinion. Even newspapers that once boasted co-operationist sentiment—or at least favored waiting to act only if "constitutional resistance fails"—slowly changed their tune as events unfolded.[42]

State support, for many Louisianians, would ultimately trump notions of national unity. Some citizens remained hopeful for a peaceful solution to the ongoing crisis. Baton Rouge resident Sarah Morgan claimed, "I was never a Secessionist, for I quietly adopted father's views on political subjects without meddling with them. But even father went over with his State. . . . I don't believe in Secession, but I do in Liberty."[43] Once the Deep South seceded, a convention held at Montgomery, Alabama, met to form the new Confederate government. Noting his concerns about the lack of political voice Louisiana residents would have at the convention, Henry E. Handerson, a Northern transplant who resided in Louisiana (and a future Confederate soldier), wrote his father, "There is considerable feeling here at the way in which our convention has conducted itself, but I presume the people will as usual submit to what the politicians dictate."[44] According to Handerson, the pro-secessionists retained a firm grip over the transpiring political events and were not willing to risk losing momentum—nor political power.

Within a few months Louisiana residents, even those individuals not keen on secession, found themselves swept up in the currents of war when Confederate forces fired on Fort Sumter. Newspapers reported, "'War, War' from the first to the last column," wrote Kate Stone. "Throughout the length and breadth of the land the trumpet of war is sounding . . . men are hurrying by thousands, eager to be led to battle against Lincoln's hordes."[45] Perhaps a group of Shreveport Jews summed up the sentiments of many Louisianians who held secessionist sympathies as they sent a message to the New York *Jewish Messenger:* "Although we might be called Southern rebels; still, as law-abiding citizens, we solemnly pledge ourselves to stand by, protect, and honor the flag, with its stars and stripes, the Union and Constitution of the Southern Confederacy, with our lives, liberty, and all that is dear to us."[46] But some Louisianians reluctantly followed their state into the Confederacy. Decades after the war, ex-Confederate Gen. Louis Hébert, claimed that he had been opposed to secession, "but my state having been put out of the Union, I had to go with it."[47] As political issues have always had a polarizing effect on many citizens, the enthusiasm and excitement of secession did not stir an emotional tempest for all Louisianians.

Though secession meant disunion, it did not necessarily mean war. However, many Louisianians were not oblivious to what they thought was likely inevitable—especially males of military age. E. John Ellis, a young Louisianian enrolled at the University of Louisiana in New Orleans, disapproved of secession and shared his personal views with his father. "Well, Pa" he wrote, "New Orleans . . . has at last disgraced herself by voting Secession—Fanaticism has triumphant [*sic*]. . . . I can see nothing before us but a long bloody war— . . . but reason and common sense forces [*sic*] the conviction upon me that . . . the North would overmatch us—I would not tell them this—If it comes to the worst, as Southerners we must fight to the last man." Though Ellis personally opposed secession, he ultimately sided with his state and the Confederacy and became an officer in the 16th Louisiana Infantry.[48]

Military-aged males such as Ellis were not naive to the severe consequences of a conflict, nor did dreams of battlefield glory blind them—especially since they would bear the brunt of the conflict's hardships, paying the ultimate sacrifice with their blood. Leery of the political leaders in charge of the secession movement, many young men watched the unfolding events with caution. They understood that their future destinies were linked to whatever political whims transpired. But with their honor at stake, many Louisianians chose to serve. To be sure, the thought of adventure and the chance to prove their manhood on the battlefield mattered to many future soldiers. However, dreams of glory and a war's reality were not the same—and many future soldiers knew the difference.

At the prospect of an impending conflict, John Foster wrote from New Orleans to his grandmother in Natchez, Mississippi, that if war came "I expect all of us young men will be bound to go. I will only go when it is absolutely necessary." He showed the ability to think clearly, without letting political passions or the growing war hype cloud his mind, remaining sober to the destructive realities of what a civil war would bring. "I have no desire to die or to be mutilated," Foster wrote, "because a few . . . politicians think it is necesary." Distrustful of politicians, he claimed "the right to think and act for myself independent of such men as Jef Davis! and men of that class. I hope we will have no war but I fear that we will."[49] In a previous letter to his father, Foster expressed his hope for a peaceful solution to the sectional crisis; however, he reiterated the reality that his services would eventually be needed if war transpired. "I know the dangers of war. For its glories I care nothing."[50] Bienville Parish resident

David Pierson reiterated his caution—but determination—to do his part to defend his home and new nation as he wrote his father: "By the time this will reach you I will be on my way . . . to join the Army. . . . I hope you will not be disturbed about my leaving so suddenly. I am not acting under any excitement whatever but have resolved to go after a calm and thoughtful deliberation as to all the duties, responsibilities, and dangers which I am likely to encounter in the enterprise. . . . I go . . . to assist as far as in my power lies in the defense of our Common Country and homes which is threatened with invasion and annihilation."[51]

Home defense, along with upholding family and community honor proved a significant motivator for some men to enlist. Glathaar argues that many White Southerners felt compelled to support the Confederacy "simply because their children, relatives, and neighbors were suddenly in harm's way."[52] Alfred Flournoy Sr. wrote to his son Charley, explaining, "This is a sacred cause you are engaged in, my son. Life, honour, and fortune depends on the result. You have voluntarily embarked in this great interprise, and now, you must not look at the consequences." Shifting his admiration of his son's enlistment to a staunch warning, Flournoy continued: "The name you bare is honourable. You must do nothing to bring reproach upon it. I could mourn the loss of a son who bravely fell in defending the rights of his country—but for one who would . . . desert his colours in the hour of conflict, I can have no love or affection of."[53] Charley was not Flournoy's only son in uniform. Alfred Flournoy Jr. also received the following advice—and warnings—from his father:

My son, you must maintain the honour of the position you occupy. . . . No man can make a good officer without untiring industry. . . . An officer who neglects his men will be remembered in all time to come. The Army is the place to try of what stuff a man is made of . . . strict discipline is the vital principle of an Army. Without it all is chaos. When you set an example of obedience yourself, you can then exact it from those under you. Ever be courteous and respectful to those in authority over you, showing them all that difference in their Rank entitles them too. Any timidity in the hour of conflict and a man is ruined forever. . . . My heart is full, my son, whilst I write these lines. I know you are surrounded by many dangers. [If] It is the will of God we never meet again, we cannot help it now. We must fulfill our destinys.[54]

William Jeter also received military advice from his father, John. In the process of raising his own company, John advised William that he would do well to educate himself in military affairs. "I will aid you to raise a company of either Artillery, Infantry, or horse, but my dear son, you ought to be reading something on the subject and if possible take lessons in all drillings as a Captain, so as to know how to command a company." He tried to instill in William the seriousness of leadership, "for it is a very great responsibility to command in time of battle" and offered encouragement to his son, "All of which I feel satisfied you can do."[55] But not all fathers held similar commitments to the cause, regardless of the motivations that prompted many men to enlist, nor were most sons going to fill the officer corps. And some men felt that offering the life of a son or relative upon the war's altar was too great a sacrifice. By the war's second year, Donald Mackay explained that his young son, Fred, was eager to join the fray despite his youth. "I tell him I fear he will be old enough before the war is ended, God forbid my fear should prove a reality."[56] Though Fred Mackay's father made him wait to join the army, many boys too young for military service found loopholes in the system by enlisting in "home protection" outfits. As the war dragged on, young recruits were usually not turned down, and many boy soldiers found themselves in an array of units and positions throughout the state and beyond.[57]

Though many Louisianians were not enthusiastic about secession, the initial excitement and prospects for adventure in the pending conflict swayed their hands to take action. As military-aged men began their sojourn into army life, their family and community connections remained strong. Local support—especially from relatives—did much to encourage these future soldiers. Many of these men faced the future with a mixture of contemplation and (after the opening shots at Fort Sumter) great excitement as they donned Confederate uniforms. Yet, even in the midst of assembling Louisiana's military forces, the complex social dynamics between soldiers and civilians remained in play. While not all Louisianians agreed with secession, most could not turn their backs on their families and home communities. Once in the military, these soldiers would strive to retain much of their prewar civilian identity—along with maintaining contact with civilians—despite their new role as warriors. Though now cloaked in Confederate nationalism and identity, a soldier's commitment to his family and community remained vital to his experience.

CHAPTER 2

RECRUITING AND ORGANIZING AN ARMY

On her way to church in Houma, Louisiana, on Sunday, April 14, 1861, Sarah Butler witnessed local soldiers marching out in full gear, possibly heading to Florida to attack Fort Pickens. She noted the town's "great excitement" and the enthusiasm of many of the men "who wished to go." The Confederate bombardment of Fort Sumter, South Carolina, had only recently ended—and with few casualties. Perhaps naive as many Americans were at the time in hopes of a short war, Butler rationalized that "it seems awful to see Brethren arrayed against one another" but exclaimed, "I think we should demand & defend our rights."[1] G. M. Lee, a Louisiana soldier stationed in Virginia, echoed Butler's sentiments as he explained to his brother-in-law back in Louisiana, "I am proud that I was one who in that trying day counted not the loss of the comforts & pleasures of this life but consulted & enlisted in the service. . . . I for one am willing that my bones shall bleach the sarced [sacred] soil of Virginia in driving the envading host of tyrants from our soil."[2] Regardless of what the future held, Lee hoped to remain steadfast to the cause.

When war became inevitable, many White Louisiana residents forged a commitment to their state's defense, regardless of their initial support for (or lack of support for) secession. The fears and uneasiness about the decision to leave the Union and the cautious attitudes some military-aged males had toward their likely roles in the brewing conflict subsided after the attack on Fort Sumter.

After Lincoln's call for volunteers to subdue the rebellion, which placed many Southerners on the defensive, numerous Louisianians of diverse backgrounds geared up for war. Growing Confederate support spread throughout the South, as one Tennessee Unionist noted how Lincoln's call for volunteers created "a tornado of excitement," which stirred many Southerners into "a phrenzy of passion." This action alone, he wrote, "has done more, and I think I speak considerably, to promote disunion, than any and all other causes combined."[3]

It was through this defensive lens—a desire and duty to protect their family, homes, and property—that many Louisianians contemplated their course of action. Despite their initial motivations, early enthusiasm for supporting Confederate Louisiana (in contrast to secession) remained high. One newspaper reported, "The Pelicans have done better in proportion to their population than any other Confederate state outside Virginia."[4] Another account claimed war fever electrified New Orleans, comparing it to the eve of the 1815 Battle of New Orleans, or the Mexican War's commencement. "The wildest military enthusiasm and patriotism prevails . . . the flag of the Confederacy is flying."[5]

While visiting New Orleans in April 1861, John T. Jeter wrote to his son in Shreveport about the growing excitement. Impressed by the military air and the sight of drilling soldiers, Jeter claimed, "Should there be a call for men to defend the city of New Orleans, while I am here, I shall surely join the army."[6] For many Louisianians, the prospect of participating in the brewing conflict proved too irresistible to not get involved. Most of the initial interaction between these newly enlisted soldiers and civilians proved productive, especially since the people left behind on the home front did much to provision their friends and relatives heading off to war. Though complexities and prejudices existed amongst Louisiana's diverse population, a cooperative network emerged, uniting many Louisianians as Confederates.

ANSWERING THE CALL TO ARMS

At the Civil War's commencement, thousands of Americans, motivated by a variety of patriotic, political, or personal reasons, enlisted in their respective armies.[7] Early volunteers joined for numerous reasons; however, the South's legacy of military tradition also contributed to wartime enthusiasm.[8] Sarah Butler and G. M. Lee's letters captured the early excitement that many Louisianians—both soldiers and civilians—harbored at the outbreak of hostilities.

The prospects of adventure, bowing to public (or peer) pressure, or a desire to prove their manhood caused many Louisianians to answer their state's call to arms.

Despite the conflict's larger, ideological causes, many White Southerners rushed to repel what they considered an invasion of their property, soil, and, perhaps most important, their families and homes. One future Louisiana infantryman told his mother that he believed his "servises as humble as they are, will be needed in defence of Southern rights, in defence of our firesides and homes. . . . Yes 'tis sweet to die for one's country so also is it sweet to die for one's parents brothers and sisters."[9] Another Louisiana volunteer, Willie Dixon, claimed, "I am willing to shed the *last drop of my blood* on the altar of my *country,* if that could be the means of saving us from northern treachery."[10] Many civilians initially supported and encouraged soldiers heading to war based on an ideology of personal or Southern honor; however, as the conflict escalated, their relatives' well-being and safety while serving at the front was what mattered most.[11] Southern independence could not be won without soldiers—and soldiers could not fight without civilian support.

As excitement mounted with the prospect of war, institutions of higher learning felt its effects as many young men abandoned their education for military service. On the eve of Louisiana's secession, West Point Superintendent P. G. T. Beauregard received a Louisiana cadet contemplating resignation. Beauregard told the young man, "Watch me; and when I jump, you jump."[12] Northern Louisiana's Mount Lebanon University fell victim to war fever as the school "deemed it advisable . . . to suspend the exercises in all but the Theological Department" because "So many of the patriotic students have volunteered their services to their country," which also included at least three faculty members.[13] In Jackson, Louisiana, Centenary College student Andrew McCollam wasted little time enlisting in the "Centenary Guards," who apparently took their military duties seriously, as these students stood out as "the best drilled company" in their battalion. However, at least for the moment, his military service remained a secondary endeavor since his unit would "be ordered into active service only in cases of eminent danger to the state."[14] But as several companies marched through Jackson heading to war, McCollam contemplated joining a unit that was ordered to Pensacola. He told his father, "It is clearly and unmistakably my duty to do so. It is a time of fearful danger to the Confederacy and every one able to bear a musket should sacrifice personal considerations to the safety of the country."[15] Heading to war would simply delay his educational pursuits, he claimed, "I can come back and graduate after peace is declared."[16] Many soldiers such as McCollam aimed to return to civilian life after a short stint in the military.

A group of Louisianians attending the University of North Carolina "unanimously adopted" a series of resolutions, which included standing up to perceived Northern political aggression that jeopardized the South's interests. These students supported and admired Governor Moore's wartime preparations and "being deeply impressed with nutriments of patriotism for the honor of our beloved state; We are ready to forsake the peaceful duties of a college life, and take up the sword." These young men publicized their devotion, sending copies of their statement to Governor Moore and to two New Orleans newspapers.[17]

Local newspapers did much to advocate for and advance the cause. The *Point Coupee Democrat* printed advertisements seeking volunteers and commanders for newly organized units, even reporting a story about how a patriotic politician abandoned his political ambitions for military service.[18] A Natchitoches newspaper captured the community's patriotic fervor: "There is scarcely a family in the old Parish of Natchitoches, who does not morn the absence of a kind father, a dutiful son, an affectionate brother, or a true friend."[19] Newspapers also gave women a public voice, which inspired enlistments. Miss Sallie Seogin addressed the "Gentlemen of the Keachi Warriors" in a north Louisiana paper, writing that the "fair ladies of our village and vicinity" were proud of the local soldiers' willingness "to fight and if necessary die in defence of a common cause."[20] Another newspaper printed "Miss Lecomte's Address," intended for the "Gentlemen of the Lecomte Guards" who "heard your Country's call, and have yielded obedience to its summons." The local ladies gave the soldiers a flag, "knowing that the solitary star which shines upon its ample folds, will cheer you on, through all trials and vicissitudes of war."[21] Reading such statements from their local women likely stirred men's desires to prove their worthiness as defenders of home and hearth. As peer pressure encouraged enlistments, the visibility of women and the possibility for some men to impress or win the approval of local ladies also remained vibrant.

Other factors promoting enlistments included parental approval and the possibility of a future draft law. Henry E. Handerson wrote to his Northern father, "I had long been anxious to visit the scene of the coming struggle, and your letter, containing permission for me to offer my services if necessary, decided me." But he offered another reason for volunteering, noting that if the conflict escalated to the point of conscription, "my services would certainly be required, and I might be drafted into a company of total strangers."[22] For many soldiers such as Handerson, an early enlistment likely meant they would serve with friends and neighbors.

Craving military action and fearing that the fighting would be short-lived enticed some men, such as William Stone, to forget raising a local company and instead to join one heading toward an active theater. His sister Kate Stone recorded his eagerness. "He is wild to be off to Virginia. He so fears that the fighting will be over before he can get there."[23] E. John Ellis noted that his youngest brother eventually made his way to the 16th Louisiana Infantry's camp at Corinth, Mississippi, enlisting shortly after arriving. "I would much rather he had remained at school," wrote Ellis, "but he was all on fire with the volunteer spirit . . . and would not remain at home."[24] Some soldiers, especially after getting a taste of army life, warned their relatives to avoid service—or at least to think twice—before enlisting. Writing from Virginia, one Louisiana soldier hesitantly told his brother, "[I] dislike very much to say anything discouraging to you but . . . if you are tired of life, if you prefer death, ah the most horrible of deaths—if this be your fancy, then I (though it be with reluctancy) say go on and join the army."[25]

However, while many young men rushed to volunteer, state authorities established regulations for creating Louisiana's military defense forces. Louisiana's military board published a pamphlet in early 1861 that described its progress in carrying out "An act to promote the formation of Military Companies and to provide for arming and equipping the same." The board also adopted "the system of Tactics for Riflemen and Light Infantry by Lieut-Col. Hardee . . . for all Companies on foot," and established instructions and regulations for a company's authorized strength. All volunteers were under orders to attend training, obey higher-ranking officials, and swear a loyalty oath to support Confederate Louisiana's laws and government.[26]

The new government orders prompted many Louisianians to take action. As one soldier told his brother, "Our Cavalry Company now numbers over one hundred members. The Gov, issued a proclamation for the organization of the militia, & good many fellows rushed into our company, so as to be saved from militia Drills, which they are feared of, like the devil."[27] Despite the emotional excitement that swelled the initial rush to arms (and the increasing government intervention), many young Louisiana men believed deeply in their new cause as state defenders. For most men, their willingness to serve spawned from a personal choice, and many took pride in their service. One St. Martinville observer, for example, witnessed "a splendid" company of soldiers who "are ready to march at any time the Gov calls for them."[28]

LOUISIANA'S DIVERSE VOLUNTEERS

When the Shreveport Greys departed from home in 1861, a local newspaper claimed that the town's "best citizens . . . make up the file of this company."[29] Romantic ideas of the state's finest young men marching off to defend the South were not only celebrated in newspaper columns. "Whilst the North is only sending the vagabonds of her large cities, a population they are glad to get clear of, we are sending the very princes of our land—men of familys,—men whose loss will be deplored by our whole community," wrote Caddo Parish resident Alfred Flournoy Sr.[30] Despite Flournoy's biased views, Louisiana's early volunteer rush was not limited to a particular group of individuals with similar backgrounds, and the state had its share of shady characters and less desirables who eventually found themselves in uniform.

Louisiana always hosted a diverse population, and regimental rosters reflected this. New Orleans, the South's largest city, became a major recruiting hub. The numerous units assembled there often included colorful individuals as some recruits had questionable backgrounds and were not always model citizens. One Louisianian told of one such unit named "the Perrit Guards," which was known as "the gambler's company—to be admitted one must be able to cut, shuffle, and deal on the point of a bayonet."[31] Another contemporary noted that a group of New Orleans enlistees were "the lowest scum of the lower Mississippi . . . adventurous wharf rats, thieves, and outcasts . . . and bad characters generally."[32]

Though perhaps not as scandalous as the examples above, the Orleans Light Horse was no less colorful. The unit consisted of a wide array of volunteers from various walks of life that included but was not limited to laborers, tradesmen, and professionals, the latter of which ranged from clerks to a facilities custodian, a rail splitter, a streetcar driver, and a telegraph operator to farmers, carpenters, real estate agents, a river boat pilot, a surveyor, a sugar refinery manager, physicians, attorneys, teachers, architects, engineers, a news-paper publisher, and a veterinarian.[33] In what became the 5th Company of the Washington Artillery, distinct social boundaries remained visible within the ranks between the unit's "members" and "drivers." Members, who came from society's gentlemen class, acted as the unit's gunners; drivers, who handled and cared for the unit's horses, were recruited from society's lower echelon and included "uneducated, recent immigrants." As one historian notes, both gunners and drivers "would live and work within sight of each other, but they would remain sharply separated by function and station."[34] But this arrange-ment remained the exception and not the rule since few Louisiana units had a prewar lineage—and elite status—as the Washington Artillery did.

Louisiana was also many foreign-born individuals' adopted home. With the Civil War's outbreak, many of these foreigners found themselves volunteering their services to Louisiana and the Confederacy. The largest groups of these transplants who joined the Confederate army from Louisiana were the Irish and Germans. Some of these foreign soldiers clad themselves with an array of uni-forms, including elaborate styles copied from European armies, which offered colorful distractions to onlookers as a variety of costumes, tongues, and nation-alities were well represented. One observer noted that a battalion, which became part of the 13th Louisiana Infantry, not only displayed the unique and colorful Zouave uniform, but also portrayed a wide range of diversity within its ranks: "Frenchmen, Spaniards, Mexicans, Dagoes, Germans, Chinese, Irishmen, and, in fact, persons of every clime known to geographers or travelers of that day."[35]

One of the many features unique to the Zouave uniform was "those great big bag briches" worn by the soldiers. One Louisiana soldier commented that the Zouaves brought "a great deal of merriment among the boys," as they jok-ingly claimed that "they are not going to carry any knapsacks or haversacks as they will put everything in their britches legs."[36] Once in Virginia, one witness claimed the Zouave-garbed Louisianians brought about the "greatest sight I have yet seen." But what really impressed him was not necessarily their foreign-looking uniforms or their drilling style. Instead, their physical "complexion that they were hard specimens before they left the 'crescent city'" stood out. For this individual, these Louisiana soldiers "were the most savage-looking crowd I ever saw."[37]

Louisiana's diverse soldiers reflected the state's unique cultural makeup and provided an array of spectacles and curiosities in both tongue and dress.

Not all foreign volunteers were enlisted men, as one German "home protection" company boasted that most of the outfit's officers had prior service "in the regular armies of Germany."[38] Some Louisiana Jews, many of whom were immigrants from central and eastern Europe, actively supported and even volunteered their services to the Confederacy.[39] Gaspard Tochman, a Polish exile who had aided his native country in its independence struggle years earlier, received permission from Jefferson Davis to recruit fellow Poles for the Confederacy and headed to New Orleans for the task. Though he recruited about 1,700 men to his ranks (most of whom were foreigners by birth), relatively few were actually Polish.[40] Another Pole, Ignatius Szymański, who found his way to Louisiana before the Civil War, commanded the Chalmette Regiment and participated in the unsuccessful attempt to defend New Orleans against Union gunboats in 1862.[41]

As men from all backgrounds joined Louisiana's Confederate forces, their languages, much like their uniforms, were not standardized and reflected the state's diversity. Even a captured Unionist witnessed a Louisiana unit's cultural differences as he wrote that his captors' "battalion was composed principally of backwoods Americans, Creoles, Frenchmen, Spaniards, half-breed Indians, &c.," with the soldiers speaking "in his own tongue."[42] And a different language did not always signify foreign birth. Many French-speaking southwest Louisiana residents were of Acadian descent who had roots in the region since the mid-1700s. Some Acadians were planters or well-off farmers who sympathized with the Confederacy (or at least held affection for the vigilante hero Alfred Mouton, who later became the leader of the 18th Louisiana Infantry); however, many did not fit into this category.[43]

The habits and customs of some of the Acadian volunteers even left an impact on a few Confederate officials. One 1861 letter to the Confederate secretary of war noted that, though many of the southwest Louisiana residents could not speak English, many likely cared less or were ignorant about politics and governmental policies. However, this Confederate official thought that these people were what the Confederacy needed. "That portion of our citizens are best able to endure the hardships of a campaign," he wrote, but, because of their lack of concern for the escalating conflict, they "are not in the field."[44] After the war, Gen. Richard Taylor recalled that the Acadians who served in the 8th Louisiana Infantry were a "home-loving, simple people, few spoke English, fewer still had ever before moved ten miles from their natal *cabanas;* and the war to them was 'a liberal education,' . . . They had all the light gayety of the Gaul, and after the manner of their ancestors, were born cooks."[45] Apparently, the tastes of south Louisiana's cuisine had already captivated an audience, and many Louisiana soldiers would exercise their cooking skills throughout the war.

With Louisiana's diverse fighting forces taking shape, language barriers sometimes caused confusion in the ranks.[46] One battalion of Zouave soldiers established that French would be used for issuing orders and commands, since many of the men and at least one of the battalion's officers could not speak English.[47] Louisiana's colorful troops often entertained onlookers; one Alabama officer, for example, admired a group of drilling Louisiana soldiers as they obeyed commands in a foreign tongue. Though the spectators did not understand what was spoken, the ceremony "presented a good entertainment for the edification of our officers and men."[48] Some of the newly formed units easily reflected their diverse ethnicities, which included names such as the Chasseurs-à-Pied, Chasseurs d'Orleans, Lützen Jägers, and the Cazadores Espagnoles.[49] Despite these units' unique names and diverse languages, some being native and others foreign-born, they were all Louisianians. Relocation to the state, whether recent or decades past, did not end the ethnic and cultural connections to the mother country, it simply reflected it. Through its soldiers, Louisiana's unique customs and cultures came on full display throughout the Confederacy.

Numerous factors lured recent immigrants to volunteer, but economics proved pivotal, especially for many Irishmen, who enlisted out of necessity because of unemployment.[50] As various motives (and later conscription) brought men into the ranks, reasons for either staying the course or deserting were also based on numerous factors. Lawrence Lee Hewitt challenges the conventional thought about foreign-born soldiers being less dedicated to soldiering and more likely to desert. His evidence suggests a soldier's prewar occupation—not origin—was the major factor that determined their "level of patriotism."[51]

Particularly with Louisiana's Irish soldiers, Laura D. Kelley notes how their display of Confederate patriotism, which was linked to economic factors, also resonated with connections to Irish nationalism. John Mitchel, an "ardent Irish nationalist and journalist," had a son who died in the Confederate service in

1864. Before dying, Mitchel's son claimed, "I die willingly for the South, but oh, that it had been for Ireland." Kelley argues that many New Orleans Irishmen had "spent . . . years constructing new lives for themselves, creating coherent communities, and building churches. All of this they saw as worth fighting for."[52] Foreign-born soldiers did not always lack dedication to their units and the Confederacy; and in some cases, these men had prior military service that would prove valuable on the battlefield.[53] And even for recent immigrants, home communities had taken root in Louisiana. Sheehan-Dean stresses how most Civil War soldiers were volunteers who "remained intimately connected to their home communities."[54] For many of the state's soldiers, regardless of their background, place of origin, or ethnicity, they had something to defend and fight for.

Southern patriotism even crossed the color line, as Louisiana's Free Black population also offered its services to defend their state. On December 28, 1860, the *New Orleans Daily Delta* noted how Louisiana's Free Blacks "have never given grounds for any suspicion, or distrust, and they have frequently manifested their fidelity in a manner quite as striking and earnest as white citizens." The newspaper went further, publishing a letter from "A LARGE NUMBER OF THEM" stating that "the free colored population (native) of Louisiana . . . love their home, their property, they own slaves, and they are dearly attached to their native land, and they recognize no other country than Louisiana, and . . . they are ready to shed their blood for her defense. They have no sympathy for Abolitionism; no love for the North, but they have plenty for Louisiana; and let the hour come, and they will be worthy sons of Louisiana. They will fight for her in 1861 as they fought in 1814-'15. . . . All they ask is to have a chance, and they will be worthy sons of Louisiana."[55] Other newspapers offered similar references to the African American contributions in the War of 1812, with one paper mentioning that many of these Free Blacks not only had skills and a hard work ethic, but also "As a general rule . . . are a sober, industrious and moral class, far advanced in education and civilization."[56] As a testament to the Black volunteers' worth—or simply as a way to reassure the state's White population that these men posed no threat to the current social order—one report stated, "Our free colored men . . . attached to the land of their birth as their white brethren here in Louisiana . . . will fight the Black Republican with as much determination and gallantry as any body of white men in the service of the Confederate States."[57]

Although a Free Black regiment, known as the Native Guards, eventually organized for Louisiana's defense, the unit did not contain the state's only African-descended volunteers. A Baton Rouge company had about thirty Black soldiers within its ranks by the end of April 1861, and two other Free Black companies formed from Pointe Coupee and Plaquemines Parishes, respectively.[58] Supposedly, one Black planter, who aimed to see his property and social rank maintained, helped finance the formation of a "white guard to help protect the parish" of Pointe Coupee.[59] Near Natchitoches, two Free Black companies organized into home guard units. An observer noted that the infantry company, Monet's Guards, needed a little work, but the cavalrymen of the Augustin Guards won the observer's praise. The local newspaper claimed these Natchitoches companies had the potential for serving as a coastal patrol or "maintaining the public tranquility."[60] Loren Schweninger estimates that over three thousand Free Blacks enlisted to aid Confederate Louisiana, which included "three out of four adult free men of color in the state."[61]

Louisiana's Black Civil War experience is unique compared with other states for numerous reasons, stemming from the colonial era of French and Spanish influence. The Louisiana militia offered opportunities for Free Blacks to serve. While the Confederacy barred African Americans from entering active service as soldiers, there is evidence that a small number did enlist, though perhaps because they were able to pass as White men.[62] To provide context for Louisiana's Civil War Free Black volunteers, a look at the state's Black military legacy is necessary.

French and Spanish control of Louisiana established a Black military tradition, which carried over, though not without issues, once Louisiana entered the Union. Colonial Louisiana's military forces used enslaved Blacks to help construct defenses, along with serving in a number of military-support occupations. The first formation of Louisiana's Black militia under the French was during the war with the Natchez Indians, and future conflicts with Native Americans saw further utilization of Black troops.[63] Colonial Louisiana's hostile environment allowed for more latitude among the Africans who provided the needed skills to build the colony and who had a sizeable portion of manpower to help defend it.[64]

Once Spain gained control of Louisiana at the end of the French and Indian War, Louisiana's Black military tradition continued. When Spain officially joined the American Revolutionary War as a French ally in 1779, many Black soldiers served—and were decorated for bravery—as they helped conduct military operations along the Mississippi River and Gulf Coast.[65] The Spanish also used the Black militia to regulate slavery, and, during a war with France in the early 1790s, were also part of the colony's defense force against a possible invasion.[66]

Once Louisiana became a state in 1812, many Black militiamen carried on their military legacy as they helped defend New Orleans against the British invasion during the War of 1812. Though he wanted White officers to command the Black battalion, Gen. Andrew Jackson issued a proclamation to the city's Free People of Color, calling upon them to enlist to help ensure an American victory. Jackson supported equal pay for Black soldiers and claimed that their service would be honored like that of Whites and that they would "receive the applause, reward, and gratitude of your Countrymen."[67] The Black militia's colonial legacy and its participation in the largest battle of the War of 1812 set the backdrop for Louisiana's Free Blacks aim to once again offer their services to defend their homeland.

By early 1861, Louisiana's military board took note of the state's Free Black population's willingness to serve. "We think it deserving of honorable mention," stated the special report, "that among our free colored population, a large number of the old veterans of 1812, and their descendants, have volunteered their services to the State."[68] However optimistic (or doubtful) Confederate Louisiana's leaders were about colored volunteers, the glory of Andrew Jackson's New Orleans victory in 1815 did not reoccur in 1862. The only volleys fired by the Free Black Natchitoches companies were in early 1862 at a local Confederate soldier's funeral.[69] While many Free Blacks occupied marginal and vulnerable positions in the antebellum South (though some obtained economic wealth), military service afforded them the benefit of protection for themselves, their families, and any property they owned.

Free Blacks strategically enlisted in Louisiana's Confederate militia, which helped alleviate suspicions of disloyalty.[70] However, their commitment remained untested until Federal soldiers arrived. Once New Orleans fell into Union hands in April 1862, Confederate forces quickly abandoned the region and told the Black troops to disband. All the publicity over the prospect of Black soldiers defending Louisiana as their ancestors had in years past came to naught. As James Hollandsworth notes, "If the Native Guards were good for anything, it was for public display; free blacks fighting for Southern rights made good copy for the newspapers." Perhaps this was true of Louisiana's other Free Black militia units. Not long after Federal occupation, the Native Guards reformed but now as a Union regiment, much to the disapproval of New Orleans's White residents.[71]

EARLY CIVILIAN SUPPORT

As regiments formed, methods of supporting them financially varied. Community organizations and patriotic citizens rallied to the call and offered donations. Wealthy planters gave their money and offered their services (and leadership) to the military, along with urging that their sons and relatives join the cause.[72] Businesses also contributed money, and some parishes passed taxes to help fund their local servicemen. Parish police juries, which were part of the state's local parish government, allocated "funds to aid womenfolk left destitute by 'their men going to war.'"[73] The Caddo Parish police jury made "the very handsome donation . . . of $2500 to each of the volunteer companys from this Parish," wrote Alfred Flournoy Sr. His son, Alfred Jr., had been a member of the police jury before heading off to war, and Flournoy told him, "I was elected to fill your place . . . and it afforded me great pleasure to aid in bringing about this measure."[74] Soldiers' social connections with civilians in various civil capacities greatly aided the state's forces. Support from sympathetic civilians reminded soldiers that their wartime exploits remained deeply connected to the home front, especially since the Confederate government often struggled to provide for its men.

Efforts to outfit, equip, and support men heading to war involved communal bonding between newly recruited soldiers and civilians—especially women. The emotional ties to the opposite sex often motivated men to take action, and one of the first items a town's ladies presented to their soldiers heading to war was their unit flag. Shrouded by ceremony, flag dedications attracted visitors who came to give their local volunteers well wishes and prayers. For many participants, this mingling was the last time they would ever see one another. A regiment's battle flag quickly became a sacred symbol, representing their ideals of honor, family, and home.[75]

William Miller Owen recalled that the Washington Artillery received its colors at Christ Church in New Orleans in the midst of "suppressed sobs of mothers, sisters, wives, and sweethearts."[76] In St. Martinville, local ladies presented a company of soldiers with a banner, flag, and "some very appropriate remarks." After a few speeches one observer wrote, "We then all went to church & old father Jean blessed both flag & banner & also made a very good little speech. The assembly then broke up."[77] Confederate flags varied in size, color, and design, and even captured the attention of some Northern civilians later in the conflict who commented on the Southern banners—and their significance. Upon entering Pennsylvania en route to Gettysburg in 1863, the sight of Confederate soldiers impressed at least one teenage girl from Waynesboro, who noted "their banners—such beautiful banners—made by mothers, wives, sisters, and sweethearts. . . . Ah, the tears and sighs, hopes and fears, stitched into their silken folds." Battle flags proved to be inspiring and powerful symbols.[78]

As men assembled for duty, a company's flag came to represent an entire regiment and not only the initial group of men to whom it was presented. For some soldiers the changing hands of a homemade flag—a symbol of *their* home and *their* loved ones left behind—to color bearers who had no connection to the flag's creators did not sit well. Officers in one company handed over their flag for regimental use. "Our men dislike it," W. H. King wrote. "They think it unfair to take our flag, & leave us behind. . . . now strangers have it, & as they do not hold it in the same sacred esteem, but seem desirous of possessing it from the same impulse that a child does a toy—to make one vain display—we feel very indignant."[79] Upset, these soldiers saw their flag's confiscation as a breach of personal honor, especially since they had emotional ties to the women back home who had made and presented them with their colors. Actions such as this reminded the volunteers that within the military their decisions were no longer theirs to make.

But women did more for Louisiana's troops than simply stitch battle flags or remain virtuous symbols of honor. They had a serious role to perform in the conflict's unfolding events. Throughout the war, numerous ladies' groups and local societies financially aided military units by organizing festivities, such as picnics, dances, plays, and concerts, along with donating their time to make these functions possible.[80] Other female organizations, which were largely made up of soldiers' wives and other prominent females, did likewise.[81] One group of ladies formed a sewing society with a preamble and decree stating, "We whose names are here unto subscribed do agree to assist voluntarily without remuneration in making clothing for soldiers in the Confederate Army the clothing to be distributed according to the direction of a majority of the society."[82] A Louisiana soldier's wife belonged to a similar club and enjoyed the fellowship with other ladies; however, their time together was not wasted as she wrote, "We have 1 hundred pairs of draw[er]s to make Friday."[83]

A soldier's proximity to sympathetic civilians often dictated the success he would have in obtaining clothing items. At least one soldier at the war's commencement sent word to his mother not to fret about his "welfare as far as clothing is concerned," noting he was well stocked and had access to more.[84] But as the war continued, homespun articles made by patriotic women became standard attire, as one soldier wrote to a friend in Opelousas, "Homespun is very much worn now by men & officers of the Army."[85] And soldiers resorted to seeking out donations—even making house calls for whatever items the local population could spare.[86]

Just as civilians encouraged enlistments, early support efforts not only physically aided soldiers but also provided an emotional sense to the men that the home front cared about their well-being. The home front's significance anchored volunteers' sense of their military obligation, especially when Louisiana's Confederate government lacked the ability and resources to outfit all of its military volunteers. Luckily for the soldiers, civilian efforts filled the gap. Without early civilian support, especially from women and the enslaved, Louisiana troops would have suffered from the lack of many of their basic necessities.[87] These wartime relationships and the cooperation between soldiers and civilians remained enmeshed as the conflict escalated. Their communal ties produced the tangible and needed items for home defense.

CHAPTER 3

CONSCRIPTION

The year 1861 had "been a remarkable on[e] in the history of the American nation," wrote New Orleans militiaman H. A. Snyder, noting Lincoln's election, secession, and the Confederacy's formation. Though the conflict remained in its infancy and Louisiana's military organization continuously evolved, this "cruel unholy war on the people of the seceded Southern States . . . continues & grows in awful magnitude daily."[1] The escalation in bloodshed did not deter nor diminish support for the war as newspaper columns captured the initial dedication many Louisianians had for the cause of Southern independence.[2] "The country here is fully aroused to the dangers that threaten us," wrote Alfred Flournoy Sr. "Never before have volunteers enlisted with more promptness. Every Parish is doing her duty. Glorious old Caddo has raised three more companies. . . . Almost our entire fighting population is gone. Our Parish is now one of the most defenseless portions of the world."[3]

On January 8, 1862, New Orleanians commemorated the forty-seventh anniversary of the Battle of New Orleans, adding to the wartime excitement of the Civil War's second year. As H. A. Snyder and his militia unit marched through the city, he described the electrifying scene, with "every available spot the galleries & balconies all along the line of march were crowded with spectators, mostly ladies & children."[4] Among the cheering and celebrations, a local newspaper noted the "thousands of men idly looking on"—men who, the reporter felt, should have been among the soldiers marching in the parade.[5] Amidst the excitement some Louisianians remained reluctant to enlist. One witness near Fort Jackson noted, "Patriotism is very Low in this parish," referring to the low turnout of men in the area for militia duty.[6] Aiming to restructure Louisiana's forces and recognizing the need to fill the ranks, the state's military affairs board now required the services of "all the free white males capable of bearing arms" without regard to citizenship and nationality.[7] Initial volunteering had been in part to defend Louisiana; however, Confederate officials transported many recruits to other fronts as the Confederacy's needs took precedence. And since not all military-aged males volunteered, this manpower shortage meant Louisiana's militia forces would fill the gap—and conscription would become law. For many young men, remaining a civilian was no longer an option.

The idea of forcing men into the army upset numerous individuals—soldier and civilian alike, including men already in the service or who eventually planned to be. Sheehan-Dean's study on Virginia soldiers notes the draft's unpopularity as many men "believed that military service was, and should remain, a voluntary act."[8] For many men, military service was not the problem; removing a man's ability to make his own decisions about serving was. And the possibility of being labeled a conscript—or being associated with one—had a negative connotation. As early as May 1861, rumors of conscription had already begun. One young Louisianian hoped to join the army before any prospective draft took effect so he could avoid being associated with conscripts "as they would be composed of the dregs of the parish." The thought of being drafted would be "very mortifying," to both himself and his family, staining his honor.[9] This Louisianian's feelings was not an exception as many volunteers (including boys) dreaded being labeled a conscript. Capt. A. C. Broussard of the 2nd Louisiana Cavalry wrote about one unnamed recruit who "has been regularly enlisted in my Company, that he is Seventeen (17) yrs of age, that the consent of his parents have been obtained, he is actually present and doing duty, and that he has never been ~~enlisted~~, Conscripted."[10]

This private was not the only young recruit who enthusiastically enlisted with the 2nd Louisiana Cavalry. Col. William G. Vincent, who commanded the unit, became a Louisiana version of Virginian John S. Mosby (commander of the famed Mosby's Rangers). Vincent's leadership abilities overshadowed his physical quirks (he was short and "wore spectacles. He looked more like a clerk than a cavalry commander"[11]), which obviously had some sway in stirring the imagination, as many southwest Louisiana "Schoolboys frequently ran away to join" his regiment. Some soldiers already in the service went absent without leave (AWOL) hoping to join the 2nd Louisiana Cavalry.[12] A unit's distinguished reputation went a long way in obtaining willing recruits. The eagerness of many young Louisianians who enlisted was even noted by a Union officer, who obtained a Confederate soldier's correspondence from a "ransacked estate" along Bayou Lafourche in 1862. Capt. John Franklin Godfrey enclosed the captured letters for his family in Maine to read, noting the soldier's dedication in the face of hardships. Impressed with the rebel's commitment, he wished "all our rich young men were as willing and earnest in the North as he is for the South."[13]

However, not all of Louisiana's sons eagerly enlisted—or wanted to be drafted—since the draft restructured Southern society and placed burdens on many families. But conscription required soldier and civilian cooperation, and thousands complied.[14] This does not imply that they went without complaint. Taking men from their homes did more than just interrupt their lives—many of these draftees had families who depended on them. Conscription also remained a class-conscious affair, which often strained the South's poorer families compared with the wealthy.[15] Kenneth W. Noe argues that the Confederacy's reluctant men who became soldiers after 1861 are often characterized as an "unwilling soldier . . . who was drafted in 1862 or enlisted only to avoid being drafted." He challenges the works of prominent Civil War soldier historians, such as James McPherson, who often cite initial volunteers as being more committed to their causes despite the fact that "half of all soldiers . . . routinely avoided battle." Placing a Confederate soldier in the context "of family leader and defender," Noe claims, "Conscription as well as voluntary enlistment thus were shaped by the needs of wives and children who needed monetary as well as physical protection during wartime. Unwillingly, even these men were fighting for their families and property."[16]

Sacher also notes the contested—but shifting—nature of Confederate conscription, as both the military and home front competed for manpower. He argues that "conscription is more accurately dubbed the most *debated* measure in the South" as it was "repeatedly modified." The debate of how best to defend the Confederacy and implement the draft often revolved around the "competing loyalties" between family and nation; however, as Sacher notes, "A southerner's dislike of conscription did not equate to the abandonment of their new nation." Protecting Southern liberties, which included their homes, families, and property, was a balancing act that demanded military service and was met with "some success."[17]

Conscription strained the early war spirit of cooperation; however, soldiers and civilians became more cognizant of and creative about how to best meet their personal needs, despite the Confederate authorities' demands. But, just like the initial wave of volunteers, the men who were soon to be pressed into the ranks also saw the growing conflict through a defensive lens; many of these men would have preferred to stay home to personally protect their families and property. Regardless of how soldiers and civilians felt about the draft, the measure remained a social experience—albeit a contested one.

NOT POPULAR ANYWHERE OUTSIDE THE ARMY

In January of 1862, Louisiana authorities passed a militia act, requiring "all free white male residents between eighteen and forty-five . . . to enroll in the state militia." Emergency situations and military necessity specified the length of service, but all militiamen could be called to statewide service.[18] Military service was no longer optional, and any eligible men not present for duty would be blacklisted "and branded as enemies of the South."[19] Interestingly, before Louisiana's government enacted this new law, some companies had soldiers above the prescribed age, which led to a force reduction; as one militiaman noted, several older men "not willing to continue . . . withdrew."[20]

In February the Confederate government authorized Jefferson Davis the power to order the collection of both weapons and men "in every State" to meet the Confederacy's needs.[21] Later that spring, national conscription took effect, which eventually included new measures, like adjusting the service age limits from seventeen to fifty years (and in some cases older).[22] New legislation also reorganized existing military units and mandated additional service from the initial volunteers who had joined for twelve months. Louisianian John A. Morgan was upset by these changes. "My opinion is that portion of our army that have been fighting as volunteers and now have been pressed for two years now will do the confederacy but little good. It would not have looked so hard if they had given us a chance to Volunteer." Another reason for Morgan's disdain was that the reorganization laws likely kept him from receiving a furlough.[23]

President Jefferson Davis believed conscription would positively affect the Confederate military's structure by requiring a soldier's service for three years.

However, military structure and morale were not the same. Though many men submitted to conscription, it was not without protest.[24] Davis realized that conscription would be very unpopular among many people throughout the Confederacy, as it "was not popular anywhere outside the army."[25] Some Southern newspapers argued that the draft acted as an equalizer, placing all eligible men on equal footing. One Alabama paper claimed it would make the "unpatriotic perform the same duty as the most devoted citizen, and brings the rich to the same level with the poor." But opinions varied, and Vice President Alexander Stephens felt "the Conscription Act was a very bad policy."[26] One Louisiana soldier claimed conscription would negatively affect the morale of soldiers already in uniform, as many of his comrades "emphatically declared that they would serve any length of time as volunteers, but that they would never serve in the degraded position of a conscript." But conscription brought some satisfaction to soldiers, who believed many "political loafers who had been such rabid secessionists . . . had never entered the army" and would now be forced to serve.[27]

Thomas B. Davidson confessed to his sister that many Confederate soldiers lacked commitment to the cause and "would rather Lincoln would conquer . . . such are renegades to honor, but they do not represent a small portion of our army; thus you see how necessary the conscript act was."[28] Upon hearing word that conscripts would now begin filling the ranks, W. H. King wrote, "We are all more or less rejoiced," as men who "were very active in procaming [sic] secession, then urging others into the army" would now be required to serve. "I do feel that conscription is just what they deserve."[29] Such opinions stood in contrast to earlier boasts some Louisianian's made about zealous volunteerism.

By the fall of 1863, backlash toward conscription remained on full display throughout Louisiana. Southwest Louisiana became a sanctuary for thousands of "deserters and runaway conscripts," and similar reports came from other regions in the state, prompting officials to mobilize soldiers to bring these men into the army.[30] Some soldiers even went to extremes to press men into the ranks; however, these were often isolated instances and sometimes involved ulterior motives that had little to do with justice or enforcing the conscription law.[31] Enforcing the draft proved burdensome, and not all men who came forth in accordance to the law proved capable—or personally keen—on becoming soldiers. One Louisiana artillery conscript used poetry to describe his feelings on the matter: "They took me for a soldier and are going to make me fight / Though I never could believe myself that shooting folks was right."[32]

Draftees commonly gave excuses, which were not always legitimate, to evade service. "Conscripts met here today," wrote W. H. King, "but none were enrolled, as many excuses (of which one alone was sufficient) were allowed."[33] King's rants about the draft continued into 1864—this time he claimed the Confederate Congress had adjusted the draft age from "15 to 55 years . . . exempting none." Unconvinced "none" would be exempt, he believed wealthy individuals—and politicians—would "find a loop hole . . . to get out." According to King, wealthy individuals, who enacted injustice and corruption at the expense of "poor men's families," would lead to the Confederacy's "irretrievable ruin."[34] Sacher also notes that Louisiana's Union occupation (which began in 1862 with the fall of New Orleans and continuously spread) delivered a severe blow to the state's morale and conscription efforts, as many residents "felt the Confederate government had abdicated its responsibility for their protection." Not only did Confederate military failure fuel resistance, but Union occupation also meant that a large quarry of the state's eligible draftees now resided behind enemy lines.[35]

As Confederate authorities pressed more and more men into the army, some soldiers believed that conscription harmed their families on the home front, especially if they relied on relatives to maintain their property in their absence. Lt. John Coleman Sibley told his wife that the draft "will take Cousin William and I will be very sorry for I was in hopes he could stay and take care of you all. . . . I don't know how you and ma could get along without some man on the place."[36] P. L. Prudhomme was saddened by the departure of a relative, who was a militia officer called to active duty, as his parting would negatively affect the family plantation near Natchitoches. He had "controle of everything and . . . his absence will be a severe trial."[37] But despite impressment, some men obtained releases for special details or for civilian positions or services that aided the state or Confederacy.[38] For example, John M. Avery from St. Mary Parish obtained permission to be "detailed as superintendant of the salt Mines," which would continue "so long as he is actually employed" in the said mines.[39] Whether serving in the ranks or on the home front, authorities saw the importance and interdependence between military service and civilian contributions.

With conscripts swelling the ranks, Governor Moore saw the need for multiple camps in strategic locations to receive the men. Sites were established in the northeast near Monroe and in Acadiana at Opelousas; however, this arrangement proved a logistical nightmare. Few facilities and tents had been procured to shelter supplies and men coming into camp.[40] And if establishing rendezvous points and basic supplies for draftees was difficult, rounding up men proved even more troublesome—perhaps proving that Louisianians' level of commitment was not as strong as it had appeared in early 1861. Later in the war, Gen. Richard Taylor noted that he frequently had to "scour the country with cavalry in order to bring conscripts to camps of instruction," claiming that sometimes men had to "be hunted down . . . and brought in tied and sometimes in irons." In parts of southwestern Louisiana, the job of bringing in draftees remained difficult because of the "universal hostility of the people," along with the fact that a language barrier existed since most of the residents there only spoke French.[41]

Assembling conscripts from north Louisiana proved just as burdensome. Louisiana Unionist Dennis Haynes recalled a violent episode in north Louisiana as conscripts and conscript hunters (some of whom were related) resorted to thievery and murder as men were "shot dead." One man, after being shot, "was literally butchered in the most cruel and barbarous manner."[42] In 1863 a group of soldiers surrounded a church in Shreveport as the congregation exited the building. They "arrested every man as he came out! What an outrage to humanity! . . . They were in search of conscripts," wrote one observer.[43]

If procuring draftees remained problematic, forcing these coerced soldiers to actually fight was yet another issue. Several Confederates who manned Forts Jackson and St. Philip on the lower Mississippi River, shifted their loyalties as the chaos of battle ensued. Many of the defenders were recent immigrants who preferred civilian life to the hardships of war. Michael Pierson argues that the Fort Jackson mutiny, which had more to do with a lack of Confederate loyalty and a will to fight, especially since the Confederate strongholds on the river remained largely intact (and sufficiently supplied) after the engagement, "guaranteed Union control over New Orleans." As this episode at Fort Jackson displayed, having uncommitted men in the ranks proved just as troublesome as not having enough.[44]

Depending on the situation, some efforts were made to appease the draftees. Authorities sometimes allowed conscripts to choose their branch of service, and, if circumstances warranted, they were placed in units made up from soldiers from their home region. Officials hoped such policies would keep these conscripted men in the ranks.[45] After reporting for duty, a draftee's physical fitness, which did not always meet military standards, had to be accounted for. Surgeon General Bartholomew Egan reported, "I have arrived at the conclusion that twenty-two and one half percent of those made subject to militia duty . . . were physically unfit for service." Governor Moore ordered surgeons to take "proper precautions," ensuring that conscripts were truly ill and not homesick or trying to avoid service. However, not all surgeons followed these procedures, as several apparently able-bodied prospects obtained discharges.[46]

By contrast, other surgeons showed little sympathy for soldiers. One Louisiana officer noted his unit's surgeon "will not discharge even a sick man if he thinks that he will live six months."[47] Conscripting officers tasked with bringing men into the ranks could also prove extreme, if not ridiculous. For example, Capt. W. C. Morrell, a St. Landry Parish conscripting officer, deemed Edmond Guidry "fit for duty"—despite the fact that Guidry only had one arm, having lost the other while serving in a Louisiana regiment in Virginia.[48] Some soldiers received legitimate discharges from military service because of their inability to endure the hardships of military life, which was sometimes linked to previous years of hard physical labor. At least four immigrant soldiers in the 1st Louisiana Heavy Artillery obtained discharges linked to their feebleness, which included men "too old and too much worn out to attend to any duty."[49]

Conscription, which was meant to pull unwilling or reluctant men into the ranks, negatively impacted efforts to defend Louisiana, as men filling the ranks were simply being taken away to other parts of the Confederacy.[50] As Union forces began their Louisiana campaigning, the regions from which to procure conscripts slowly shrank, further intensifying concerns about the Confederacy's ability to defend the state.[51] In the fall of 1862, Rep. Lucius J. Dupré wrote to Jefferson Davis explaining the state's plight and the need for soldiers to defend its own borders. He claimed that the Louisiana regiments stationed in Virginia "cannot be filled with conscripts from home unless the state is drained of all her men between 18 & 45," especially as the regions for procuring replacements (such as New Orleans) were already under Union occupation, or under the imminent threat of invasion. Responding promptly, Davis acknowledged Dupré's concerns but claimed that the current situation in Virginia was dire as "Genl Lee's army . . . is now in the presence of the enemy." Removing "any portion of his force" would have negative consequences. Though Davis denied the request for transferring Louisiana soldiers back home, he told Dupré that if the situation in Virginia changed, troops would be redeployed to Louisiana. "When it can, it will be done," he wrote.[52]

Confederate authorities did not discredit concerns for home and state defense; however, they made it known that the nation's needs came first. The Confederacy needed Louisiana's soldiers to defend Richmond and the territories its commanders deemed of high strategic value. Though several Confederate Louisianians (and later historians) critically pointed out the folly of losing New Orleans, Louisiana's officials—and its soldiers—complied with national defense. This does not necessarily imply that home defense bowed out to Confederate nationalism. Ultimate victory, whether near Richmond or elsewhere, meant soldiers could return home.

Finding conscripts was not the only manpower problem the Confederacy faced. Wavering militiamen, such as H. A. Snyder, who had been called into state service, turned down the opportunity to volunteer for active Confederate service, preferring "civil life with their families at home, to a life of warefare among the Confederates."[53] In late 1862, another Louisiana militiaman wrote, "I felt it my duty to stay at home as long as I could," insinuating his desire to put his family's needs over national service in the Confederate army.[54] As wavering militiamen attempted to evade active service, so did conscripts. Several local residents questioned draftees' contributions and abilities, especially on the battlefield. In one 1862 engagement near Thibodaux, the soldiers in the 18th Louisiana and Crescent Regiment performed admirably, but "the conscripts did not see their good example," wrote one St. Martinville resident.[55]

The quality of soldiers mattered and having uncommitted men in the ranks could prove as bad as having too few. Sacher provides an example of the presence of cultural clashes between Confederate authorities and southwest Louisiana's Acadian population, as several of these men sought to avoid service. Though many Acadians viewed the conflict as not their affair, several thousand were eventually drafted.[56] When the Confederate government refined the draft, even adjusting service age limits, Union soldiers picked up on their desperate situation. On January 21, 1864, Yankee soldier William H. Whitney wrote his brother, explaining the rebels' recruiting and logistical problems, which plagued the Southern war effort. He mentioned that a group of captured Confederate cavalrymen had aimed "to seize conscripts. . . . You know that every able bodied male citizen in the Confederacy is drafted and ordered into their army."[57]

Though Whitney recounted what he saw as desperate Confederates looking to fill their ranks, the Union army also needed men, and rumors of the Federal draft circulated among the Confederacy.[58] By 1863, the Federals began drafting male Louisiana "Unionists"—or their sons—into the Yankee fold and hiring a substitute was not unheard of.[59] For the state's Confederates, Union conscription aided recruitment and alarmed residents, such as Hélène Dupuy, who wrote, "[Many men] fear the Yankee conscription and would be ashamed to serve in the Yankee army . . . more than 1,000 men from Ascension and the neighboring parishes have already crossed the lines and will join the Confederate army."[60] However, not all Federal actions forced Louisiana men to don Union blue. Under Federal-controlled New Orleans, Union officials gave passports to individuals who wanted to trade in the city, which commanded the passport holder to not support the Confederacy. Governor Moore took note of this, stating "The Confederacy and the State recognize but two classes—its friends and its foes," placing the detested passport holders in the latter category.[61]

CONSCRIPTION AND THE HOME FRONT

"Oh this cruel war it is bringing distress & trouble on us all," wrote one soldier's wife on March 8, 1863. "They have now called on all from 17 to 50 years of age & are going to force them I dont see what will become of the country & people it is dreadful to think of."[62] As the Confederate draft restructured Southern society, Drew Gilpin Faust argues that a large portion of "the Confederate homefront became a world of white women and of slaves."[63] Thavolia Glymph notes the irony of such a notion since the slaveholders who helped bring on the conflict "to protect white homes and white women" led to much of the destruction of these homes and the social order that supposedly upheld the virtue and protection of White women. But she also notes that plantation mistresses had previous experience managing—and punishing—slaves. Ex-slave testimonies present evidence that many slaveholding women were well versed in such actions that made plantations a "war zone," as one historian described them, rife with "barbaric responses from slaveholders," both male and female.[64] However, not all Southern women came from slaveholding families.

The war—and the draft—forced many women to alter their lives and lifestyles, along with taking on new roles, responsibilities, and occupations. Confederate women not only bore the brunt of the chaos and commotion the war caused on the home front, but were also subjected to the political, economic, and social changes that ensued.[65]

As not all men dutifully honored the draft laws, the same was true of women—prompting some Louisiana ladies to take matters into their own hands. Decades after the war, ex-slave Rebecca Fletcher recalled how women aided their husbands in dodging conscription. "When the war came on they conscripted men to go to fight, white men," she stated. "Some didn't want to go and they had they wives to hide 'em under a bed or in a chim'ley or some place to keep from gwine to war."[66] Conscription evasion could also turn violent. One Louisiana woman noted, "Many bad patriots refused to enlist," claiming their families' welfare would be jeopardized if they were obliged to serve. Some of these men "revolted . . . and prepared to resist those who would try and capture them."[67] A group of over seventy Washington Parish men organized and "declared openly that they would rather die than serve in the army of the Confederacy."[68] Draft resistance stirred strife among the population and Confederate officials, sometimes leading to the mishandling and abuse of conscripts.[69]

Despite this social restructuring and resistance, many women accepted these circumstances (though oftentimes grudgingly) for the good of the cause, which ensured that the cooperative network between soldiers and civilians would continue. Accustomed to hard work before the war, many women were very capable of taking care of themselves and their families.[70] One Louisianian's 1863 account of how his wife's honorable conduct in the face of enemy soldiers stands as a testimony to the stern resolve of many Southern ladies who remained on the home front. "No other woman could stand such an ordeal as she passed through," he wrote. "Had the Confederate Generals and Officers who commanded the troops of Louisiana had just one tenth of the Bravery moral and physical courage of my dear wife, Louisiana would never have been in Federal hands."[71] Other Louisiana soldiers held similar views of their women's resolve and capabilities.[72]

Married soldiers, though now in the army, sought to retain their role as household head as they continued to instruct their wives on various domestic matters via letters. This does not imply that Confederate women had no say in running their homes. Many soldiers fully trusted their wives and felt them capable of carrying on home-front operations. Women did what they felt was best at the time, but they likely remained cognizant of their husband's preferences and desires when making decisions. Throughout the war, Laure Stagg from southwest Louisiana received instructions, advice, and suggestions from her soldier-husband on how to manage the family plantation, which included addressing topics such as hiring workers, caring for (and selling) slaves, harvesting crops, maintaining structures and fences, and raising and tending livestock.[73] Though absentee husbands provided input, it was ultimately up to Southern women to run the household. "I would have asked your advice," wrote one Louisiana soldier's wife, "but I did not have time to wait for your answer, I hope what I have done will meet with your approbation for I do the best I know how."[74] Another Louisianian's wife tended to her husband's affairs of ginning and selling cotton, which she took seriously. "There is a good many of the neighbors told me particularly not to let him touch it until paid for," she wrote of an untrustworthy cotton dealer. "It is a trick but I intend to be smart enough for him. . . . I am going to keep my pistol and gun both loaded and if he dares to touch the cotten he will get a ball in the head." Apparently, this woman had other qualms against the cotton dealer, as she claimed he "has treated me shamefully and is talking about me all over the neighborhood."[75]

Women exercised control of their husbands' property while they soldiered—whether voluntarily or unwillingly, often winning their approval. In 1864, one Louisiana soldier claimed he had "so much confidence. . . . I congratulate myself even in moody moments that I must be a fortunate man at least so far as the wife is concerned."[76] Indeed, the Confederacy was truly indebted to the large numbers of tough and self-willed Southern women who simultaneously cared for their families and tended to home-front operations. Both husbands and wives saw that their sacrifices over family separation and enduring the hardships brought on by the war constituted a cross that the state and the Confederacy forced them to bear. "But as we have so often said to each other," wrote one Louisiana officer serving in Tennessee to his wife, "we are separated by duty & will bear it. May God grant you strength to do so!"[77] But wartime stress and responsibilities often caused frustration for some Confederate women—even as early as 1861. One Louisiana soldier's wife wrote to her husband in Virginia complaining, "I am tired of attending to your affairs. I have my hands full, I am going to make you pay me giv [*sic*] wages when you come home."[78]

While many Southern women admirably rose to the challenge of independently managing the home front without their husbands, the draft, which some authorities—and soldiers—felt would act as a leveler, forced many more civilians to pick up the slack from their relatives who were now in the ranks. It also stirred class tensions (even among Southern women); one historian noted that social discrepancies remained visible.[79] To help alleviate tensions, Confederate authorities advanced the idea that soldiers fought to protect the homes and honor of Southern White women, which fostered some unification among the classes. And many Southern families (as least in part since their relatives were in the ranks) remained loyal and steadfast to the Confederacy.[80]

Louisiana's militia laws granting concessions to slaveholders stirred protest; one Confederate general, for instance, argued that such measures harmed the state's war effort. He claimed that granting exemptions to planters "would reduce the patriotic contributions of the nonslaveowner, destroy harmony, and display inequality and injustice toward the less fortunate."[81] On the national level, the passing of the "Twenty Negro Law," which allowed one White male per plantation of twenty or more enslaved people to be exempt from military service, had less to do with aiding the privileged slaveholders than with ensuring that vital plantation production continued. The law also attempted to contain the strained power structure on large plantations as most of the White male population, who customarily regulated the forced labor, were off fighting and left the tough task of running plantations to women.[82]

Indeed, friction between Southern social classes existed well before conscription took effect. In the summer of 1861, a Winnfield, Louisiana, newspaper reported, "The non-slaveholding population think that the slave-holders are not doing their duty, and therefore, should be made to do it." However, further research has uncovered that by 1862 the slaveholding population pulled its weight.[83] In some cases, wealthy individuals put their social status aside and fell into the rank and file. Louisiana militiaman H. A. Snyder noted the ritzy makeup of his "Regiment composed principally of men of wealth, many of them millionair accustomed to all the ease, luxuries, comforties wealth can produce, harnessed up in uniforms, marching in the ranks as common soldiers."[84]

IMPRESSMENT OF BLACK LABORERS
FOR THE CONFEDERACY

Conscription not only affected Louisiana's White population. The Confederate government also saw the importance of Black labor. The contributions made by bondsmen allowed able-bodied White men to fill the Confederate ranks and enslaved people's toil on plantations would "not leave the material interests of the country in a suffering condition."[85] African Americans were also highly visible among Confederate forces as they performed a range of activities that included constructing military fortifications and loading and unloading supplies.[86] But impressed slave laborers also required provisions and supervision, which increased the demands on Confederate soldiers.[87] F. A. Prudhomme wrote to his father explaining, "We are here encamped on the banks of the bayou Teche and my company is guarding a lot of negroes who are engaged in government work . . . throwing up fortifications."[88] Guarding or obtaining enslaved workers was no easy task. Pvt. Isaac Dunbar Affleck told his mother he and his comrades obtained ten "negroes" near Alexandria, but only "after a great deal of trouble," especially since the region had been devastated by the fighting and enslaved laborers were scarce.[89]

At the war's commencement, bondsmen came onto the scene as Confederate laborers. A little over a month after the war's opening shots at Fort Sumter, a small number of Confederate enslaved laborers deserted to the Union lines. Slave agency, even in the conflict's infancy, played a major role in wartime developments.[90] Some Federal commanders saw the value enslaved individuals could perform for the Union cause, which also caught the eye of some Confederates.[91] Both armies questioned the exact role of African American laborers, which one historian argues opened the door for eventual emancipation.[92] Union general Benjamin Butler capitalized on the idea of labeling enslaved people as contraband and his confiscation of them and willingness to encourage other bondsmen to desert their enslavers wreaked havoc on the Confederate labor force. Once Butler reached Louisiana, his reputation would be well-known by many residents.[93]

For Louisiana, the first legislative measures authorizing the impressment of slave labor for Confederate defense projects, which aimed at protecting the Red River, came in 1862. Police juries received authorization to create a census of the region's able-bodied slaves between the ages of eighteen and forty-five (the same age requirements of military conscription), along with the ability to not only obtain the needed individuals for each project (regardless of their owners' consent) but also "demand sustenance, working tools and instruments . . . as were necessary." Any slaveholder or overseer who did not comply with the law could be fined, and Confederate officers received orders to use "military force . . . to procure negroes from the planters who have neglected or refuse to furnish their quota." The military also relied on the parish police juries, which were part of Louisiana's local parish governments, to cooperate.[94]

Confederate authorities offered compensation for slave laborers; however, performing the military's fatigue duty took slaves off a plantation, possibly creating an opportunity for resistance or escape.[95] Numerous planters who lost their human chattel to labor conscription also worried for their slaves' health and well-being as physical abuses likely occurred. Indeed, planters' concerns over their enslaved workers well-being grew to such an extent that Confederate authorities passed legislative action ensuring protection.[96] Confederate author- ities "assured" many planters "that their slaves were handled with care while they worked on defenses"; however, the situation's reality proved less benevo- lent. Soldiers who witnessed the impressed laborers in action were not fooled by any Confederate authorities' half-hearted statements. One soldier claimed that the slaves "are worked from day break untill dark in chains and Sunday all the time."[97] Another soldier wrote, "Oh how I pity these poor negroes here . . . They work from daybreak until dark [and] about half feed them[.] They look so bad[.]"[98]

Throughout the entire Confederacy, enslavers protested their enslaved peoples' treatment and exposure to extreme conditions (including diseases), fearing such treatment would affect their monetary value, at the hands of Con- federate military officials—and many planters demanded the return of their slave property.[99] Supplying slave laborers for the Confederate army also took its toll on plantation production as well as on protection against flooding. Many alarmed planters along the Tensas, Black, Little, and Ouachita Rivers requested and received cooperation from their police jury for the return of their slaves for levee maintenance.[100] However, even before the war, the use of slave labor was not always a cooperative affair. Jobs off the plantation not only interrupted daily routines, but also provided opportunities for the enslaved to undermine the institution.[101] Once the fighting began, opportunities to escalate the institution's demise quickly became apparent. One historian notes that "slaves—men and women—took slowly increasing advantage of white men's departure for war to test the sovereignty of slaveholders." Even slaveholders who attempted to protect their chattel property by pulling up stakes for lands undisturbed by war brought disruption to antebellum routines and wartime production.[102]

Planters, such as those from Morehouse Parish, sought to ensure they could reclaim their impressed slaves at a nearby fort. The planters wanted "the Overseers we send to take charge of the negroes. . . . And that they shall not be given any other duties which may cause them to leave the Post so long as our negroes remain there." The enslavers even requested separate accommodations be established for their bondsmen, along with their medical treatment to be under "the Physician employed by the Planters."[103] And for conscripted slaves who remained at their posts when battles loomed, they sometimes found themselves caught in the fray. One Louisiana soldier stationed at Vicksburg wrote his wife about the close calls he and the enslaved workers faced under Yankee bombardments as one explosion "would have buried me & all my niggers if we hadn't been working somewhere else at the time."[104] Confederate authorities made their case that the war effort needed slave laborers—and took them. However, officials sometimes attempted to explain to Louisiana planters how the military impressment of their chattel property aided the cause, hoping to foster cooperation.[105]

Coercing slave laborers remained problematic for Confederate authorities, especially when dealing with unwilling planters away from the watchful eyes of their enslavers—and close to Union lines—many slaves took the opportunity to liberate themselves. One Union officer noted the irony of the situation transpiring before him in Louisiana, as slaves were "flying from their masters . . . thoroughly impressed with the idea of being free. The doom of slavery is already written." He claimed the secessionists "must stop the rebellion to save their country from destruction and servile war, and perhaps themselves from negro domination and a Black Republic. What a terrible punishment."[106]

However, escaping remained a complex endeavor for the enslaved, and it did not always offer satisfactory results. William R. Pritchard's study of African American mobility in Civil War–era Louisiana provides a detailed look at the familial effects of emancipation, which often meant relocation, displacement, and separation. Reaching Union lines sometimes meant permanent separation from families, neglect, and suffering, which was often linked to diseases. Even in Federal-occupied New Orleans, Black mobility often remained limited, especially as fears of insurrection loomed.[107] While serving in Louisiana, Texas Confederate soldier H. N. Connor noted how he and his men, "Captured hundreds of Negroes from the swamps, all in the state of starvation." The suffering African Americans told the Texans that their condition of "Disease and starvation . . . in place of freedom" was such ever since the Federal troops placed them in that location. Connor claimed that, after providing relief for the runaways, "they appeared to be very happy, and wanted to go to their homes, or ours if we chose to take them."[108]

If a newspaper account is to be believed, one Federal officer stated, "The strength of the South is in its slaves . . . it has become a military necessity to take them away." According to an "intelligent lady from Alexandria," she wrote that when the taken slaves "'entered the yankee lines, everything they had was taken from them by their friends and sympathizers,' . . . when husband and wife were separated, parents and children, they shrieked and screamed, and begged them for God's sake to let them 'go home to their masters,' . . . the men went one way . . . —poor creatures!'" This newspaper account begs questions of how Northerners could support such actions. Despite the Yankee atrocities mentioned, the article is obviously one-sided and self-serving, as disturbing scenes such as this commonly occurred before the conflict at antebellum slave auctions.[109] But despite these episodes, slave agency remained in play and resistance proved effective.

Near Donaldsonville, F. A. Prudhomme wrote home after hearing word of Union Gen. Benjamin Butler's "drama," stating that "a perfect reign of terror pervades all hearts . . . by public demonstrations to insurrection and destruction."[110] And as African Americans joined the Union ranks and fears of insurrection mounted, one Federal major lay the blame of the social upheaval on the rebels, claiming, "Did you expect to march into that country, drained as you say it is by conscription of all its able-bodied white men without leaving the negroes to show symptoms of survile [sic] insurrection? You are in a country where now the Negroes outnumber the whites ten to one."[111]

Not all Union soldiers embraced the idea of setting slaves free, nor did the Emancipation Proclamation end the institution, as slavery remained legal in the border states and areas of the Confederacy already under Union control, which included parts of southeastern Louisiana. But the proclamation's effects could not be ignored—and Confederate soldiers knew it.[112] Louisiana soldier W. H.

King, who was captured by Union troops near Brashear City [present day Morgan City] in south Louisiana, claimed, "Many of the Yankees assent they are not in favor of freeing the negro, & would fight no longer if they knew such to be the purpose of their gov't." He questioned these Federal soldiers' sincerity. Pointing out groups of African Americans en route to Brashear City to his captors, King "asked those of the Yankees who said they were opposed to freeing the negroes, what that meant if their gov't did not intend to free the negroes. The ready reply is, 'It is not the real intention of the gov't to free the negroes, but it finds it necessary to take the negroes from their owners for the present to crush the rebellion. When that is effected, we have no doubt but the negroes will be returned to their proper owners.'" King remained skeptical, claiming the soldiers were misguided, stating, "Such is their delusion. They are caused to believe the gov't does not really intend to free the negro, to encourage them to fight."[113]

Unfortunately for some enslaved individuals who made it to Union lines and became soldiers or laborers, abuse remained a fixture in their lives, which sometimes included the lack of adequate food and provisions.[114] Several Union soldiers disliked the idea of being emancipators, and they made their opinions on the matter known. As one private wrote, "There is one thing the men in general don't like, that is freeing the niggers."[115] One Union soldier witnessed the prejudices African Americans faced in a Federal camp, noting, "The men in our camp treat them [the Negroes] worse than brutes."[116] Rumors of such treatment made it to Confederate camps; one Louisiana officer told his wife, "The yankees have shot and hung several negros for disobedience. It seems that the negros who went with the yankees have got into a bad pickle."[117]

Louisiana Confederate soldiers remained watchful for rumors of violent developments as the institution began to break down. In 1862 an armed clash occurred in New Orleans between the police and a Black gang that numbered "about twenty-five or thirty . . . marching up the levee . . . in a sort of semi-military style, armed with formidable cane knives and pistols." The incident resulted in many casualties from both parties.[118] About sixteen months later, a Louisiana soldier wrote in his journal that it was "Rumored that the negroes have rebelled against the Federals at N. Orleans, & taken possession of the City." Though this might have been a similar instance as the August 1862 riot or just a lie, the soldier claimed, "Good if true, but I do not believe a word of it." He later found out the "great rebellion" was only a "small difficulty in Fort

Jackson, in which about 30 Federals were killed."[119] Other violent encounters between runaway bondsmen and law enforcement transpired that involved Union soldiers, and their actions sometimes mimicked those of slave patrols.[120] As both Union and Confederate soldiers noted the growing violence and racial disorder, one Louisiana soldier stationed in Mississippi wrote, "I heard that the runaway slaves have done more harm than the Yankees themselves, they say they have burned and pillaged several plantation[s], and that they steal all the livestock."[121]

David Gleeson argues that the Civil War eventually became "the largest slave rebellion in modern history," but not from a large-scale internal rebellion—"the real threat to slavery was the external one of Union armed forces' incursion, invasion, and occupation." Gleeson's research reveals that much of the rhetoric surrounding slave-insurrection fears in Georgia were often linked to men attempting to avoid military service. He claims that "plantation security," even with fewer White men at home, remained intact; however, it was the arrival of Federal troops that made Georgians uneasy. Even in 1863 and 1864, when Georgia remained under the threat of Union invasion, Confederate laws continuously restricted exemptions, forcing more men into the ranks. According to Georgia's officials, the best way to ensure slavery's survival was to "halt 'the enemy.'"[122]

Despite the initial excitement caused by the arrival of Union troops and the Emancipation Proclamation, rumors of freedom did not always produce cheers of jubilation from the enslaved. Indeed, some planters openly read the proclamation to their bondsmen, which left many African Americans pondering their new predicament. What exactly did the proclamation mean to them? And, based on their understanding of it, what was their best course of action? Running to Union lines or joining the Union military remained options for some enslaved individuals—but only if Federal forces were located nearby. However, even these actions sometimes proved futile.

One slave decided not to wander from the plantation, claiming, "I see no use of us going and getting ourselves into trouble. . . . We think it betterer to stay home on the plantation, and get our food and our clothes. If we are to get freedom, dare we are! But if we run away, and go to New Orleans, like dem crazy niggers, where is we?"[123] Indeed, some historians note that "for many freed people the realities of freedom often looked similar to or worse than" their experiences in slavery. Even as escaped slaves reached New Orleans, hoping to improve their circumstances and gain their freedom, Federal officials, who could not logistically provide for these individuals, turned many away.[124] E. John Ellis recalled his interpretation of the effects of the Emancipation Proclamation on both the Union and Confederacy, writing, "Lincoln's policy of war and subjugation of pillage and confiscation, his proclamation of emancipation, the arming of negroes, the insults to our women and the excesses of the Federal soldiery, all proved to me that the war was for the negro and not for the Union. . . . Lincoln's policy has <u>united</u> a <u>divided</u> South, has <u>divided</u> a <u>united</u> North, and Southern independence must, <u>can only be</u> the result of the struggle." If anything, Lincoln's policies would escalate the conflict and make the Confederates fight harder.[125]

Though the initial volunteer wave subsided by the war's second year, many White Louisiana civilians continued to answer their state's call for military service—even if it was forced and unpopular—helping to fill the manpower shortage. Assembling men for military service required civilian cooperation and support, especially from the women and planters left on the home front. Attitudes toward these measures varied as some soldiers (and authorities) saw the draft as a social leveler, but placed a major burden on the numerous families left behind. However daunting (or, in the war's earlier stages, exciting) raising troops—and providing for them—might have been, transforming the state's volunteers and draftees into soldiers (and slaves into military laborers) remained an interdependent feat. And as the war's demands restructured Southern society, both soldiers and civilians remained cognizant of the importance of the Confederacy's enslaved population's labors. Without their coerced contributions, the Confederate war machine would have crumbled.

CHAPTER 4

CAMP LIFE

"This war has done me good in many ways—It has taught me patence [*sic*] and endurance," wrote 16th Louisiana Infantry officer E. J. Ellis, noting the discomforts of soldier life. "I think I have seen the dark side of soldiering and although it is tolerably hard, yet there aint any use of calling it intolerable."[1] Other soldiers, such as Frederick Taber, expressed his frustration and disgust about camp life, which, to him, was proving unbearable. Taber told his family that Camp Benjamin, which was located near New Orleans, "is the D——mist hole on earth. . . . God pity the poor Soldiers for our Officers do not."[2] In the unstable world that the war shaped, camp experiences transformed civilians into soldiers. Even in the midst of complaints, many soldiers accepted their lot as fighting men and adapted to military depravations. One Louisianian claimed, "We cannot grumble of camp life, it is a thing past & gone with us—we know nothing but march, march, and halt and sleep in wet blankets & mud."[3]

Enduring physical and mental discomforts hardened these men, which would prove necessary for them to wage war. However, as separation from loved ones and privations became the norm, many soldiers reconstructed some semblance of civilian life within these spaces, and their interaction with civilians remained a major part of their military service. They often reflected the complex dynamics of Southern society's social class structure, especially between enlisted men and officers. Porous spaces, camps often served as meeting places for soldiers and civilians—reinforcing the social reality that defined Civil

War soldiers' experiences. Historians have discussed many aspects of Civil War life in camps, which varied in size, location, and condition, and were inseparable from the soldier's wartime experience as men spent most of their time in them.[4] Confederate camps, which acted as training grounds and campaign staging areas, proved to be much more.

SOLDIERS, CIVILIANS, AND UNIT FORMATIONS

Assembling men from the same locale proved a morale booster for many soldiers, as William Paxton explained to his wife that he and others anxiously waited for the arrival of companies from back home in northwestern Louisiana. "If we could get them," he wrote, "we would have a full Regiment half of the men of which were well acquainted with Each other before they left home— Such an association you can well imagine would be very pleasant."[5] E. J. Lee mentioned his excitement when men from his home parish of Union arrived at Camp Moore. "We have been very lively since they come."[6] High morale made some soldiers believe they were destined for greatness; one 9th Louisiana infantryman, who held his officers in high esteem, felt his "regiment will certaninly make a name in history."[7]

Assembling units was exciting and also granted soldiers a small measure of autonomy in their military regimen, resembling yet another aspect of civilian life. Volunteers welcomed familiar faces. Having kinsmen in the ranks or in leadership positions offered comfort for many soldiers who were far from home. However, in the case of Charley Flournoy, it did not translate to favoritism. "Do not presume the forbearance of your Captain because he happens to be your brother," wrote Flournoy's father. "Your Captain has to do his duty and cannot show partiality."[8] Providing leadership to newly formed regiments proved a daunting task. Citizen-soldiers, who were more inclined to be citizens than soldiers, elected their officers, and these elections resembled political campaigning. Soldiers running for leadership positions vied for votes from their comrades, and oftentimes the results were not unanimous.[9]

Finding (or choosing) officers to lead soldiers was not easy. William H. Russell, a foreign visitor who reported for the *London Times,* noted the relaxed military standards at Camp Moore. "The militia of Louisiana has not been called out for many years, and its officers have no military experience and the men have no drill or discipline."[10] One Louisiana officer blamed "the long and profound peace" that preceded the Civil War, which led to this "almost entire decay of the militia."[11] Undisciplined behavior remained visible even on the cusp of the Union's invasion of the state, as several soldiers—regardless of their rank—engaged in dueling and other blood-letting activities.[12] William Russell also credited Louisiana forces' lack of professional military leadership with their methods of choosing their commanders. Despite a soldier's military credentials, or lack thereof, men campaigned to become officers. This electioneering, which "has made the camp as thoroughly a political arena as the poll districts in New Orleans before an election," did not have the soldiers' best interests in mind. Russell stated that these so-called "heroes" who sought leadership roles were "in reality only laying pipes for the attainment of civil power or distinction after the war."[13] W. H. King feared electioneering "will prove of injury to us . . . the spirit of seeking positions of honor & lucrativeness has spread widely throughout the Confederacy."[14]

However, not all officer appointments were by ballot. Eugene Janin received his second lieutenant's commission in a company of the 10th Louisiana Infantry after Captain Hewitt "wrote me to ask if I would accept it." Before accepting the appointment, Janin visited the company, finding it "had the reputation of being the most orderly & best drilled company in the reg." Along with the perk of joining a disciplined company, Janin noted that many of the unit's officers were "old acquaintances," further prompting him to accept the commission.[15] Becoming an officer demanded a certain level of dignity in dress and appearance as Janin noted: "An officer has to appear as a gentleman," which included "a quantity of clothes . . . sword, pistol," along with other trifles and expenses that went with the position.[16] Other officer commissions came from the Confederate War Department; however, this method (just like electioneering) was not always popular among the men.[17] Though officers obtained commissions by different means, Andrew S. Bledsoe claims that junior officers, like their lower-ranking enlisted soldiers, were *citizens* first and were "influenced by, the persistent citizen-soldier ethos of republican tradition." Regardless of military rank, citizen-soldiers often saw themselves as social equals to their chosen leaders. Among these men, social bonding and cooperation mattered.[18]

Some enlistees became disgruntled when they failed to obtain a commission, believing their subordinate military rank did not match their civilian social status. One Louisiana soldier told his sister that "I will never be a private soldier after my term of enlistment expires. I must have a commission. . . . I cant tolerate officers over me who are in every way my inferiors." Social rank mattered to this soldier, but he felt that his predicament—which was self-inflicted—was a necessary sacrifice for the South's independence. "I gave up for the time my social position, and <u>condescended</u> to take for associates and peers, men for whome I have as much affinty, as heat for cold. . . . I hold it dishonorable to stay at home . . . while my countrymen and neighbors are risking their lives for my defence. . . . I came for action."[19] Indeed, some officers looked down upon enlisted men, which brewed animosity between them. One soldier wrote that some of the officers in his company "generally thought that a private did not have any humane feelings and were treated like dum brutes."[20] Amos Anselm, an 8th Louisiana infantryman, compared soldier life to slavery as he complained about his camp's strict regulations. Despite not always agreeing with strong disciplinary measures, he admitted they were "necessary. If I had the making of the law I would make it just as it is—can't get along any other way."[21]

Becoming an officer offered a mode of escape from the injustices among the rank and file in military life, though not all enlisted men desired promotions. An officer's workload entailed too "much labor to perform with too little compensation," wrote Frank Richardson. He claimed that as long as his physical needs were met and that he continued to "remain on freindly terms with my company . . . I am content to go through life as private."[22] Though Richardson might have been content with his low rank, he also echoed the disdain between officers and enlisted men that many soldiers felt, claiming, "The life of a common soldier is a most hard and rough one it is a great deal worse than that of a common field negro but those commissioned officers they are just like the owners of slaves on plantations they have nothing to do but to strut about dress fine and enjoy themselves." As a soldier and a son from a slaveholding family from southwest Louisiana, Richardson well knew the comparisons; however, he too understood that to maintain discipline most "common soldiers have to be treated as negros or they will not obey and besides they are a very low set of men being composed of these low Irish and the scum of creation." Diverse as Louisiana's forces were, contempt for the privileges of officers and prejudices against a fellow soldier's background or nationality remained present among the troops.[23]

While conversing with a Union prisoner, Capt. E. John Ellis of the 16th Louisiana Infantry noted that the Yankee was a recent Irish immigrant. According to Ellis, the Union soldier was shocked to hear that many of Ellis's fellow Confederates "were my earliest and best friends and that the best and wealthiest citizens of the south were, many of them, privates in the armies." The poor Union Irishman "could not comprehend how anyone with plenty of money and a comfortable home should engage in the war and endure the hardships incident to the lot of the private soldier."[24] Indeed, that a financially stable individual would endure the hardships and privations of war as an enlisted soldier might be admirable, but it must be remembered that Ellis was an officer, and, as the evidence shows, much grumbling and complaining existed within the ranks.

OBTAINING WEAPONS, SUPPLIES, AND TRAINING

Within weeks of the firing on Fort Sumter, Gen. P. G. T. Beauregard from Louisiana departed Charleston for another assignment. Before leaving he told the Charlestonians that "whatever happens at first, we are certain to triumph at last, even if we had for arms only pitchforks and flintlock muskets, for every bush and haystack will become an ambush and every barn a fortress."[25] Though the general's rhetoric inspired applause and cheers, the question of obtaining and maintaining firearms proved a constant chore for the Confederacy—especially for Louisiana's quickly forming regiments. Learning the art of war was a new experience for many Louisianians and obtaining supplies relied heavily on civilian support, sometimes with mixed results.[26] One officer at Camp Moore told his wife of the "unfortunate" weapons shortage, claiming, "there are at least five or six companies here without arms."[27] William Paxton echoed the same predicament, claiming that one reason for the soldiers' inferior or nonexistent weapons was because the governor answered the pleas of other Confederate States and sent thousands of arms for their assistance. While Paxton and his compatriots lacked firearms, he did not blame the governor, writing, "Of course I do not censure him for those guns have long since been doing good service in the common cause."[28] Even though some companies remained armed, not all soldiers shared Paxton's sentiments.[29]

Other units throughout the state faced similar challenges. The 10th Louisiana Infantry Battalion, nicknamed the Yellow Jacket Battalion since many of the soldiers wore "home made yellow cottonade suits" had at least one hundred weaponless men. The battalion later received "225 double-barreled shotguns," but only about 158 proved serviceable.[30] W. H. King also hinted at the weapons shortage in the spring of 1862, noting that his unit originally organized "for

State defense for a term of twelve months, on condition we equip ourselves with double-barrelled shot-guns." Many of the enlistees did not report with their firearms as the company formed a detail to "collect guns."[31] Pleas for firearms came early in the war from high-ranking state or Confederate officials. Louisiana newspapers also relayed the message as Confederate agents sought cooperation from local citizens to donate "many thousands of tried guns that lie unused in your houses." To quell fears that these weapons would be needed for home defense, the newspaper assured citizens that "the surest way to prevent the necessity of using them at home is to place them in the hands of the thousands of brave men who are now chafing with anxious desire to stand as a wall of fire between you and the invading foe."[32]

Governor Moore also expected New Orleanians to answer the call for arms, authorizing Lt. Col. George W. Logan "to seize every shot gun, rifle, musket pistol or other fire arm in the city." Moore directed Logan to provide receipts to the owners promising that the firearm would be returned "in the condition in which it was received, or to pay its appraised value."[33] A few firearms (at least in the war's earlier months) remained available for purchase. One Texas soldier, for example, wishing to obtain a sidearm noted that he found some pistols for sale in New Orleans, "but they asked 50 or 60 dollars a piece for them." Apparently, they were out of his price range as he continued shopping after arriving in Nashville days later.[34] Louisiana soldier Edwin Fay wrote his wife from Tennessee that he obtained "a large sized Colt's revolver" for forty-five dollars. "I was determined to be as well armed as any of the company and if I could buy another I would do it. . . . Money is nothing where my safety is concerned." Fay apparently was a good shot with his new pistol, as he claimed he could "kill rabbits with it almost as well as if I had a rifle."[35]

Some Louisianians, especially those with relatives in the ranks, did what they could to help. "I want to give all I can," wrote a sugar planter (who apparently was a former soldier) to his brother, which included both weapons and soldier accoutrements. "All of these things I wish to contribute to the company," but "My two pistols and sabre and whatever else you need keep for yourself, and let the rest go into some good hands."[36] Though citizens helped, Louisiana's residents could not make up for the weapons shortage. Even as late as 1863, some regiments, such as the 2nd Louisiana Cavalry, turned to the Confederate Capital for assistance as they sent an officer to Richmond to "procure pistols for the Regt."[37] Confederate Louisiana's authorities' continuous

battle to procure enough firearms for their men—even with the assistance of
civilians—proved a logistical fiasco.

The Confederacy had great need of contributions from its residents with
means—monetary or otherwise—highlighting the dependence that soldiers
had on civilians for the necessities to wage war. Decades after the conflict, one
former officer of the 26th Louisiana Infantry recalled how much of a soldier's
clothing "was received from our friends, or obtained by our own efforts from
private sources, by gift or purchase." Self-sufficiency ruled the day as the officer
also remembered that "we had to take care of ourselves . . . save what we might
procure individually, from patriotic citizens."[38] One Louisiana soldier noted his
personal equipment included socks, flannel drawers, and shirts, along with "a
pair of very showy aligator shoes which I had purchased in New Orleans for 6
½ dollars." Though "showy," these shoes "proved very little worth as they do
not refuse to admit water to my feet."[39] Civilian supplies, despite their varying
quality and ability to withstand the rigors of war, not only aided in outfitting
Louisiana's troops for the field but also reminded them of their civilian connections.

ESTABLISHING CAMPS

As the initial volunteer rush and conscription swelled the ranks, Confederate
authorities established camps to provide spaces for these men to transition
into soldiers. Officials hoped that isolating camps from populated areas would
prove beneficial as it would "not only afford the men more personal comfort
but will banish the soft feelings to which they are daily condemned . . . by the
daily visits of their relatives and friends."[40] Keeping some distance between
civilians and soldiers in camp would likely limit a soldier's distractions and
help maintain discipline. However, camps were only semi-secluded and never
totally isolated, nor were civilian visits forbidden—in fact, they were usually
encouraged.[41]

Regardless of a camp's location, they oftentimes reflected the soldiers' Louisiana connections, which included christening these spaces with the names
of familiar places and people. While serving in Virginia, the Washington Artillery's camps displayed their Louisiana roots with names such as Camp Louisiana, Camp Orleans, and Camp Beauregard.[42] Louisiana's infantry regiments
in Virginia also made use of names associated with their home state, such as

Camp Carondelet (named after a Louisiana Spanish colonial governor) and Camp Stafford (named after Louisiana Gen. Leroy Stafford, who was killed at the Battle of the Wilderness). Environmental elements and supply shortages led some Louisiana Tigers to give their camps nicknames based on their poor conditions, likely to add humor amidst their misery. Soldiers in the 5th Louisiana Infantry referred to their camp near Yorktown as "Camp Starvation" because of food shortages, and Louisiana troops stationed near Port Royal combatted winter conditions by "burrowing into the ground like animals," earning their camp the nickname "Camp Hole in the Ground."[43] Camps and forts within the state of Louisiana obviously reflected their share of names of famous soldiers and politicians, but also included an array of names associated with well-known landmarks and waterways.[44]

Arrival at a camp of instruction marked the beginning of a recruit's (or conscript's) transition from civilian to soldier. One soldier described Camp Moore, which was named for Gov. Thomas O. Moore and was the state's major instruction site located about eighty miles north of New Orleans, as "a pleasant place." Camp Moore replaced Camp Walker, the ill-suited training site of the Metairie Racetrack, for numerous reasons, especially related to health concerns and discipline.[45] The new locale provided raw recruits with fresh water, clean air, and distance from big city vices. The camp's environmental surroundings offered soldiers leisure activities, such as fishing, which men eagerly took advantage of; one soldier told his wife that "if there are fish to be caught, we will have them."[46] But access to fresh water meant more than fishing. Robert Patrick noted that the Mississippi River was their previous water source at Camp Walker, and they collected water in "old pork barrels, and in addition to being warm and muddy, the old grease and salt that had been in the barrels previously gave it a very bad taste." Camp Moore's water proved both literally and figuratively refreshing.[47]

One (exaggerated) account noted that soldiers' access to fresh water greatly improved camp health and hygiene as "10,000 men can bathe in this beautiful stream at once and then 10,000 more without inconvenience to any."[48] And Camp Moore was not the only Confederate base with water access, both for recreation and bathing.[49] Yet, even with clean water, reports of camp deaths continued, often related to illnesses, environmental exposure (such as heat stroke), or accidents associated with carelessness or drunkenness. And despite the common bonds men shared as soldiers, ethnic prejudices remained a fixture in the ranks; one soldier, for instance, felt little sorrow for two men who died at Camp Moore, writing that "they were both Irishmen and were not greaved after much."[50]

Over time, Confederate authorities established other camps throughout the state for the purpose of training new soldiers. In southwest Louisiana near New Iberia, Camp Pratt (named after Louisiana Militia Gen. John G. Pratt) became an instruction center for local soldiers and conscripts who aimed to learn the art of war to assist "in freeing this section of the country from the polluting tread of the Lincoln hordes."[51] Campaigning soldiers sometimes set up camps close to residents' homes, as one Texas soldier noted, "We have been camping in a grass lot in front of a lady's house for the last few days. It is a nice country."[52] Soldiers who camped near civilian homes were sometimes lucky enough to be welcomed with open arms. One Louisiana lady captivated her bittersweet feelings of parting on good terms with soldiers as she wrote, "I was very sorry to see them go. Will miss them. . . . I dislike to see any of the soldiers leaving the place. I miss the tents when I go in the yard or on the gallery."[53] In November of 1861, a soldier in the 24th Louisiana Volunteers optimistically wrote from his camp along Bayou Teche that "we are likely to have a nice time here for the citizens are inclined to be kind to the soldiers."[54] Another soldier wrote his father about his unit's new camp near the Atchafalaya River, noting, "The people are generally verry hospitable to us. they have Sent us . . . all kinds of vegetables potatoes and one or two bbles of molasses Since we have been here."[55]

But not all Louisianians shared these friendly sentiments toward soldiers. David Waters, who lived in Amite, Louisiana, had first openly welcomed the Confederate troops setting up camp near his home; however, he soon regretted his decision to cooperate. After the soldiers began stealing and damaging his property, he warned them but to no avail. Aiming to end the shenanigans, Waters eventually shot and killed one of the soldiers, unleashing the Confederates' wrath. The retaliating troops destroyed much of Waters's property, leaving him financially ruined—even putting fear into his neighbors that the upset soldiers would continue their destruction on other inhabitants in the area. In cases such as this, civilian cooperation with soldiers became more aligned with fear than patriotism.[56] And if civilian encounters in camps such as the Waters incident could be deadly, diseases proved much worse.

Regardless of a camp's location, the less-publicized and unglamourous reality of these spaces was the growing filth and waste, which resulted from the large number of men living in close confines. Reubin A. Pierson wrote that "camp is one of the filthiest places I have ever been permitted to see." Even with soldiers policing the camp and "removing filth. . . . The flies are so thick until you have to be careful in carrying a mouthful from your plate to your mouth. . . . This is no exaggeration statement but will receive testimony on its truth from all who have visited this camp."[57] Soldiers—and their officers—constantly battled camp filth and all the negative effects associated with it. Issued orders made the soldiers "strictly accountable for the cleanliness and Police of their respective Camps," which included cleaning, sweeping, and garbage collection.[58] W. H. King led a squad of camp "policeman" who performed various tasks, especially cleaning up after his unit's officers. Making known his disdain about this detail, he recorded the following descriptive account of his experience:

> It was a filthy job, filthy in the extreme. It seemed that all scraps, odds & ends, entrails of fowls, & whatever other animals might have been brought into camp; together with feathers, fish heads, scales, &c., &c., had been thrown around indiscriminately, & none removed from their first arrival. Maggots were found in abundance—in some places not less than a quart, perhaps more, could be scooped up at once—and they the bigest of the big, & the fatest of the fat of their kind. All of this, & much more, we had to move out, while the buck negroes of the officers stood around, & grinned significantly. The picture needs no varnish, & my comment is, what could be more humiliating?[59]

King's comments highlight how the waste buildup—including excrement— contributed to camp illnesses that killed many soldiers. "Sad to think of; our men are dying in the attempt to serve our country, but are doing it no good."[60] However, camp life had also reversed the social roles for many Louisiana troops. Maintaining cleanliness, which was once of little concern to civilian men—especially those from the privileged slaveholding class—now became a despised part of a soldier's routine since their very lives depended on it.[61] But soldiers were not the only individuals who suffered. Civilian interactions with camps also spread diseases. Faust claims that the conflict "generated significant movements of peoples that served as deadly disease vectors. Contagions and epidemics that flourished in army camps spread to surrounding populations."

The Civil War soldier's social encounters could also be deadly ones—for them and their civilian counterparts.[62]

One Louisiana soldier explained to his wife, "Actual war has comparatively little danger in itself. The great majority of deaths are from sickness."[63] A Louisiana resident's wife who remained in South Carolina during the war also acknowledged, "Disease . . . proves as much if not more fatal than the bullets."[64] Frank Richardson, who suffered from a number of camp maladies, summed up a sick soldier's agony as he wrote, "A sick soldier is the most miserable animal on earth. . . . How I wish the war was over. There aint a bit of fun in it."[65] Edwin Fay believed a soldier's "life is not regarded as any more than a dog's, hardly as much. . . . I hope I may never be sick enough to need attention from any one."[66]

Sometimes soldiers blamed medical personnel for camp deaths. One 2nd Louisiana Cavalryman, for example, "died from the effects of an overdose of morphine . . . given by a mistake of the nurse."[67] Soldiers had various opinions of their surgeons, ranging from praise to disgust. One disgruntled Louisiana soldier at Port Hudson remained astonished at the "amount of ignorance there is amongst the Medical fraternity." Unsatisfied with their prescribed medical practices, the soldier claimed, "I am suffering now from the treatment of ignorant, sap-headed physicians."[68] But however incompetent surgeons could be, many men retained confidence in their abilities, and numerous soldiers testified that diseases, not surgeons, were the main culprit for camp deaths.[69] Kathryn Shively Meier argues that soldiers who distrusted military surgeons often turned to self-care, which "was more effective at keeping soldiers fit than the official army systems." The superiority of a soldier's self-care, Meier argues, was in the "ability to prevent illness," which contrasted with nineteenth-century medical professionals, who "focused instead on palliative care."[70]

As disease and illness ran their course, there were self-inflicted diseases as well. John A. Harris explained to his wife that "those who dye are men who would run after bad women, get bad diseases, then take measles, expose themselves in every way, and this is sure to bring on death." Harris's detailed description of camp sufferings continued as he mentioned a sobering visit to the hospital. "I cannot joke. For God noes, if any Man can come here and See the Suffering of human beings And then write jokes and nonsense back home, I dont no What kind of a heart he has," he told his wife. "I went to one Hospittle yesterday to See for my own Self, Their Were 27 [?] men in it Sick.

Their disease Was from Measels down to the rottenest disease that Man can take, from (women.)"[71]

One 9th Louisiana infantryman told his brother that "I never read or heard of such prostitution as I find in some parts of this country. . . . I do abhor & detest to see a woman throw herself upon a level with the brutes. When they do this they are truly the lowest of God[']s creation."[72] Prostitution, and its likely byproducts, sexually transmitted diseases, was not uncommon during the Civil War, plaguing both Union and Confederate armies. For the unlucky soldiers who contracted a sexually transmitted disease, which indicates civilians were nearby, they not only had to battle physical anguish, but also they became the subjects of camp gossip, which sometimes made its way back home.[73]

Alcohol consumption among soldiers remained prevalent in camps throughout the war. As Megan L. Bever notes, both the Union and Confederacy manufactured alcohol and its people consumed it—but its largest social impact linking soldiers and civilians was that it "broadened the conversation . . . about the relationship between drinking, patriotism, and national duty." Attitudes varied toward the use of alcohol. Both sides' soldiers fought against drunkenness, especially as it often "disrupted their duties or caused a misuse and the abuse of manpower and resources"; however, they also defended its use, arguing that alcohol held medicinal qualities and "fortified their bodies and minds and kept them able to serve in and survive the war."[74]

For the Confederacy, alcohol's availability determined the amount soldiers would consume. Regulated usage often remained linked to medicinal purposes, acting as a disease preventative and a major agent in soldier self-care, along with assisting in comforting the sick, wounded, or "to stave off the effects of exposure and fatigue." However, camp boredom and the social interaction between soldiers, which often included their partaking in conversations, games, and reminiscing about home, led to the consumption of spirits.[75] Confederate troops stationed at Port Hudson were apparently successful—or had connections with local civilians who assisted them—in obtaining (or making) alcoholic beverages, which often led to unruly behavior. The bastion's officers did all in their power to destroy alcohol's presence within the camp, much to their soldiers' dismay.[76] Excessive drinking led several Louisiana soldiers to take creative measures to obtain and conceal their libations, especially as officers attempted to enforce temperance; however, when available, soldiers eagerly obtained all they could get.[77]

One Texas officer complimented the 3rd Louisiana's leaders, but he also noted the "turbulent" behavior of the regiment's enlisted soldiers, as they were "desperately fond of whiskey."[78] Even as Louisiana officials authorized the production of medicinal whiskey, abuses continued, as some men felt it "their patriotic duty in testing" it.[79] Holidays offered soldiers a chance to enjoy a few libations, especially when celebrating Christmas, which helped them forget army life and remember home.[80] One Louisiana soldier serving in Virginia noted that his officers "gave a fine nogg to the whole camp" for Christmas. We had a "merry time while the effects of King alcohol lasted," he wrote.[81] Some Port Hudson soldiers enjoyed access to "Louisiana Rum," however, its taste apparently proved too strong for some men; one soldier believed it was "the vilest stuff a man ever tried to drink."[82] To some soldiers, the sin of excessive drinking and drunkenness threatened their nation's survival—and that of the people they so strongly wanted to protect, their families. A Confederate officer claimed, "If the South is overthrown, the epitaph should be *'Died of Whiskey.'*"[83] Such detestation of alcohol would remain vibrant among some soldiers well into the postwar years.[84]

There were many aspects of camp life that invited discomfort—and worse. For example, insects and other pests wreaked havoc on soldiers in camp, and their infestations were linked to Louisiana's geography and topography—and the location of a campsite.[85] In addition, lack of equipment, supplies, and nutritious rations led to some illnesses, but the army made efforts to combat the spread of diseases via vaccinations. One soldier claimed small pox was "creating some alarm . . . but I do not think there is much of it in camp" since "most of the men have been vaccinated."[86] Other soldiers also noted the positive effects of vaccinations, which prompted Confederate leadership to take further action. Writing from his camp near Fredericksburg, Virginia, 2nd Louisiana infantryman Winter Posey told his sister: "The health of the army is very good. We have had several cases of small pocks in the brigade but none in the Regiment as yet. . . . I was vaccinated about a month ago. It took very well. . . . There has been a general order for the whole army to be vaccinated, those that have not been."[87] The order eventually spread to other theaters, along with assigning a medical officer to ensure the soldiers in each respective "Department or Army" obtained the vaccination.[88]

Widespread camp vaccinations prompted some soldiers to take action by sending scabs home to be used on the home front. One Louisiana soldier stationed in Mississippi sent his father "a scab of Vaccine matter," which he felt could "be of service," while another soldier sent his wife a scab to give to a local doctor near Minden for vaccinations.[89] Some Confederate officers also made vaccinations available for enslaved individuals who labored near camps and posts. One commander requested "some vaccine matter to vaccinate the negroes in the fort," as he obviously knew the benefits of taking such actions to ensure maximum output from the enslaved Louisianians—and the likely protection from spreading diseases to soldiers.[90]

But even as soldiers battled camp diseases and uncleanliness, camp improvements and preventative self-care reflected a soldier's ability to think for himself and act in his own self-interest, even within the confines of army life. Soldiers recreated some semblance of home and civilian life by "trying to make themselves as comfortable as possible," wrote militiaman H. A. Snyder, even by planting "trees, bushes, & lillies from the Swamp to ornament their avenues." This camp's civilities somewhat resembled a café as "awnings were spread in front of tents . . . rough tables were spread—& dishes placed there on." These men apparently obtained various assortments of foodstuffs as they served appetizing meals to "their guests—with chamepaigne, wines, & Liquore."[91] The fact that this unit was a militia company "composed of cotton factors and members of the Boston Club, all of mature years" emphasized their desire for home comforts and their ability to obtain them.[92] But not all soldiers relished their camp experience, nor had any special attachment to their temporary home. Frank Richardson excitedly wrote about how happy he was to leave Camp Moore—and the illnesses it bred. At one time his morale was so low that he even acknowledged that he had contemplated desertion to escape camp miseries, but these were just thoughts in moments of weakness. "I will fall doing my duty," he wrote.[93]

While Civil War camps were fairly relaxed, structure and discipline still ruled the day. One correspondent who visited Camp Moore in May of 1861 noted that the "sentinels suffer no Volunteer to leave the precincts of the camp, even to bathe, without a pass or the word."[94] Apparently at the Washington Artillery camp near Richmond, even President Jefferson Davis could not get by without at pass. When Davis questioned whether the sentry recognized that he was the president, the Louisiana artilleryman replied, "I know no one. I only know my orders. Go round by the guard tent: you can't pass here." Unoffended, Davis admired "this display of discipline."[95]

In some cases, camp regulations sometimes mimicked—or exceeded slave regulations, as a few soldiers compared their military experience with the conditions of slavery.[96] Reid Mitchell notes how the many "rules and restrictions of the army reminded the Confederate of the humiliation of slavery," citing Edwin Fay who claimed, "No negro on Red River but has a happy time compared to that of a Confederate soldier." Fay later claimed that in the service he was "a bond slave worse than any negro, in fact I would deem myself fortunate to exchange with any slave I ever saw."[97] Most soldiers expected some restrictions on their personal liberties once they entered the military; however, some Louisianians felt that their commanding authorities went too far. Amos Anselm of the 8th Louisiana Infantry wrote to his mother in St. Landry Parish that "guards are kept day and night to keep us in camp. We cannot go more than 50 yards without a pass written just like a negro's pass." Upset at the strict standards for passes, he noted that "Three men have to sign it" for soldiers, but "one man will do for a negro."[98]

Transitioning from civilian to soldier proved a taxing experience for many Louisianians. Indeed, some men embraced their new life and excelled in the disciplined environment; but for others, soldiering remained a tough ordeal. Becoming a Confederate soldier demanded the sacrifice of their individuality and the familiarity of home. Some of the earlier forays of soldiering not long after Louisiana seceded had been a joke compared with obtaining proper military instruction and discipline. For example, Wilson's Rangers, a New Orleans cavalry unit, took a very cavalier approach to training. Despite being well equipped, well armed, and well dressed, their daily drills consisted of following their commander's orders: "Dismount! Hitch horses! March! Hunt shade! Begin playing!" Once evening approached, the commander ordered, "Cease playing! . . . Prepare to mount! . . . March!" Crowds, who believed the soldiers "had been out drilling in the hot sun, preparing . . . to protect their homes from the Northern invaders," eagerly cheered the returning men.[99]

In stark contrast to Wilson's Rangers, extreme cases of drill and training existed. Some soldiers felt their commanders were immune to their personal suffering—even forcing men "to drill whose looks clearly prove them not to be able." W. H. King wrote how he "heard Lt. Marks say to Marion Shaver, whose very appearance proves him to be totally unable for duty—'I will take you out & double-quick you 2 hours, & if that does not cure you, I will give you 3 lbs. of Blue Mass, work you out thoroughly. It is a perfect shame to have 75 men here,

& never have more than 25 or 30 for duty.'" Apparently, this officer's methods
for curing pain and weakness had little sympathy for the physical welfare of his
men.[100] But as more and more men found their way to a camp of instruction,
the day-to-day drilling, routines, discomforts—and sufferings—mentally and
physically transformed them into soldiers. Future participation in the war's escalating violence demanded mental and physical toughness, but it did not mean
total separation from civilians, nor the total abandonment of civilian attributes.

DRUDGERY AND DISCIPLINE OF CAMP LIFE

As the war continued, soldiers tired of camp and longed to return home—despite the efforts men took to make their existence tolerable, if not comfortable.
While serving in Louisiana, Pvt. Isaac Dunbar Affleck spoke for most Civil War
soldiers as he told his mother, "A fellow dont know how to enjoy good living
while at home, but let him stay in camp a short time and it makes his mouth
water of what they have there, and that he too could be enjoying it if not for
this blarsted war."[101] Louisiana soldiers stationed throughout the Confederacy
shared similar experiences with their brothers-in-arms who remained within
the state. E. L. Stephens, who served in the 9th Louisiana Infantry, explained
to a friend, "I am becoming very much disgusted with the life of a Soldier" as
he rambled on about his miseries. Realizing his need to explain no further he
wrote, "I guess you are becoming tired of hearing the truth I will stop it."[102]
Edwin Fay told his wife that "I could tell you of camp life and if I could give a
true picture you would be miserable."[103] Camp life took its toll on many soldiers as some men regretted their decisions to join the army, especially if they
left behind families with dependents.[104] The urge to escape military service
remained so strong for one Louisiana soldier that he hoped his self-inflicted
wound would be his ticket home.[105]

Evidence of both a lack of discipline but also sometimes overly obsessive
discipline among Louisiana soldiers during the Civil War provides historians
with a labyrinth of viewpoints to decipher. The ill-treatment and tyrannical
discipline that some Louisiana troops (especially conscripts) underwent was
even noted by Union admiral David D. Porter after the surrender at Fort Jackson. Despite the long absences from their families, "a large portion of them
had been pressed into a service distasteful to them, subject to the rigor of a
discipline severe beyond measure," Porter wrote.[106] No patriotic sentiment

came from these captured Louisiana soldiers, only tales of their mistreatment and suppression by their officers, who, during the battle, "stood over them with loaded revolvers and would shoot them it they did not fire," wrote one Union soldier.[107] For some Louisianians, being captured by Union forces meant a chance to abandon the war and return to civilian life. Overall, military discipline, despite the groanings of soldiers, proved beneficial for the cause. Weak officers who had little control over their men were sometimes responsible for the breakdown of camp discipline.[108] One Louisiana soldier greatly appreciated and openly welcomed the initiation of order and structure put out by his captain. His support for enforcing discipline was well founded, as he wrote, "Confusion has ruled supreme since our arrival here, & as there are enough of other troubles to encounter I am rejoiced . . . of the abolition of that trouble."[109]

Some officers claimed a soldier's ethnicity or background produced his self-discipline and ability to follow orders. After the war, one Louisiana officer recalled that many soldiers under his command were of French descent, followed by Americans, Irishmen, and "very few Germans." He particularly favored the French "Creoles" since they "were brought up in the Roman Catholic faith. Subordination to 'the powers that be,' was the earliest lesson of their childhood; hence they were easily governed."[110] An 8th Louisiana Infantry officer also claimed, "The Creoles are great favorites," but not necessarily for their ability to obey orders but because they usually proved good natured and entertaining.[111] In contrast, a soldier's ethnicity or nationality sometimes became a mark of disdain and made maintaining discipline proved problematic. Camp Chalmette hosted a scene of insubordination of "several companies of a Dago regiment called 'Cazadores,'" wrote H. A. Snyder. Sent "to arrest and bring into subjection" these men, Snyder noted that the incident ended when some of the insubordinate soldiers "agreed to obey orders . . . the rest, not willing to go were forced to surrender unconditionally—laid down their arms, & became our prisoners—thus saving us the task of shooting them." Luckily for all involved, the only shots the soldiers fired in the melee were into the Mississippi River to discharge their arms.[112]

Being absent without leave (AWOL), whether for a short time period or permanently, became an option for soldiers who wanted to escape military discipline and camp life. Reasons for going AWOL varied from homesickness to a lack of resources, comfort, or pay.[113] Louisiana soldiers' punishments for such infractions greatly varied, but mirrored those of other soldiers of the era.[114]

William Kennedy, who was stationed at Port Hudson, explained to his wife that some fellow soldiers' punishments included confinement and wearing a "barrel four hours each day." Kennedy also personally endured camp discipline. "I am on double duty my self for the day i over stayd my time," he wrote.[115] Other punishments included confinement, being "bucked and gaged with a bayonet," which uncomfortably binded a soldier's hands behind him to his knees with an object in his mouth (in this case a bayonet) to keep him from speaking, along with other abuses such as being "tied up by the thumbs . . . so that only the tips of his toes reach the ground." Some soldiers were "marched through the streets twice a day preceeded by a drummer," along with having reduced rations. Publicly shaming soldiers in front of their comrades was also common. In one instance, a group of soldiers found guilty for being AWOL was required to wear a sign stating, "I left my command without leave. Good men remained & performed their duty."[116] One Louisiana cavalryman once guarded a fellow soldier forced to "mark time" while carrying "a Railroad beam (?) for firing his gun in camp."[117] Accused of stealing items from an officer, one Texas soldier serving in Louisiana received six months hard labor and was forced to wear a twelve-pound ball and chain.[118]

But perhaps the most serious crime a soldier could commit was desertion. Many loyal soldiers found themselves tasked with bringing back men who had abandoned the cause, oftentimes with success. One captured Union officer, who was held at Camp Pratt near New Iberia, witnessed Confederate desertions by those who had "not much stomach for fight." He claimed that "desertions were quite frequent, sometimes as many as thirty or forty stampeding in a single night. But they would be caught, brought back, made to wear a barrell [sic] for a week or two, and were finally broke in."[119] By the end of 1863, one Louisiana soldier near Shreveport reported over fifty deserters had been captured and brought to camp. Though "desertions are common," he wrote that "they are constantly being caught & returned."[120] Searches even spanned into Texas as numerous men sought to escape the army's woes by forging passes and wearing civilian clothes to evade capture. But feelings toward the whole debacle of hunting deserters remained distasteful for many soldiers.[121]

Possible serious consequences awaited deserters who returned to camp, including death by firing squad. "A private was shot a few days since for desertion. Several men have been shot recently for desertion," wrote W. H. King.[122] Another Louisiana soldier noted that "two privates were shot . . . for desertion," but since he was in charge of the camp guard at the time, he (fortunately) "did not witness the execution."[123] One Louisiana officer serving in Virginia recalled the grim details of a deserter's execution as "Nine balls pierced his head and one his heart, and his death was instantaneous. I hope that I may never witness a like scene again."[124] Writing from his camp at Avery Island, one Louisiana lieutenant told his wife that he pitied two deserters who were shot, but felt their execution was "an example to others. I am sorry for them and hope they have no wives and children."[125] Another report from southwest Louisiana told of weekly executions for desertions "on Fridays. Fifteen men have been shot at one time recently for desertion."[126] Though desertions continued, executions did deter some men from abandoning the ranks. As one Louisiana soldier wrote, "I have seen one deserter shot so I don't think I'll desert."[127]

Not all men who went AWOL were deserters and had legitimate reasons for not being at their post. One Louisiana soldier, stricken with a serious case of "The Chronic Diarrhoea," opted to remain put as "the crowd with whom I was traveling had of course gone." Though unable to continue, he wrote that he would likely be listed as or "arrested as a deserter," since his proper paperwork had left with his companions.[128] Some AWOL soldiers felt their absence was warranted because of their interpretation of Confederate patriotism and commitment. Weitz highlights how most Confederate soldiers were "yeomen who left farms and families that were dependent on them for essential labor." As the war lingered and their families and property suffered, many of these yeoman-turned-soldiers sometimes left the army because "the nation they were fighting for proved unwilling or unable to provide what their families needed." As Weitz notes, many soldiers believed that the "real root of patriotism is 'home.'" To many Confederates who left the ranks, they were not necessarily abandoning the Confederate cause, but they had a different interpretation of what the cause entailed.[129]

But for soldiers who unlawfully returned to civilian life, serious consequences awaited. And the death penalty was not always reserved solely for deserters. Capt. E. John Ellis of the 16th Louisiana Infantry noted how a soldier was shot for the "direct violation of a stringent order," which "was against plundering and robbing citizens of their property." Apparently, Gen. Braxton Bragg had little tolerance for soldiers preying on civilians, as some Confederates were "fast becoming an armed mob," as Ellis claimed, "The firm and prompt measures of Gen. Bragg alone saved it."[130]

A lucky few Confederate deserters sometimes received pardons. Such was the case of Pvt. Joseph Hébert, who "is hereby ordered to be released and will resume the discharge of his duties as a soldier."[131] The Trans-Mississippi Department attempted to offer some leniency toward its AWOL soldiers by issuing an amnesty order, stating, "All deserters . . . who will return to their respective commands before the 1st day of February, 1863 will be restored to duty without trial."[132] But even as desertion persisted, some Confederate officers attempted to shame the missing men into returning to the ranks by publishing their names in local newspapers for all back home to see. Public shaming and striking at a soldier's personal honor could ruin a man's reputation among his family and community should he ever return home. And this tactic proved twofold: while shaming the deserter, it also served as a deterrent for other men who contemplated abandoning their posts.[133] However, striking at a soldier's honor only worked if he valued it over life itself.

For soldiers who returned to the ranks, Weitz notes that Confederate authorities sometimes took into account an absentee's "intent" in leaving to "determine if he really meant to stay away indefinitely." But such policies often bred confusion for the high command, especially if some soldiers abandoned their units only to rejoin a company closer to home, or if these men simply sought amnesty from the death penalty.[134] For deserters wishing to fully abandon the Confederate cause, finding employment within Union lines or galvanizing—that is, joining the Union army—became an escape option, albeit a dangerous one. If captured and recognized by their former comrades, the consequences for becoming a turncoat proved fatal.[135]

THE PRESENCE OF BLACK LOUISIANANS IN CONFEDERATE CAMPS

Even as some Confederate soldiers compared army life with slavery, the institution remained a fixture within the Confederate military.[136] Tasked with various duties, African American laborers were a common sight in Confederate camps, and their labors did not go unnoticed as they freed soldiers from many unpleasant and menial tasks.[137] A number of enslavers brought their bondsmen to war with them to act as camp servants. "We have plenty of servants in the mess," wrote 2nd Louisiana Cavalry Lt. John Coleman Sibley, "and I will not have much drudgery to perform as I am cooked for by the Capts. servant."[138] Soldiers from one 9th Louisiana Infantry company from Bossier Parish brought along "nine slaves with them into the service."[139] Gen. Richard Taylor recalled how body servants were a fixture in his family's military legacy, specifically naming his servant Tom, who accompanied him to Virginia and had previous service in military campaigns in Florida and Mexico. Taylor claimed that Tom "was a model servant. Tall, powerful, black as ebony, he was a mirror of truth and honesty. Always cheerful, I never heard him laugh or knew of his speaking unless spoken to." He also possessed superb skills in making fire and coffee, along with the ability to perform other camp chores, making him a valuable fixture in the general's headquarters.[140] Gen. P. G. T. Beauregard rented an enslaved South Carolinian named Frederick Maginnis while in Charleston at the war's commencement. Maginnis was said to be "a very white intelligent fellow" and obviously had some sway with Beauregard's affairs as he supposedly "talked freely about the general's future plans, and posed as a confidant."[141]

African Americans in camp also reminded slaveholding soldiers of home. One Louisiana soldier wrote, "I hear that Tom Murphy [?] takes care of Archy. I would give a good deal to see that darkey, his old familiar face would remind me of home more than any one else up this way."[142] Regardless of their acquaintances with soldiers, these African Americans were brought along or in the case of Free Blacks (and some slaves), hired to perform labor. In a letter to his wife, John A. Harris wrote, "You spoke of clothes. I will not need any thing unless its pants for 3 months. I will have General Scott the negro to make me some shoes unless H sends me a pr. first as I wrote him about it."[143] At Camp Roman, near Carrolton, Louisiana, one soldier told his relatives, "You need not be worried about my going to the River to wash when the Capt. told me to give my dirty clothes to his niger to wash at any time."[144] The mother of a young Louisiana officer, E. John Ellis, had a body servant named Stewart sent to him, "which relieved him of the 'toils' to army life."[145] Writing to his wife, one Louisiana officer noted that his quarters were "comparatively quiet, for Walter is writing by my side & his darkies are brushing boots, & doing other little jobs."[146]

Frank Liddell Richardson wrote to his father from Camp Moore requesting him to send his slave "Monday down here as waitor to the company and myself. I have asked the captain and some of the company about it and they all say he could do them a great deal of service," which included cooking, performing "odd jobs" around camp, and "wait[ing] on myself in case I should get sick."

Monday was obviously trustworthy, as Richardson claimed he "has traveled by himself and when you give him a pass and the necessary directions he can get here safe."[147] Eventually, a Richardson family slave named Allen arrived in camp and "has been and is getting on swimingly, he guards the provisions tent where he sleeps sometimes and cleans up muskets and shoes for the boys, from whom he gets a good deal of money for his services . . . he sends his compliments to his wife and all the black folks."[148] Later, Richardson decided to send Allen home since "I, occupying the position of private do not need a servant as we all can easily do what we have to do ourselves . . . Allen can be of more service to you at home in the sugar house." Richardson noted that Allen's service was appreciated, and he had "done his duty faithfully." But his camp workload was apparently light compared to "a common negro, he being smart enough to make all work as light as possible." Within weeks, Richardson regretted sending Allen home as the camp chores mounted.[149] Nearly six months later Richardson requested another body servant since "all the negroes in camp have invariably proved faithful to their masters even when near the yankees."[150] Elements of paternalism remained visible in the soldier-body servant relations; Edwin Fay, for example, noted that while his servant Rich "does do tolerably well . . . he is carless and inattentive."[151]

William Miller Owen, an officer in the Washington Artillery, remembered that nearly "every mess had its two or three servants, or 'boys,' as they were universally called. . . . They were expected to black the shoes, forage for provisions at times, rub down private horses, etc. Many were accomplished body-servants, good barbers, and the like." Not all of the artillery battalion's servants remained with the unit throughout the war, as "some deserted to the enemy when it was bruited amongst them that the war had set them free."[152] And the presence of body servants in Confederate camps offered soldiers a constant reminder of how their disciplined army regimen mirrored that of slaves.

Perhaps some enslaved men saw that the position of a body servant in a Confederate camp offered incentives and opportunities, including the ability to travel, which was likely more desirable (though often uncomfortable)—and less taxing—than laboring on a farm or plantation. But traveling could prove dangerous—one body servant, for example, drowned on his way to a Confederate camp near Bayou Boeuf.[153] Even if the chores and routines of camp life provided a break from agricultural pursuits, body servants retained their status as chattel property—and their susceptibility to abuse remained. One Louisiana soldier noted how his servant was not panning out, especially since he "seems to know nothing about cooking." The previous Sunday, this soldier wrote, "I had to flog A[lex] . . . for his insolence."[154] Louisiana soldier Edwin Fay gave "a good whipping" to his body servant Rich, along with other forms of abuse that included hitting Rich's head "against a hogshead of sugar" for abandoning his camp duties to chase women.[155]

For some Confederates operating in Louisiana, body servants came to them as spoils of war. In one instance a Texas soldier found himself surrounded by the enemy as he obtained water for a surgeon at Milliken's Bend. Being quick-witted, Private Schultz took advantage of the Union commander's confusion from the fight and led the Union soldiers toward Confederate lines, resulting in the capture of the White officer and his "entire company of 49 negroes." As a reward for his actions, Schultz's commanders allowed him to choose one of the Black soldiers to "cook and wash for him and his mess during the war, and to work for him as long as the negro lives."[156]

Black Louisianians, both male and female, also provided short-term services for Confederate soldiers in their vicinity, such as cooking and delivering food.[157] Performing camp chores and being associated with the Confederate army did not make these laborers and servants soldiers in the eyes of the White men in uniform; however, some Blacks found themselves close to the action. Frank Richardson, who participated in the Battle of Shiloh, noted that his body servant "brought a carpet bag & a knapsack full of clothes away" from the Union camp during the engagement. Though the body servant was present "he did not go near enough to the enemy to get hurt. I think he is getting use to soldiering."[158]

The presence of body servants in Confederate camps had both physical and psychological reverberations. Their presence reminded many soldiers of home, especially if soldiers personally knew them. However, psychologically, enslaved body servants also reminded soldiers that their military-disciplined lives mirrored those of slaves. A few African Americans in Confederate camps also enjoyed some satisfaction by seeing White soldiers perform menial duties and taking orders from their superiors. Peter Carmichael notes that camp slaves kept class conflict between Whites visible, especially between officers and enlisted men.[159] The presence of body servants proved a double-edged sword. They helped soldiers—but also reminded them of a way of life that was fast disappearing.

Army life offered many Louisiana troops new experiences, discipline, and many discomforts. However, their military existence was not an isolated one, as it was oftentimes viewed as an educational opportunity, exposing soldiers (and many enslaved African Americans) to experiences they likely would have never had if they remained home. One Louisiana soldier informed a friend that since departing home, "my pathway has been chequered with exciting scenes, and I have tasted of many of the evils and pleasures of the world since. There is no school in which one learns as much as the dear bought school of experience."[160] Soldiers incorporated familiar elements of civilian life into their military regimens, and Southern civilians who sympathized with the Confederacy did much to aid and comfort these men in uniform.[161] Though away from many relatives and friends, most Louisiana soldiers were not totally alone. Their regiments consisted of many men from the same parishes and towns, and they remained engaged with the civilian world as Confederate camps and military operations remained in close proximity to civilians. These numerous camp experiences reinforced a soldier's sense of community, whether with their own homes or with the areas where they campaigned.

CHAPTER 5

PHYSICAL INTERACTIONS

"My life . . . was gladdened by a visit from my father," wrote E. John Ellis. "I had not seen him for four months which was a longer period than had ever before separated me from him." This visit provided Ellis not only a small reunion, but a wonderful distraction from the drudgery of military life.[1] Total isolation from civilians was impossible. Camp visits from friends or relatives remained a common practice, which provided solace, improved morale, cultivated civilian relationships, and offered soldiers a chance to reminisce about home. And soldiers, too, found ways to reach the populace. "The only general complaint among both officers and men is an unending desire to go to the city," noted one New Orleans newspaper, referring to the troops stationed at Camp Moore. Apparently, the soldiers' reasons for leaving camp proved creative, as they gave "anything in the world for an excuse to get to town."[2]

Time off allowed soldiers to engage in a wide array of entertainment, some of which were less becoming of gentlemen. While waiting for transportation to Tennessee, one Texas soldier camped near New Orleans felt, given their proximity to access the city's vices, that it "will be very hard to keep some of the men straight as some of them are inclined to get drunk and cut up."[3] Louisianian Frank Richardson received a pass to go into New Orleans, found friends and relatives, and remained away "a long time after my leave of absence had expired." His punishment of extra duty made him reconsider his actions, claiming, "I think I will be more careful next time how I stay over my time."[4]

Once together, soldiers and civilians engaged in various activities, including social functions such as dancing and balls, which one soldier stationed in north Louisiana claimed was "all the rage down here."[5] Games, performances, and music, which one Louisiana soldier claimed "always cast a spell over my soul and my heart," offered diversions for soldiers and civilians, often reminding them of home.[6] For some soldiers stationed near New Orleans, their civilian encounters also included visiting fortune tellers. Excited at the prospect of knowing the future, Isaac Hall paid a New Orleans fortune teller two dollars to hear her prognostication. "Mary," he wrote to his wife, she "described you as well as I can to save my life," though he became skeptical at her report that his wife's "height was five feet two inches. I want you to measure yourself and write me if she was correct." The fortune teller also claimed that Hall "would have four more children," but unfortunately for him this information proved untrue. Hall's wife wrote back noting that she was two inches taller than what he had been told, and he never had a chance to produce more offspring: he died of an illness the following summer while participating in the Vicksburg Campaign.[7]

Campaigning soldiers also remained in close contact to civilians, even when serving in a different state. Claiming kin to nearby residents offered some soldiers an opportunity to obtain good company and provisions. Texas soldier Isaac Dunbar Affleck became acquainted with distant relatives while serving near Alexandria, Louisiana, writing his mother, "I claimed kin with two families up there, but forget their names, they traced the connexion up but I could not write it down if my life depended on it. I was perfectly well satisfied, it enabled all of us to get a good meal at each place, and it was all we wanted."[8] Many soldiers in the Washington Artillery remained orderly and neat while serving in Virginia "as the command had, or claimed to have, cousins and aunts in every city or hamlet in the whole of the eastern part of the Old Dominion," wrote William Miller Owen. "The best rooms everywhere were opened to them, and the land flowed with eggs, chickens, milk, and 'wild honey.'"[9]

While these interactions created a support network to help maintain a soldier's ability to continue fighting, it affected more than just his ability to serve. Physical encounters not only stimulated their senses but also provided soldiers with a powerful reminder of their reasons for—and understanding of—their wartime sacrifices. As many soldiers interacted with local civilians, they often socially and emotionally bonded, making them more willing to keep fighting. And the more they interacted, the more solidified those bonds became, reinforcing many soldiers' beliefs that this conflict was about defense—of families, homes, and property. Even as several Louisiana troops served far from home, their contributions ensured that families and property—whether their own or their fellow Southerners—would be protected. The ideologies of national defense and home defense remained intertwined.

CONFEDERATE SOLDIERS, CULTURE, AND CLASS

Unlike the examples above, most Louisiana soldiers serving outside of their home state had no relatives in their vicinity of operation. And in the case of some Louisiana troops, their reputations preceded them. Wartime calamities and destruction did not begin when the troops arrived on the battlefield. For some Louisiana soldiers, their first battles were between themselves, their commanding officers, and civilians. Louisiana soldiers sent east to serve in what became known as the Army of Northern Virginia eventually earned the nickname the Louisiana Tigers as their conduct cemented a brave—and rowdy—reputation both on and off the battlefield. Even before engaging the Yankees, Louisiana soldiers established their association with chaos and their love of fighting.

En route to Virginia by rail, a group of Louisiana warriors went berserk at Grand Junction, Tennessee. Upon arrival "open mutiny broke out, and the men turned against each other with perfect ferocity, entirely disregarding the authority of their officers." It took their commander's iron will—and pistols—to bring them to heel. Even with such force, gaining control proved a difficult task since the men grew wilder and more destructive before the fiasco ended, resulting in at least seven deaths and the wounding of nearly twenty men.[10] This was not the Louisiana troops' only railroad adventure. Another unit, Coppen's Louisiana Zouaves, hijacked a train in Pensacola, stranding their officers. By the time the frazzled leaders reached their rabble-rousing soldiers in Montgomery, a Georgia unit had been called in to restore order. The armed and fearless Zouave officers proved their mettle as effective leaders and ended the chaos. One observer recalled that the soldiers had obviously taken a beating, as "many a fez was drawn far down over a bleeding forehead, and many a villainous countenance was lighted by one eye, while the other was closed and swollen." The Zouaves continued their trek to Richmond but not without incident. Casualties continuously mounted from undisciplined actions and carelessness.[11]

As many Louisiana soldiers reached their duty stations, some of their reputations with civilians remained in limbo. One group of Louisiana soldiers "gained such a reputation for pilfering and general loutishness that as soon as anyone sees them coming they bolt the doors and windows. Usually any affiliation at all with the Louisiana boys is enough to assure one a cold welcome no matter where he shows his face," wrote Chaplain Gache, who ministered to these rowdy men in Virginia.[12] Louisiana soldiers had a similar reputation when interacting with Northerners. In 1863 as Louisiana troops made their way to Gettysburg, Pennsylvania, a unit of Confederate "cavalry, when they passed thro, told everybody that the La. tigers would kill, burn & destroy every thing & every body in the country." One local lady fainted shortly after she learned that a soldier who entered her home (who had requested food) was from a Louisiana regiment. Once the woman recovered, it took some convincing to prove that this Louisiana warrior "was not a cut throat."[13] Another Pennsylvania lady won renown from Louisianian Thomas B. Reed as "the worst scared woman I had ever seen." Seeking food, Reed claimed the woman aimed to provide him with something to eat, but as more and more soldiers arrived, she "was almost crazy."[14]

Despite these colorful episodes in Louisiana Tiger lore, not all Louisiana soldiers heading east were ill-disciplined or rowdy. One Louisiana soldier claimed, "We have been received with the greatest hospitality, and enthusiasm throughout the entire route, except in Tennessee, where they are in a very cold and luke-warm state." Perhaps these Tennesseans heard about or witnessed the fiascos caused by other Louisiana troops. But "In Mississippi, Alabama and Virginia, we were cheered . . . covered with perfect showers of boquetts of flowers" by the local civilians, sometimes even obtaining food and refreshments.[15] Rueben Pierson told his father back in Bienville Parish that his trip to Richmond was "one of great excitement . . . We were applauded and cheered by Ladies at every station and from the windows and galleries of every house we passed. I have never seen such demonstrations of true love for southern rights."[16]

The Civil War brought many individuals of various social classes into close contact as military service provided soldiers with travel opportunities most men would not have had outside of the army. Within Louisiana, some troops found hospitality among the state's wealthy families, but the poorer classes also paid tribute to the needs of Confederate soldiers. Near Alexandria, Felix Poché documented his contact with a poor, "pitiful family." Despite their small one-room dwelling, the family offered him what they could. He noted that "to my surprise they gave me a very dirty bed, next to the rest of the family. . . . Never in my life have I ever seen such an impressive and disgusting view of such truly terrible misery as in the abject, ignorant, half-civilized family."[17]

For Louisiana soldiers serving out of state, their interactions with the populace and other soldiers in their areas of operation were no less colorful—and obviously tainted with prejudices. Writing from Knoxville, Tennessee, Frank Richardson told his mother of the cultural differences existing between other sections of the country and Louisiana. "To a novice like myself, the manners of these worthless hoosiers appear as strange as those of a foreign nation which he has never seen." His dislike of these men continued in great detail; he stated they spoke English "almost as bad as the cornfield negroes, the majority of them I believe, a good many of them I know, have just as much knowledge as these same honest natives of Africa of writing or reading." Lacking education was only the start, as Richardson pointed to their other faults. They "dont take care of themselves, and need someone to force them to wash themselves and put on clean clothing," along being "men which for the most part compose our sick and fill up our Hospitals. of course though there are many . . . who are men of as much worth as any in the army . . . but . . . are scarce to the number of ignorant dirty hoosiers . . . Georgia & Alabama seem to be the native place of most of these men."[18]

Though some Louisiana soldiers held contempt for their fellow Southerners, their opinions of fellow Louisianians hailing from other parts of the state sometimes fared little better. While traveling through Trenton, Louisiana, W. H. King noted filthy streets and the lack of cleanliness, and his opinion about the surrounding countryside reflected that of the town. "The country . . . looks to be very poor, & from appearances . . . at that time, there was no good reason to believe the citizens would make bread. The land is thin, & . . . weeds & bushes had almost completely . . . possession of the fields. Surely laziness prevailed."[19] The conflict sometimes blurred the boundaries of the state's social classes, especially when many residents found themselves in society's lower echelon, thanks to the war's destruction. One soldier's unit made camp in northwestern Louisiana near Campti at "the ruins of a magnificent plantation." This Confederate noted that the Yankees had "with one broad sweep" destroyed the place, leaving a widow "houseless, homeless and a beggar, Houses, Negroes, Furniture, Stock, Cotton; all gone, and by whom, ? by the GREAT United States."[20] Even among Acadian families in southern Louisiana, the war acted as a social leveler. Carl A. Brasseaux explains how the conflict's destruction sapped the region's inhabitants of their wealth as "the crestfallen genteel Acadian planters of the river parishes and their plebian western cousins, the prairie ranchers, faced the same bleak future."[21]

Providing services to soldiers also cultivated interaction between Confederate troops and Louisiana's residents. In January 1862, William Edwards Paxton told his wife about hiring a cook who "is a very poor one" along with sending his dirty clothes to a washerwoman.[22] At Port Hudson, local women aided soldiers with their cooking, along with the hiring of "negro cooks." Indeed, Christopher Thrasher notes that the civilian presence at Port Hudson in 1863 remained so prevalent that Confederate authorities urged the garrison's commander, Gen. Franklin Gardner, to "force civilians to leave."[23] Finding personnel to prepare meals became so highly valued in some Confederate camps that W. H. King wrote how one general authorized "the enlistment for 4 cooks to each company—either white or black, to take charge." The hope was that these cooks would boost soldier morale and possibly improve the men's health.[24] The Washington Artillery had good luck at the war's commencement when it lured a French cook away from his New Orleans restaurant, but this arrangement did not last long as he "soon tired of camp life" and returned home.[25] The position of camp cook was also open to both free or enslaved persons, "provided, however, that no slave shall be enlisted, without the written consent of his owner."[26] Some enslaved (or free) cooks—or their owners—had no choice in the matter. One Louisiana officer had to cut his letter home short on account of his "mess cook is quarreling because I don't come to supper," he wrote. "He is a negro that we captured . . . and made a mess servant of him."[27] For some soldiers from privileged backgrounds, having civilians or slaves in camp performing domestic chores helped maintain ties to their prewar social status.

Sometimes Confederate troops offered civilians their services, which often varied, including providing protection. Especially after the Union invasion, many White Louisianians found comfort when Confederate soldiers reoccupied captured territory, regardless of the length of their stay.[28] In July 1864, Gov. Henry Watkins Allen sent a boatload of corn to needy citizens near Alexandria. Needing protection for the provisions against "the depredations of the soldiers" stationed nearby, officials requested an armed guard. A Confederate

officer planned to send six soldiers led by a noncommissioned officer to ensure the civilians received the corn.[29] Confederate troops in north Louisiana
engaged in rescue operations after a "government saddle shop, in Shreveport"
collapsed with people trapped under its roof. Wasting little time, the soldiers
who were encamped nearby rushed to the scene, but ended up performing
little service because, as one soldier wrote, "There was nothing we could do."
Their sense of urgency and concern quickly deflated as "many were standing
around apparently unconcerned, joking as though nothing serious had happened. The officer directing the operations was using the bitterest oaths over
the bodies of the dead & the wounded."[30]

While soldier services to civilians remained irregular, they did offer people
in need compassion and charity. A fire in Charleston, South Carolina, drew the
attention of soldiers in the Washington Artillery, who aimed to provide "for
the relief of the sufferers." The battalion collected and donated over $1,500.[31]
Assisting needy civilians allowed soldiers to physically and emotionally bond
with them sometimes, and such interactions reminded soldiers that they were
not the only ones suffering from wartime discomforts; civilians suffered too.
Exposure to these realities forced soldiers to reflect on their reasons (or understanding) of why they fought. Protecting their homes and hearths also extended
to offering a helping hand to civilians in need, who likely reminded them of
their own families back home.

After Union troops arrived in Louisiana, many civilians remained en-
trapped in the seesaw of advancing and retreating armies that sought territorial
control.[32] For the Louisiana troops stationed within close proximity to their
homes, these men relied on their sister Confederate states to send soldiers.
Many men who found themselves deployed to the Pelican State came from
neighboring states, especially Texas. Opinions of these outside soldiers varied,
which often reflected differences in culture and mannerism. One onlooker at
Cheneyville, Louisiana, remained unimpressed at the sight of a group of Texans, noting that the "soldiers passed here this morning . . . the[y] dont at all
look like soldiers . . . the[y] look more like Baboons mounted on gotes than
anything else."[33] A Louisiana priest also held a low opinion of Texas soldiers,
claiming, "It was difficult to meet one who was a good sort. They seemed
uncivilized."[34] Despite these criticisms, Sarah L. Wadley noted that she and
a friend waved and shouted at a group of Texas cavalrymen passing through
their area. One soldier told her, "I will bring you two Yankees home." Not im-

pressed, the girl replied, "I will not thank you for so few as that." The Texan responded "enthusiastically, 'God Bless your little Jeff. Davis rebel soul.'" Apparently, these Louisiana belles made a favorable impression on these men, as Wadley recorded another incident when a group of ladies shook hands with a captain, who told them that "if I survive this war, I shall certainly call again."[35] Though both soldiers and sympathetic civilians identified as Southerners and Confederates, culture played a role in how (or if) wartime relationships developed. Louisiana's cultural diversity, especially with the heavy use of the French language in southern Louisiana, stood in stark contrast with what many soldiers were accustomed to.

Out-of-state soldiers serving in Louisiana (especially southern Louisiana) often found themselves in the midst of a culture shock—but they too could provide an entertaining spectacle. Texan William Nicholson wrote from New Iberia to his sister, "The country is very thinly settled, until we get in about 25 or 30 miles of this place, and they are all French. There are a good many Americans here, the most of them are French."[36] Once Nicholson and his unit reached New Orleans, they "created considerable excitement," he wrote, "as everybody wanted to see a Texas Ranger. Some of the little boys in N. O. gathered around Capt. Walker who was dressed in a buckskin suit, and a Mexican hat. They called him a real Texan or some of them would say Texican."[37] Other Texas soldiers caught the attention of Louisiana's high-ranking officers. One Louisianian claimed the men belonging to the 13th Texas Cavalry Battalion "were superbly mounted, well armed, and thoroughly equipped for war." Confederate Louisiana needed many more men such as these.[38]

Just as Louisiana's soldiers who served throughout the Confederacy, the state's civilians, too, often offered non-natives a cultural spectacle. Out-of-state soldiers and Louisiana civilians both noted their cultural differences and prejudices toward one another; however, both groups also found attributes they admired. Some Texas soldiers noted the dedication and beauty of some Louisiana women, just as many Louisiana residents admired the Texans who projected a tough persona—an image that these men could protect and defend them. Physical encounters, like a picture, only provided a representation that conjured many misconceptions. But physical interaction fostered a sense of community and understanding between soldiers and civilians. This was especially important since many of Louisiana's diverse soldiers and civilians, though different, often found commonality when interacting with fellow Confederates.

CHRISTIAN SOLDIERS, CIVILIANS,
AND CHURCH SERVICES

"I am altogether a different youth now than when I left home," wrote a soldier in the 4th Louisiana Battalion, referring to his growing Christian faith. He wished his relatives "could only witness the grand spectacles of our camp. Imagine every night when duties will permit, the weary and exhausted war-worn veterans assembling around a cheerful fire singing praises and offering up prayers . . . you will have a true picture of the interest and feelings now existing among many of our brave defenders, and I am proud to say it is almost daily increasing."[39] Spiritual matters concerned many Louisiana soldiers, especially amid the war's uncertainties. And for some individuals, their spiritual faith proved a common bond that connected soldiers and civilians. As religion took root among many of the men, church services and camp meetings provided another avenue for soldier and civilian interaction.

While army chaplains remained highly visible throughout the war, many civilians also ministered to soldiers' spiritual needs in both traditional and un-conventional settings. Confederate army chaplains often ministered to both sol-dier and civilian congregations, even venturing from camp to local churches—which were often well attended—to deliver their sermons. One female diarist noted that an army chaplain from Port Hudson delivered a captivating message at a local Baptist church as "quite a large congregation" attended.[40] In 1863, the 14th Louisiana's chaplain, Rev. James B. Sheeran, claimed that during one service in Virginia his congregation of soldiers and civilians was so numerous "that I feared the galleries might break down."[41]

Religious service locations often varied; however, some soldiers had the luxury of attending local churches near their duty stations. Felix Poché wrote that he attended "old Father Foltier's church. There was a very large atten-dance of Ladies and soldiers. . . . I took my seat on the benches reserved for the use of soldiers. . . . Since I have separated from my sweet little wife, I have never had such pleasant reminiscences of her, as I did this morning when I knelt during the holy sacrifice, and read the same prayers which we, every Sunday, read together in our old parish church."[42] Capt. E. John Ellis attended a Methodist church while serving in Tennessee "and heard an eloquent and impressive sermon by the Rev. Dr. Quintard," who was a chaplain on Gen. Leonidas Polk's staff. Ellis's attendance allowed him the pleasure of interacting with at least one female civilian who shared her hymn book with him and engaged in conversation afterwards.[43]

Military service also offered many Louisiana soldiers the opportunity to interact with civilians and other soldiers from different denominations. Such intermingling of the faiths remained common throughout the war. One historian notes that "southern ministers of every denominational ilk" heeded the call to minister "to enormous gatherings of soldiers, [attend] to the wounded and dying, and in some cases [lead] successful religious revivals."[44] If a preacher, priest, or chaplain could be found, a Catholic or Protestant service commenced. Such exposure caused some soldiers to reflect on their own faith, while others curiously looked on. W. H. King noted how he "attended the Catholic Church to-day, the first time I was ever inside one." Intrigued, the "exercises" and traditions the Catholic churchgoers performed left him pondering, "Who can judge as to which party is right? All may be right in some things, but all can not be right in every thing."[45] John A. Harris wrote his wife and children, "You would laugh Becky if you could See the Old women here, They are called sisters of charity, They have on White bonnets the tail of which Stands out just like a Busard Suning himself—They look strange to one who never saw the like before."[46]

The war's demands kept Lt. John Coleman Sibley from routinely attending church services, and among the few services he did attend he noted that at least one of them contributed little to his spiritual growth, claiming, "I heard a priest in some language that I could not understand."[47] Chaplain James B. Sheeran noted that while conducting a service, "The Protestant portion of my audience with the exception of two persons behaved very well. These two, I think, will know better how to behave themselves the next time they attend Catholic service."[48] Gardiner H. Shattuck Jr. argues that the Civil War "had a crippling institutional effect on the churches" in the South, which involved a lack of financial support and decreased church attendance. However, he notes that clergymen realized that Confederate camps were "a more promising field for their labors."[49] The efforts of both army chaplains and civilian clergymen exposed soldiers to various Christian denominations, something not likely to occur during the antebellum years. Civil War historiography that centers on religion and camp revivals often emphasizes the soldiers' experiences; however, these events were usually affairs that included civilian and soldier interaction.[50]

If church services often brought soldiers and civilians together, pious behavior was not always on full display. John E. Hall wrote from Camp Moore about the church services that took place there; however, he also did not hesitate to point out the immoral and ungodly behavior that ran rampant in camp, which he admitted "is enough to call down God's wrath."[51] One Louisiana officer explained to his wife how he cherishes the time he is alone so "I can write in peace to you & then read my Bible, kneel down, & pray." Camp life offered little time for such activities as he claimed that "my only opportunities for secret prayer are when walking or sitting by myself Then I try to lift my head up to God." Distractions in camp were many, as "one's ears become perfectly accustomed to obscurity & profanity & the Sabbath is so like other days, that sometimes one hardly knows that it is Sunday."[52]

Other soldiers, such as R. J. Causey, noted similar incidents. He frustratingly wrote, "There is so much cursing and swearing in camp that it makes me feel very bad."[53] Jacob Frierson noted the blatant disrespect that some soldiers displayed one "sunday while the preacher was preaching; some soldiers instead of listening, were running chickens in twenty steps of him."[54] One Louisiana soldier serving at Vicksburg also noted his disgust at the lack of reverence some of his compatriots had for both religious and funeral services. He simultaneously witnessed "some men playing cards, our men burying their deceased comrade, and Mr. Bray preaching. The gambling in open view of both. How can we expect peace when we are guilty of such wickedness. Lord, save us or we must perish forever."[55]

Just as soldiers sometimes displayed irreverent behavior in full view of clergymen, not all ministers, who claimed to care about soldiers' spiritual wellbeing, remained steadfast to the Confederacy and its soldiers. Excited at the prospect of hearing "the distinguished Rev. C. K. Marshall of Miss. preach," 8th Louisiana Infantryman Amos Anselm, in the midst of writing a letter to his mother, explained, "After I return I will finish my letter." After putting his desire to hear God's word above writing home, he was sadly disappointed as the preacher failed to appear.[56] "It looks like the preachers thought that soldiers were past saving or were not worth it," wrote Lt. John Coleman Sibley to his wife. "When I was home preachers were tolerable plenty and now . . . there seems to be no preachers that care about preaching. In fact I hardly even see a preacher." According to Sibley, the hardships and depravations of war kept these ministers away. "They must have some aversion to the whir of bomb shells or to corn bread and blue beef."[57]

But despite a soldier's or clergyman's level of devotion (or lack thereof) regarding spiritual matters, camp meetings and church services (though sometimes inconsistent) remained a fixture in connecting soldiers and civilians. Religion, just like military service, acted as a unifier, bringing soldiers and civilians together for a higher calling. Though beliefs often remained personal, the outward expression of a soldier's or civilian's faith, which resulted in physical interaction between the two groups, further cultivated their spiritual and emotional bonds. The religious themes of sacrifice, service, and love also linked Christian soldiers and civilians, who often thought of their wartime trials in religious contexts. To these individuals, their triumphs and sufferings had a deeper meaning.

CONFEDERATE SOLDIERS AND WOMEN

Near Natchitoches one soldier noted the warm greeting he and his comrades received from "all the citizens in our Route," which included "The ladies."[58] One Louisianian en route to the eastern front noted that the local women made quite an impression on him, claiming, "I would not be surprised that I did not call to see some of them after I got through playing soldier."[59] Near Baton Rouge, many emotional women cheered a group of Confederate soldiers as they marched by, "waving their handkerchiefs, sobbed with one voice, 'God bless you, Soldiers! Fight for us!'"[60] Local girls offered many soldiers a pleasant distraction from army life. Female visitors often reminded them of the wives, sweethearts, or mothers they left at home, and, for several single soldiers, these encounters provided hope for future relationships in a postwar era.

Interaction with women often had positive effects on the soldiers, and physical attraction or ties to a man's patriarchal duties to protect women often remained a constant theme between both soldiers and female civilians. J. D. Garland, a Texan stationed near Harrisonburg, Louisiana, wrote: "There are some of the most attractive young ladies in that Swamp that I most ever saw."[61] Indeed, Louisiana hosted an array of appealing women, as another soldier stationed at Camp Moore claimed, "Tangipahoa women are as beautiful as Creoles." Some of these girls hurt their ladylike image as "one sees only Irish and German women, who have the masculine habit of smoking."[62] Virginia belles offered Louisiana soldiers quite a spectacle, as William Miller Owen remembered "enjoying Richmond society very much, riding and dancing with the pretty girls. . . . I don't believe there ever were so many pretty girls to the square inch as there are now in Richmond; it is remarkable."[63] Even on the eve of General Lee's surrender in April 1865, Louisiana soldiers continued obtaining furloughs to visit their local sweethearts, one of whom a Donaldsonville artilleryman affectionately called "my angel."[64]

Women, regardless of their looks, also provided lonesome soldiers with companionship. Near Washington, Louisiana, Sydney Harding recalled how she and some other ladies "took a ride to camp" and met a group of soldiers stationed there. She noted the soldiers' excitement at the prospect of female visitors and, as a testament to her desired presence, "begged" her to stay.[65] One group of Louisiana cavalrymen in camp beheld an agreeable spectacle of "several young ladies" who sang songs and threw flowers, wrote one officer.[66] Such occurrences stirred an emotional tempest within many men, and for at least one group of soldiers stationed in north Louisiana, their overexcitement in the presence of ladies fostered ungentlemanly conduct. W. H. King wrote that "many of the men are behaving shamefully" as they were "crowding around the ladies, starring at them vulgarly. Indeed, many are climbing saplings & trees, & whatever object near that will enable . . . them to get a view of the ladies." For the sake of decency and morale—and the well-being of the female visitors— King felt the "officers should stop such behavior; [f]or . . . such base conduct will stop true ladies from visiting our camp, & their moralizing influence, to a considerable degree lost," duly noting his fears if the ladies' visitation ceased. He reiterated his faith in the mystical powers that female fellowship had on soldier morale and moral conduct, claiming, "If something is not done to improve the morals of our men—I mean the whole Confederacy—I humbly think our cause is lost beyond redemption."[67] However, some soldiers disliked visiting with local women as one Louisiana soldier told his wife they "only serve to remind me of you and our separation and I don't care to see them."[68]

Women not only offered soldiers opportunities for visiting, but, if the girl lived nearby, it might include the hospitality of a meal.[69] Sydney Harding noted throughout her diary that many soldiers (mostly officers) dined with her and her family. On one occasion, she explained how a soldier gained an invitation to stay with her and her family for the night as they were "awakened by a knock . . . there was the cavalier . . . containing excellent news. Lee's victory over Meade. . . . I asked him to stay all night. After a little hesitation he said yes. I sat on the gallery talking to him. . . . Sis F. asked if he was a native of La. No, born in N.Y. Oh, my I was quite dumfounded, but . . . had been here six years. Had fought at Shiloh, been injured. Proved himself a good southerner. Son of an Episcopal clergyman . . . has elegant manners and remarkably handsome."[70] The mention (usually in the privacy of a letter or diary) of having a physical attraction toward a soldier was not uncommon among females. On another occasion, Harding mentioned that, after the 1864 Battle of Mansfield, she and her family met with an officer en route to their home. She wrote that in the evening five soldiers dined with her family, including a major who "is very fine looking and a great talker and laugher."[71] Ellen Louise Power from East Feliciana Parish met two New Orleans artillerymen from Fenner's Battery who were "such nice young men," she wrote, and "one of them was so handsome."[72]

An Alabama soldier stationed at Port Hudson recalled how a soldier's insignia also attracted female attention. He claimed that "if there was anything on earth that a Southern woman, during these days, could not resist it was a Confederate soldier with brass bars and stars on his coat collar"; however, he also mentioned that "there was some fascination even with a corporal's stripes." According to this Alabamian, rank had its privileges.[73] A soldier's looks were not the only attributes young ladies sought in a potential suitor. By the war's end, one Louisiana woman wrote to her cousin Lt. John Coleman Sibley, explaining her dire situation of not having a marriage prospect and felt a soldier would make an agreeable spouse. She encouraged Sibley to "pick one out and tell him he has to come, for the boys are getting scarce," she wrote. To prove the severity of having few available prospects, she claimed, "What there is left of them they are marrying all the old widows. There was a boy seventeen years old married and old lady over thirty."[74]

While many women associated with Confederate soldiers, not all of these ladies had good reputations, good motives, or good effects on the men. Indeed, one Louisiana officer documented that some of his comrades from home had "been rascals" by mingling with prostitutes and contracted "the secret illness."[75] And women of disrepute could prove violent. A group of Texas soldiers who went to Alexandria and Pineville ran into many women whose behavior reflected the "low characters of the fair sex" as one woman "struck one of our men in the arm, with a large knife, and inflicted a very serious wound." Actions such as these made isolated camps more appealing for Confederate commanders as their men "might be more easily controlled."[76] Another incident of female aggression occurred near Shreveport as W. H. King described an altercation "at the houses of two women of ill fame. At one, three men were severely beaten, but . . . no life was lost, notwithstanding 7 pistols were discharged." King obviously disapproved of the violence as he wrote, "Such behavior should be severely dealt with."[77]

As many women and soldiers shared a mutual affection, many ladies, especially those from elite slaveholding families, were constantly reminded that they had much to lose from the war. Many women felt the Civil War concerned not only soldiers in the field but also themselves as one woman claimed the fight was "certainly ours as well as that of our men."[78] As Faust explains, for the Confederacy to triumph, women had to do their share. "Women had to become patriotic, had to assume some of the political interests of men, and had to repress certain womanly feelings and expectations for the good of the Cause." Faust notes that Southern women, in many ways, had to show "self reliance" and "self denial," along with fostering patriotic and pro-military sentiment within their communities.[79] Ward argues that Southern White women actively (and defiantly) "marked Confederate space" once Union occupiers arrived.[80]

The presence of soldiers constantly reminded these women of what was at stake. One steadfast Louisiana woman, Sarah Morgan, remained sympathetic to the South in the face of Federal opposition. When Union soldiers arrived in New Orleans, they ordered that "All devices, signs, and flags of the Confederacy shall be suppressed." Morgan defiantly claimed that no Yankee order was going to keep her from displaying Southern patriotism as "I devote all my red, white, and blue silk to the manufacture of Confederate flags. . . . Henceforth, I wear one pinned to my bosom—not a duster, but a little flag; the man who says take it off will have to pull it off for himself; the man who dares attempt it—well! a pistol in my pocket fills up the gap. I am capable, too."[81] Edwin Fay wrote his wife about a Tennessee woman who stood ready to defend her property against Union troops—even at the peril of her personal safety. Her aggressiveness and courageous display (with a pistol) ensured that "she was entirely unmolested." Fay instructed his wife to follow suit if the Yankees arrived and "treat them, if they should come, civilly and whenever they overstep the bounds of civility have a pistol ready with a will to use it."[82]

Though perhaps not as daring or outspoken as Sarah Morgan or the Tennessee lady Fay wrote about, Lizzie Fitzgerald had her experiences with Union sympathizers and soldiers. In the spring of 1862, Fitzgerald's education remained uninterrupted by the conflict; however, varying opinions and sympathies existed on her campus. She explained to a friend, "Our school is still progressing very fast some of the scholars got mad because Yankee Doodle was played and stoped [*sic*]. Miss Waters the music teacher played it both my teachers are from New York and another one of them are for the North. . . . I am so tired [of] going to school."[83] A few months later Fitzgerald encountered more Union sympathizers, and these wore blue uniforms and carried weapons. She wrote that upon the arrival of two boatloads of Union soldiers, "the Yankees called me a . . . rebel, and one had the imprudence to kiss his hand at me." Luckily for Fitzgerald the canal's dropping water level forced the boat-borne Union soldiers to leave, shortening the confrontation's duration.[84]

Despite the various conditions or circumstances, soldiers usually jumped at every opportunity to interact with civilians, especially women. Even if no long-term romance evolved, soldiers relished the thought of kindling a relationship—or at least a flirtatious conversation, with local females. Romance aside, the sight and physical interaction with women also reminded soldiers of relatives and friends back home, which likely conjured up images of their prewar lives. Women were also a major reason soldiers fought—defense of their homes, family, and property. And women, especially from the upper class, knew of the importance of their wartime support roles as Confederate defeat would end their privileged status. The fight for victory was a mutual endeavor.

VISITS AND FURLOUGH

As the war's demands and lengthy separations from loved ones took a psychological and emotional toll on many Louisiana warriors, what men desired most was to return home. When granted leave, soldiers cherished whatever time they spent together with their loved ones. Coming home on furlough—or even receiving a short pass—offered soldiers a chance to catch up with relatives and friends and, as long as military campaigning was at a far distance, enjoy some resemblance of civilian life. The perceived promise of furloughs also caused strife in Confederate camps if they were not granted. On occasion, soldiers took matters of heading home into their own hands—especially if they had been promised leave. One 19th Louisiana Infantryman wrote in December 1863 about the feelings of "dissatisfaction among our troops" and how many soldiers "deserted because they were denied the furlough promised them when they were conscripted and retained in the service."[85] In the spring of 1862, one Louisiana soldier noted how his colonel did not have authority to grant leave "without a commission" and warned his men he would consider them "deserters if they go home." A standoff between the regiment's soldiers and officers ensued since their gear was already packed. Luckily, the men submitted but the "spirit of leaving prevails."[86] The business of granting furloughs frustrated commanding officers, too, as one Louisiana soldier felt the obtaining a leave of absence was a lost cause. Wanting to avoid his commander's wrath, David Pierson told his father, "The Gen.'s quarters swarmed with privates after discharges & furloughs, & he raved and cursed at being annoyed so much. So I concluded not to bother him."[87]

Despite upsetting episodes of reneged furloughs, awarding soldiers with time off proved beneficial. To boost morale and troop strength, the officers of at least one company in the 2nd Louisiana Cavalry promised a sixty-day furlough to any soldier who brought in a recruit "under seventeen years of age." At least four men from Company E procured recruits and received their furlough.[88] In a Texas regiment stationed near Marksville in 1864, William Tamplin wrote that his colonel promised a sixty-day furlough if he could "get a man to enlist." He solicited the aid of a female friend, telling her that "if you see lon tell Him if He Will come and join the company I Will give Him $300 dollars." Tamplin's request was urgent as he feared, "they Will Stop the system of furloughing in a month or to."[89] Hopeful for leave, one Louisiana officer wrote his wife that if any "Officers shoud be sent home on business, I am to be the one." But his commitment to duty remained steadfast; he reminded his wife that receiving a furlough was not his choice—"you know our motto 'Gods Will.'"[90] During the last year of the war, a few Louisiana cavalrymen serving near Alexandria requested furloughs, each promising he could "remount myself immediately" if allowed leave. Their efforts, while likely self-serving, also kept the army's needs in mind as fresh horses would not be unwelcome in a cavalry unit. The men received their furloughs.[91]

For the lucky soldiers who obtained a furlough or pass, it usually allowed time for mental and physical rest and relaxation—within the presence and comfort of civilian company. Furloughs also allowed soldiers to get reacquainted with loved ones after long stints of separation, such as one 8th Louisiana infantryman, who had not seen his sister in nearly three years.[92] Wounds or illnesses helped many soldiers obtain a leave of absence, allowing time for recouperation and recovery.[93] With the war's glamour quickly fading, some men welcomed the prospect of injuries, which would likely result in a trip home. As one Louisianian explained, "Oh! wouldnt it be nice," he wrote, "to get a 30 days leave and go home and be petted like a baby, and get delicacies to eat . . . and then if I ever run for a little office I could limp and complain of the 'old wound.'" He even claimed he would harbor no ill-will toward the enemy; on the contrary, he would "consider the Yankee . . . a good kind fellow."[94]

Once home, a furloughed soldier's leisure activities varied. Time off enabled W. H. King to reflect—and harbor animosities towards the people he felt were responsible for the war: "Spent the day most agreeably with my family, eating fruits, reading letters, & writing in my journal.—Just now I feel that I would rejoice to know that those who caused the war, had to assemble in one vast field, & fight the battle of their own making—not until one party had whipped, but until the extinguishing of the last man. I want a 'Kilkenny cut fight' of it. After such an event, I believe families might retire to their former vocations in peace & quietude—but not till then."[95] The prospect of returning to duty after a leave of absence proved a difficult thought for many soldiers. "The painful duty of parting from my family, is again forced on me," wrote W. H. King. His love for his family ran deep as he questioned individuals who separated from home for long stints who sought "pleasure; or, even 'fortune,'" as he made clear his life's sole desire was to remain in his family's embrace. "Give me my family, my beloved family, with but the absolute necessaries to sustain life, & they may have all the rest." For many soldiers a visit home, which often ended in sadness as he once again departed, served as a strong reminder of what they were fighting for. Indeed, King spoke for many soldiers when he wrote, "Nothing save the sacred honor of myself & family, could induce me to separate from them as I have done."[96]

Even short visits provided some soldiers (and their families) with a mental reprieve that made them feel all was well. But for others, the joy of returning home to what they hoped would resemble prewar normalcy and familiarity was shattered after witnessing the war's destruction on the Louisiana home front. As wartime destruction escalated, many soldiers and civilians realized that sometimes there was little that distinguished the battle front from the home front. Stephen V. Ash argues that Union occupation created three spheres of influence within captured Confederate territory. The "garrisoned towns" became the Union forces' operational base; the "Confederate frontier" remained in Confederate hands and saw enemy activity "only sporadically"; and there was a "no-man's-land," which was not under constant Union occupation, but was "beyond the pale of Confederate authority and endured frequent Yankee visitations" since it surrounded "the garrisoned towns." A Federal foothold on Southern soil disrupted daily civilian routines and, when fighting occurred, forever changed the physical and social landscape.[97] "I remained at home a little over three weeks," wrote one furloughed Louisiana soldier near Clinton in 1863, "but everything looked so gloomy that there was little or no pleasure in remaining."[98]

Times of mourning or loss also provided civilians and soldiers opportunities for interaction. For some furloughed soldiers their visit home would be short—and their last. One Louisianian came home from Virginia "with consumption & died from it." The soldier's father took it hard, mourning his "baby boy!"[99] Without the presence of a soldier's family, fellow comrades or strangers took it upon themselves to offer the recently departed a respectful ceremony, often stirring personal emotions. In an 1864 letter, Amelia Faulkner notified her friend, Henrietta Lauzin, that her brother Paul had been killed in action near Bayou Lafourche. Henrietta's brother was "buried in a gentlemans yard about 12 miles below Donaldsonville . . . some citizens knowing his family were Catholic had requested not to have him buried deep as they wanted to bury him in the Catholic Church Yard. He was shot through the breast and died instantly, it was the first fight in which he was engaged after leaving home."[100] W. H. King described a soldier's funeral procession, noting that their unit's chaplain "executed his part well, & the men behaved with excellent decorum." King hoped "the exercise will have a beneficial influence on all who attended. How solemn it is to witness the funeral ceremonies of a fellow soldier far from loved ones at home!" The absence of family and friends—especially a soldier's wife—was, to King, "one of the most solemn thoughts I have ever encountered."[101] Such sad examples show the deranged realities of war. In the midst of the conflict's death and destruction, soldiers and civilians still took it upon themselves to show compassion by expressing their personal feelings and emotions toward the fallen and those they left behind.

Hospitals also offered civilians an opportunity to interact with soldiers and provide comfort in their hour of need. H. N. Connor, a Texas soldier serving near Vermilionville (present-day Lafayette), highly praised the women who helped care for the sick Confederates stationed nearby. "The Methodist Church was turned into a hospital, also a number of private houses, and the ladies attended them day and night, providing them all that was in their power." Connor even recalled how "Mrs. Mouton (the former governor's wife) acquitted herself as a southern lady should toward a sick soldier. She had received the blessing of many a poor 'gray-breeched Rebel,' even if some of them did steal her spoons."[102] One Washington artilleryman's wife, who had been appointed as a vivandière back in New Orleans, accompanied the unit to Virginia. She won the battalion's affection as "many a sick or wounded fellow has felt her motherly hand."[103] Hospitals also became meeting grounds for old friends. One ill soldier stationed in Natchitoches requested that his sister "tell mother I met up with one of my old School mates Heare [*sic*] He is Surgeon of the Hospittle. . . . He was glad to See me and treated me like a brother."[104]

When hospitals were nonexistent, soldiers turned to civilians for care. A sick Louisiana soldier traveling through Alabama met civilians willing to aid him as he battled his ailment by loaning him money and providing lodging, meals, and care. "I can say that I could not have been better attended to evin at home," he wrote, as a testament to their generosity.[105] Whether all obliging civilians were Confederate sympathizers is not always recorded, but many who came into contact with soldiers who were ill or in need—which sometimes included their enslaved body servants—provided assistance.[106] Sarah L. Wadley noted that a sick soldier stayed at her house for about a week, claiming the soldier kept mostly to himself, but "he was an honest, quiet and modest person, seldom conversed, but very sensible."[107] Some civilians who helped sick soldiers expected compensation. One ill Louisiana soldier under civilian care in St. Mary Parish received the aid of a local doctor, but for a price. "I expect my Dr. bill will not be small," he wrote.[108] And civilian home care did not always result in a recovery. Sarah L. Wadley helped care for a soldier who "is very ill indeed . . . and groans constantly, it is pitiful to hear him." Though she and the soldier's wife did their best, the man died.[109] Civilian contributions toward soldiers in need cannot be overstated. A sick soldier greatly appreciated civilian help, which brought real meaning and purpose to his wartime service and sacrifices, perhaps reminding him that he was appreciated and not forgotten.

CONFEDERATE SOLDIERS AND BLACK CIVILIANS

Throughout the Civil War, soldier and civilian interactions were not limited to the South's White population. African Americans had contributed to the Confederate war effort since the conflict began—some willingly, but most by coercion. Many Confederate soldiers frequently interacted with the South's enslaved and free African American population in various scenarios, situations, and engagements.[110] With the Union's shifting war goals, which eventually included slavery's abolition, the role of African Americans in the conflict varied. Even as numerous escaped slaves and some Free Blacks offered their services to the Union, many African Americans remained within Confederate lines. However, slave agency—and in some cases their ability to strike against the institution physically—became more apparent as the war escalated. What some Confederate soldiers originally saw as docile or compliant servants and impressed enslaved laborers shifted as the slave system eventually broke down.

As the raging war took its toll on the land and economy, soldiers' relatives, especially wives, played a crucial role in maintaining slave control while slaveholding soldiers were off fighting. In comparison, Georgia's Confederate officials felt "the threat of servile insurrection was minimal" even as late as 1864, as they continuously pressed men into the ranks. Though few males remained on the home front, women "who often expressed the greatest fear of slave violence still managed slavery."[111] Soldiers often saw or heard of slavery's breakdown when Union forces operated in the vicinity. Some planters abandoned their plantations and became refugees, seeking a place to rebuild their fortunes.[112] A few New Orleans slaveowners left the city, forcing their enslaved men and women to fend for themselves. Other slaveholders who fell on hard times told their slaves "to go to the Yankees" to seek aid until they could once again provide for them.[113] Still others who remained in areas that Union troops invaded saw much of their workforce disappear to the Federal lines. In the summer of 1862, one planter wrote that Union troops "are taking all the Negros off the Plantations . . . but a few oald ones."[114] One Confederate soldier serving in Louisiana noted that as the Union army got closer to their location, "there are very few places that will make more than a support for the negro women and children, as you are aware that all the men that is worth anything have gone to the Federals."[115]

When enslaved laborers escaped, plantation production declined. Planter Isaac Erwin claimed, "The Yankeys have taken off nearly all the Negros on the coast and wherever they go the Negros have left their Masters and run to them our whole cuntry will be devastated and I see nothing but starvation and great distress to fall upon us much as has never been heard of." By the spring of 1863, Erwin continued recording instances of how Union soldiers disrupted plantation life.[116] Such actions not only disturbed the home front's social and racial order, but it also affected plantation production for the Confederate war effort. A little farther south near Opelousas, the Union troops conducted similar operations.[117] Civilian suffering and restructuring also meant severe consequences for Confederate soldiers. Every slave laborer who ran away meant less agricultural production or laboring for the Confederate army—along with the mental anguish soldiers held for the safety of loved ones who remained at home amid the growing chaos.

But not all enslaved individuals who tried to liberate themselves were successful. Lt. John Coleman Sibley noted in his diary: "The Regt was called out to witness the execution of a negro who was shot for trying to get to the enemy and render them assistance."[118] In a letter to his wife, Charles D. Moore wrote: "Yesterday morning my picket captured a negro who was trying to get to the Yanks."[119] Slaves sought freedom on their own terms, and some favored remaining on the plantation rather than running to advancing Union troops. Lizzie Fitzgerald wrote to her friend and explained that the Yankees "did not take any pour nigroe as ma, had them all run back in the woods." Apparently, they evaded the Federal troops who "went four miles back in the woods hunting for nigros."[120]

Captured by Union troops in southern Louisiana, W. H. King noted how he saw numerous African Americans while in Federal captivity. "I heard one say to the Yankees," referring to a visiting slave, that "he did not intend to leave his master . . . his master had always furnished him what he wanted, & treated him well in every respect." King claimed the Union officer who commanded the soldiers guarding the captured Confederates told the enslaved man, "You are the most sensible negro I have met with."[121] One enslaved man named Sandy observed a Union gunboat off the river bank in north Louisiana and asked a "negro who was in the skiff if any body could go on board that boat that chose (meaning the gunboat)," wrote Sarah L. Wadley. She claimed that "the negro said no, asked Sandy if he wanted to go . . . Sandy told him no, that he had had no hand in bringing on the war, and was not going to have anything to do with it!" Though Sandy apparently did not run to Union lines, Wadley remained uncertain as to what her family's other enslaved laborers might do.[122]

Nonetheless, many of Louisiana's enslaved population abandoned servitude when an occasion presented itself. One planter near Opelousas recorded that numerous enslaved families "all left for the Yankees. . . . A Steam Boat stopping opposite Plantation to take them on—Yankees."[123] Despite disillusions of his bondsmen's loyalty, planter Isaac Erwin wrote, "My Negros are looking hourly for the Federals to take them away and I think they will all go." A few days later, his frustration grew: "Negros took today without saying a word for Holliday and say they are Free and have as much law in their favor as I have. I let them go on hoping the Federals or some one will come and take them away. Some few want to work but Most of them are unwilling to do anything." Not long afterwards, he noted, "Some 25 Confederate soldiers came . . . Arrested all my Negros and took away 4 men and 3 Women by forse saying they were dangerous Negros."[124]

For enslaved African Americans attempting to gain their freedom, obtaining resources and food became a chore, requiring creative tactics. On at least one occasion, a group of runaways used the excuse of aiding the suffering of Southern soldiers to obtain some milk for their own use. Sydney Harding noted that the slaves "told us when they were wounded who they were and everything. We felt so sorry concluded to ride down and bring them up—The soldiers were surprised when we asked. Said none had been there All a story of negroes."[125]

As bondsmen fled slavery, many Whites—both Southerners and Union soldiers serving in the region—feared the possibility of slave insurrections. Indeed, to White individuals living in a slave society, any evidence pointing to a possible uprising brought a swift response. In June 1861, one St. Martinville resident wrote to her brother, telling him of the hanging of a "white man bent on urging slaves to revolt," along with "six of the Negroes," who were supposedly involved in the plot.[126] A group of enslaved Louisianians near Bethany Institute "had everything planned and were going to murder the people at nine o'clock," wrote one female contemporary, "but the gentlemen found it out a few hours before the appointed time and caught some of them. . . . We are afraid to go to bed now."[127]

Fears of slave revolts were real. And the conflict's early years saw an increase in slave regulation as local militia units sometimes acted as slave patrols. Parish police juries also passed various laws and ordinances attempting to maintain a high state of order among the enslaved; however, as C. Peter Ripley notes, military demands and slave agency initiated the unraveling of the institution.[128] In 1863, one Louisiana soldier's wife in the Florida Parishes wrote to him about brewing fears associated with the local bondsmen. "The people generally think that the negroes will turn out boldly and go off to the yankees." She mentioned some troubles with a couple of their neighbor's slaves who were "trying to steal there guns and horse[s] . . . they had a terrible stir over that way and whipeped some of the negroes very bad. there was five brought to Jail la[s]t friday night from off Tickfaw they will be hung." Apparently, these individuals had organized into "a company of 125" and were "ready Just as quick as the word was given to go to work." Though the woman's account is sketchy, the uprising ended in bloodshed with several bondsmen killed. "I am afraid we will have troublesome times down here the men are patroleing all the time but the men are so few in the country that they can not do much good."[129]

Concessions and exemptions, such as the "Twenty Negro Law," which aimed more at keeping experienced overseers at work managing slave laborers to produce war necessities, were not enough to keep slavery intact.[130] This uprising in southeastern Louisiana showed the real threat that rebellion posed to Confederate authorities and to the White inhabitants who remained on the home front. Susan O'Donovan notes in her study of wartime enslaved individuals in Georgia that the loss of the South's White male population to military service "put the whole slaveholding nation at significant risk," since such scenarios "appeared to invite . . . insurrection."[131] The war's escalating tempo and the Confederacy's growing manpower shortage eventually ensured slavery's doom.

Federal commanders also harbored similar fears of insurrection, as "Women and children, and even men are in terror" of a possible slave uprising. However, widespread violence never materialized.[132] Union occupation forces in some Louisiana towns, such as Jackson, served as a quarry to swell the Federal ranks, as soldiers attempted "to gather up all the negroe men they can, to put in the army."[133] For freedmen who found themselves wearing Union blue or laboring for the Federal army, their conditions sometimes mimicked a plantation—especially for men accused of disobedience, as floggings and other abuses among the Black Union ranks were common.[134]

Both Union and Confederate soldiers noted the growing violence and racial disorder. One Louisiana soldier stationed in Mississippi wrote, "I heard that the runaway slaves have done more harm than the Yankees themselves, they say they have burned and pillaged several plantation[s], and that they steal all the livestock."[135] But not all African Americans in Louisiana during the Civil War found themselves involved in violent predicaments, nor were all who interacted with Confederate soldiers enslaved or impressed laborers. For example, among the various businesses and "shanties" near Camp Moore was "old Aunt Mary's restaurant—old black Mary of Craps street."[136] Soldiers often frequented Aunt Mary's establishment, as one soldier claimed, "We often go to 'Aunty's' for a diversion . . . the most popular restaurant at Camp Moore. Everything is in order at her place. The tables are solidly settled on barrels; the candles . . . are set in the necks of bottles. . . . Yesterday evening, our little group was eating an excellent chicken gumbo made with ham and beef."[137]

Louisiana soldiers serving near Vermilionville visited an establishment "kept by a free colored Lady," who charged the men "the moderate price of $13.00 for supper, lodging, breakfast and stabling for my horse and mule."[138] Free Black business owners were not uncommon in the area. Some Creoles of Color in southwest Louisiana had made economic progress before the Civil War, obtaining status as business owners, some of whom owned slaves, and ran hotels, brothels, and coffeehouses.[139] Perhaps even more curious than Confederate soldiers interacting with Black entrepreneurs were soldier interactions with a shop owner of Asian descent. Along with "Aunty's," Camp Moore also hosted a businessman of half-French, half-Chinese lineage. "Tatout," wrote one soldier, "is the proprietor of the major store. . . . He is some sort of Chinese-Frenchman . . . anywhere between 30 and 70 years old. His infernal babble is as incessant as that of the general's parrot." His small shop "reveals to astonished eyes a thousand and one articles, each one more useless than the other, but which the soldiers cannot dispense with. . . . While selling us his merchandise at five times what its worth, he manages to persuade us that he is giving them to us at half price."[140]

Whether in camp or on campaign, according to many Civil War historians, soldiers remained separated from civilians and the comforts of civilian life. However, separation is not isolation. Physical and social exchanges between soldiers and civilians remained a fixture in their wartime experiences, even if such encounters sometimes challenged the perceived notions of good will both groups had toward each other. The relationships soldiers formed with both Black and White civilians catered to their psychological needs as these interactions played a major role in maintaining a soldier's ability to wage and perhaps to understand why they were waging war. Communal and family ties remained strong, which was in large part due to soldier and civilian physical interactions that continued throughout the war.

CHAPTER 6

―――◦◇◦――

SOLDIER PROVISIONS AND TRADE

―――◦◇◦――

On the same day Louisiana seceded from the Union, the Secession Convention passed a resolution recognizing "the right of free navigation of the Mississippi River and its tributaries by all friendly States bordering thereon," along with allowing "the right to egress and ingress of the mouths of the Mississippi by all friendly States and Powers."[1] However optimistic this "free navigation" measure seemed in 1861, much changed as the war unfolded. The Mississippi River proved key to both Confederate and Union war strategy and success. Even Abraham Lincoln saw the importance of controlling the Mississippi, which would cut the Confederacy in two—and allow Union forces to freely trade, ship, and transport its resources.[2] Fearful of New Orleans's vulnerability to Union attack, Governor Moore remained concerned about its lack of defenses, even voicing his concerns to Jefferson Davis, describing not only Louisiana's seemingly indefensible geography, but also urging the placement of a more "active, energetic [younger] commander" in charge.[3] But while Louisiana's Confederate officials emphasized military command and strategy, trade and the ability to obtain supplies and provisions remained essential to soldiers and civilians alike.

When the army failed to provide provisions—or if the amount provided remained insufficient—soldiers took matters into their own hands and turned to civilians. For their relatives back home, soldiers did what they could to offer advice on the issues of trade, commerce, and survival. Providing for soldiers involved navigating a labyrinth of shifting economic and military developments that sometimes put military authorities and civilians in competition. Soldiers benefited from—and relied on—civilians (especially women) for provisions.[4] The same energy that mobilized men for war also had a similar effect on civilians wanting to support their new nation. At first, provisions abounded; however, as the war continued, the economic strain from shortages and the passage of the Impressment Act forced soldiers to walk a fine line between being property protectors or takers. Perhaps this aspect of a Civil War soldier's social experience proved most threatening to their relationships with civilians. Impressing civilian property for military use—taking provisions civilians needed to survive when many families had sent husbands and sons to the front—disrupted the reciprocal relationship between soldiers and civilians.

Illicit trading between Union and Confederate forces and civilians distributed an array of items and supplies throughout the Confederacy, but it also made authorities question the traders' patriotism and loyalty. Ludwell H. Johnson notes that the contraband trade put both the North and South in precarious situations—it could aid their war efforts, but also it could damage it. For example, he argues: "Without cotton," Northern economic (and diplomatic) interests might suffer, while the Confederacy had much to gain in resources from trading; however, among Southerners it could "produce confusion in the public mind, suspicion of corruption and favoritism by civil and military officials, and resentment against speculators." Confederate authorities also feared that enemy trade could potentially distract the army from fighting and provide a way for military intelligence to leak.[5]

Confederate government and military officials had no consensus on how to handle illicit trading, which, Johnson argues, could be blamed on Jefferson Davis's inability to develop "a clear and consistent policy" for Confederate officials to follow.[6] The lack of a cohesive Confederate policy against illicit trading failed to curtail the practice. But the irony of it all was the belief that obtaining goods through illegal trade would demoralize soldiers and civilians while they simultaneously suffered from a lack of resources. The encroachment of Union forces into Confederate territory, not to mention the growing economic woes brought on by the conflict, alarmed many Confederates. As Ash notes, the numerous economic problems—even as Federal troops took over a region—impacted everyone, often threatening civilians with "widespread privation."[7]

If high-ranking Confederate officials remained in limbo over the issue of contraband trade, some of its soldiers and civilians did not. To many Louisianians, ensuring that their relatives obtained provisions—regardless of the methods used—equated to home defense, not disloyalty. For many Confederate soldiers and civilians, illicit trading allowed their family—and indirectly, themselves—a way to survive. Though despised by some and engaged in by many, illegal trading (to some degree) benefited ordinary people.

SOLDIERS, CIVILIANS, AND PROVISIONS

At the war's commencement, many residents with Confederate sympathies happily catered to—or at least willingly complied with—the needs of their local soldiers.[8] Agricultural shifts from cash to food crops began in 1861, which helped account for an abundance of produce. Some planters saw the wisdom of such actions, as one contemporary proclaimed that food production would be as important as weapons of war since a well-fed population "can defy the world in arms."[9] Lt. P. L. Prudhomme wrote to his father in Natchitoches, commending the region's planters, who "have made not only ample provisions for themselves but enough to furnish the Government with the necessary provisions to carry on the war."[10] Farmers in southeastern Louisiana did likewise by decreasing cotton production and "tripling their output of corn."[11] But converting fields into food crops did not end cotton and sugar cane production, nor did all planters accommodate soldiers who sought provisions. Jonathan Knight, who served in Walker's Texas Division, explained his frustration with local planters, noting, "I have tried to buy [necessities] and cannot for these big planters wont sell nothing they have got because they have to take Confederate money." Knight's efforts, though largely unsuccessful, did not leave him empty-handed since he managed to obtain some "watermelons and sugar cane."[12] Many civilians' early attempts to assist soldiers shifted as the Union blockade, shortages, and headaches with trade strained interactions and cooperative relationships.

As Louisiana troops mustered for service in 1861, most Confederate camps maintained adequate provisions. Writing from Virginia, one Louisiana soldier noted that food was in great abundance as "I am as fat as pork & crackers"; however, a home-cooked meal proved more desirable: he wished his mother could mail him "a real good country dinner . . . a good peach cobbler for instance it would go down faster than rain."[13] Back in Louisiana John A. Harris wrote from Camp Moore, "I can live as healthy here as at home. We have enough to eat."[14] Fredrick R. Taber answered his sister's inquiry, "You asked me how I like camp life? Well I will tell you in the first place we have better meat here then you have in St. James in the Second we have Ice. Water & Coffee three times a day."[15] Camped near the Atchafalaya River, Silas White assured his father that all was well and that he was "Still in the land of liveing fat and healthy."[16]

Soldiers quartered near sugar plantations often had access to sugar cane—sometimes in seemingly unlimited quantities. E. J. Lee noted how his excellent health continued after reaching Chalmette, claiming, "I am fatning every day. I get plenty of Sugar cane to chaw down here."[17] One Texas soldier overindulged on the available cane crop, which resulted in "a little headache." More importantly, his overeating made him too full to take up an invitation by a local resident for a meal, so he claimed, "I wished then that I had never seen any sugar cane."[18] Near Alexandria, another Texas soldier, Isaac Dunbar Affleck, wrote that he and his comrades had access to an "abundance of sugar," making a variety of dishes and pies, "also candy, and syrup which we eat until every one makes himself sick."[19] Lt. John Coleman Sibley, who served in the 2nd Louisiana Cavalry, wrote from camp in Avoyelles Parish, "We have been several days among the sugar plantations and the way we make the cane fly is a sight to the planters." Sugar was not the only abundant ration, as Sibley claimed he and his men received meal, meat, and salt, along with "twenty five ears of corn by the day for each horse and five bundles of fodder."[20] Plantations, at least during certain months of the year, could boast a plethora of supplies and provisions.

Soldiers who found themselves in Louisiana's secluded terrain sometimes foraged for wild grown delicacies. Soldiers near Opelousas, for instance, "cut down some trees, or one tree rather, for grapes. We got all as many as we wanted."[21] But a soldier's diet, while sometimes plentiful, did not always offer much variety, nor was it always appetizing. One soldier claimed, "This fat pork dont agree with me so well, those hard crackers too are not the most pleasent things."[22] Writing from Camp Moore, Louis Stagg told his wife that "there is not much choice in meals here; I would give anything to be home eating a good gumbo, milk, butter, things i've not seen since i've been here." Despite longing for a home-cooked meal, Stagg continued "to grow fatter."[23]

Amid the poor quality or taste of some military rations, the abundance of 1861 waned. By the spring of 1862, many soldiers complained of the dwindling food supplies. John E. Hall provided his wife with a vivid description of the issued "rations for one man," which, he noted, "is entirely unfit for any human to eat."[24] Another Louisiana soldier wrote from Vicksburg, comparing his ration's quality and quantity to that of the enslaved. "I only get half enough to eat," he wrote, "and it is not as good as the Negroes eat."[25] Encamped at Avery Island, T. J. Shaffer wrote in disgust, "We have to live on corn bread and salt junk," along with having little to no clothing and money. Shaffer and a group of soldiers supplemented their diets by attending an officers-only ball, "which was as fine a one as could be gotten up in time of peace."[26] But holding a commission did not guarantee an invitation to an officers' social function. Lt. John Coleman Sibley knew his place—both in a military and civilian setting—claiming that "common stock have no business eating cake and drinking wine. They do better on beef and potatoes or corn bread baked in an oven without any lid."[27]

Some Louisiana soldiers disregarded both military and social rank when such formalities stood in the way of a meal and a full belly. Ned Phelps, a Louisiana private serving in the Army of Northern Virginia, cared little for rank—and even less for formal protocol. Upon entering a farmhouse after a foraging expedition the night before, he noticed an empty chair at the table in the midst of a group of his superior officers preparing to eat. A general asked the uninvited Phelps if he knew whom he was sitting with. "Before I came soldiering I used to be particular whom I ate with," replied Phelps, "but now I don't care a damn—so [long as] the victuals are clean." Shocked and amused at his reply, the general allowed the soldier to stay.[28]

Soldiers foraging in large groups sometimes hindered their efforts to obtain provisions by overwhelming civilians and their capabilities to assist. W. H. King noted how he and a group of comrades planned "to keep ahead of the main body of the Company" to obtain something to eat, possibly hinting that their civilian benefactors were not always accommodating—at least not to large crowds.[29] Home front shortages also took their toll on local residents. "This cruel war still continues," wrote Louisiana planter Isaac Erwin in the fall of 1863. "One thing for certain Louisiana will soon be in a state of starvation for Meat."[30] While the quality and quantity of food varied, many soldiers and civilians learned to do without or found substitutes.[31] Lt. John Coleman Sibley explained his recipe for coffee substitution, which required "two table spoons full of sugar," water, and milk. "I like it very much if it is done rite [sic]."[32]

But substitution did not always mean scarcity, and some Louisiana residents remained in a position to feed Confederate troops.[33] Louisiana's numerous waterways also provided both soldiers and civilians with opportunities to supplement their dwindling food resources with fresh fish; however, with varying degrees of luck—catching and fishing are not synonymous.[34]

For many Confederates, food scarcity depended more on location rather than time. Near the war's closure, many Confederate soldiers suffered for lack of proper food and necessities; however, sometimes men did without in the war's first year because of logistical hiccups. And some soldiers had the good fortune of having access to adequate supplies much later in the war as some men received bountiful provisions as late as 1864.[35] Nonetheless, shortages (regardless of when they occurred) often tested a soldier's patience—sometimes causing disorderly conduct. Frustrated by the lack of desired items found in local shops near Camp Moore, one soldier and his compatriots wandered into an establishment named "Soda Water & Coffee." After a long wait, the soldiers helped themselves to the available beverages and pledged "not to pay in order to punish the proprietor for having made us wait." When soldiers returned the next day, again finding the proprietor missing, they "repeated the same manoeuvre."[36]

Actions such as this remained common throughout the war, but they often ended in physical confrontation—especially when alcohol was involved.[37] And soldiers taking what they wanted foreshadowed the future impressment law. In the fall of 1861, William Edwards Paxton explained what happened when a contractor failed to supply beef to Camp Moore. "We had quite a lively time of it," he wrote, as between fifty and a hundred soldiers "tore down several sutler's shops and gutted them of their provisions. No interference by the officers except to persuade them to desist which they did as soon as they got as much as they wanted to Eat." This rowdiness soon prompted authorization of a foraging party, who obtained "four beeves very much to the delight of their hungry companions."[38]

Complaining of the food quality at Port Hudson in February 1863, one Louisiana soldier wrote, "I must say that never since I have been in the army have I fared so badly and in truth I have been almost starved. If better food is not provided for the troops we will certainly lose a great many men from this cause alone."[39] Washington artilleryman Alexander Pierre Allain noted his scant rations while serving in Georgia in 1864. "These are trying times indeed on the poor soldier," he wrote, noting that the region was "so played out that it is impossible to buy, steal, or borough anything."[40]

Throughout the Confederacy, military logistical issues abounded. Supplying food to troops often met with delays—or failure, which resulted in soldiers suffering.[41] When this happened, soldiers often took matters into their own hands, usually with the aid of civilians. At Port Hudson a well-meaning colonel "not having the fear of red tape before his eyes" sought to obtain supplies from the surrounding countryside and constructed "store houses" to protect the collected items. However, his plans were "interrupted sooner than expected . . . warehouses for the protection of corn and meat never were built," wrote one officer. Frustrated, many Confederates "frequently remarked . . . 'If Port Hudson falls, we will have to thank the commissary department for it.'"[42] Even the enlisted men stationed at Port Hudson noted the lack of protective structures to store provisions and the wastefulness they encouraged. John A. Morgan and his comrades "had to work day and night" unloading supply boats in vain. "I suppose that there is between 30 & 50,000 barrels of corn now laying out exposed to the rain on account of not having any place to put it under shelter."[43] When Port Hudson eventually fell into Union hands, a local resident wrote, "It is sad news for us. I know if they [Union forces] have it, they starved our poor men out."[44]

Confederate bureaucracy and Union assaults combined to create hardships. Some soldiers took creative (or desperate) measures for feeding themselves when the army failed to do so—especially when actively fighting. Once Confederate troops exhausted their meat rations at Port Hudson, they resorted to eating mules—and more. One officer wrote, "Far from shrinking from this hardship, the men received their unusual rations cheerfully, and declared that they were proud to be able to say that they had been reduced to this extremity." These hungry soldiers were not particular of what they ate—or had exotic tastes. One paper reported, "Many of them, as if in mockery of famine, caught rats and eat them, declaring that they were better than squirrels."[45]

As many Confederate soldiers fended for themselves, their actions sometimes caused innocent civilians to suffer. In September 1864 a squad of Confederate soldiers near Trenton, Louisiana, commandeered a hog from a nearby resident who threatened reprisals if he were not compensated for the stolen and eaten animal. The squad's sergeant paid the man but was promptly repaid by his men, as the soldiers had "killed the hog, not for the pecuniary profit, but because they were hungry, & had no other means of getting the meat."[46] Many Louisiana soldiers were not bashful in seeking out civilians who might be sympathetic to their dietary needs. One Washington artilleryman attempted to obtain "*only a snack*" from one Virginia lady as she prepared a meal for the unit's officers. The soldier's large appetite redefined the definition of a "snack," since he consumed "half a chicken, a 'pone' of corn-bread, some ham, and a hard-boiled egg."[47] These actions strained soldier and civilian relationships, sometimes eroding mutual respect. Assisting soldiers out of abundance was easy; however, civilians forced to provide for soldiers when their own needs were not met proved burdensome.[48]

BLOCKADE AND TRANSPORTATION

"Your prospects for a cotton crop is better than usual," wrote Alfred Flournoy Sr. to his son in June of 1861. "It will be hard for old Lincoln to starve us out the next twelve months with all his blockages."[49] Though Union officials announced the Federal blockade in 1861, Louisianians took little notice as many months passed before it became effective.[50] But as time continued, the blockade's noose slowly tightened causing a growing economic sting to throb. By January 1862, Louisiana militiaman H. A. Snyder noted the blockade's increasing effectiveness, which reflected his personal perceptions and not reality. He explained that not all entrepreneurs were financially ruined by the Federal attempts to strangle the South since "some have gone into business more extensively than ever." These merchants' ability to sell goods "at enormous advances in prices," allowed handsome profits to flourish. Noting these successful ventures, Snyder, who had been a "moderate scale" merchant, claimed he had "been successful & done well—but might have done better had I studdied wisdom & been more prudent."[51] While some merchants prospered, many consumers suffered. As one Louisiana soldier wrote, "Nothing is for sale here except at Blockade prices."[52]

Supplementing a soldier's provisions often called for civilian cooperation and money—and more of it as prices rose. One Texas soldier in Louisiana noted, "Everything is high here, and previsions getting scarce. Our beef is very poor, corn meal very course. . . . I will never get tired of beef and corn bread when I know I can do no better."[53] Pvt. Isaac Dunbar Affleck told of the "enormous price" he paid for flour and bacon ("$2.75 per lb. for flour and $4.00 per lb. for bacon") and noted that his money is "all most useless."[54] Even as early as the autumn of 1861, one Texas soldier passing through southern Louisiana noted the "very high" price of coffee, which ranged between forty to fifty cents per pound.[55] By the winter, coffee prices had reached a dollar per pound, and numerous other items became scarcer and more expensive.[56]

By comparison, Louisiana soldiers stationed outside of the state also noted soaring prices. "I expect times are hard back in Louisiana," wrote one soldier from a Richmond hospital, "but they are flush here. Everything is at an extravagantly high price. The Confederacy should remember the men who are making fortunes out of the necessities of our people at this time."[57] By the war's second year, one Opelousas resident concurred that "Every thing here is exorbitantly high"; however, the Louisianian remained optimistic, stating that "home industry is showing itself here. . . . In the country the people are at work in many places in good earnest."[58] Some soldiers blamed counterfeiting for the escalating inflation. In late 1862, Lt. P. L. Prudhomme wrote home to Natchitoches from Mississippi, noting, "The paper currency here (shin plasters) is very plentiful, and what is worse. . . . One cannot tell a good note from a counterfeit." Prudhomme mentioned the Confederate government should have passed laws to combat counterfeiting by not allowing individual notes to be printed. "This superabundance of paper currency tends to the depreciation of our national currency," which "is the ruin of the country."[59]

The effects of the growing shortages and high prices placed a growing burden on many women on the home front. Southern ladies from all social classes took the reins managing homes, businesses, farms, and plantations. Their diligence, skill, and ability to think and make decisions did much to ensure their and their families' survival.[60] Such actions by Louisiana's women to supplement and substitute began in 1861, several months before Union troops arrived. One Livingston Parish woman commented on how hunting, along with access to hogs, supplemented home front diets; however, not all Louisianians had access to these resources, as "a good many of them live entirely without meat." She also noted that not all animals were fit for consumption because of diseases (such as rabies), claiming, "We have plenty of mad dogs down this way . . . one of our neighbors has a horse that has been bitten also a hog, they have not gone mad as yet but will of course." To further compound home-front problems, the lack of knowledge also plagued this lady's survival operations. "Tell Ma I am going to begin soap making pretty soon," she wrote. "I only wish

I had her here to show me how. I expect hard times will make us learn a great many things. . . . I believe I shall have to quit writing I have so much to do." Indeed, this woman had her hands full. She also cared for—and disciplined— her strong-willed children without her husband's aid.[61] For many Louisianians on the home front, their wartime experience continuously gravitated to their personal survival and less to the political debates about nationalism and loyalty. Just as soldiers on the front lines hoped to live to fight another day, civilians instinctively fought the home-front war to survive. Without the efforts of both soldiers and civilians, which remained complex but cooperative, the Confederacy would have quickly collapsed.

When resources were available, soldiers and civilians relied on both the Confederate government and private efforts for the transportation and distribution of provisions. Subject to wartime demands, the Confederacy's lack of shipping venues proved troublesome, as military supplies and troops had priority in transportation. One sugar planter complained, "I fear we shall not be able to do anything with our Sugars—As there is no way of Distributing them throu the Country—The Blockade & the Railroads all rushed with carrying Troops and Supplies."[62] At the Civil War's outset, steamboats, which had brought great wealth and commerce to antebellum Louisiana, were giving way to developing railroads.[63] Railroads proved a vital link that not only transported soldiers to the front, but also played a major role in the trade and distribution of provisions and supplies—connecting both soldiers and civilians.[64] Soldiers' sympathy (at least on the surface) toward the hardships civilians faced helped divert some of this blame off of the army, especially since soldiers also suffered and lacked supplies. For example, by early 1863 several Louisiana Tigers suffered so much from the lack of shoes that the 5th Louisiana Infantry's commander canceled drill because of the "horrible condition" of his soldiers' feet.[65] As the further demands for sacrifice became apparent, many Louisianians, often in the name of survival and self-preservation, rose to the wartime challenges.

CONFISCATION AND IMPRESSMENT

On the surface, soldier needs trumped civilian desires, but this situation proved more complex. Soldiers knew that confiscating supplies from civilians also affected their own families. As the state's Confederate government continuously relied on civilians to keep Louisiana's troops provisioned and equipped, obtaining these items and necessities sometimes proved troublesome as the situation became muddled between the willingness to endure patriotic sacrifice versus forced confiscation. Whatever provisional items remained on the home front could be taxed or taken by Confederate authorities. Cognizant of what was taking place, many soldiers warned relatives to safekeep anything that could be of use to the warring armies. In this sense, they sought to protect their property while simultaneously confiscating items within their areas of operation. This is where nationalism and loyalty clashed with individual self-preservation and survival. And to many Louisiana residents who had relatives in the ranks, survival and self-preservation did not equal disloyalty.

In 1863, Lt. John Coleman Sibley warned his wife, "If the army gets anywhere near you, you must look out. . . . The soldiers will press everything they want." Though Sibley did not specify *which* army, confiscation—regardless of who conducted it—took its toll on civilians.[66] By 1864, both armies had cemented a reputation for pilfering. Louisiana soldier Joseph Texada warned his wife, who had been in the company of a group of Texans stationed near their home, to keep her guard up, as these soldiers were a "terrible set of men." He claimed, "If you do not be very watchful you will [be] 'eaten out of House and Home.' . . . I am afraid the 'Infernal Texans' will steal everything you have got."[67] Texada even compared the Texas soldiers to the enemy, writing they "are equally as hurtful to our country as the Yankees. Their conduct everywhere they go in such as to bring down upon them the just condemnation of the people at large."[68] Because soldiers operated with the power of government agents who demanded what the law required, residents oftentimes despised their very presence. Ironically, the soldiers who were fighting to protect Louisiana and the Confederacy were the ones enforcing unpopular measures to obtain provisions. Such actions showed how volatile confiscation had become.

The Confederacy's balancing act of retaining civilian support at the expense of military necessity kept tensions between the two groups high, especially as soldiers realized their own families faced similar fates. Some soldiers treated civilians fairly, while others took advantage of their power wielded by wearing uniforms and toting firearms.[69] Felix Poché witnessed the corruption and cruelties associated with confiscating supplies, explaining that some soldiers "do not limit themselves to taking only what they need . . . the love of pillaging, encouraged by the soldiers, is spread also to certain citizens of elastic conscience. . . . This state of things is deplorable, and one must hope that something will intervene to put an end to this system of stealing and pillaging."[70]

Once New Orleans fell to Union forces, many irate Louisianians blamed their incompetent leaders. Confederate officials hoped that this tragedy, combined with "the barbarism of the Yankee invaders," would inspire the rebel spirit and calm the growing wave of dissension among the state's Confederates.[71] One Louisianian noted how the city's fall would keep Confederate sympathizers from obtaining goods and items from within and would allow the enemy to be "emboldened by no resistance whatsoever," along with becoming "troublesome."[72] Despite the Confederacy's loss of the city and eventual loss of control of the Mississippi River, the Confederate governors of Louisiana, Texas, Arkansas, and Missouri did not lose heart or signal defeat. These men acknowledged that the river's loss was detrimental, but they argued it was not fatal, offering their citizens a seemingly honest statement. "We will not attempt to disguise the change in our position by the fall of our strongholds on the Mississippi River. . . . We now are self-dependent, but also self-sustaining." They called upon their citizens, including their "Allied Indian Nations," to rise to the challenge of continuing the war effort without the support of "our sisters east of the Mississippi." In closing, the governors ensured that these temporary trials and tribulations would "only strengthen the ties which bind us together."[73]

However, in the wake of the fall of New Orleans many civilians who had once hailed the Confederate army—and their leaders—as saviors and protectors had a change of heart.[74] Louisiana's wartime problems only escalated as defenses remained inadequate, its largest city was in Union hands, and its antebellum prosperity waned as economic hardships abounded. The 1863 Confederate Impressment Act forced many Louisianians to turn over needed supplies and goods to Confederate officials and agents at a designated, "reasonable" price. Complaints abounded as a "Great dissatisfaction prevailed" throughout Louisiana as many farmers were not left with much, if anything, that would allow them "to make a crop," wrote Henry Watkins Allen. "Under this pressure the people have become, if not disloyal, at least indifferent . . . to the cause."[75] This was not a new development; some soldiers had observed this attitude of growing indifference as early as 1862.[76]

Near Alexandria, a Texas private recalled the local populace's waning enthusiasm toward Confederate troops. He explained that many residents "feared for their commissaries and forage of their fruitful farms." One civilian wrote that neither the Yankees nor Confederates (referring to the Texas soldiers) were welcome in their vicinity. Although one civilian wrote that he admired these Texans for being "good soldiers, brave and daring, and as fearless as one could desire," he cut to the chase: the real issue he and others held against them was that "they would confiscate property as badly as any Union soldier who ever served in this section."[77]

While confiscating military resources and food was bad enough, some Louisiana residents fared worse. One Confederate officer led a raid in Alexandria and "entered houses of private citizens, brutally practiced extortion and out-rage[,] and . . . spread terror among the people."[78] One sugar planter along Bayou Teche despised Gen. Alfred Mouton's troops who camped on his property. "Our troops have stripped me, by robbery, of nearly every resource for living from day to day," he wrote. "From a condition of ease comfort and abundance, I am suddenly reduced to one of hardship, want & privation."[79] In Natchitoches Parish, one local planter noted that a group of Confederate soldiers had robbed him of "two carriage horses, a saddle pony, and a saddle mule."[80]

One Confederate Missouri soldier who was stationed in Louisiana admitted that he did "something I was allway's ashamed of we took some lumber from an old house to build houses this served as a good Joke on one and I heartely repent of my rashness afterwards."[81] Sometimes civilian property destruction was done in the name of military necessity. For example, Lt. John Coleman Sibley told his wife how they "burnt the finest house on the Bayou," which would "allow good range for our artillery."[82] Other Southern civilians and their property fell prey to Louisiana troops operating in their vicinity. A Virginian homeowner confronted a couple of soldiers taking boards off his house. One soldier failed in his efforts to blame their crime on men from another state—his French accent gave away his Louisiana origins.[83] A Texas officer wrote of the destruction he witnessed, stating that "if the war lasts much longer this country will be a complete wreck . . . there is always men along in an Army mean enough to do almost anything in the world."[84] Vandalizing homes, especially abandoned plantations, knew few bounds. One Yankee soldier sympathized with the Southerners who faced widespread property destruction, writing, "The amount the people have lost must be incalculable. Northern people do not understand how thankful they ought to be that their section of the country is not the seat of war."[85]

Witnessing wartime destruction negatively impacted civilian morale. Governor Moore asked both Jefferson Davis and the Confederate secretary of war, "How much longer is Louisiana to be considered without the protection or beneath the consideration of the Confederate government?" If Louisiana "is to receive but the shadow of Confederate support . . . let not the sensibilities of her people be offended and their rights and liberties be disregarded."[86] Moore also criticized the state's impressment law, admitting that it did more harm than good.[87] Even Confederate foragers from other states arrived in Louisiana to prey on residents. Moore condemned these "armed men" who "seized property, entered houses of private citizens, brutally practiced extortion and outrage, and with bullying and threatening language and manner spread terror among the people and disgraced the service." This predicament resembled the proverbial rock and a hard place as Louisianians faced the Yankees under General Butler in the South and Confederate foragers in the North "committing the same outrages," Moore noted. His solution favored "self-protection" and called upon local militia units to help preserve personal property.[88]

On the surface, Confederate confiscation, impressment, and the perceived disregard for citizens' rights and property galvanized some Louisiana residents to become turncoats and switch allegiances to the Union.[89] But it must not be forgotten that many of these people had relatives in the Confederate ranks and taking the oath was not always genuine. Some Acadian planters in southwest Louisiana took the oath for personal and economic reasons to "retain their Negroes and purchase some provisions," writes Brasseaux. He claims that even though some south Louisiana planters had apparently galvanized, "They nevertheless clandestinely assisted Confederate raiders" and did much to continue their support to the Confederacy.[90] Survival—not disloyalty—often motivated wartime actions.

Many civilians knew that their sacrifices benefited many of their own relatives in the army, but some civilians felt that the Confederate authorities—and their unpopular measures—were too extreme. In 1863, one Louisiana soldier's wife offered her husband a grim reality of the sacrifices she and their children were making, not to mention the hardships that often compounded their problems and stress. "I was even taxed on what little wool I had and a part of it was taken from me. . . . I told him [a soldier] how little I had and he said he hated to take it but said he was compelled to do it by law he said it was a heavy tax on us I told him I thought so when people did not have enough for their own use."[91] Desperate times called for desperate measures, especially when civilians believed government actions were unfair. After gathering the corn harvest, the soldier's wife exclaimed, "I did not trouble those potatoes in the corner of the field . . . we are so heavily taxed on everything that we gather I thought it would be best to leave them for to fatten the hogs." Her actions were well played—especially with the increasing demands of Confederate taxation and confiscation, as the unharvested potatoes also helped preserve their precious corn supply "that was left me after the tax was paid on it."[92] As this woman's account testifies, many civilians understood and accepted their role in providing for soldiers, but they despised unfair and despotic policies. Perhaps one Louisianian best summarized the confiscation predicament numerous civilians found themselves in, stating, "All take what they require and pay very little or anything for what they take—So between the two contending Armies all of our worldly things movable, have taken wings."[93]

Both soldiers and civilians realized that their sacrifices meant the preservation of the other; however, soldiers were not oblivious to the negative effects confiscation had on local residents. Civilians, too, realized that their relatives in the army also suffered, as the war became less about operating within the strict confines of (failing) government policies and more about merely surviving. For Louisiana's Confederates, competing for resources, not disloyalty, held the greatest danger for the Confederacy because it could sever the social bonds between soldiers and civilians.

COTTON AND ILLEGAL TRADE

The growing illicit trade, which found accomplices among both soldiers and civilians, provided tangible compensation and access to resources. Though some planters switched to growing food, cotton production—and trade—did not cease.[94] As the war increasingly disrupted the daily lives of Louisianians, this question of who benefited from illicit trade—along with the meaning of Confederate loyalty—remained a contested topic between authorities, civilians, and soldiers. One Louisiana soldier hoped the Confederate government would focus on defending the South and not on economic profit, telling his wife, "Let [?] our country look to their defense and not to cotton bales, (perhaps it is better not to grow any cotton)."[95]

The Confederate government made efforts to cease all cotton trade, even encouraging its destruction if it was in danger of falling into Federal hands.[96] To discourage enemy trade, government officials in Richmond made it illegal to export "products" to ports other than those within the Confederacy. Once Union forces captured New Orleans, Gov. Thomas O. Moore reiterated the importance of Louisiana residents not doing business with the Union. He wrote, "To each loyal citizen of Louisiana and of the Confederacy, every citizen of the country hostile to us is our enemy. . . . We cannot exchange our corn, cattle, sugar, or cotton for their gold. . . . It is a rule recognized as imperative by all writers of public law, and universally administered by authorities of nations at war."[97] Moore ordered Louisiana's residents near "areas in danger of enemy occupation" to destroy their cotton stores, which, along with sugar and alcohol, including ships and steamboats, burned all along the Mississippi River that spring, as levees became altars of sacrifice.[98]

For many Louisianians, the Union advance into the state only spelled disaster as wartime destruction and Confederate resolve to destroy anything that might be useful to the enemy wreaked havoc. Lt. P. L. Prudhomme sympathized with his father, writing, "I am of your opinion in regard to the Yankees going up Red River . . . it will be the ruin of that flourishing & fertile country. Their mode of warfare inaugurated on the Mississippi & else where justifies this opinion."[99] But much of the early destruction of Confederate resources was self-inflicted. Wartime diarist Kate Stone's family suffered financially from these actions, especially their cotton crop's destruction. "We should know," she wrote, "for Mamma has $20,000 worth burning on the gin ridge now; it was set on fire yesterday and is still blazing."[100] Near Baton Rouge, Sarah Morgan "went to see the cotton burning . . . All were busy as though their salvation depended on disappointing the Yankees."[101] Confederate support proved a great financial sacrifice for many Louisianians who sought to keep their property out of Federal hands. But much of the disappointment promoted internal discontent and bitterness among civilians toward Confederate policies, not necessarily toward Confederate soldiers.

In protest, many Louisiana residents favored hiding but not destroying cotton, hoping to find a market or buyer, despite what Confederate officials dictated.[102] One Union soldier wrote how "the woods and up small Bayous" offered ideal hiding spots as he claimed he and his comrades found nearly "10000 or 12000 bales" at one particular location alone.[103] To ensure residents obeyed government policies, Confederate troops sometimes acted as policemen, keeping illicit trade and smuggling operations at bay. Even Quantrill's Raiders, Missouri's infamous guerilla force, policed the cotton trade in northeastern Louisiana; however, as Daniel Sutherland notes, many residents questioned—and feared—their conduct as "they made few distinctions between friends and foes."[104] Striving to put the Confederacy first, Governor Moore attempted to combat the illegal trading and inspire patriotism. Noting his strong stance on the issue, he claimed, "Tories must suffer the fate that every betrayer of his country deserves."[105]

Felix Poché noted how one group of soldiers had orders "to intercept . . . some cotton which is being sent to the Yankees."[106] As late as March of 1865, he even led a squad of soldiers near Bayou Barbe to capture smugglers, cotton, and the Federal troops who operated in the region.[107] One Confederate officer saw the negative effects illegal trading had on the residents in Louisiana's Florida Parishes, as they had lost confidence in the Confederacy's ability to "protect and provide for them."[108] Confederate leaders' fears of losing civilian support revolved around the question of what to do—or how best to use—their available resources.

But not all Confederate authorities favored destruction. Some Louisiana officials and officers, such as Henry Watkins Allen and Richard Taylor, were against destroying property because it caused additional suffering to many Louisiana residents.[109] Other Louisianians, such as Auguste Donato, a Creole of Color planter from St. Landry Parish who actively supported the Confederate war effort, brought a civil case to court to receive compensation for "wrongful or unjustified litigation" concerning cotton confiscation.[110] Officials who encouraged enemy trade claimed it benefited the Southern war effort. Confederate Inspector Gen. Jacob Thompson argued to Jefferson Davis that trade with the Union did not equal Confederate disloyalty. Allowing Southerners to trade with Union contacts "will enliven our people and greatly aid our army." The reality of the situation, Thompson wrote, was that many a trade item "finds its way to the army in one way or another."[111]

Illegal trading, which spawned both support and opposition, was not limited to an internal struggle within the Confederacy. The Union also had its supporters of illicit trade, which included Abraham Lincoln, who felt the trade would assist Southern Unionists "in occupied areas." Reasons for wanting to trade with Confederates had much to do with Northern economics, European diplomacy, and attempts to nurture existing Unionism among Southern loyalists.[112] One historian noted that cotton was absolutely vital to the Northern economy, writing, "Massachusetts depended almost as much on cotton as did South Carolina and Mississippi."[113]

Even as trade remained a contested topic, the illicit activity continued—oftentimes with the knowledge or consent of the high command.[114] Union Gen. Nathaniel P. Banks, who commanded the Red River expedition, noted the extent of the illegal cotton trade, as he wrote, "Cotton is king, for the army is doing nothing but gathering cotton . . . the rebels were furnishing us with supplies to be shipped."[115] Cotton procurement, for instance, was a major objective of the Red River campaign; one Union soldier proclaimed that "the private speculation and precuniary motives of men in high places, making cover of the army movements, to conduct a vast scheme of Cotton Stealing made legitimate by Government sanction." The entourage of wagons to be used for cotton confiscation helped confirm this soldier's observation.[116] Months after the fall of Vicksburg, Confederate soldier J. D. Garland noted the boat traffic on the Ouachita River, "going up and down every few days carrying 'forage' to the army above here. . . . I believe there are some goods in Monroe but they ask such exhorbant prices you have no idea. They keep up a trade with the Federals at Vicksburg. The most of the citizens in here side with the Feds I think."[117]

Shortages caused many Louisianians to prefer trade rather than with doing without. However, once the Union gained control of the Mississippi River by the summer of 1863, it did not equal "free navigation" as wartime operations, which meant killing, continued.[118] Despite Confederate guerilla activity along the Mississippi River, illicit trading—and sometimes bribery—between Union and Confederate forces proceeded. Confederate soldiers continuously crossed the "Big Drink," a common name for the Mississippi River, to drive cattle to Mississippi. Louisiana soldier Joseph Texada participated in an 1864 cattle drive, noting how "our trip going and coming was rather a hard & tiresome one . . . we succeeded tolerably well crossing over about 2800 beeves & bringing back some eight (800) hundred more." This successful river crossing was not simply luck. Texada explained, "The talk in camp is that Howard has bribed one of the gunboats which patrols that particular part of the River."[119] Despite the increasing presence of Union troops and military campaigning, Confederate trade—both with sympathetic Southerners and Unionists (civilians and soldiers) continued.

As Union forces obtained a firmer grip on Confederate territory, Johnson notes that the developing Federal trade policies eventually placed the US government in a position to monopolize the cotton trade via Union agents. Though not necessarily their intention, Johnson claims that cotton speculators had an easier time with illegal trading with the Union's new laws. In perspective, Confederate blockade runners who smuggled cotton to a foreign port obtained "the price of an entire crop in peacetime." If the North obtained the cotton, it would benefit Northern economic interests and disrupt some of the foreign trafficking.[120] Jarret Ruminski's research of the contraband trade in Mississippi notes how these illicit actions provided the state's residents with "an abundance of goods normally sold in the regular marketplace but made scarce by the Union blockade and general wartime privation." He argues that while Confederate civilians and soldiers benefited from the trade, its drawbacks included "depreciating Confederate currency, funneling valuable cotton to the Union, and compromising many Confederate nationalists' ideas of self-sufficiency." Rumunski claims that the Mississippians participating in the trade did so because of "multiple loyalties to self, family, neighborhood, and nation." To them, trading meant survival, not disloyalty.[121]

For many Confederates, illegal trade provided everyday supplies and provisions—items the Confederacy could not supply (at least in prewar quantities), and many of the trade items often benefited Confederate soldiers. But when luxury items often found their way into the hands of high-ranking Confederate officers, many soldiers felt betrayed. Felix Poché took note of "not only with the necessities, but with all the delicacies of the New Orleans market" that a general and his staff had in their possession. The sight of items, such as "coal oil lamps, which are of the principal profits of the speculators in the large trade in cotton with the enemy" disgusted Poché, as he noted that the local populace were the real losers in this illegal dealing. He fumed that one day, judgment, whether from "their administration if not to their superiors at least to the Supreme Being who will not allow such injustices to go unpunished."[122]

Rank had its privileges, and high-ranking Confederate officers were apparently not discreet in their activities. Just as some Southerners held disdain for planters who received concessions for their status as slaveowners (i.e., "Twenty Negro Law"), some lower-ranking soldiers felt such actions were unjust. Knowing well the privileges of rank, W. H. King bluntly wrote, "If a private, or citizens, engage in such business, the act will be regarded as a high crime," unlike the Confederate officers partaking in the trade, who were "apt to get large sums of money for the cotton."[123] King later concluded that these officers' actions and privileges confirmed—at least for him—that "this is a 'rich man's war, & a poor man's fight,' needs no further proof."[124] Texas Pvt. John Simmons claimed that from all the cotton sent North the return was "Fine boots and calico for the officers and their wives! But there is not a thing for the privates who have borne the burden of the war."[125] Another Texan encamped near Marksville in February 1864 noted the constant exchange of items between Union and Confederates lines. "Our officers," he wrote, "are trading With the yankeys everry day."[126]

Though many high-ranking officers engaged in illegal trading, they were not the sole participants. Frustrated soldiers also blamed illicit trading on Southern civilians. Disgusted over illegal trade operations near Natchez, Mississippi, one Confederate officer serving in southeastern Louisiana had little sympathy for the civilians who partook. He claimed that the "out-and-out immeasurable, uncompromising secessionist . . . who in '61 were for 'War to the Knife' and 'Knife to the Hilt'" had turned coat on the Confederacy by engaging in illicit trade.[127] Felix Poché believed illegal trading undermined the Confederate war effort and blamed the "contemptible speculators, mostly Jews" who were in league with the Confederate officers conducting the trading. This, he claimed, undermined the loyalty, welfare, and sacrifices "of the farmer and soldier the two elements that form the foundation of all countries."[128]

Capt. Elijah Petty of Walker's Texas Division also had suspicions of the cotton trade and also accused "civilians, especially Jewish merchants" of engaging in the illegal activity. "They take the oath of allegiance (I suppose) to both governments so that they can pass in & out and smuggle and steal. They care nothing for obligations or any thing else but the almighty dollar. They have neither country, character or honor."[129] One officer recorded that, with all the soldiers pouring in and the heavy construction taking place at Port Hudson, "it was not a very difficult undertaking to get in and out of the lines. Although it had become a military post, it was still a port of some commercial importance. . . . Speculators, almost exclusively the children of Israel, were constantly passing in and out, and the gates of travel were not shut against peddlers and sojourners."[130] While the Jewish speculators were not held in high regard in these examples, numerous Jews did support and fight for the Confederacy. The stereotype of "the Wandering Jew" was not necessarily the rule, nor was choosing sides in times of war and participating in the conflict the exception.[131]

According to W. H. King, the *Monroe Register* ran an article about the Confederate Congress "taking steps to ferret out frauds practiced by quartermasters & surgeons, some 400 having been reported as delinquents." Thinking this a necessary action on the government's part, he proclaimed, "I think some such work might be beneficial in this part of the Confederacy," referring to the questionable legalities of their regimental quartermaster. An officer in King's unit claimed that "he could, & did buy hams at 20 cents per lb., & the quartermaster charges him 25 cents per lb., & swears it is cost."[132] Louisiana soldier John E. Hall observed the questionable legalities of individuals who sought personal gain from the conflict. "The army," he wrote, "is nothing but a bridge for speculators to pack their wealth over, and a hiding place for Office seekers, from what I see God will certainly curse us as a people."[133] While in camp in St. Mary Parish, one Louisiana officer wrote how his personal finances would flourish "If I was out of the army and was willing to speculate. . . . Almost anything that can be brought here in the way of army supplies sells for a very high price."[134] And it was the high prices that kept mostly officers, not lower-paid soldiers, in a position to obtain trade items. One soldier told of a dry-goods auction, which led to little dealing as he noted many "soldiers and families were most entirely debarred from buying as the lots were too large to allow their buying anything."[135]

By contrast, officers defended their participation or at least pretended to turn a blind eye to it; Richard Lowe claims that the trade was "absolutely critical" in providing for "the Trans-Mississippi treasury, income that would help them to continue the war. . . . Ironically, the same policy that enabled Trans-Mississippi officials to carry on the war also created resentment and harsh mutterings from the very people the policy benefited."[136] Though many Louisiana soldiers disliked their officers' trade actions—from which these high-ranking Confederates personally benefited—not all transactions had impure motives. Some Confederate generals "sold tons of cotton through the lines in order to purchase needed supplies for the trans-Mississippi army." This trade brought in large sums of money—"$250 per bale in Liverpool, about four times its prewar price" and a New York bank "offered to buy $500,000 worth of cotton . . . and haul it through the lines themselves."[137] Illegal trade's true contribution to the Trans-Mississippi Confederate war effort was that it kept the conflict alive.

Even though several soldiers harbored animosity toward illicit trading, others felt that their family's participation in the trade could likely provide economic relief. Soldiers, if not active participants in trade, acted as advisors to their relatives back home, encouraging them to protect their own economic interest and well-being in the face of the conflict's uncertainties. Cavalryman F. A. Prudhomme noted wartime cotton trading's profitability as he wrote his mother, "It would be a shame to lose our cotton because it's worth so much. Mr. Champlain, Sr. told me that he had bought 400 bales of cotton for which he paid 65,000 dollars in confederate money and he converted 128,000 dollars into gold. If we could have the chance to sell our cotton at that price we would be prosperous."[138] In early 1864, one Louisianian participating in the cotton trade received word that his cotton was to be sold "for the best and hope to give you a satisfactory result." Quality mattered and every bale contained a varying degree of profitability.[139]

Unsurprisingly, women, who already played a prominent role on the Confederate home front, often engaged in illegal trading. Meeting their family's needs, which did not mean turning their back on the Confederacy—the very nation many of their husbands and sons were risking their lives for—was what mattered most when participating in illicit trading.[140] And many Confederate women had previous roles in resisting the enemy—often at the risk of their own safety, which included smuggling.[141] Several female residents near Clinton, Louisiana, actively participated in the "illicit trade," which was "carried on to an astonishing extent." Women hauled cotton to Baton Rouge, as it "was never carried . . . by the men—the women always took charge of it. . . . The guards would allow the women to pass"—but trading came with a price. The cavalrymen guarding the roads charged the traders between ten and twenty dollars per cotton bale on their way to Baton Rouge. The traders' return trip to Clinton "with their wagons laden with the articles they purchased with the cotton" once more came under the soldiers' demands, and they confiscated some items. However, preying soldiers were not the only men who vied for their cut in the cotton trade. These "*cotton tollers*" and "*Jay hawkers*" were "nothing more or less than regular highwaymen," as they stole cotton from the local planters and gained vast amounts of wealth. The Louisiana soldier who learned of these activities claimed, "Nearly everybody seemed to have lost all sense of right and wrong and *Honesty* the jewel was decidedly at a discount."[142]

One Louisiana soldier's wife explained that a nearby trader "buys the cotton at his house and take[s] all the responsibility on himself if it is burnt before he gets to Baton Rouge it is his loss not ours." She obviously felt that it would be worth her effort to trade since she would receive something for their cotton without having the risks—or hassles—of transporting it, especially since it was only "about thirteen miles to his house." This arrangement also seemed to have fit her busy schedule as the weight of the farm—and family—fell on her shoulders.[143] A Louisiana soldier stationed at Vicksburg encouraged his wife to engage in trading "cotton for sugar and molasses" since he felt destroying it was simply a waste which would do his family no good.[144]

Illegal trading, which many soldiers had once seen as unpatriotic, disloyal, or self-serving, became more accepted when placed in the context of benefiting their families back home. At best illegal trade meant prosperity; at least it meant a means of survival. The rise of illegal trading remained a factor in keeping the Confederate war machine operating and, as Johnson notes, "unnecessarily prolonged" the conflict.[145] Placing personal or familial needs over the dictates of Confederate authorities did not equate to abandoning the cause. Both groups sacrificed—and continued to do so—as survival and self-preservation remained central to their wartime experiences. These assertive and contested activities surrounding trade and obtaining provisions provide a true picture of the Civil War's complexity. While operating within these complexities of duty and loyalty versus survival and self-preservation, soldiers and civilians remained socially interdependent—and communal ties remained strong.

An unidentified soldier in a Confederate uniform, holding a musket and sporting a belt with a Louisiana state seal buckle. Liljenquist Family Collection, Prints and Photographs Division of the Library of Congress.

A chromolithograph, after a painting by C. W. Chapman, of Confederate soldiers in camp—a location troops spent most of the war. Civilians often visited these spaces, offering soldiers a pleasant distraction from military life. African Americans were also a common sight in Confederate camps. M. & N. Hanhart Printers. Prints and Photographs Division of the Library of Congress.

Louisiana Zouave soldiers and their unique uniforms, which caught the eye of their fellow Louisianians and Confederates, 1861. Prints and Photographs Division of the Library of Congress.

Alexander Pierre Allain of 5th Company, Washington Artillery, photographed by Anderson & Turner between 1862 and 1865. Liljenquist Family Collection, Prints and Photographs Division of the Library of Congress.

Thomas Isaiah Booker of the 28th Louisiana Infantry, displaying equipment and apparent pride of Confederate service; however, over the course of the war, not all Louisianians held their leaders in high esteem. Liljenquist Family Collection, Prints and Photographs Division of the Library of Congress.

Sergeant A. M. Chandler of Co. F, 44th Mississippi Infantry Regiment, and Silas Chandler, a man enslaved to the Chandler family. Though this image depicts a Mississippian and his body servant, such pairings would have been familiar in Louisiana Confederate camps as well, as African Americans acted as servants or laborers. Liljenquist Family Collection, Prints and Photographs Division of the Library of Congress.

Sketch of the Louisiana Tigers in action at Gettysburg. *Attack of the Louisiana Tigers on a Battery of the 11th Corps*, 1863, by Alfred R. Waud. Prints and Photographs Division of the Library of Congress.

Edwin Francis Jemison of the 2nd Louisiana Infantry was one of the many young Louisianians who fought—and died—for the cause. Jemison was seventeen years old when he was killed in 1862 at Malvern Hill, Virginia. Prints and Photographs Division of the Library of Congress.

These Louisiana Tigers who fell at Antietam offer a grim reminder of the reality—and price—of war. Both soldiers and civilians would have witnessed such scenes. Photograph by Alexander Gardner, 1862. Prints and Photographs Division of the Library of Congress.

Louisiana Tiger officer Francis T. Nicholls was wounded twice, losing an arm and foot during the war. His image serves as a reminder of the fate of numerous other Louisianians who survived the conflict, but returned home with empty sleeves. Prints and Photographs Division of the Library of Congress.

CHAPTER 7

〰◇〰

WARTIME COMMUNICATIONS

〰◇〰

"I saw in Greenwood yesterday a company from Jefferson," wrote one Louisiana woman to her husband serving in Virginia in 1861. "I saw their tents, and all of their cooking untensils [*sic*]. . . . I thought of you so far away, and Oh, how sad I felt. . . . I dont know why I feel so sad unless it was seeing those soldiers."[1] Soldiers and civilians treasured letters and letter writing as they offered comfort, consolation, and a way to communicate and remain emotionally connected with one another, especially as the war progressed and separations lingered. "Writing to you is one of my most delightful occupations," wrote Lt. John Coleman Sibley to his wife.[2] Soldiers highly valued letters from home, which one Louisianian claimed were "worth more than gold to me."[3] Another Louisiana soldier writing from Vicksburg in the spring of 1862 assured his wife that his thoughts were with her. "Dear Effie, bad pin, uneasy position, makes an unsightly letter," but he continued:

But this is me and you are sitting beside the window or perhaps by candle light. I now see your silent bosom, your feelings of love, joy and peace in reading this. Could I tap you on the shoulder, way would go cold letters that seemed so warm. You do as I do I suppose I read over and over, them. Hunt to see if I might not find another sentence yet. . . . I sometimes almost forget every thing, for this reason, I have thought over, and over, until every thing would get into a whirl. Oh that I could once more get peace of mind, rest to body & mind as I have had beside you my dear wife. If I could just hold your hand as once again I did what pleasure. . . . My Dear Wife What else can I say to you! you know my heart[.][4]

Soldiers and civilians expressed their feelings and thoughts in letters, along with venting their wartime frustrations. Though private, a soldier's correspondence sometimes made its way to the public arena, as friends and relatives spread (by word of mouth or publication in a local newspaper) what had been written. Camp visitors or comrades heading home on or returning from leave did their part in keeping this communication network alive. Letter writing proved a powerful force that kept friends and relatives emotionally and spiritually connected, reinforcing the concept that a Civil War soldier's wartime experience was a social one.[5]

The Civil War offered its participants two fronts for waging war: the physical realm (on a battlefield or the home front) and the psychological realm within an individual's mind. The anxieties over the fear of not knowing a relative's fate, the toll of long periods of separation, and the likelihood of witnessing combat dimmed their once vibrant affections toward one another. These stressful feelings and situations created mental or emotional battles with which soldiers and civilians contended. This inner war might have proved insufferable—or psychologically fatal—to both groups without the presence of letters and correspondence. Michael E. Woods argues that "historical analysis of emotion" is vital to understanding the Civil War, along with how "emotions directly affected Americans' perceptions of themselves, their friends and foes, and their interests and ideals."[6] For Louisiana's soldiers and civilians, their inner emotions expressed through correspondence proved immensely important, as they often interjected their opinions, beliefs, viewpoints, and speculations. The ability to express their true thoughts about their experiences to relatives and friends via the privacy of a letter enabled them to share those thoughts and experiences, connecting individuals on both the home front and front lines.

WELL-BEING AND WORDS OF LOVED ONES

Of all the home-front items traversing the Confederacy, news from relatives and friends was what soldiers craved most. Camp visitors, who often carried news from home, were always a welcome sight.[7] But not all Confederate soldiers had the good fortune of a constant stream of well-wishers visiting their camp, especially as authorities continuously shuffled men across Dixie. Letter writing attempted to remedy the long distances separating loved ones. Pvt. Isaac Dunbar Affleck, who served in Louisiana, spoke for most Civil War soldiers as he pleaded for his mother to write to him. "It is so lonesome here in camp that a fellow will get home sick directly if he does not get a letter occasionally to cheer him up."[8] Writing from Virginia in June of 1862, E. L. Stephens requested that his parents "give me all the news for I am anxious to hear from home."[9]

Even before Louisiana residents faced extreme wartime hardships, soldiers worried about their families' security. By the fall of 1861, one Louisianian stationed in Virginia told his wife that upon arriving at his present "seemingly God forsaken camp . . . I had not received a single letter." A short time later, "news came that I had two letters. . . . My heart leaped with joy, but still I went with fear and trembling. I could not help thinking maybe all is not right at home."[10] For this soldier and countless others, a Federal invasion of their home state was not their only concern. Louis Stagg feared his wife in southwestern Louisiana had forgotten all about him. "I really believe you no longer think about me at home, for I have been here nearly a month, and have thus far received only one letter from you." He explained his discouragement, telling her that "no one sends me any news of my family, when the very least little bit of news from you is so precious to me."[11] Even if a soldier did not receive a letter, having a comrade from his same town or parish who did, remained an exciting and welcome experience. "I am sure if our 'home folks' could see how eagerly the boys gather around one just from our parts to catch every word he speaks, they would spare no trouble in order to send us news," wrote a Louisiana soldier serving at Vicksburg.[12]

Letters from home (and receiving visits from familiar faces) apparently had healing effects on soldiers, wrote Frank Richardson: "Frank Thompson arrived here . . . you may be assured I was glad to see him, I was lying down at the time under a tree, quite sick, but as soon as I saw him and Allen [a slave] coming I jumped up and recovered suprizeingly after they came and after I had read those refreshing letters of yours and Pa's, which were like ice water on the parched tongue."[13] Correspondence in the midst of wartime uncertainties also quelled rumors and fears. Hearing of the heavy casualties at Corinth, Mississippi, one Louisiana soldier feared his two brothers were killed, "but I hope and trust to God that they were not," he told his wife. "Mary, you don't know how glad I was when I got this letter from you. It did me lots of good for I had begun to get out of heart."[14] A simple confirmation that all was well back home kept many soldiers at mental peace amid the war's physical carnage and chaos.

Longing for a relative's presence sometimes caused an outpouring of emotions, which could be heart-wrenching, as the ink flowed—even in the war's first year. Alfred Flournoy Sr. wrote a heartfelt letter to his son but caught himself before getting too emotional. "It fills heart with sadness," explaining his concern for his "brave boys exposed to all the hazards of war" and the possibility they might never return. He quickly changed the subject stating, "I will try not to write a letter calculated to make you feel melancholy; letters from home should be cheerful."[15] Soldiers encouraged loved ones to write, promising to eagerly respond, especially as the war continued. William J. Walter told his nephew, "Write often & I will repay you by *long* letters if not *interesting* ones."[16] One Louisiana soldier serving in the Army of Northern Virginia asked a female companion living in Virginia to write soon and often "as you can hardly immagine how I feel when I read one of your letters write soon and I will not fail to answer them."[17] Writing from Vicksburg, Edmond Vige told his wife, "I wish that you would write to me as soon as possible, & tell me all the news." His plea was yet another voice echoing numerous other Louisianians who instructed friends and relatives back home to write.[18]

Civilians, too, craved information about their friends and relatives in uniform. They desired any information of wartime events and of their soldier's personal well-being. At the beginning of the war, Louisiana Confederate Congressman Alexander DeClouet Sr.'s son, Paul, who attended school in Virginia, had joined a local company and subsequently saw action in the western part of the state. Fearing for his son's safety, DeClouet greatly stressed over not knowing Paul's whereabouts and condition, writing, "For God's sake let me if possible hear from you soon."[19] DeClouet's anxieties and concerns, experienced by numerous other Southerners, were well-founded. Texas soldiers serving in neighboring Louisiana also lacked consistent contact with their relatives. A father writing from Nacogdoches, Texas, to his son noted, "My anxiety has been great about you. I have heard that there has been several battles out there & can't hear nothing of your fate."[20]

Amid active campaigning, many soldiers had little time or supplies to frequently write letters. Texas cavalryman A. L. Grow wrote from Louisiana, explaining to his sweetheart, "I will try to write evry week but do not blame me if you do not get letters this often as if I should not be able to do so we are frequently out of writing materials and . . . at times we are so busy that there is not time to write."[21] The lack of proper writing materials plagued many soldiers throughout the Confederacy. One Louisiana soldier stationed in Virginia wrote to a friend asking her forgiveness of "my pencil writing for you know a soldier is deprived of ink and even those he loves."[22] For many civilians far from the battlefield, stories of soldiers' wartime exploits—whether eventful or not—found their way home.[23] And time constraints, the stress of soldiering, and fatigue often took their toll on the number of details relayed to loved ones. One Texan serving in Louisiana spoke for many soldiers as he wrote, "I have passed over much that I should like to relate . . . we do not have much time for writing as we are stil on the march."[24] For most campaigning soldiers, especially as the war continuously evolved and escalated, letter writing remained secondary to the army's demands.

While letters emotionally connected soldiers and civilians, military service also fostered deep friendships between soldiers in the field. Soldiers, in turn, described their affectionate bonds between one another to their friends and family back home. For civilians on the home front, knowing that fellow soldiers looked after their loved ones' well-being and safety helped ease their mental burden. Writing from Virginia to his friend's relatives back in Louisiana, W. Ezra Denson explained, "I can assure you and your family" that Edmond, who was recovering from an illness, "will never suffer for attention as long as his friend Ezra survives. Since we left home, the warm friendship that we entertained for each other has ripened into the love of brothers."[25] The vast amount of time soldiers spent among their comrades, especially in camp, cultivated deep friendships—another social aspect of soldier life. The little personal time soldiers scrounged were "employed in visiting his brothers-in arms, enjoying his *mess chums* pipe, & strolling far & near," wrote one Louisiana Confederate soldier. Ensuring that these activities were time well spent, he continued, "These strolls have furnished me with a number [of] jokes, anecdote[s] and incidents which I have carefully stored away in my budget to regale you all upon my honorable discharge from my country's service, or when she shall have no further use for men and the grim paraphernalia of War."[26]

The time soldiers spent together—the humorous occurrences, the drudgery of military life, and the war's hardships—forged them into a band of brothers. This support system created by comradery expanded to larger portions of the army, which sometimes developed identities based on an esprit de corps seen through all organizational levels of the military. Sheehan-Dean notes that for many Virginia soldiers, the "local nature of enlistment . . . would be of central value in keeping men in the ranks," as it linked soldiers with civilians who knew one another—and would know of their wartime deeds.[27] Similarly, for many Louisiana soldiers, their comradery and social affiliation began well before their enlistments. Carmichael uses the term "extended family" when describing how soldiers bonded, noting, "Their survival depended on their mutual cooperation and support to endure difficult times of privation." He also claims that these extended families "originated within community-based networks of support," which were strongest if "a soldier's home was within the orbit of military operations."[28]

Affectionate writing about their relatives and brothers-in-arms, whom soldiers viewed as their equals, were not always the only individuals on a writer's mind. For slaveholding soldiers, their letters reflected their paternalistic relationship—and for some men, even a level of trust—toward their chattel property. In 1861, one Louisiana soldier wrote from Virginia to his wife, "Tell all the negroes I think of them every day. Tell them they talk about hard work, but ask them what they think of my trotting fifteen miles through the hot sun and dust with a blanket, sword, and a big pistol in three hours and a quarter. . . . Tell them if I live to get home, I will bring home five boxes of the best tobacco for them."[29] According to the soldier's wife, his bondsmen apparently had some affection for him as she wrote, "The negroes ask me often when their kind good master is coming home. They want to see you very much."[30] Perhaps these bondsmen were biding their time. Glymph notes that "slaves understood as a signal that" the conflict might result in their emancipation. Such notions sometimes stirred a "war within" plantation households, pitting the enslaved against their enslaver, helping to instill fears of insurrection, ensuring a breakdown in the system. However, she also points out another complexity. As slaveholders went to war, "masters . . . asked slaves to protect white women and white homes," along with continuing their daily toils. In this sense the war had also established a communal effort (albeit a coerced one) on behalf of the master and slave, as the former's military service and the latter's domestic service both aided the Confederacy.[31]

From Camp Moore another Louisiana soldier instructed his wife to tell his slaves that "I confide my trust in them, that one day they may see their masters face, and bless the hour of his arrival."[32] One can only speculate as to how his bondsmen responded. R. J. Causey's paternalistic attitude contained a spiritual element as he told his wife to "tell the negroes that I am [proud?] to heare that they are getting along and doing so well for I have prayed to God for them that he would bless them and save them." Causey also instructed them "to continue to attend to their buisiness and not to get into trouble."[33] Absentee slaveholders-turned-soldiers, regardless of their paternalistic views, expected their laborers to perform. As spring approached in 1863, Lt. John Coleman Sibley told his wife to instruct his slaves to grow as much corn as possible, despite the poor conditions the previous year. He intended to hold them accountable as "I expect to be home in June or July to look at their crop."[34] Some soldiers even entrusted a reliable bondsman to oversee his plantation's operations during the war. Though recorded years after the conflict, ex-slave Hunton Love recalled, "When ole Marse went to war, he left me overseer of the plantation." He apparently had full authority over disciplining his fellow laborers as he told his interviewer, "Yes'm I did—some of the slaves wouldn't mind and I had to whip 'em. . . . Besides I had to show 'em I was boss, or the plantation would be wrecked."[35]

But not all slave performance was related to agriculture. Edwin Fay told his wife in Louisiana to tell their slave Cynthia that he expected her to get pregnant or "when I come home that I'll either whip her most to death or sell her to the meanest man I can find on Red River. . . . I bought her to breed and . . . she shall or I won't own her long." Fay later wrote his wife that his enslaved body servant Rich told him that Cynthia had gotten sick "from the effect of medicine she had taken to procure abortion."[36] Even though an (absentee) enslaver made demands, enslaved agency remained in play.

Soldiers counted on their relatives (and for some, their enslaved workers) to maintain home-front operations; however, they also looked to them for emotional comfort and support, which often came in the form of letters. The sheer volume of Civil War letter writing by both soldiers and civilians produced an astounding amount of mail.[37] Though delivery difficulties existed, which sometimes included mail censoring, many soldiers remained confident that their fellow comrades going on or returning from leave could deliver correspondence—and even enclosed money—to its intended destination.[38] Receiving word from relatives brought much comfort to both soldiers and civilians—oftentimes swelling emotions. "I was so glad to get your letter," wrote a soldier's wife from southeastern Louisiana in 1863. "I had just got to the house from a walk in which I had a big cry about you and you may believe it helped my feelings a great deal."[39] Especially as the war lingered and grew bloodier, relatives on the home front longed for any news from their soldier. One Louisianian wrote to her brother in 1864, "I pray God every day for you my dear brother I hope that you will come home soon. . . . I would give any thing in the world to see you."[40]

In 1863, R. J. Causey's wife pleaded with him to try and obtain either a discharge or furlough to come home. "I do want to see you so bad. . . . I thought my poor heart would break in spite of all I could do."[41] About a month later, this Louisiana woman's melancholic mood remained difficult to shake. "I again attempt to send you a letter but I have sent so often and you have never received any letter from me that I feel like it is hardly worth while to write." As her lengthy letter closed, she told her husband "that you are dearer to me than everything else on earth, and if we never meet again you may rest assured that I love you as hard as a woman ever loved a husband."[42] Venting frustrations, which often proved useless in encouraging change, at least had a psychological effect on soldiers and civilians who felt the urge to release their resentments emotionally through letter writing.

Both soldiers and civilians (especially husbands and wives) engaged in emotional letter writing, sharing a range of human feelings with one another. Though meant for private interaction, emotional letters also allowed for women to shed nineteenth-century gender formality and present a realistic and honest view of what they felt and thought about their wartime experiences. Sharing their inner emotions, remained (so they hoped) private. Safeguarding their correspondence from prying eyes—and ridicule if exposed—remained a priority for many soldiers and civilians, especially women, who sometimes burned their letters if enemy troops approached. Having the autonomy to correspond on their own terms and about topics that mattered to them kept soldier and civilian ties strong despite physical separation.[43]

Along with letters, relatives and friends also sent care packages to their soldiers, which remained a common practice throughout the war. LeeAnn Whites argues that the household's significance and centrality to the conflict—especially when sending letters and supplies via the "household or domestic supply line"—proved critical not only as a morale booster but also as an avenue to strengthen soldier and civilian relationships under the stress of separation.[44] Edible reminders of home were sometimes enclosed—and greatly appreciated by the receiver. "All my provissions which you and Ma prepared at home arrived here safe," wrote Frank Richardson, "and were demolished in double quick time."[45] Receiving another care package several months later, Richardson assured his parents that "there is no use telling you that I am a grateful boy."[46] One Louisianian stationed at Camp Moore in 1862 received a package containing "Paper Ink and pens." He claimed he "was very glad to get it for I was nearly out and could not get any here." Thanks to his relatives' thoughtfulness, his letter writing would continue.[47] Several soldiers serving in the Washington Artillery's 5th Company in Georgia remained grateful to their friend Moses Greenwood, who sent "packages through the lines—containing books, money, socks, and handkerchiefs," along with "vegetables and fruit."[48]

Louisiana's Confederate authorities made efforts to ensure that soldiers received their packages. One Louisiana officer stationed in Virginia told his father about a state-appointed agent who would "receive forward goods for the La. troops. . . . The best way to send packages to La. troops in this state [Virginia] is to address them to him."[49] By receiving packages and correspondence, a Civil War soldier's social interaction thrived, for every letter or package required an individual to deliver it, and the arrival of a mail carrier, whether a fellow soldier or civilian, stirred excitement and appreciation. W. H. King noted how a furloughed soldier returned to camp and presented "me with a letter from home, containing the news of the good health of my family & friends. Consoling news."[50] P. L. Prudhomme excitedly wrote from a camp in Mississippi, "To our great joy and satisfaction Emile Cloutier arrived here last Saturday. . . . The many letters he brought were eagerly perused and thousands of questions were asked . . . you may imagine how great was our contentment at seeing him."[51] The welcome sight of a familiar face in camp—along with his toting correspondence from home—provided soldiers with a short respite from the drudgeries of military life. Enslaved African Americans often assumed the role of couriers by delivering letters, supplies, and messages to soldiers from slaveholding families.[52] When soldiers saw someone from home, they vicariously derived real pleasure and feelings from these encounters, which kept their emotional bonds between family and friends on the home front alive.

Amidst the high volume of letters sent between soldiers and civilians, the guarantee of delivery remained erratic. As Whites notes, "The domestic supply line was only as successful and strong as its ability to deliver necessary items."[53]

The inability to receive letters and packages from home dampened soldiers' spirits. One frustrated Louisiana soldier stationed on the Gulf Coast wrote: "The Mail Boat has not made her regular trips for the last week and there is no garantee that she will for the Capt of her is such an infernal coward that he will not run any risk at all to bring the mail."[54] For Louisiana's soldiers and civilians, their mail frustrations were only beginning.

Serious changes erupted in 1862 as Union forces arrived in the state. However, Union activity and occupation in or near Confederate territories did not necessarily halt all deliveries. After the Union occupation of New Orleans, Lizzie Fitzgerald was "very glad indeed" to receive a letter from her friend. "I thought we could not get any more letters after New Orleans was taken," she wrote.[55] One Louisiana soldier expressed concerns about his wife receiving his letters after the Federals occupied New Orleans, writing, "This may not reach you, owing to the turmult[?] and confusion, yet I hope it may." She received the letter.[56] A hopeful Louisiana soldier serving in Alabama wrote home, noting that since Baton Rouge had been retaken "and the enemy have been hemed in so closely to New Orleans, we will again have the benefit of the mailes and I will have the pleasure of receiving and sending letters to you as oftern as I desire without fear of their not reaching you."[57]

With the Union noose tightening across the Confederacy as early as 1862, the failure to deliver correspondence and the chaos of active campaigning strained relationships. Texas cavalryman A. L. Grow wrote from south Louisiana explaining to his friend Mary how Yankee forces sometimes disrupted deliveries intended for Confederate troops. "I feared your letter had fallen into the hands of the enemy as one of my letters was lost in that way. I am thankful it was not yours." Indeed, Grow's anxieties over receiving Mary's letters were linked to his growing affection for her. "I cannot wait until I see you for all that I would tell. . . . I must write it, I love you." As the rest of his letter testified, he even proved an able poet.[58] Writing from Louisiana, another lovestruck Texan wrote to his sweetheart describing himself as a "man Who is deeply in love." He regularly admired her "ambrotype," which "I take out 8 or ten times a day and look at it and Kiss."[59]

Louisiana soldiers serving outside the state remained tense, especially when they received little word from the home front. "Our greatest misfortune in our troubles and anxieties is to be without news from home and no means of corresponding with those so dear to us," wrote Lt. P. L. Prudhomme.[60]

Deliveries across the Mississippi River sometimes proved difficult after the Confederate bastions at Vicksburg and Port Hudson fell to Union forces in July of 1863. Many Louisiana soldiers questioned whether their correspondence made its way home; as one officer told his mother, "[W]hat will you say when I tell you that its [*sic*] been ten months since I herd [*sic*] from you or anyone from home?" But despite these frustrations, a furloughed soldier became the main mode of transporting letters to loved ones. Indeed, even newspapers aided mail delivery. One Opelousas newspaper, for example, notified local residents in St. Landry Parish that any correspondence they wished to send to Louisiana soldiers stationed in Virginia were to be delivered to "Mr. Posey, in Opelousas, or Mr. Millspaugh in Washington. Lt. Thomas D. Cooke, 8th Louisiana Infantry, will forward to their destination."[61] Men fortunate enough to obtain a furlough kept their comrades in mind as they took it upon themselves to bring the ever-precious letters from loved ones back to the front.

NEWSPAPERS AND RUMORS

While soldiers and civilians craved home-front correspondence, they also hankered for newspapers that could tell them about any wartime developments from distant theaters. And, like letters, newspaper deliveries often remained sporadic. Fredrick Taber had access to outside news in his camp as "newspapers . . . are sold in camp every morning (the first thing you hear is the cry here the morning papers)."[62] By contrast, a soldier serving near the Atchafalaya River had little to no access to outside news sources, "which has almost rendered us perfectly ignorant of what is going on among the Federals as well as among the Confederates."[63] One Louisiana soldier claimed he had inconsistent access to a Memphis newspaper, and he wrote his mother, "I cannot get the papers often I wish you could send me a Planters Banner once and a while."[64] But sometimes it was a soldier who provided civilians with the latest newspaper, as one Louisiana soldier wrote, "I send you a La Democrat, and Gov Moores proclamation the only papers I can get."[65] News mattered to soldiers and civilians, and whoever obtained it did their part to pass it on.

As soldiers and civilians devoured a newspaper's contents, many individuals read with a skeptical eye since much printed material proved erroneous. While serving in Louisiana, Pvt. Isaac Dunbar Affleck wrote about what he heard from Virginia, stating that at the Battle of Cold Harbor General Lee had pushed back General Grant "forty miles with heavy loss . . . Grant himself was killed. If the news is true Johnston will make the last big fight of the war, and it will not be long in my opinion before we are all at home agane." Updates of the unfolding events (although, false, as this example depicts) kept Affleck's hopes—and curiosities—high.[66] In August of 1862, E. L. Stephens wrote, "I had heard that Vicksburg was Surrendered to the Yankees & Knew nothing better until I recieved your letter."[67] One soldier stationed in Louisiana told a friend, "I have no important news . . . reports from the east but nothing reliable, hope the war will soon be over, but fear it will be a long time before . . . pease is made & that we can return home to friends & sweat harts."[68]

The rumor mill constantly churned among Civil War troops. Events and military actions shaped soldiers' lives—and kept many soldiers and civilians pondering the war's outcome. "There are a thousand and one rumors here," wrote Edwin Fay to his wife in Louisiana as he attempted to pass on information about a recent battle near Memphis. Deciding what—or who—to believe remained a constant chore.[69] Writing from south Louisiana, Texas cavalryman A. L. Grow claimed, "The enemy are at New Iberia . . . still no one can tell what may take place. There are rumors that Texas has been invaded and that our brigade has been ordered home should it prove true I shall try to come by." Grow took this information with a grain of salt as he refused to be fooled by false information.[70] W. H. King also remained skeptical about camp gossip. "Almost any thing may be heard in the way of news. Many fabricate whatever their brains are capable of producing, & tell it to witness the effect . . . it is impossible to know what is, & what is not true."[71] And the more rumors spread, the more skeptical soldiers became. As one Louisianian serving at Vicksburg wrote, "I have heard enough of camp rumors to know how much credit to give them."[72] He was not the only soldier of this opinion.

Louisiana's civilians also remained cautious of what they believed about reliable wartime news. "You requested me to write all the news," wrote one Louisiana soldier's wife. "There is no news that I can hear that can be relied upon."[73] Writing from Caddo Parish, Alfred Flournoy Sr. told his son, "We get no reliable news from the papers. Everything is so misrepresented, we know not what to believe. The only hope we have of anything like correct information is from those who are in the service. Letters from the Army are read with great avidity . . . every mail day we meet at Boughs Grocery and talk. . . . The man who has the last letter from the Army receives the most attention."[74]

Many Southerners discredited Northern newspapers as propaganda. Sarah Morgan claimed Northern newspapers actively ridiculed and insulted the South, exclaiming, "I grow sick to read these vile, insulting papers." On another occasion, Morgan doubted what she read about Lee's defeat at Gettysburg. "He may have been defeated; but not one of these reports of total overthrow and rout do I credit."[75] While on picket duty, one soldier stationed near Bayou Vermilion in Lafayette Parish apparently obtained some Northern newspapers through a flag of truce with Union soldiers. Writing to his sweetheart, he told her the papers contained a "good deal of war news, but for your sake, I will not trust it to paper."[76] Even Union soldiers lacked confidence in what was sometimes published in their own newspapers. One Yankee stationed in Baton Rouge "saw in a Salem paper" an erroneous account of how two regiments who assaulted Port Hudson "were all cut to pieces." Clarifying the false information, this anonymous soldier wrote that "if you see any such account in the best paper ever was, put it down as incorrect."[77] Both soldiers and civilians remained discouraged—and disgusted—by false or erroneous reports, but they were not necessarily distraught. Many individuals simply waited for a confirmation or rejection of the rumors.

When newspapers were nonexistent, civilians sometimes personally delivered the latest news and rumors about the war. One report told how a Vermilionville resident named Mr. Theogine Hébert passed on hearsay from "some men who are trustworthy." His report included erroneous rumors that Union troops had killed Gen. Ulysses Grant while he led a charge against Confederate lines.[78] Hopes and rumors of peace also abounded, especially since an end to hostilities would mean a welcome homecoming. A 2nd Louisiana Cavalry officer, F. A. Prudhomme, wrote, "The general impulse of the brigade is for speedy announcement of peace. It is rumored in camp that France and England have recognized our independence."[79] W. H. King wrote, "Great excitement in camp! News of peace propositions. Rumored that Mr. Lincoln proposes to president Davis to give up the Cotton States, & let the border states decide for themselves—decide which power they will unite their destinies with."[80] By 1864, one Louisiana soldier hesitated to spread rumors about the war's end to his brother. "No news. Every body confident of Peace shortly. . . . I assure you that every one in the army is so confident of it, that if we were not to have it that it would be a great disappointment, and would cause more of a discouragement, than the loss of a great battle."[81] Rumors, albeit false ones, often gave hope or a pretense that reinforced what soldiers wanted to hear. Without the ability to quickly confirm or deny whether the latest news was true caused much disinformation to spread.

While Confederate soldiers and civilians traded the latest developments, Federal troops also passed on information to their foes. P. L. Prudhomme wrote to his father in Natchitoches about an engagement near Iuka, Mississippi, where the Confederates under Gen. Sterling Price clashed with Union forces. "On the 19th the enemy came down in force and preparations were made to attack. . . . A flag of truce was sent in by Rosancrantz asking the surrender of our force to prevent bloodshed stating Lee and Jackson had been whipped in Maryland and our cause was lost. Price answered he did not believe in the defeat of our Generals and that were it so, it was a greater inducement for us to fight so much the more obstinately."[82] Sometimes news, whether true or false, provided incentives for Confederate troops to continue fighting—even to the point of further solidifying their resolve to fight harder.

Word from distant theaters also provided a glimpse of how soldiers stationed in Louisiana reacted to and viewed Confederate commanders. In late 1864, Louisiana soldier Joseph Texada explained to his wife that there was "No news of the Enemy," but "I understand the Yankees are steadily advancing their works in Virginia." Even though things looked bleak near the Confederate Capitol, Texada claimed that "my confidence in Lee is firm and unshaken."[83] Many Confederates often criticized their military leaders, but confidence in Gen. Robert E. Lee's leadership remained steadfast. In the summer of 1863, one soldier noted how a De Soto Parish resident claimed "the old men at home . . . discuss the abilities of our Generals—know more than any of them—except General Lee only. They admit him to be a great man, but all the others do wrong all the time."[84]

These comments by Louisiana residents far from the eastern theater speaks volumes about the growing fame of and faith Confederate civilians had in Robert E. Lee. However, not all Confederates praised Lee's decisions. Henry Ginder, a Louisiana soldier serving at Vicksburg, told his wife in a letter dated June 28, 1863, "I am almost sorry to hear of Lee's progress Northward; for it looks as if the importance of Vicksburg were not understood." Ginder criticized Lee's offensive push into Pennsylvania, claiming, "Our existence, almost, as a nation, depends on holding this place. Why not then remain on the defensive & send troops hither, instead of employing them on useless expeditions

. . . having no decisive results. Our rulers seem to have gone clean daft . . . for it is only owing to the total efficiency of the enemy that we are not already captured.[85] Such understanding and foresight frustrated soldiers, such as Ginder, who knew that high risks—and mistakes—by the Confederate high command only prolonged the war, keeping men away from their families.

EMOTIONAL TOLLS OF HOMESICKNESS AND SEPARATION

Of all the Civil War engagements fought, perhaps the most wrenching for both soldiers and civilians was their mental battlefield. The longing for loved ones and replaying images of home took a heavy toll on many soldiers and civilians. Unlike the sporadic battles or infrequent shock of combat, many soldiers' and civilians' minds remained active with the omnipresent sympathy and compassion for their loved ones. Their thoughts about the hardships and potential dangers their relatives faced, whether at home or on the battlefield, fostered waves of anxiety. Within a few months of his enlistment, Frederick Taber suffered from homesickness and grew desperate. "Mother," he wrote, "can't you try & get some excuse for me to come up and see you say for instance that you are sick But it must be a good one or else the Col will not let me come."[86] Separation caused much distress for soldiers; as Alfred Flournoy Jr. wrote from his camp near Richmond, "Maybe you think I write too often, but I can't help it. All my thoughts are about home. It is my thoughts by day and my dreams by night."[87]

Many soldiers attempted to escape the war by dreaming about home. Transcribing their dreams in letters, what one historian terms as "dream reporting," helped soldiers and civilians remain vigilant in their affections for one another and offered them a coping mechanism for dealing with the stressful situations.[88] Some soldiers even felt the strain of separation from their new friends and acquaintances who lived near their camp's vicinity. One 8th Louisiana infantryman wrote to a local Virginia belle, expressing how he missed her and dreamed about being in her presence. "I am going to relate to you a dream that happend night before last while in a deep and profound Slumber." He claimed he was in the presence of her "Dear Parents & Friends amusing ourselfs as we did some few evenings ago. . . . I had seen every thing as Natural as if my person was there itself but by misfortune I was awaked by the sound of the Bugle and find myself on a pile of straw."[89]

Writing from Mississippi, Edwin Fay told his wife, "The Bugle reveille waked me from a dream of you. . . . It was too hard to be awaked to war's stern, sad realities."[90] One Louisiana officer encamped near Nashville, Tennessee, wrote his wife, "The further I get from you, the dearer do you Seem to grow." Writing was his top priority as he relocated to new quarters, claiming that "the first thing I did was . . . take out this paper, & commence this letter to you."[91] Cultivating dreams and emotions—via letter writing—proved a powerful combination for soothing many soldiers' state of mind. It allowed them to temporarily disconnect from the drudgery and shocks of military life and refocus their thoughts and emotions on what they missed most—their loved ones.

For many soldiers, writing became therapeutic, which impacted their mental health as they found solace in keeping a diary or journal writing. "When I came into the army," wrote Lt. John Coleman Sibley, "I expected to keep a record of all important events but have put off beginning it from time to time. . . . A few days ago I mentioned my intentions to one of our company W. J. Rusk and he presented me this blank book that I might have no excuse."[92] Without Rusk's gift, Sibley's wartime experiences—and those of his comrades in the 2nd Louisiana Cavalry and the civilians he met and interacted with—might never have been recorded. E. John Ellis of the 16th Louisiana Infantry also saw the value in documenting soldier life; however, he too got a late start. "I have often regretted that I failed or neglected to keep a journal or diary from the time of my enlistment. . . . What small trouble and inconvenience it would have cost me." Luckily for posterity, Ellis eventually recorded his wartime observations—but only after becoming a prisoner of war in Ohio. Along with noting his time in prison, he also provided a "rapid review" of his wartime experiences up to his captivity, which "have most impressed me . . . and which consequently remain freshest in my memory."[93]

While letter and journal writing gave many soldiers a way to communicate and record their martial adventures, some soldiers turned to writing poetry. Mississippian James Addison Boyd, who was killed in Louisiana defending Port Hudson, kept a journal and, among his entries, wrote poems depicting various aspects of his military experiences. While stationed at Port Hudson, he wrote poems titled "Address to My Fellow Soldiers" and "The Flag of the South," which included patriotic verses, such as "By the flag of the South . . . Never may it trail, even may it wave, A type of liberty, born of the brave." Even in the midst of fighting, Boyd penned a poem titled "The Battle of Port Hudson, Mch 14th '63," which described the "pending storm" of battle between the Confederate defenders and Union troops.[94]

Though poetry and expressive writing proved entertaining and provided a mental reprieve for some soldiers, many others simply wanted to use writing for communication, especially with relatives. Joseph Texada, who served in the 2nd Battalion of the Louisiana State Guard, wrote from his camp near Franklin, Louisiana, asking his wife about the well-being of his "Darling little boy." Texada claimed, "I have been almost afraid even to ask you. I have been so low spirited about him—I have had the blues to-day . . . when I think of Home I get very melancholy."[95] But the Confederacy demanded service, and time away from loved ones remained upon the altar of sacrifice. "Were my country free," wrote Lt. John Coleman Sibley, "I would have no inclination to stay here one day more but would hasten to my quiet home there to meet those I love and spend the rest of my days in quietude. But alas my country is not free any more than myself."[96] But sometimes camp loneliness or the quietness of guard or picket duty afforded soldiers solace to dwell on home, rendering the "comfort and satisfaction to know," wrote John Coleman Sibley, "that while I toil on and wear my way through many disadvantages of a camp life there are those at home who still love and remember me."[97]

Many soldiers' thoughts transformed nostalgia into future hopes of a life without war. One Louisiana officer explained, "I miss the quiet of home and crave for a personal enjoyment of those attentions and marks of affection that render life so agreeable. . . . I live not in the present, it is forgotten in the past and the past is the dream of [the] future."[98] Years earlier, he had even explained how "the influences of memory" forced him to recollect the images of young ladies, regardless of who they were or how well he knew them. "I verily believe I now love every Miss I ever met or heard of," he wrote. "Why, I have apportioned a day to be devoted to every young lady of my acquaintance . . . to love all the time! Remarkable is it not?"[99] Keeping their personal spirits high proved a chore, but it was necessary in order for some soldiers to stay focused on their military mission.

Separation from a spouse was tough, but for soldiers who had children, the stress and anxiety was only compounded. One Louisiana soldier serving in the Spartan Guards became emotional as he wrote a letter to his wife from New Orleans: "Mary, I tell you I fare bad here. I am worried almost to death about you and the children. . . . I can't write for the tears in my eyes and my heart is nearly broken."[100] Another Louisiana infantryman longed for more than just his wife and children: his pet canine obviously meant a great deal to him, as he wrote, "If I ever get back I want to sea my dog. I would give a thousand dollars if . . . this war was endid."[101] Apparently, affections for all his family (including pets) remained heavily on his mind. A soldier's emotional stress only escalated as the war dragged on. In 1864, Edwin Leet wrote to his wife back in Bayou Sara, Louisiana, telling her to "kiss all the children for me and the Baby twice. . . . I hope to be home. I do want to See you and the children So bad."[102] A few months later, Leet's mind remained fixed on his family's welfare, "With a thousand prayers that you all may get along well," he wrote.[103]

Sheehan-Dean argues that Virginia soldiers "experienced great difficulty finding the right balance between their competing obligations" of protecting their families and the new nation. He notes that in the first half of the war, soldiers viewed leaving their families and joining "military service as the most effective way to protect their families," despite the situation's irony.[104] However, a sense of helplessness sometimes shrouded soldiers' thoughts as they lacked daily physical contact with their loved ones and relied solely on written correspondence for their comfort. A Louisiana officer stationed in Mississippi remained on edge when he learned of the Federal invasion near his home in southwest Louisiana. "You cannot imagine how anxious I am to have news of you," he wrote his wife. "I would like to know how they treated you. . . . I am almost persuaded that, unless they behaved differently in our home than everywhere else, they stole all they got their hands on. I am sure they must have burned the house and everything in it."[105]

The feelings of fear and helplessness tormented many soldiers who knew not the fate of their loved ones back home. The fear for his family's safety was so strong for at least one soldier that "the thousand anxious moments I have had has been worse than death" as not knowing "what situation you are now perhaps in is perfectly harrowing. . . . I would give everything in the world to see you and find you . . . well."[106] But relatives on the home front also worried about their soldiers at the front. "Oh you have no idea how uneasy I feel it makes me so miserable to know that you are exposed to so many dangers & I cant hear from you I dont know how I am to stand this dreadful suspense," wrote one Louisiana soldier's wife.[107]

The enemy's encroachment into Confederate territory often spread a series of rumors of atrocities, which many local residents usually took at face value—

especially if they remained in close proximity to the unfolding events.[108] It was episodes such as these that struck fear in the hearts and minds of Confederate soldiers stationed far away without the ability to protect their family members and friends physically. Whether the news or information they received proved true or erroneous mattered little. Their families' welfare remained their utmost concern.

For some soldiers stationed away from home, they connected with local civilians who lived near their camps. Affections often developed between soldiers and civilians, which, for some, blossomed into something more. Such relational developments sometimes proved problematic, especially for married soldiers. One Louisiana soldier's wife heard an upsetting story about her husband "flirting with the girls" near his camp in Virginia. She displayed her apparent jealousy, telling her husband's visiting comrade, "I did not believe a word of it and if he did not want to make a lasting enemy of me, to not say another word."[109] Making friends with female acquaintances frequently occurred—sometimes with multiple ladies. Frank Richardson explained that at the prospect of a battle his comrades gave him "all their valuables letting me know where to send them if they were killed . . . one poor fellow gave me two or three hundred dollars, and an address to his sweetheart, telling me to tear up all those letters to other ladies as they might heart [sic] her feelings should she see them."[110]

A Louisiana lieutenant also had affections for more than one woman—however, his situation ended in disaster. A Richmond newspaper relayed the story that, although this officer had a wife and children back home in Louisiana, he had recently married a lady "who was a few miles away from camp." After writing to both women, "he sent the wrong letter to each, so that his lovely bride got the letter intended for the wife . . . and she the other. I guess that made a 'fuse in the family,' if not in both families."[111] At least one Louisiana infantryman's short-lived encounter with a local Virginia lady did not last long enough to breed true affections or letters. As the 8th Louisiana Infantry entered Winchester, Virginia, one lady proclaimed that they were too late to capture the retreating Federals. Then "a tall Creole from the Teche" took the woman "in his arms, and imprinted a sounding kiss on her ripe lips, with 'Madame! je n'arrive jamias trop tard.'" Supposedly she quickly departed the soldier's arms "with a rosy face but merry twinkle in her eye."[112]

While correspondence provided separated soldiers and civilians a way to communicate and cultivate emotional bonds, it paled in comparison to a physical visit and embrace. Short homecomings provided soldiers, such as Lt. John Coleman Sibley, with a chance to reunite with his wife and children. Upon arriving at his house, he noted the toll that long absences took on family relationships. "Found my wife and little babes glad to meet me once more. That is my wife and oldest babe was." Sadly, he admitted, "I don't think my Little Belle knew me. She was only a little over two years old and I had been absent nine months and eighteen days."[113] Over a year later he described his growing frustration at his seemingly never-ending absence as the war continued. "What will become of soldiers and soldier's wives and soldier's children? . . . My little babe is growing up without the benefit of a fathers' instruction. My wife is lamenting my absence. I am growing grey in the service and still there is no peace." However, he acknowledged that he and his fellow Confederates must continue on. Wives, too, had to remain devoted, especially by rearing young children, especially in religious and spiritual matters without the aid of their husbands.[114]

Relying on God's power helped some soldiers deal with the pain of separation. Stationed near Memphis, one Louisiana officer wrote his wife, "As I look out on the River, how I long to take a boat for home. But now is the hour of our Country's necessity every man should be at his post & every woman should by her labors, be words of encouragement, & her prayers should cheer a[nd] urge him on." His duty and honor remained steadfast, and this officer's letter highlighted his confidence in God's wisdom as he wrote, "You know I never have 'the blues' . . . I feel all things are in God's hands & therefore All is well."[115] While wartime separation remained emotionally taxing and arduous for soldiers and civilians, the news of a loved ones' death brought immense sorrow. While losing a husband or son was hard enough, the effects of losing a father in the conflict greatly impacted his children he left behind. Some Civil War soldiers never met their sons and daughters who were born during the conflict, placing the burden of care—and the joys of parenthood—solely on their surviving relatives. Such was the case for many Louisiana families. Noting the "first death that occured [sic] in our company," Lt. John Coleman Sibley sympathetically explained how he laid his comrade, A. J. Whitely, to rest. "I was very sorry . . . for he left a poor widow and one little babe which he never saw."[116]

But while soldiers courted death in camp and on the battlefield, civilians back home also met death at unexpected times. Such occurrences added to wartime stress and caused another emotional burden for soldiers to bear as they remained helpless to offer physical comfort or solace to their surviving relatives. "I lost My Wife," wrote one Louisiana infantryman to his sister who lived in the North. "She left Me with two as lovely little Children. . . . I thought I had Seen trouble before but I Knew nothing of it but thank god I have many friends that dident forsake me." A family friend took in his daughter, and a relative took care of his son in his absence. His son came "to see me . . . Stayed Several days" but his departure was heart wrenching as "it was like death to part with him when he Started home."[117]

Sometimes children passed away, often when their fathers were absent from home while serving on the battlefield. For many absentee fathers, the devastating news of a child's death brought great sorrow. After receiving word that his baby daughter Ella passed away, Lt. John Coleman Sibley, crushed by the news but comforted by his faith, wrote, "I shall see her no more on earth; she has gone to swell the angelic throng around the Savior's throne. Sweet little one I did not think when I kissed your rosy lips good bye . . . that I should see your bright eyes no more. Oh! My babe how sad to give you up . . . may we meet in heaven to part no more is the prayer of grief stricken papa."[118] Still grieving the death of his young son after a month of his passing, Louisianian Edwin Fay wrote from his camp in Mississippi that "my heart bleeds afresh to feel, to know that my darling is no more, that I can never see him again, that he can never again climb upon my knees and throw his arms around my neck and show me how much he loved me. . . . I cannot stand it, Why did my child die?"[119]

Communication proved a double-edged sword; while it could relieve a relative's mind about their loved one's well-being, it could also exacerbate their anxiety, fostering more uncertainty and tensions. But despite this contention, letter writing remained a critical part of a Civil War soldier's social interaction. Such communication kept soldiers and civilians emotionally connected and their communal bonds tight. For without it, and the emotional, physical, and psychological benefits associated with obtaining correspondence and home-front news, a Civil War soldier's suffering would have drastically intensified.

CHAPTER 8

◇◆◇

SOLDIERS AND CIVILIANS AT WAR

◇◆◇

By 1864, Louisiana and its people had endured the sobering, long-term effects of warfighting, and the "country here is quite laid waste," wrote one Louisiana soldier.[1] Lt. John Coleman Sibley wrote how "the horrors of war" remained—even months after a battle. Viewing the carnage along Bayou Teche, Sibley left an unpleasant description. "We found several bodies still almost entire and looking as if they had lain there but a short while, some were intirely [*sic*] gone and naught but the bones remaining." Destruction "was everywhere to be seen," as he noted military hardware and equipment of all sorts, along with "Several of our brave soldiers" littered the field.[2] Battlefield survivors quickly realized their mortality; as one Texan who fought near the Sabine River claimed, "I never Want to get in as dangerous a plase as that any more for they come verry neare Killing me."[3]

Exposure to the war's violence and destruction left many soldiers and civilians in awe. "The distruction of property from Natchitoches to Monetts' Ferry is indescribable," wrote Louisiana soldier Lucien Flournoy in 1864. "This whole country is an utter waste."[4] W. H. King gave a similar report for northeast Louisiana, claiming the region near Monroe was "one continued scene of devastation. . . . Every thing presents a gloomy aspect."[5] Even for individuals who never witnessed the chaotic scenes of death and suffering, the war remained on their minds.[6] Louisiana residents such as planter Isaac Erwin observed the war from a safe geographical distance at least at the war's

commencement; however, information about military events was not necessarily listed simply as an afterthought.[7] The war mattered for Louisianians
on the home front, even though the state remained virtually untouched by
Union forces until the conflict's second year. Transpiring events stirred many
residents' emotions of vulnerability and insecurity, especially since Confederate
authorities sent large numbers of Louisiana's troops to other states. Residents
with relatives in uniform also suffered from the familial strife connected to long
stints of separation.

The effects of combat also took physical and psychological tolls on all its
participants. However, as McPherson notes, Civil War soldiers, despite witnessing the horrific scenes of combat, continued to fight. In *For Cause and
Comrades,* McPherson centers his study on soldier motivations and ideology,
and his attention to the soldier-civilian interaction focuses on the distant relationships between the civilians on the home front and the battle-tested soldiers.[8] Soldiers often turned to civilians to relate their combat experiences,
allowing them to decompress psychologically their combat stress. But civilians,
too, contended with wartime atrocities and destruction, and soldier-civilian
relationships did not always follow an assailant vs. victim scenario. Historians who debate the Civil War's level of brutality and destruction often draw
different conclusions.[9] When the chaos of combat ensued, the lines between
the home front and battle front melted away, especially when the fighting took
place near populated areas. And a Union presence in a populated area would
likely escalate hostilities. Ash notes that enemy occupation did not end Confederate resistance: "It endured and by so doing radically altered the course of
occupation and, indeed, of the entire war."[10]

Despite the conflict's degree of savagery, its participants remained socially
intertwined. Most Civil War engagements occurred near cities or towns, and
battle names easily reflect this. Soldiers and civilians remained in close proximity (especially in hospitals), even when battles raged as this cooperative network remained vibrant in the midst of active campaigning. Soldiers provided
defense and protection, while sympathetic civilians filled support roles, such
as providing information or working in hospitals. Just as physical encounters,
correspondence, and communal cooperation played a major role in soldier-
civilian relations, combat proved the ultimate test of these bonds. Civilians
witnessed the soldiers' bodily sacrifices amidst the chaos of battle. The sight
of blood and amputated limbs, the painful screams and shrills of the dying and

wounded, the wake of property destruction that remained when the smoke cleared all resonated with civilians of the sacrifices their soldiers made. Such scenes reminded civilians that, despite their criticism of Confederate authorities or Confederate government policies, it was the Confederate soldier whom they truly appreciated—or pitied. Escalating violence brought new meaning to home defense, as it became more than just a sense of duty or an excuse to go to war. Serious consequences followed such actions.

Louisiana's Federal invasion and occupation exposed the state's manpower shortage, forcing Confederate authorities to not only seek support from neighboring states but also from their own civilians. Raising irregular forces who served close to home—and who needed civilian support—brought a new dimension to the term *citizen-soldier*. Waging war required a cooperative support network from both soldiers and civilians—even as both suffered. In his study of middle Tennessee in the Civil War, Ash argues that wartime devastation created a "democracy of devastation," as the destruction "mitigated class discord among whites by punishing and humbling high and low alike."[11] Louisiana's soldiers and civilians had similar experiences.

THE LURE OF BATTLE

When the Civil War began, excitement gripped the minds and emotions of many men who itched to prove their manhood and win battlefield laurels and accolades from their friends and family. Shortly after parting from home, many men quickly realized that not all wartime episodes were colorful, glorious, or heroic; nor did all Louisiana volunteers find themselves destined for a battlefield—at least at first. When the 4th Louisiana assembled in 1861, "the highest hopes were entertained . . . that it would soon make its mark upon the field of battle." However, the military's needs shattered this unit's aspirations, as its men were stationed "upon a barren island" off the Mississippi coast. Disappointed, the "restless and discontent" volunteers could not understand their lot, since "one of the finest regiments ever formed for the Confederate service" now acted "as a coast guard!"[12]

Writing to a friend, one of the regiment's disgruntled members claimed, "I am . . . not by any means satisfied. I am willing and ready to join any company or battalion (under good officers) for the war just to get out of the 4th Regiment. I am tired and sick of it. We are here on, (must I say it?) dead expense to the Southern Confederacy."[13] Another soldier concurred. "If I can get a discharge . . . from the crab catching Reg I intend Joining some other company," he wrote.[14] The 4th Regiment did not remain inactive long. Its soldiers saw action at Shiloh, which offered a sobering reality check of what war was really about.[15] Such would be the fate of several other Louisiana regiments.

Many soldiers who remained anxious to get into action often criticized Confederate authorities for not sending them straight to the front. Envious of their fellow Southerners who had already engaged with the enemy, several Louisiana soldiers made their feelings known to their relatives back home: they remained dedicated to the idea of defending their homes and families. For many men, not seeing action hurt their masculine personas as capable—and willing—defenders, an image they tried to cultivate when initially enlisting. One Louisiana soldier told his sister that he aimed to participate "in a battle, I left home to fight,"[16] while another Louisiana infantryman Granville Alspaugh wrote to his mother, "I want to shoot a Yankee so bad I don't know what to do."[17] Killing, at least before it actually transpired, seemed to be an anticipated sport.

Oblivious to the reality of taking another human life, one 8th Louisiana infantryman told his mother: "Tell Miss Francis and Miss Lacombe I will try . . . and kill as many Yankees as I can."[18] Not seeing combat in the war's opening months frustrated numerous Louisiana troops, especially those heading to Virginia. Eugene Janin told his father, "Our battalion has been decidedly unlucky thus far. We were the first to leave the State and have as yet seen nothing but the most monotonous & tedious parts of a soldier's life, while others, starting long after we did have their share of victory of Manassas & will soon no doubt join in a triumphal entry into Washington City." Downtrodden by not seeing action, Janin remained hopeful. "Our turn may come by and by but appearances are against us."[19] He was later killed at Second Manassas.

But for many men, this anticipation gave way to inactivity. Some Louisiana soldiers, such as Benjamin Smith, who served in Virginia, loathed his regiment's idleness. "I loaded my musket once or twice with the expectation of hurting somebody," he wrote, "but was disappointed. . . . As for my bayonet it had only been stained by the blood of a unfortunate pig, who was foolish enough to tempt a hungry soldier. I devoutly hope, that, he was a Yankee pig." Since being away from home, Smith claimed there is "not so much gas about exterminating unfortunate yankees," as he and his comrades now focused on "a great deal more solitude about our bodily wants and comforts."[20] The desire for solitude and comforts, often with the companionship of civilians, became more desirable for campaigning soldiers, especially when the bullets began flying.

Several Louisiana units quickly cemented their reputation as hard fighters. One South Carolinian claimed Major Roberdeau Wheat's Louisiana company, named the "Tiger Rifles," seemed to always be "continually fighting with each other. They were always ready to fight, and it made little difference to them who they fought."[21] Another account told of how these same soldiers not only effectively wielded their firearms, but also resorted to hand-to-hand combat as they unleashed "unearthly yells and [when] they drew their knives and rushed to close quarters, the Yankees screamed with horror."[22] A Virginia soldier claimed the Louisiana Tigers "were a dangerous, blood-thirsty set." Even a Yankee soldier noticed the Louisianians' ferocity in battle: "D——n those Louisiana Tigers—born devils, every one of them!"[23] After the Battle of Chancellorsville, one Louisiana soldier told his father that the Union prisoners "said they knew we were the La. boys as soon as we screamed. They said they had rather fight a whole Division of Virginians than one of the La. brigades."[24]

Newspaper reports often told of Louisiana regiments' heroic feats and accomplishments on distant battlefields across the Confederacy, adding luster to their reputations. One newspaper published a soldier's letter from the 1861 Missouri battle of Oak Hill. "It is admitted by all here, that the Louisiana Regiment met with the hottest fire, and did the most damage in the ranks of the enemy," the soldier told his uncle.[25] Another published letter in the same newspaper recounted the Louisianians' Missouri exploits, but ended with a somber reminder that a soldier "will shed tears, for those who have been left dead and wounded on the field."[26]

Coming out of an engagement alive brought individual rejoicing, but dealing with the horrors and psychological scars of witnessing the deaths and maiming of friends and relatives in the ranks stirred an emotional tempest. As the conflict escalated, so did the casualty lists. By the winter of 1861, Louisiana soldier George Lee told his sister, "I have witnessed scenes that would strike your hearts with terror." He reminisced about the days before the war "of our own Louisiana, where I have spent the happiest days of my life. . . . Oh! may the time soon come, when the desolating of war will be rolled back."[27] Psychologically, the soldier-civilian network cultivated by correspondence allowed

Louisianians a way to relate their horrific battlefield experiences to their loved ones. Combat not only destroyed bodies; it potentially destroyed the mind. As soldiers mentally suffered with the oppressions of war, their civilian connections remained a vibrant coping mechanism with dealing with traumatic stress. Relating their struggles to a friend or relative helped ease their mental burdens, especially when they turned their attention off of them and onto a fellow comrade who was potentially in worse shape. However, such news would likely not remain private, which could affect a soldier's social standing back home.[28]

WAR COMES TO LOUISIANA

In the spring of 1862, news reached Louisiana of the Battle of Shiloh's carnage. Reports offered the newly formed companies training at Camp Lovell a sobering account of how bloody the war had become.[29] Upset by the heavy casualties—and their inactivity, soldiers from one company in the 26th Louisiana Infantry petitioned their former commander to lead them "to the scene of action . . . to avenge the death of our brothers and friends."[30] Many of their slaughtered friends had served in the 18th Louisiana Infantry under the command of the Acadian Col. Alfred Mouton, which suffered 211 casualties.[31] One Louisianian in the Orleans Guard wrote, "It was truly horrendous . . . to see on all sides those unfortunate men of the Eighteenth . . . bathed in their blood; some had been wounded in the face, others, in the body, arm, etc. They fled into our ranks, asking us for water and help."[32]

Frank Richardson wrote home after the battle, reassuring his family about his safety; however, he made it clear that many of his comrades met a different fate.[33] Heavy casualties forced Louisiana's forces to restructure, as regiments such as the 4th Louisiana suffered heavily. One soldier wrote that "the poor fourth are very unfortunate out of 900 men when they first came, they had not over 300 men for duty." In one company, "all their officers have died of disease since the battle."[34] The growing death toll was not simply a statistic. Serious psychological consequences awaited the survivors who experienced and witnessed horrific battlefield trauma.

Many soldiers found they lacked the words to accurately express what they felt when under fire, so relating their strife to civilians proved no easy task. After Shiloh one Louisiana artilleryman honestly explained his personal fears to his wife. "I tell you May! I have never had such feelings in my life and would have given a great deal several times, if I could have been away."[35] For this soldier and countless others who participated in a major battle, distance from the active conflict would have been a blessing. Perhaps E. John Ellis of the 16th Louisiana Infantry captured many Louisiana soldiers' feelings after seeing battlefield horrors by claiming that "after being under fire once I was never very anxious to be there again."[36] Shiloh's level of carnage shocked both the nation and Louisiana; however, the worst was yet to come.[37]

A few weeks after Shiloh, disaster struck Louisiana as Union forces captured New Orleans. Both soldiers and civilians criticized Confederate leaders for the city's loss; however, a few soldiers believed the city had a fighting chance.[38] This strategic blunder also illustrates how both soldiers and civilians remained in dialogue about Louisiana's transpiring events, often with various opinions. Before New Orleans was captured, E. J. Lee enthusiastically noted how he and his compatriots "are all Ready for the Yankees to attack N. O . . . we have the city so well fortified that the Yankees can never take it." Lee later relocated to Camp Chalmette and saw New Orleans's defenses firsthand. "We are at the spot where Gen Jackson whiped Packanham."[39]

Standing in the shadow of Andrew Jackson's 1815 victory and reinforced by false confidence in the city's defenses and security did not convince all residents and soldiers of the city's safety. Dosie Flournoy wrote to her husband stationed in Virginia that she heard that "New Orleans is in great danger and the people are so indiferent [sic], they have been very negligent in providing for the defence."[40] Writing from Camp Moore, John E. Hall bluntly told his wife, "Now to see the people of New Orleans living in perfect security, in luxury, thoughtless of danger, and as we all know they will be surrendered on the approach of the enemy, it has caused more than myself to murmur."[41] For Confederate Louisiana, New Orleans's defense would not repeat Jackson's 1815 precedent; nor would this be the Confederacy's last blunder. Contending with setbacks and disappointments, many residents often voiced their discontent and frustrations; however, many also remained steadfast to the cause. Their soldier-relatives who remained in harm's way on other fronts needed their continued support.

The opening shots fired against Louisiana's defenses at Forts Jackson and St. Philip along the Mississippi River not only ended in a Confederate disaster, but it also provided a bloody spectacle. Albert Patterson, an ex-slave who witnessed the engagement, recounted decades later: "I remember when de

gunboats come up de river an' took Jackson an' St. Phillips Fort, an' General
Butler took New Orleans. I see some bad things," he told an interviewer. "I
seen de Rebel soldiers run, wid their leg most cut off to de knee, or de arm
hangin',' de blood pourin.' De Colonel, he make me carry dem in de buggy, so
they could come here to de hospital, an' then some o' them start cussin',' an'
insist they goin' right back to de battlefield even with their arm cut off so they
can't carry a gun."[42] The city's surrender upset Confederate Louisianians, such
as Kate Stone, who remained distressed that "the greatest City of the South"
easily fell without stiff resistance. "Such was not its fate in the days of Jackson," she wrote.[43] This defeat ushered in a new wave of frustration for Louisiana's Confederate soldiers and civilians.[44] Writing from Mississippi, Lt. P. L.
Prudhomme asked his father, "Why does not the Government come to the
assistance of our state? Really La seems to have been forgotten."[45] Louisiana's
military commanders complied with the Confederacy's demands as best they
could, even as Governor Moore voiced his concerns to Jefferson Davis.[46]

Both soldiers and their commanders remained at the mercy of higher military and political authorities. Many Louisianians, like P. L. Prudhomme, vented
their frustrations on pen and paper but continued to serve. Home defense,
which soldiers viewed as their top priority, was still linked to Confederate nationalism. If the nation survived, even with the loss of territory, it was a win for
home defense. Voicing criticism of Confederate policies or authorities was not
disloyalty. Several soldiers and civilians realized that the conflict was going to
be long and that disappointments and setbacks would occur; morever, many
Louisianians knew that service required sacrifice and that their actions (they
hoped) would ensure ultimate victory.

IRREGULAR WARFARE

As Union forces encroached deeper into Louisiana, the battle front became a
local matter for soldiers and civilians as the Yankee noose tightened. On August 18, 1862, Confederate Gen. John L. Lewis proclaimed to soldiers in the
Lafourche region that the invading Yankees would meet their doom. "Wherever and whenever he dare pollute our soil with his accursed and dastardly [sic]
foot-prints and menaces our fire sides, let every place of natural protection and
defence [sic] that surrounds your homestead . . . contain men of unerring aim
ready to do or die."[47] Louisiana's Confederate officials took drastic measures to

rally men to the cause. Both state and national forces, which sometimes operated as rivals, sought to repel the Union invaders. Much like the prejudices volunteers held against conscripts, not all soldiers viewed one another as equals.[48]

A soldier's status, whether in the militia, state guard, or national service,
sometimes became equated with their dedication to the cause and perhaps
their level of training, toughness, and discipline. But as the conflict escalated,
the distinction between militia and regular forces sometimes blurred, especially
if the military components worked in conjunction. The Assumption Parish
Regiment's leader, Col. W. W. Pugh, felt his militia force would need a supporting military element "of sufficient magnitude" if it was to have any success
in an engagement. "There is serious doubt, whether the militia as a body can
be brought into active service without the aid of a sustaining force," he wrote
in July of 1862.[49] Pugh's reservations were well warranted, but Louisiana's
militiamen could fight. Earlier service was performed by a militia unit, the
Chalmette Regiment, which saw action against Union gunboats that steamed
up the Mississippi River to capture New Orleans. Though the regiment failed
in preventing the Union boats from entering the city, it *fought* before surren-
dering. One historian notes that these militia soldiers were from the very region
they defended, likely having family and friends in the vicinity, and would not
have wavered in their loyalty. According to the regiment's commander, Ignatius
Szymański, the surrender only occurred after "losing some 30 min killed and
wounded, without a possibility of escape or rescue."[50]

One Texas soldier praised the Louisiana militiamen who participated at
the Battle of Pleasant Hill in 1864. "In justice to the Louisiana militia, I will
state, that not withstanding they were past the years of enduring the toils and
hardships of a soldier's life, no braver or nobler body of men ever went into
action."[51] Joseph Texada, who served in the 2nd Battalion of the Louisiana
State Guard, performed picketing duty and faced the common hardships—
and enemy fire—of any soldier of the era. He expressed his frustration at his
plight of "doing duty for the Confederacy . . . with all the hardships" but, as a
soldier in the state guard, received "none of the priviledges of a Confederate
soldier," which included being exchanged if captured. Becoming a prisoner
under state service risked the possibility of being labeled or "perhaps treated as
Guerrillas," as Texada claimed, "The New Orleans' papers style us nothing but
a band of Bushwhackers and Guerrillas." He hoped his unit would be "taken
from here or turned over to the Confederacy."[52]

In 1862, Governor Moore called on citizens to raise "companies of experienced woodsmen . . . with their trusty rifles and shot-guns [to] harass [the enemy's] invading columns," later reiterating that "every able-bodied citizen must hold himself in readiness for immediate active service. . . . Let every citizen be an armed patrol. . . . Let all our river-banks swarm with armed patriots."[53] Using imagery of woodsmen—tough men who could care for themselves—related well to the warrior profile Confederate authorities used to promote guerrilla warfare. The Partisan Ranger Act (passed within days of the Conscription Act in April 1862) became a way Governor Moore hoped to fill Louisiana's defensive void and to retain social order from both foreign (Yankee troops) and domestic (Louisiana Unionists and enslaved insurrectionists) enemies. But regulating how these guerrilla forces would develop and function left many officials to wonder. Arkansas's governor, Harris Flanagin, knew that sanctioning guerrilla warfare was a double-edged sword for the Confederacy to contend with. "Soldiers do not enter the service to maintain the Southern Confederacy alone," he wrote Jefferson Davis, "but also to protect their property and defend their homes and families." Especially with guerrilla troops, home defense remained an integral part in serving the Confederacy.[54]

Irregular forces (whether partisans or guerrillas) brought a new meaning to the term *citizen-soldier*. Historians classify partisans as legal combatants with ties to a nation, while guerrillas were local forces with personal, not national, interests in mind. However, Federal intervention also had a hand in escalating guerrilla operations, especially in the West.[55] Historians have generally portrayed Civil War guerrilla warfare as chaotic, savage, and, perhaps more importantly, as a side show to the big show. Nevertheless, the guerrilla war proved more complex than simply irregular soldiers wreaking havoc on whomever they personally declared war against. These Southerners, though they adopted an unconventional style of fighting, sought to display their masculinity, defend their families, uphold their society's social order, and fight the war on their own terms. And, like their conventional brothers in arms, these men believed they fought "for the good of the community."[56]

As Ash notes, violence was no new phenomenon in the South. While Southerners engaged in various activities to resist Union occupation and aid the Confederacy, only "true redemption for self and community meant killing Yankees." Irregular warfare was a communal affair that encompassed "members of every social class." A partisan or guerrilla was "not a footloose adventurer but a longtime resident of the community." To these irregulars, protecting their family and community—by any means necessary—mattered most.[57] However, even when Federal forces withdrew from a region, targeting Union sympathizers and destroying their personal property—especially in acts of revenge—sometimes continued. Capt. Dennis Haynes recalled how Unionists who lived along the Red River near Alexandria in 1864 suffered at the hands of local Confederates, who "were on hand as soon as the Federals were out of the way; and they did the work of destruction with celerity and cheerfulness." Haynes referred to the "many dark and bloody deeds committed on both sides" in Louisiana as a "Reign of Terror." Atrocities, such as "cold-blooded murders . . . thefts and robberies; the barbarity with which these acts of violence were committed" (sometimes against "their nearest relatives") bear testament to the brutal nature of Louisiana's irregular warfare.[58]

By 1863 Lincoln's administration adopted the "Leiber Code," named for international law expert and university professor Francis W. Leiber, which sanctioned "all measures" deemed "indispensable for securing the ends of the war." The code labeled guerrilla fighters as outlaws, even permitting punishments for civilians involved in aiding said belligerents. Rooted in antislavery ideology, the Leiber Code provided legal protection for Lincoln's "hard-line war initiatives—martial law, suspension of habeas corpus, confiscation of the property of the disloyal, and emancipation."[59] While condemning guerrillas as illegitimate combatants, the code labeled partisan forces and their commanders (such as John S. Mosby and his rangers) as "authorized" belligerents who functioned under "the main army."[60]

Hyde notes how in the Florida Parishes, at least one Confederate officer helped form a "citizens' militia," which "called for the creation of home-guard units . . . to act as local reserves" when needed. What made the citizens' militia (not the state's "militia, which recognized the authority of the regular army") unique was that it remained "independent of any civil or military control."[61] And the fighting that transpired between Louisiana's irregular forces and Union troops made isolation from wartime violence nearly impossible for some civilians, especially since irregular warfare required soldier and civilian cooperation. Whether such actions actually benefited civilians remained in question; however, their participation in aiding local irregular soldiers was an integral part of guerrilla operations. Indeed, one Union officer commented that the local civilians near Ponchatoula "would hardly treat me civily; they are terribly enraged against us." Another Union officer, Gen. George Andrews, fumed that over one hundred Federals had been captured in one engagement "through the aid of so called citizens."[62]

Just as the war's initial excitement launched a wave of patriotism and co-operation between Louisiana's soldiers and civilians, the invading Union army had a similar effect; however, support was more out of necessity than from new-found love for the cause. Even if civilians sometimes disliked having Confeder-ate troops nearby disturbing their property, the Yankees' presence often posed the greater threat. To some residents, ridding the region of Yankees equated to a smaller Confederate presence to contend with. And with the rise of irregular warfare, many of the civilians-turned-irregular soldiers meant their personal stake in the fight was their literal defense of their family, homes, and property. By the spring of 1863, one Louisiana Confederate soldier favored raising "the black flag at once," as the Yankees "are fighting almost upon that principle. We, I think ought to take some measure to retaliate. There is no reason to fear that they will do more, for they are doing all they possibly can now."[63] The Confederate war effort benefited from guerrilla operations— whether or not the state or national government officially sanctioned and recognized these irregular troops. Michael Fellman notes that despite the ambiguity surrounding guerrilla operations, these men remained "a threat to the enemy."[64]

Civilian aid in irregular operations cannot be overstated—it brought a literal meaning to the term "household" war. Without civilians, especially women, and their support, partisan and guerrilla forces could not conduct war. Their intimate connections among themselves—and other guerrillas and their civilian supporters—kept their reasons for fighting communal and tight knit.[65] Support came in various forms, and, just like regular soldiers, guerrillas often interacted (or caroused) with women while serving the cause, reinforcing their ideology of communal defense.[66]

Motivations for civilian support ranged from individuals who were either die-hard Confederates or bystanders who became supportive after falling prey to Union confiscations or atrocities. Irregular actions also complicated Union strategy as Confederates used the civilian front to conduct war. Andrew F. Lang's study on Civil War military occupation exposes the chaotic nature of unconventional tactics. "Guerrillas and combatants dressed as private citi-zens" as they unleashed violence "in the streets of towns and in the desolate countryside where traditional rules of engagement and 'civilized' combat rarely

occurred." Such actions complicated the role and tactics of Union occupation, along with the "changing nature of American military culture." In 1862,
Union Lt.-Col. John A. Keith sought to punish the Terrebonne Parish guerrilla
forces responsible for killing wounded Federal soldiers—and mutilating their
bodies. After arrests and interrogations, the Union soldiers discovered that a
local "prominent attorney and newspaper editor" had been behind the activity.
Fuming, Keith made it known that his troops would dispense future retaliation
if similar actions occurred, claiming that "not a vestige of the town of Houma
shall be left . . . and the plantations in the parish of Terrebonne shall suffer in
a like degree."[67] If properly executed, guerrilla tactics, characterized by "surprise, mobility, and stealth," proved effective.[68]

Another factor relating to Confederate guerrilla activity was its ability to
possibly quell slave insurrections. The chaos created by the war often left the
home front without large numbers of White males to regulate the enslaved
workers since so many Louisiana soldiers served abroad. However, guerrilla
and home-guard troops filled the gap. Their presence—and likely their reputations for using unconventional violence—helped keep social order. Sutherland
notes that "the principal task of guerrillas in all circumstances was to defend
against potential enemies," which included not only Unionists and Union
troops, but also rebelling slaves.[69] In 1862, a group of escaped slaves entered
Union-controlled Baton Rouge and reported on the brutality of such guerrilla
attacks. One Federal soldier noted the irregular soldiers had shot one slave,
then "tied another one by the neck and heels and threw him into the river as
an example to deter other darkies from crossing to the Union lines." For the
enslaved individuals who sought freedom among marauding guerrilla bands,
getting captured had serious consequences.[70]

CONFEDERATE SOLDIERS, CIVILIANS, AND UNION BLACK TROOPS

Compounding Confederate Louisiana's manpower shortage, the shocking
scenes of the Union army enlisting ex-slaves as soldiers stirred great anger
among the state's Confederates.[71] Word of the 1863 exploits of African American soldiers operating in Louisiana (and elsewhere) brought harsh criticisms
from Confederates, both soldiers and civilians. White Southerners viewed such
actions as an armed revolt against the slave system; however, not all Confeder-

ate soldiers desired the opportunity to fight against—and possibly be defeated by—former slaves. Joseph Texada told his wife he hoped his unit would be sent "south of the Red River for many reasons. One particular one is that I have no fancy to fight Contrabands when Yankees are in abundance elsewhere in the state. The Black Flag has no charms in my opinion and not much glory in thrashing out negro troops, but on the contrary a good deal of disgraced in being defeated by them."[72]

By 1864, other Confederate troops took notice of African American soldiers' bravery and willingness to sacrifice their lives in the cause of freedom. One Texas soldier, Samuel Watson, who helped hold the line at Petersburg, Virginia, wrote that "them Bloody Niggers of Grant made a charge on us and a charge it was . . . the boys litterley coverd the ground with Dead nigs, dont think I am braging for it is so."[73] Black men fought, and facing armed ex-slaves complicated a Confederate soldier's interpretation of combat. While some men believed in the honor of sacrificing their lives for the cause, getting killed by former enslaved laborers now in uniform held no allure. And the question of the Confederacy using bondsmen as soldiers sparked heated debate between soldiers and civilians.[74]

For civilian Confederate sympathizers, they counted on the rebel soldiers in their vicinity for protection.[75] Fighting the enemy—along with keeping bands of marauding Jayhawkers (outlaws consisting of Union and Confederate deserters, draft dodgers, and runaway slaves) in check—were not the only tasks given to Confederate soldiers. Sometimes their services included acting as a police force and making arrests in domestic affairs, especially when unruly citizens got out of line.[76] The inability or the perception of Confederate forces to protect local citizens against a Union attack or marauding bandits caused great alarm for many residents. One Louisiana woman claimed that marauding Jayhawkers "commit all kinds of outrages upon men, women and children, rob, murder, rape. Oh, it is dreadful!"[77] In the face of Union threats and destruction, civilians sometimes felt Confederate forces failed them. As one Louisianian noted: "I wept bitterly for it seemed as if our Confederates had forsakened abandoned us . . . the streets were continually filled with Yankees . . . my poor eyes were soar and tiered of seeing blue."[78]

In southeastern Louisiana, a "band of helpless women—we, the mothers, daughters, and sisters of your soldiers" from St. Helena Parish pleaded to Confederate generals for soldiers to remain nearby for protection. Referring to nearby Camp Moore, these ladies felt abandoned, as "scarcely a soldier remains to shoulder a musket in our behalf. All gone—transported, 'tis true, to scenes of more active and stirring interest, but leaving us to the somber realities of our perilous position."[79] Near the war's end, one Louisiana woman claimed, "I will turn Yankee," telling her friend, "I have seen some mean mean Confederates since I left St. Landry, I did not think there were such men in the world as there is in the army at home. come and murder innocent citizens. all the time that yankee fort was there not one of those negro soldiers were killed, nothing but citizens, that were not in the army."[80]

Civilians took notice when Confederate soldiers directed their violence toward them. Such actions created a fluid environment that disrupted support; however, Confederate sympathies among civilians usually revived once Union forces adopted hard-war policies.[81] Reports of Union atrocities against the state's civilians greatly disturbed many soldiers. One Louisiana officer, William J. Walter, fumed at the calamities his family faced at the hands of the Yankees in 1864. "The mere thought of the outrages of my family makes me mad beyond controll," he wrote his sister. "I will return your avengers or not at all."[82] Wartime atrocities, depending on which side committed them, often shifted civilian sympathies and support. Louisiana's Civil War experience illustrates how this see-sawing of civilian support was often connected to their treatment by the warring armies.[83] Soldier-civilian relationships were interdependent—but could also be contested.

CASUALTIES, PSYCHOLOGICAL EFFECTS, AND MENTAL COLLAPSE

Writing home after an engagement in Mississippi, P. L. Prudhomme mentioned the death of a friend who "was a most excellent young man and liked by all the boys." Though sympathetic to the loss of his comrade, he well knew the demands and costs of soldiering, noting that nearly 40 percent of his regiment had become casualties. "But such are the chances of war," he wrote, "and we must humbly submit to the will of our Maker."[84] For many Christian soldiers, their views of combat and loss had an eternal perspective. As Sarah L. Wadley spoke with a group of visiting Confederate officers, their conversation turned to discussing "wounded soldiers . . . and their desperate condition, deprived as some are, of both hands or both legs." Stating she would "rather die than live thus," one officer offered deep contemplation about the afterlife, noting that "mortal hopes and pleasures" were temporal and eternity was long.[85]

Numerous wartime accounts attest to Louisiana's soldiers' bravery, and, despite their high casualties in all theaters, they fought on.[86] Sometimes soldiers bragged about their battlefield performances to relatives back home, but this did not mean that they remained unaware of the seriousness of their deeds. For example, Washington artilleryman Billy Vaught wrote to his sister about his participation in the Battle of Farmington, Mississippi, in May 1862. "I fired a cannon, in one instance, at a single enemy. . . . *The shell burst in his face.* I have become passionately fond of gunnery and have attained great skill." He even told of another shot "fired at a wagon galloping across [his] position a mile off," which hit its mark. Vaught did not think himself "hardened" or heartless at his enemies' misfortunes. Remembering his own mortality, he wrote, "I am a better (I hope & believe) & more religious man. My time is in His hands. He only knows when I may be called."[87]

Vivid combat descriptions, which oftentimes painted the grim—and gory—realities of war, offered sobering reminders that war was hell. Louisiana Capt. William J. Seymour recounted how the third day at Gettysburg "was a most terrible scene and made one believe that truly 'Hell was empty, and all the devils were there.'"[88] E. John Ellis recalled his experience at the Battle of Stones River, Tennessee. "I saw one of my company just ahead of me . . . he fell forward on his face. I stopped, turned him over but poor Coffman was dead—a ball had passed through his head and his brain was oozing out on the ground." Bullets were not the only Union armaments that took Confederate lives that day as one artillery shell hit close and "killed 6 men. The skull of one of the miserable men was blown off with the quivering brain still attached." As if the transcribed details were not already too gory, Ellis added that the skull fragment "flew several paces and fell upon the body of one of his comrades who was lying down."[89]

In the spring of 1863, 2nd Louisiana Cavalry Lt. John Coleman Sibley recorded the carnage he viewed near Franklin, Louisiana. It was "a desperate fight," he explained, "in which many of our gallant men fell," which included his commander, Col. William Vincent, who received a neck wound. Enemy losses were also "considerable, probably two hundred."[90] Soldiers constantly relayed news of casualties to relatives and friends back home. One 8th Louisiana Infantryman in Virginia notified a local friend of the death a comrade who was killed during "a little Fight on the Rapidan," along with a report that another companion was badly wounded at Fredericksburg. Luckily for "me," he claimed, "I am still a lieve. and enjoying a purfect health."[91]

However, soldiers were not the only individuals who witnessed or experienced wartime carnage. Civilians, too, often saw the armies' destruction first-hand.[92] One Louisiana soldier serving in Mississippi recorded an incident in which "Two Sisters & 3 children were fleeing from the scene of bloodshed." Canister from an exploded shell flew "around in every direction—one of which entered the side of one of the ladies; who was the Mother of the 3 poor little girls," he wrote. "Some of our boys carried her to Mr Huff's house near-by—She lived only about 20 minutes."[93] Wives and children of some of the soldiers stationed at Port Hudson were visiting when the Union bombardment commenced. As the civilians fled the attack, at least one "woman and child drowned" as they fell into a nearby stream attempting their escape.[94] One Texas officer claimed Louisiana's Red River region was a terrible sight to behold, as many people "are *in the woods* without food, shelter or clothing." He affirmed his report "to be true, for I see them with my own eyes. And what a sight!"[95] Soldiers who struggled psychologically with combat stress and suffering were not alone in their discomforts.

Battlefield trauma did not end when the smoke cleared. The pain of hearing of a soldier's death caused many Louisiana residents much heartache and sorrow. Both soldiers and civilians had to come to terms with the bloody realities and losses that the war continuously produced. Louisiana militia officer W. F. Pugh wrote a eulogy for his relative, Francis Welman Pugh "having attached himself to the 2nd Louisiana Cavalry," who died from an illness while in Union captivity. Pugh's mournful prose also reflected his unwavering commitment to the cause, claiming his relative "gave his life to his country 'A flower when offer'd in the bud, is no vain sacrifice.'" At the time of his death, Francis was only about two months shy of his sixteenth birthday.[96] One Louisiana soldier serving in Virginia told his sister of his melancholic thoughts as he pitied his dead comrades "whose lifeless bodies the soil of Va. now lies with nothing but the head boards to tell who lies beneath," along with the "grief [of] fathers & mothers, brothers, and sisters, and oh the bereavement of widows and orphans. Sad, sad indeed."[97] After one 1864 engagement in Georgia, Washington artilleryman Alexander Pierre Allain noted the loss of "three of [the] best and bravest boys" whom he regarded as "The flower of our company. . . . Poor boys your fates were sad ones."[98]

One Louisiana couple received a letter bearing the sad news that their son, E. L. Stephens, had died in Virginia. "It is my most painful duty to inform you of the death of your son . . . who fell in one of the late bloody battles near Richmond," the letter began. "He was attended during his last hours by the kind ladies of Staunton . . . he was decently buried in the family graveyard of Mrs. M E Measellar[?], and his friends can without difficulty find the spot that contains his mortal remains."[99] Bad news for the Stephens family continued; another letter arrived a few weeks later recounting that friendly fire likely caused their son's death, along with news that Ezra Denson—a good friend to their entire family—had "fallen in defense of his country" while carrying his regiment's battle flag. "Some of his blood now stains the center star of our flag and even now when looked upon by anyone of the Regt you will here them say never was a better boy or souldier ever fell," wrote 9th Louisiana infantryman Henry M. King, who had served with both of the young men. King listed other friends in the unit who had also been killed, as "Co. 'C' looks very small now only 29 men for duty." The remaining men "deeply sympathise with your & Mrs. Denson families in the loss of their beloved boys."[100]

Such news produced waves of mourning, but the soldiers or civilians who took the time to express heartfelt sorrow and sympathy for a grieving family highlight the wartime bonds that developed between soldiers and civilians. R. A. Allen, a soldier in the 4th Louisiana Battalion serving in the Army of Tennessee, had the unpleasant task of notifying a father that his son had been killed in action at New Hope Church. After describing the details of his comrade's death, Allen wrote, "Being a mess mate and a particular friend of mine I deeply deplore his loss and sympathize with you in your bereavement . . . but trust in his eternal gain. He was much respected by his brother soldiers as a good soldier and a true patriot. He died like a hero at his post of duty falling for a holy cause."[101] One Washington Artillery officer expressed his personal grief to the mother of one of his soldiers who died fighting in Georgia. "Since the death of your son I have been anxious to write you expressing my deep sorrow and sympathy . . . he was at all time cheerful & ready to do his duty be it what it might be and was always to be found at his post. His loss to us is great; to you it is irreparable. . . . God alone can comfort & solace you in this dark hour."[102]

Civilians, too, often wrote letters for soldiers too crippled or incapable of performing the task. A nurse serving in a Gettysburg hospital wrote a letter for a young Louisiana officer who lost "both of his legs and the loss of his eyesight." The dying Louisianian saw his plight as a waste. "How does my dying make us free? . . . If you should ask how I died, and are told 'at peace' it would be a monstrous lie."[103] The realities of war—wounds, killings, deaths—offered onlookers and participants anything but a romanticized view of the conflict. Helping wounded soldiers write letters proved no easy chore as the soldiers and civilians who often wrote letters for the men who could not had to recall the grim—and oftentimes gory—circumstances.

To shelter the wounded and dying, both soldiers and civilians set up makeshift hospitals in camps or nearby towns, using any available structure capable of serving the purpose. Sydney Harding described the poignant scenes while visiting the hospitals after the Battle of Mansfield: "Oh what a dreadful sight. Our poor men just lying on the floor in cotton. And such an odor. And they bore it so bravely. Not a groan was heard, all so cheerful. I only went to one church. There are more than a thousand wounded. Every house in town like a public building and every private house full. . . . Went the next morning to hospital. As we were coming out a missourian asked me to please go see the Missouri boys They like to see ladies. So of course we went. Poor fellows they did seem glad. . . . Oh the sickening sights. Some shot in face, both eyes out, head bent arms, legs, everywhere."[104] For wounded soldiers, their care and comfort remained largely in the hands of sympathetic civilians, many of whom were ladies. At Vicksburg, one Confederate chaplain commented on the plight of "a young man from some Louisiana Reg. that was dreadfully wounded . . . by a shell. Nearly all of the flesh from one of his shoulders, down towards his back was removed." However, this Louisianian had the good fortune of receiving special care from his company commander's wife, who was in Vicksburg during the bombardment. "She was a particular friend to the one who was wounded," the chaplain wrote. "She attended him to the hospital & for several days did not leave him day nor night. . . . No matter how severe the shelling was, she came as regular as the rising of the sun." Thanks to her care—and bravery in the face of danger—the wounded Louisiana soldier "improved."[105]

Wounded and writing from a hospital in Baton Rouge, John A. Morgan told his sister about the exceptional care he and his fellow soldiers received from "the Ladies who . . . are very devoted to the wounded soldiers." He continuously praised these women, noting that they "have been here allmost all of the time day and night ever since we were wounded. I never saw persons take more interest in any one than they have taken in the wounded soldiers here." Morgan's letter also hinted at a possible romance brewing, stating, "I have fallen in Love with Baton Rouge or some one here I do not know which but am inclined to think that I will try and find out which when the war is over."[106] Combat, much like other aspects of the war, did not always occur in isolation. Though soldiers did the actual fighting, civilians were left with helping restore their devastated communities—along with caring for the men who were left wounded or dying.

Even while facing death, some Louisiana soldiers solicited sympathy from caring females. At least one mortally wounded Louisiana officer at Gettysburg charmed some Northern women in his last moments on earth and received a kiss from each of them.[107] But incubating romantic feelings between soldiers and female nurses was not the purpose of a Civil War hospital. The blood, stench, suffering, and merciless cries of pain and loss vastly overshadowed romance, and one soldier noted, "All the houses in Mansfield are filled with wounded. You should see the suffering of those with amputated arms and legs. This is one of the worst battles which we have had since the war began."[108] One Confederate, who was at Mansfield "but not an active participant," told his wife he "came out unhurt," but many of his comrades did not share the same fate. "Many of our friends and acquaintances were killed and wounded."[109] Groups of wounded men reminded all who looked upon them of the war's brutality. And their suffering—whether physical or psychological—continued for the rest of their lives. Brian Craig Miller's study on Civil War amputations emphasizes that the sight of wounded men and amputated limbs "made such a deep impression on everyone who saw" them. These impressions served as living war memorials years after the conflict ended.[110]

In some cases, the bloodshed became so common that individuals became numb to the shocking sights and sounds caused by the fighting. Kate Stone wrote, "Death does not seem half so terrible as it did long ago. We have grown used to it." On another occasion, she explained, "People do not mourn their dead as they used to. Everyone seems to live only in the present—just from day to day—otherwise I fancy many would go crazy."[111] One historian notes, referring to Walker's Texas Division, that it was surrounded by "dens of suffering" throughout the Civil War. After the unit had seen action at Milliken's bend, very

"Few of the Texans, grimy and stinking with sweat and dust and gunpowder, thought about bouquets and cheering ladies and bands playing 'Dixie' on the march back." The realities of death and destruction for those who witnessed it left a lasting impression.[112]

And the "dreadful field-hospitals" remained a constant reminder of the war's agonies. "The screams and groans of the poor fellows undergoing amputation are sometimes dreadful," recalled William Miller Owen, as "the sight of arms and legs surrounding those places, as they are thrown into great piles, is something one that has seen the results of battle can never forget."[113] Another Louisiana soldier noted a box "so full" of amputated limbs "that two horrible and bloody feet protruded out of the top."[114] Witnessing horrific scenes caused many soldiers to feel compassion for their fellow man—even if he happened to be an enemy. Years after the conflict, a 2nd Louisiana cavalryman's daughter related her father's humanity after the Battle of Yellow Bayou. "He said his heart was wrung at sight of the silent friends, and foes. . . . He was so overcome at the sight . . . he wept aloud, all alone on the field. He saw one Union soldier fatally wounded . . . lifted him to a more comfortable position, gave him water from his almost empty canteen. The poor fellow soon died, his last moments soothed by a weeping foe."[115]

But Civil War battles did not only result in dead or wounded soldiers. After an engagement, many soldiers remained unaccounted for. Labeling a soldier as missing in action produced great psychological stress for a soldier's loved ones, who were unsure of his fate. John A. Morgan's cousin Davis remained missing after the Battle of Baton Rouge in August 1862. Not knowing whether he was dead or alive, Morgan wrote that Davis could have been wounded or captured—or both.[116] One Louisiana soldier received word that his brother serving in the Army of Northern Virginia "is missing, and we are left in suspense regarding his fate."[117] Even among enemies, some men tried to notify relatives of a soldier's fate. Attempting to contact the family of a dead 7th Louisiana Confederate who died of his wounds at Gettysburg, one Union officer sent home a photograph of three children found in the rebel's pocket to help identify him. The story eventually made its way into *Harper's Weekly* but to no avail; however, years after the war a stroke of fate helped solve this mystery.[118] The confusion and uncertainties concerning a loved one's safety after a battle kept many relatives and friends in a state of anxiety, especially since many Louisiana soldiers had been sent to distant theaters. Unfortunately, not knowing a missing soldier's whereabouts was a common occurrence.

Wartime trauma caused many individuals to reflect personally on what they had seen or experienced. For soldiers, thoughts of home offered a mental respite from the conflict's bloodshed, but oftentimes failed to sooth their anxieties. One soldier stationed in Louisiana unsuccessfully dreamed about a life of peace. "I waked to find myself stretched uppon a rough blanket with the horrors of war pressing its self upon my once undisturbed mind."[119] Receiving letters from home sometimes further cultivated anxiety for soldiers. Encamped near Allen, Louisiana, one soldier noted how the recent letters he received reminded him that his loved ones were "surrounded by Yankees." He longed for the day "when the scenes of blood-shed, and the devastations of war, may be driven from my deer old state, as from all our southern homes." This, he claimed, could be accomplished by "the devotions" of Confederate leadership and "the well directed valor" of the South's fighting men.[120] "I hope some day is near at hand," wrote 8th Louisiana infantryman John McCormick, "Which may bring us the glad tidings of peace when every poor Soldier may return home and enjoy himself Oh how I do wish for that day to come."[121] Another Louisiana soldier also longed for the war's end, writing that "when will this terrible war of trial and trouble be over? When will our Seperation from our loved ones at home be over? . . . I can See nothing but a prolongation of our strife."[122]

While serving in Georgia, Louisiana soldier Robert Patrick also kept his thoughts on home—along with his reason for participating in the conflict. He mentioned how he "passed the grave of a Yankee who died yesterday" and felt no remorse at the "very small spot of earth" the corpse now occupied. Patrick's disregard for the Union soldier's fate stemmed from his belief that the Yankees had "come to the South to murder our citizens, burn our houses, desolate our homes and lay waste our country; to make war upon women and children, turning them out to die of cold and want." He further stated that this Yankee soldier met his "just reward, which is a grant of land from the Confederates of three feet by six, in an obscure spot . . . nothing to mark the spot except a small hillrock of red clay, which a few hard rains will wash away and it will disappear forever."[123]

The rigors of combat took both physical and psychological tolls on the men. "Three years in Confederate States service this day, and very tired," wrote one soldier. "I might say I am surfieted, in point of fact I am all most ready to 'holler 'nuff.'"[124] Battle stories varied from soldier to soldier, and not all men told of heroic actions or glory.[125] The battlefield of the mind tightly gripped the thoughts and emotions of soldiers and civilians separated and affected by war. As soldiers suffered, so did their civilian counterparts. But even in the midst of bloodshed, compassion remained visible. Waging—and surviving—the Civil War relied on the cooperative network between soldiers and civilians. Combat and its aftermath not only strengthened soldier and civilian communal ties but also became the agents for binding groups from different backgrounds. Though their wartime experiences remained complex, they were also inseparable.

EPILOGUE

The opening months of 1865 saw the Confederacy suffering—but not defeated. Soldiers continuously remained vigilant, even conducting examinations of their officers to test tactical proficiency. "I fear for my self," wrote Lt. John Coleman Sibley, "I have never given tactics much attention, and as I have had no book and [have] not been with the drill in several weeks I feel unprepared."[1] But major events transpired in Virginia that placed the war in its final throes. Americans, including Louisianians, were about to witness and undergo vast changes. The Confederacy's defeat and demobilization—just like camp life, trade, and combat—operated along social as well as political lines for Civil War soldiers. And the wartime bonds between soldiers and civilians would remain vibrant in the years to come.

Richmond's capitulation in early April brought mixed emotions from Louisiana's Confederates. Sarah L. Wadley noted that the crumbling Confederacy was "lost, lost, my God what a word, our country gone, I feel as if all were gone. I had never felt the possibility of this blow."[2] Confederate soldier Joseph Renwick wrote his wife from Shreveport that Richmond's fall was "very bad news indeed." However, he remained steadfast. "I have been expecting it for some time. & am not much disappointed. . . . I am not whipped yet." Too much was at stake for Renwick and like-minded Confederates to easily surrender as the consequences of defeat included economic and social upheaval.[3] Remaining defiant, one Missouri Confederate officer claimed that "the fall of everything east of the Mississippi don't warrant ignominious surrender of this department;" he argued that the Trans-Mississippi troops should "contest every inch of soil from here to the Rio Grande."[4] However, this was not to be. Dwindling supplies, high desertion rates, and growing demoralization plagued the Confederacy. The unfolding events of the spring of 1865, at least in the East, suggested the end was near.[5]

On April 9 General Lee's Army of Northern Virginia, which included what remained of the famed Louisiana Tigers, surrendered at Appomattox Courthouse. Upon receiving word of the event, Sarah Morgan sadly wrote, "Everybody cried, but I would not, satisfied that God will still save us."[6] Shocked at first upon hearing the news of surrender, 26th Louisiana Capt. Jared Young Sanders wrote, "Great God, grant that all this is false."[7] Capt. E. John Ellis wrote from prison camp that Lee's surrender brought a wave of disappointment to him and his fellow prisoners, claiming, "It is impossible to tell what we felt then. Many, aye, the majority of the prisoners said that all was lost and that our cause had failed."[8] Such a blow to the Confederacy's most celebrated army and commander dampened any hopes of victory as most Confederates began to accept defeat, even in the Trans-Mississippi theater.[9]

Many Louisianians hoped that Lee's surrender would also mean peace.[10] But peace for many Louisianians—and the nation—did not come with the events at Appomattox Courthouse. Just days later, a Louisiana planter wrote, "President A. Lincoln was killed. . . . Great God what is our poor suffering people to do or think of such a thing."[11] E. John Ellis recalled the responses to the news of Lincoln's assassination among Confederate prisoners as he wrote, the "announcement was received with silent regret by all the prisoners, with, perhaps, half a dozen exceptions."[12] Priscilla Bond also noted Lincoln's assassination and the surrenders of generals Lee, Johnson, and Taylor in her diary. "I think the Confederacy," she wrote, "must be pretty nearly played out."[13]

General Lee's defeat sounded the Confederacy's death knell and unraveled the logistical, political, social, and military issues that had plagued the Confederacy during the war. William Marvel argues that Lee's soldiers' demoralization and high-desertion rates in the spring of 1865 led to this military failure.[14] Though many Louisiana troops remained in the field awaiting orders for further action, it was the surrender at Appomattox that unleashed Confederate frustration—even in Louisiana. This does not suggest that Louisiana's Confederates desired defeat, shed their Confederate identity, or embraced the

Union; instead, the war years—marred by much suffering, numerous deaths, and unimaginable chaos—had mentally and physically wore them down.[15] What soldiers and civilians had once given freely (or were forced to give) to preserve their nation they now took back.

By May 1865, Confederate soldiers and civilians—including women—in Shreveport raided government storehouses. Whatever could be gathered by the looters was taken; one veteran noted a "scene which beggared description. Government stores, of every imaginable description, were seized, the streets filled with goods, official papers, etc., scattered everywhere. It was awful, terrible beyond portrayal."[16] Writing from Alexandria, Asst. Adj. Gen. David F. Boyd told the 7th Louisiana Cavalry's commander, "The fact can no longer be concealed that the whole army and people, with scarce an individual exception, are resolved to fight no more, and to break up the army at all hazards. All is confusion and demoralization here, nothing like order or discipline remains."[17] Soldiers and civilians fought the war together, and now they ended it together.

Even before Appomattox, some Louisiana civilians believed the war had been already lost. A year before Lee's surrender, some Louisianians wrote to their loved ones in uniform, urging them to come home. One Louisiana mother explained to her son that widespread destruction, misery, and death, not honor and glory, was the only outcome of the conflict.[18] E. W. Moore, a planter residing in Washington, Louisiana, summed up his destitute situation to an uncle as he explained, "The closing of the war . . . leaves us all in a very exhausted and ruined condition and I anticipate much suffering—as for myself—I have been completely ruined."[19] Noting the toll the war had taken on his property, one Louisianian told his children, "Our old place looks desolate Enough and it will be a long time before it is in order again."[20] The South's social restructuring led to many new challenges, especially in getting plantations and farms back into operation. Land value declined during the postwar years, with some areas losing more than half their value.[21]

Though denying defeat lingered in the minds of some soldiers, the desire for peace—and to return home—proved a strong motivator. In the waning days of war, one Union officer witnessed the growing discouragement and poor performance among his Confederate foes, as he wrote that "they do not fight as they did."[22] Many Confederates serving in the Trans-Mississippi theater realized that further resistance would likely unleash the full might of the Union army on them. Continuing the fight also hindered a soldier's ability to reunite with his family. As with other instances during the conflict, impatient soldiers took matters into their own hands.[23]

Lt. John Coleman Sibley noted that the troops encamped in central Louisiana were "teribly [sic] demoralized. 2 hundred deserted from the forts at Alexandria and the 5th La. Cavalry in three days." Seeing the writing on the wall, officers allowed soldiers to "leave and go home . . . but all are asked to remain and see what the winding up will be," wrote Sibley.[24] Civilians noted the large numbers of soldiers returning home. Priscilla Bond wrote on May 21 that "soldiers are leaving their commands by companies—even regiments leave." She longed to see her husband and hoped he would be among the soldiers heading home.[25] Writing from New Orleans, Henry Rightor hoped for an official end to "this wicked war" and for the nation to reconcile. He noted the subsequent surrenders of Generals Johnson and Taylor, which "if this is all true the war is virtually Ended."[26]

Louisiana's largest surrender occurred in Washington in late June. As these men laid down their arms, the surrendered soldiers who had served in the Eastern theater began arriving home. Union authorities instructed Confederate parolees to remain at home, not take up arms against the United States, obey the law, and wait until properly exchanged. Also, these men could no longer wear their Confederate uniforms in public.[27] As the Confederacy crumbled, the long-awaited end of hostilities, which meant soldiers could return to civilian life, had finally come. High-ranking Confederate officials bid their parting soldiers farewell and reminded them of their sacrifices and shared struggles.[28] Soldiers, who had remained vigilant during the conflict and obeyed orders, were given their final commands as Confederates. Instead of resisting, Confederate commanders promoted cooperation with the United States. Cooperation would provide some stability in the war-torn South and hopefully make their transition back to civilian life a little smoother.

What remained of Louisiana's Confederate government quickly dissolved. Writing from Shreveport in early June 1865, Gov. Henry Watkins Allen issued a statement to his "Fellow Citizens" of Louisiana. "I have thought it my duty to address you a few words in parting from you, perhaps forever. . . . The war is over, the contest is ended, the soldiers are disbanded and gone to their homes, and now there is in Louisiana no opposition whatever to the constitution and laws of the United States." Allen's address offered solemn words to the state's war survivors, explaining to his fellow Louisianians, "You, who like myself, have lost all (and ho, how many there are) must begin life anew. Let us not talk of despair, nor whine about our misfortunes, but with strong arms and stout hearts adapt ourselves to the circumstances which surround us."[29] Opinions varied on how best to overcome the Confederacy's loss, but soldiers and civilians together had to come to terms with their defeat.

The sights of disbanding and returning Confederate soldiers remained common throughout the summer. One steamboat passenger heading up the Mississippi River from New Orleans noted that "at many points on the river we were hailed by disbanded Confederate soldiers, en route to their homes, who wished to be taken on board. . . . At West Baton Rouge some 1500 disbanded Confederate soldiers were encamped, awaiting transportation." One group of Louisiana soldiers in North Carolina aimed to get home by railroad. Those less fortunate in obtaining a ride via steam power resorted to walking, and New Orleans became a major hub for returning soldiers. One newspaper reported that the Confederates seemed worn down by years of fighting: "A hard life seemed upon their faces, bronzed upon their features. It is seen in the curl of their fingers when at rest, fingers that are used to handling the cartridge, pulling the trigger, limbs that have sloughed their way night and day through many a long and weary march."[30] For the surrendered Confederates, their return home proved their final foraging expedition. Just as during the war, soldiers sought civilian cooperation. One Louisianian remembered obtaining "some corn-bread and milk from a kind-hearted old negro woman."[31] Without civilian support, demobilized Confederate soldiers would have confronted increased suffering.

Louisiana's residents paid a high price in the cost of lives during the conflict. Many homes were without husbands, fathers, and sons—and Louisianians from all walks of life felt the sting of wartime suffering. Catherine Cornelius, an ex-slave who lost a brother in the conflict, spoke for many Louisianians when she told an interviewer, "Ah nebber want to see anudder war."[32] For the returning Confederates, the decision to obey the Union's laws and instructions remained an individual one. Many Louisiana Confederate officers took the amnesty oath, promising to support all "Laws and Proclamations which have been made during the existing rebellion, with reference to the emancipation of slaves."[33] A handful of extremists decided to abandon the reunited nation altogether and seek citizenship in (or offer their military services to) foreign countries.[34]

Reconstruction, which included rebuilding the war-torn South, legally

abolished slavery; however, offering ex-slaves civil rights would prove a long—
and violent—road. For some White Louisianians, even the idea of being reconstructed brought on disgust, and resistance towards reunification, which meant
bringing the former Confederacy back into the Union, began well before the
military campaigning had ended. The following excerpt from Sarah L. Wadley's
journal entry on October 27, 1864, provides insight into the resistance attitudes
that many Louisianians like her harbored. "The very idea of 'reconstruction,'"
she wrote, "sends a thrill of horror and disgust through my veins. Oh! what a
shame to our principles, what a wrong to those who have nobly fought and died
for our cause; and to the thousands of brave men now in arms, to admit such
an idea, if our grievances were so great in time of peace that we could not bear
them, what hope of honourable union can we now have! honourable union! I
scout the words, there is none such, there is only shame for us, subjugation and
national death in the idea of reconstruction."[35] Many Southerners feared that a
new social order only spelled disaster, especially with the potential disruption of
the South's racial order. One Louisiana officer wrote to his sweetheart in 1864,
"The negroe will never be our equals while they live—when dead the poore de-
luded race may commingle their blood with an inferior race—the Yankees,—but
never, forbid it God, with Southern, *whites*. The[y] can never be our equals,
though they may attain a superiority over the Yankees."[36] Facing the wartime
devastation and violence that transpired throughout the state kept grudges alive,
and the remaining presence of the Union army in Louisiana, which would be
used to enforce reconstruction, did not help matters.[37] But as politics remained
a contested field during the Reconstruction Era and beyond, many veterans
wished to put the war behind them. These ex-Confederates sought to carry on
with their lives, but for many Louisiana veterans, especially those maimed by
the war, this proved a difficult task.[38]

Reconciliation efforts between Union and Confederate veterans continued throughout the latter nineteenth and early twentieth centuries with some
success. Especially for the famed Louisiana Tigers, who served in the Army
of Northern Virginia, the legends of their heroic actions—and fighting spirit—
remained affixed to their wartime service, even gaining notoriety from both
veterans and civilians from across the nation. One Kansas newspaper noted
how association with the Louisiana Tigers, "that band of heroes in the rough is
the highest distinction. Sometimes as a gray and bent man passes slowly along
a quiet street in New Orleans loungers under the awnings of the other side

point him out and say to each other: 'He is one of them.'"[39] Veteran and battle-field reunions—far removed from the bloody war years—provided ex-soldiers a chance to reminisce about the conflict, often showing good will toward their former foes. However, these veterans were not alone. Their reunions and cer-emonies occurred in the midst of civilian onlookers.[40]

The intermingling of veterans and civilians in the postwar years, which had also been a common sight during the conflict, highlights how the Civil War was and the memory of it remained socially connected. While remembering and celebrating soldier comradery was common in the postwar years, many veter-ans also reminisced about the bonds they formed with civilians during their time in the service—bonds, in some cases, which remained strong. Louisiana Capt. Alexander Hart, who was wounded at the Battle of Antietam, owed the preservation of his left leg to a Virginia woman, who had urged the surgeon to hold off on amputating it until she could have a go at mending it. Charmed by Hart's good looks, she claimed, "So young and handsome a man should not lose a leg." Hart's friendship with the lady continued well after the war as he made annual trips to Virginia to see her.[41]

Some soldiers who served in the 8th Louisiana Infantry remained in contact with Maggie Williams, a female companion from Winchester, Virginia. "Having arrived to my native home once more It is with great pleasure that I take my pen in hand to write you a few lines hoping they will reach you and find you and your family all well," wrote Emile E. Delseries. Much of his conversation turned to the troubles of readjusting to civilian life, along with getting used to the social restructuring initiated during Reconstruction.[42] Reminiscing about the conflict was a common theme in the postwar letters written to civilian friends made during the war. "I often think of our struggling for independence the many hardships & privations endured By southern soldiers & how many hard trips we had up & down that old Valley," one Louisiana ex-soldier wrote.[43]

Forever changed by their wartime experiences, different fates awaited Lou-isiana's Confederate veterans as they demobilized and rejoined society. For some soldiers, their lives ended in financial failure, suicide, accidental or un-timely death, or the violence surrounding Reconstruction's political turmoil. By contrast, other ex-Confederates found success in business and agricultural ventures or engaged in meaningful and charitable service as medical profes-sionals or clergymen.[44] New York–born Louisiana militiaman H. A. Snyder had abandoned the Confederacy long before the war's end. He rekindled (or openly displayed) his love for the Union once Federal troops arrived in New Orleans. Having returned to running his New Orleans business, he and his family eventually returned North.[45] After the 2nd Louisiana Cavalry's disbandment, Lt. John Coleman Sibley returned home to his wife and surviving children in Sabine Parish and entered the mercantile business. Though his young daughter Ella passed away while he was in the service, Sibley and his wife had the joy of bringing another child into this world before his death in 1870.[46]

After taking the oath of allegiance to the Union on June 13, 1865, Capt. E. John Ellis prepared to leave Johnson's Island prison camp. He hoped for a better life, writing, "Rise once more the curtain of hope and active life. Hail 'Home Sweet Home.'" Before his death in 1889, Ellis got involved in politics and became a Louisiana Congressman, serving from 1874 to 1885.[47] W. H. King relocated to Texas after the Civil War and "held meetings and lectures on phrenology," which is "the study of the structure of the skull to determine a person's character and mental capacity." He later became a druggist and postmaster. King married twice, losing both wives (who were sisters): the first by death, the second by divorce. He eventually left Texas to live with his son in Oklahoma, where he died in 1903.[48]

Before dying in 1920, Frank L. Richardson returned home after the war and later graduated from the University of Louisiana (today's Tulane University) in 1870. He became a lawyer in New Orleans and became involved in Reconstruction politics. Richardson was an organizer of the White League and participated in the infamous Battle of Liberty Place in 1874. He supported Francis T. Nicholls (a maimed Louisiana Tiger officer) for governor, stood against the state lottery, and served in other political and civic organizations. Richardson also helped to reorganize the Louisiana Historical Society, and his charitable contributions aided suffering families affected by the 1878 yellow fever epidemic. In 1885, Richardson wrote his wartime memoir. He dedicated it *"To my little son, Frank. He will learn from this record the hardships through which his father passed and will appreciate the blessings of peace."* Sadly, his son—like many of Louisiana's Confederates years earlier—died in the flower of his youth.[49]

Indeed, much had been lost by Louisiana's Confederate soldiers and civilians who now reckoned with defeat. Their wartime experiences occurred together—fighting the Civil War had only been possible with cooperation. True, many soldiers depended on one another (and in many cases themselves) when the Confederate government failed to provision them. However, these men depended even more on local civilians for basic needs, which often made a nebulous distinction between the home front and the battle front. Whether physical or psychological, civilian support played a major role in sustaining the Confederate war effort—even though tensions between (and within) the two groups existed. For the war's survivors, their relationships continued, as former soldiers and civilians during wartime remained in contact, keeping their interaction (physical or through correspondence) alive. Reflection and reminiscing replaced their wartime memories and miseries, and, much as times had been during the war, the future remained uncertain. For Louisiana's Confederate veterans and their civilian counterparts, their final test of cooperation now lay with how to respond to the Union and its Reconstruction policies. The task of moving forward fell on their shoulders.

NOTES

1. Lee quoted in Glatthaar, *General Lee's Army*, xiv.

2. Gary Gallagher argues that many Confederates believed that success lay in both military victory and a "tenacious popular will rooted in a sense of national community." Confederate nationalism had roots in community ties. See Gallagher, *The Confederate War*, 5.

3. Weitz, *More Damning than Slaughter*, 26–27.

4. Glatthaar, *General Lee's Army*, 24. LeeAnn Whites explores the role and importance of civilian support, which she calls the "household or domestic supply line." Whites also argues for the importance of viewing aspects of the Civil War through the lens of a "household" war as female civilians played active roles in supporting guerrilla operations in Kansas and Missouri. See Whites, "Written on the Heart: Soldiers' Letters, the Household Supply Line, and the Relational War," in Frank and Whites, *Household War*, 118–19; Whites, "Forty Shirts and a Wagonload of Wheat," 56–78. J. Matthew Ward also examines the central role the household played in Civil War Louisiana, along with civilian relationships—and responses—to both Confederate and Union occupation. Government and military power, along with the fluidity of loyalties and allegiances between nation and state, remained visible (and contested) within Civil War households. See Ward, *Garden of Ruins*, 4–14.

5. For a detailed and captivating study on the Louisiana soldiers who served in the Army of Northern Virginia, see Jones, *Lee's Tigers Revisited*, and his previous work *Lee's Tigers*. Other works on Louisiana soldiers and their wartime exploits include Mingus, *The Louisiana Tigers in the Gettysburg Campaign;* Stalling, *Louisianians in the Western Confederacy;* Hewitt and Bergeron, eds., *Louisianians in the Civil War.*

6. Paul Escott argues that the Confederate "military affairs and civilian life . . . was unusually close," and military necessity often trumped the needs and comforts of civilians. See Escott, *Military Necessity*, 72, 165–77. The idea of a "household war" drove the conflict and heavily impacted its course. For some historians it was the home front—and its people—that shaped wartime events. See: Frank and Whites, *Household War*, 1–5.

7. Weitz, *More Damning than Slaughter*, 5.

8. Winters, *The Civil War in Louisiana*, xi, 428; Booth, comp., *Records of Louisiana Confederate Soldiers and Louisiana Confederate Commands, vol. 1, 3, 6–7.*

9. The parish figures cited above are not definitive but are meant to give a general representation. They are based on Louisiana's Confederate companies that displayed their parish of origin and are found in Bergeron, *Guide to Louisiana Confederate Military Units 1861–1865.*

10. Jones, *Lee's Tigers Revisited,* 20, 393–415. The statistics cited are from Jones's appendix data for each Louisiana unit that was sent to Virginia. Also, to further complicate these wartime statistics, it must be noted that some soldiers originally hailed from different parishes throughout the state but were mustered into Confederate service in New Orleans, which inflates the city's contributions.

11. Sacher, *Confederate Conscription and the Struggle for Southern Soldiers,* 4; Sacher, "A Very Disagreeable Business," 144.

12. Woodward, "Marching Masters," 260, 269–77.

13. Glymph, "Noncombatant Military Laborers in the Civil War," 26–28.

14. Ward also explores the relationships of Louisiana's diverse population during the Civil War through a "household analysis" as both Confederate and Union forces occupied the state; however, my work focuses on Louisiana's Confederate soldiers' wartime experiences and interactions with civilians (at home and abroad) within the framework of both the military and their households and communities. See Ward, *Garden of Ruins,* 8–13.

15. Roland, *Louisiana Sugar Plantations,* 118; John Guild letter to sister, July 21, 1863, John H. Guild Letters, 1862–1864, Mss.3204, Louisiana and Lower Mississippi Valley Collections, LSU Libraries, Baton Rouge, Louisiana (hereafter cited as LSU). Union loyalty—even among soldiers—sometimes shifted. A Union soldier stationed near Baton Rouge wrote that a cavalryman "deserted . . . he was a southerner and enlisted on our side." See Anonymous letter to Isa, April 18, 1863, Folder Misc.: A, April 18, 1863, Mss. 2824, Anonymous Civil War Letter, LSU.

16. Frank Richardson to Mother, October 8, 1862, Folder 3, Frank Liddell Richardson Papers, 1851–1869, Series 1, 1862–1867, #631, Southern Historical Collection, Louis Round Wilson Special Collections Library, University of North Carolina at Chapel Hill (hereafter cited as UNC).

17. D. A. Morgan letter to Cousin, October 12, 1861, Box 1, Folder 2, May–December 1861, Mss. 1712, John A. Morgan Papers, LSU.

18. Lisa Tendrich Frank makes gender central to Sherman's raid and notes that Sherman hoped to break the spirit of the elite slaveholding women, especially since he blamed the war on the South's slaveholding class. See Frank, *The Civilian War,* 4–18. For studies on wartime policies and the effects toward Southern civilians, see Grimsley, *The Hard Hand of War,* and McCurry, *Confederate Reckoning.*

19. Escott, *Military Necessity,* xiv; "Why Louisiana Should Commemorate the Civil War," *Morning Advocate,* January 22, 1961, Larry Crain Collection, box 21, folder 6, Center for Southeast Louisiana Studies and Archives, Southeastern Louisiana University (hereafter cited as SLU).

20. For a study on the debate about when the Civil War really ended, see Downs, *After Appomattox.*

21. According to the 1860 census, Frank Richardson was sixteen years old and from a wealthy slaveholding family. His father's real and personal estate was valued at $100,000 and $80,000, respectively. The UNC Southern Historical Collection's archival finding aid lists

Frank Richardson's regiment as Company I of the 2nd Louisiana Regiment; however, according to Booth's *Records of Louisiana Confederate Soldiers and Louisiana Confederate Commands,* two entries exist for Frank Richardson, and one for F. L. Richardson. Though all entries are for the same man, Richardson originally enlisted in the 13th Louisiana Infantry, then transferred to the Washington Artillery's 5th Company, and finally to the 2nd Louisiana Cavalry. See Booth, comp., *Records of Louisiana Confederate Soldiers and Louisiana Confederate Commands, Vol. III, Book 2,* 309.

22. Booth's records list William H. King as a private in Company B, 28th Louisiana Infantry, enlisting at Monroe in 1862. He was captured at Bayou Teche and later exchanged and paroled. See Booth, comp., *Records of Louisiana Confederate Soldiers and Louisiana Confederate Commands, Vol. III, Book 1,* 71. King also served in the 4th Engineer Regiment as a sergeant in Company H. For more information on King's family, life, and military service, see Joiner, "No Pardons to Ask nor Apologies to Make," 30–50. See also King's full-length published journal: Joiner, Joiner, and Cardin, eds., *No Pardons to Ask, nor Apologies to Make.*

23. The 1860 census lists "H. A. Schnieder's" birthplace as New York. He is a married twenty-eight-year-old clerk with one daughter. Snyder's diary also discusses camp life and the Union takeover of New Orleans. For his service record, see Booth, comp., *Records of Louisiana Confederate Soldiers and Louisiana Confederate Commands, Vol. III, Book 2,* 642.

24. The 1860 census for Sabine Parish lists John Coleman Sibley as a married twenty-four-year-old, working as a clerk in the district court, and having real and personal estate value at $3,500 and $1,000, respectively. His two-year-old daughter, Ella, will sadly pass away while he is serving in the 2nd Louisiana Cavalry. Sibley enlisted in Natchitoches in 1862, originally as a 1st sergeant before getting promoted to 2nd lieutenant nearly a year later. He was captured and exchanged in 1864 and paroled at the war's end on June 13, 1865. See Booth, comp., *Records of Louisiana Confederate Soldiers and Louisiana Confederate Commands, Vol. III, Book 2,* 561.

25. Listed as Ezekiel J. Ellis, he served in Companies F and H, 16th Louisiana Infantry Regiment, as a 1st lieutenant and later captain. He enlisted on September 29, 1861, at Camp Moore, was captured at Missionary Ridge in 1863, and became a POW at Johnson's Island, Ohio. Ellis took the oath of allegiance to the United States on June 13, 1865. Buck, "A Louisiana Prisoner-of-War on Johnson's Island, 1863–65," 234–35. For his service record, see Booth, comp., *Records of Louisiana Confederate Soldiers and Louisiana Confederate Commands, Vol. II,* 769.

1. LEAVING THE UNION

1. Sherman quoted in Bragg, *Louisiana in the Confederacy.* Future Confederate general P. G. T. Beauregard, who had sons attending the Louisiana State Seminary of Learning, casually wrote to Sherman and noted that the political turmoil over secession would likely subsist. See Williams, *P. G. T. Beauregard,* 44.

2. Benjamin quoted in Hewitt and Bergeron, eds., *Louisianians in the Civil War,* 75.

3. Bragg, *Louisiana in the Confederacy,* 26–27. Aaron Sheehan-Dean questions the idea of widespread Southern support of secession as he notes that, although secession won out with over 50 percent of eligible voters, it was "often just barely." See Sheehan-Dean, *The Calculus of Violence,* 31. Van D. Odom noted that Louisiana's secessionist convention's "popular vote—

17,296 for the Cooperationists and 20,448 for the Secessionists—indicates that the voice of the people of Louisiana was not too strong for separation from the Union." Odom, "The Political Career of Thomas Overton Moore," 26.

4. Hearn, *The Capture of New Orleans, 1862,* 16.

5. Dew, "The Long Lost Returns," 358; Dew, "Who Won the Secession Election in Louisiana?" 18–32. Sacher argues that Louisiana's partisan politics during the antebellum era was linked to the national stage, and the preservation of slavery and white liberty eventually shifted the state increasingly into the Democrat camp. See Sacher, *A Perfect War of Politics.* Roland also argues how the debate over slavery and the institution's preservation came to dominate Louisiana's politics. See Roland, "Louisiana and Secession," 389–99. Grimsley discusses the views of Northerners toward Southern secession, which for some individuals was rooted in social class and legal debates. See Grimsley, *The Hard Hand of War,* 8–17.

6. McPherson uses the French term *"rage militaire*—a patriotic furor" to describe early Civil War soldiers' motives for volunteering. He claims that though the initial war fever "eventually cooled," waves of it reoccurred later in the war. See McPherson, *For Cause and Comrades,* 16–17. For more on citizen-soldier ideology relating to antebellum America and republican virtues, see Lang, *In the Wake of War,* 4–8.

7. W. H. Pearce letter to John W. Gurley, December 3, 1860, Mss. 507, Box 1, Folder 2b, LSU (Louisiana Digital Library).

8. Warren A. Durant to Cousin Hal, December 26, 1860, Folder 12, Slack Family Papers, Subseries 1.1, Correspondence, 1860, #3598-Z, UNC.

9. Henry Slack to Hal, December 10, 1860, Folder 12, Slack Family Papers, UNC.

10. Warren A. Durant to Cousin Hal, December 26, 1860, Folder 12, Slack Family Papers, UNC. Future Confederate general Robert E. Lee noted the brewing political tension that quickly engulfed both Northern and Southern extremists. Despite the growing polarization— and his willingness to put state loyalty before the nation—Lee hoped political moderates would quell the upheaval. See Horn, *The Man Who Would Not Be Washington,* 98–99.

11. Rosen, *The Jewish Confederates,* 149.

12. Frazier, *Fire in the Cane Field,* 22–23, 29.

13. Ward, *Garden of Ruins,* 20. Bragg highlights the importance of the national debate over the expansion of slavery; however, he notes it was the wealthy slaveholding Louisianians who led the secessionist charge. See Bragg, *Louisiana in the Confederacy,* 8. Winters argues that "Secession had not come to Louisiana unexpectedly. . . . The social, economic, and political crisis of 1860 had finally produced a feeling of hopeless defeat and ruin for the slave-owning aristocracy of the state." See Winters, *The Civil War in Louisiana,* 4–13. For a detailed study on secession and its political and ideological debates on the national level, see Freehling, *The Road to Disunion, Volume II;* and Nelson and Sheriff, *A People at War,* 48–52.

14. Shugg, "A Suppressed Co-Operationist Protest Against Secession," 4–5.

15. Haller Nutt letter to Alonzo Snyder, December 16, 1860, Mss. 655, Box 11, Folder 44, LSU (Louisiana Digital Library). King Cotton was a serious money maker for Louisiana, the South, and the entire nation—disrupting its economic productivity was a serious matter. One bale had the value of "more than most people earned in a year." See Edmonds, *The Guns of Port Hudson, Volume Two,* 4. However, Stève Sainlaude claims that Southern secession—at least in France's viewpoint—held great trade potential with the removal of tariffs. From an economic

standpoint, Sainlaude notes, "The Southern states had everything to gain from secession. Their valuable resources were just waiting to be exploited." See Sainlaude, *France and the American Civil War,* 84–85.

16. H. Safford letter to Mary, January 10, 1861, Box 1, Folder 5, Safford Collection, Northwestern State University Watson Memorial Library, Cammie G. Henry Research Center, Natchitoches, Louisiana (hereafter cited as NSU).

17. Edward J. Gay letter to L. Janin, January 17, 1861, Mss. 1925, Box 40, Folder 378, LSU (Louisiana Digital Library). David Plater notes that Gay's sympathies were with the South, but he realized that the Union would better protect his property and financial interests. See Plater, *The Butlers of Iberville Parish, Louisiana,* 164–67.

18. Shugg, "A Suppressed Co-Operationist Protest Against Secession," 6, 7. Other individuals who voted against secession during Louisiana's secession convention shared Taliaferro's sentiment of keeping their state tied to the western states. J. A. Rozier and Christian Roselius both opposed secession and harbored fears that the secessionists did not represent the Louisianians' best interests. See Bragg, *Louisiana in the Confederacy,* 45.

19. In southeastern Louisiana's Florida parishes, Samuel C. Hyde Jr. notes that "slightly less than 41 percent of voters in the plantation parishes supported immediate secession" compared with "a 53 percent majority in the piney woods voted" for disunion. Hyde claims a variety of reasons existed for the region's pro-secession sentiment. See Hyde, *Pistols and Politics,* 105–6.

20. Sarah Lois Wadley Journal (typed transcription), 77–78, Folder 7a, in the Sarah Lois Wadley Journal, Volume 1, #1258, UNC, hereafter cited as Wadley Journal. Anyone suspected of harboring abolitionist sympathies, which included visitors and businessmen, was sometimes met with threats and violence. See Ward, *Garden of Ruins,* 22.

21. Caskey, *Secession and Restoration of Louisiana,* 21.

22. Roland, *Louisiana Sugar Plantations,* 20.

23. Hewitt and Bergeron, eds., *Louisianians in the Civil War,* 9–10.

24. W. H. Pearce letter to John W. Gurley, December 3, 1860, Mss. 507, Box 1, Folder 2b, LSU (Louisiana Digital Library). Pearce's newspaper did not misrepresent the preachers. Benjamin Palmer and W. T. Leacock were both ministers who advocated for secession and "defended the institution of slavery and upheld the right of a state to resist." Winters, *Civil War in Louisiana,* 8. William A. Blair notes how ministers "ranked among the most important proslavery ideologues," especially in the Deep South. See Blair, "Extremists at the Gate: Origins of the American Civil War," in *Struggle for a Vast Future,* ed. Aaron Sheehan-Dean, 29.

25. Wadley Journal (typed transcription), 85–86, Folder 7a, Volume 1, UNC. For a detailed analysis of the role of religion and the pro-slavery arguments of Leacock and Palmer during the secession crisis, see Nguyen, "Preaching Disunion: Clergymen in the Louisiana Secession Crisis" in *The Enigmatic South,* ed. Hyde.

26. Governor Thomas Overton Moore, "Inaugural address of Governor Thomas O. Moore: delivered January 23, 1860 to the Legislature of the State of Louisiana" (Baton Rouge: J. M. Taylor, State Printer, 1860), 5. An early 1860 newspaper report cited Moore's support and strong ties with other Southern states: "I am sure, however, that Louisiana dearly as she loves the Union will never separate herself from her sister slaveholding States." Odom, "The Political Career of Thomas Overton Moore," 20–21.

27. Frazier, *Fire in the Cane Field,* 21; Sacher, "Our Interest and Destiny Are the Same," 267.

28. Unpublished diary by Isaac Erwin, entry for January 27, 1861, Juanita Henry Collection Bound Volume 179, Bound Volumes, Melrose Collection, NSU (hereafter cited as Isaac Erwin Diary, NSU).

29. Mimmie to Cousin April 2, 1861, Folder 13, Slack Family Papers, UNC.

30. John S. Foster letter to Grandma. January 30, 1861. Folder 1, 1861, #2184, Foster (James and Family) Correspondence, 1861–1866, LSU.

31. Bragg, *Louisiana in the Confederacy*, 47. Though Grivot's report related that numerous Southerners sought to join the Confederate war effort, at least one Louisiana newspaper in August 1861 found space in its columns to note three Louisiana natives who received commissions in the Union army. See "Native Louisianians in Lincoln's Army," *South-Western* (Shreveport, LA), August 21, 1861.

32. The Baton Rouge arsenal was under the command of Maj. Joseph Haskins, a one-armed Mexican War veteran who was undeterred by the militia infantry force sent to take possession of the post. Haskins, who had artillery, claimed, "I've lost one arm in the defense of my flag and I will lose the other or even my life if necessary before I surrender to that lot of ragamuffins on the Boulevard." Governor Moore sent for a detachment from the Washington Artillery to satisfy Haskins's resolve and provide a scenario for his honorable surrender. See Dufour, *The Night the War Was Lost*, 20–21.

33. Bragg, *Louisiana in the Confederacy*, 49–50. On January 17, 1861, Sherman received $500 in funds "to provide for the transportation and storage of arms" and another $500 allotment for his "one year's salary as Ordnance officer" on January 28, 1861. See *Special Report of the Military Board to the Legislature of the State of Louisiana* (Baton Rouge: J. M. Taylor, State Printer, 1861), 7.

34. Ward, *Garden of Ruins*, 26–28.

35. Taylor, "Discontent in Confederate Louisiana," 410.

36. Roland, *Louisiana Sugar Plantations*, 22–23.

37. Stone, *Brokenburn: The Journal of Kate Stone, 1861–1868*, ed., Anderson, 19.

38. Julia LeGrand, quoted in Frazier, *Fire in the Cane Field*, 25.

39. Frank, *The Civilian War*, 24–25.

40. Wadley Journal (typed transcription), 129–130, Folder 7a, Volume 1, UNC.

41. Bragg, *Louisiana in the Confederacy*, 33.

42. Dufour, *The Night the War Was Lost*, 16.

43. Dawson, *A Confederate Girl's Diary*, ed. Robertson, 32.

44. Handerson, *Yankee in Gray*, ed. Cummer, 87–88.

45. Stone, *Brokenburn: The Journal of Kate Stone*, ed., Anderson, 14.

46. Rosen, *The Jewish Confederates*, 38. About three hundred Jews lived in Shreveport by 1860 and about seventy-eight (most of whom were recent immigrants) joined the Confederate service. See ibid., 174.

47. Louis Hébert Autobiography (typed copy), page 6, Folder 1, Louis Hébert Autobiography, #3047-Z, UNC.

48. Winters, *Civil War in Louisiana*, 17–18. While a POW, Ellis recalled his opinions about the war's opening scenes in his diary as he claimed that even after all the secessionist excitement "I did not yet partake of the revolution; I still hoped that every difference might be accommodated and the Union saved from impending peril." See E. John Ellis Diary, entry titled "A Ret-

rospect," 2. Box 1, Folder 1:2, v. 3 (typescript), E. John Ellis Diary, 1862–1865, Mss. 2795, LSU, hereafter cited as Ellis Diary, LSU.

49. John S. Foster letter to Grandma, January 30, 1861, Folder 1, 1861, Foster (James and Family) Correspondence, LSU.

50. John S. Foster letter to Pa, Dr. James Foster, January 11, 1861, Folder 1, 1861, Foster (James and Family) Correspondence, LSU.

51. Thomas W. Cutrer and T. Michael Parrish, eds., *Brothers in Gray,* 13.

52. Glatthaar, *General Lee's Army,* 24.

53. Alfred Flournoy Sr. letter to Charley, March 7, 1861, Folder 28, Mildred McCoy Collection, NSU.

54. Alfred Flournoy Sr. letter to Alfred Flournoy Jr. June 16, 1861, Folder 28, Mildred McCoy Collection, NSU. According to this letter, Flournoy seems to have had four sons in the service as he claimed, "A few days ago I wrote to William and Charley—today I write to you and Lucien." In another letter written by Alfred Jr. to his wife, Alfred Jr. states his father, Alfred Sr., "has three sons risking their lives every day." See Alfred Flourney letter to wife, September 22, 1861, Folder 28, Mildred McCoy Collection, NSU. In a letter written by Lucien to Alfred Sr., Lucien is a nephew. See Lucien Flournoy letter to Uncle (Alfred Flournoy Sr.). April 26/27, 1864, Folder 28, Mildred McCoy Collection, NSU.

55. John T. Jeter letter to William, June 25, 1861, in the Annie Jeter Carmouche Papers and Reminiscences, 1853–1915 (microfilm), #M-3022, UNC.

56. Donald Mackay letter to Margaret Butler, April 14, 1862, Mss. 1068, Box 1, Folder 3, LSU (Louisiana Digital Library).

57. Winters, *The Civil War in Louisiana,* 30–31; Wadley Journal (typed transcription), 87–88, Folder 7b, Volume 2, UNC.

2. RECRUITING AND ORGANIZING AN ARMY

1. Sarah Ker Butler letter to Margaret Butler, April 16, 1861, Mss. 1068, Box 1, Folder 2, LSU (Louisiana Digital Library). While no soldiers were killed during the actual engagement at Fort Sumter, one soldier lost his life and five others were wounded after a cannon burst in a salute to the Union withdrawal from the fort. See Williams, *P. G. T. Beauregard,* 61. Louisiana soldiers heading east to defend Florida brought about serious concern from Louisiana's political leaders, especially as the Confederate government continuously demanded supplies and arms. Governor Moore feared an invasion (via New Orleans) but the Confederate secretary of war claimed that Pensacola was under a higher threat. See Odom, "The Political Career of Thomas Overton Moore," 33–34. Some Louisianians applauded the action of sending troops to take Fort Pickens as one patriotic individual claimed, "I had me a fine Secession flag made, & as soon as we hear of the taking of Pickens, I am going to hoist her up on top of the house." See Alex de Clouet letter to Paul, May 9, 1861. UAAMC-COLL-22, Box 1, Folder 17, DeClouet Family Papers, University Archives and Acadiana Manuscripts Collection, Edith Garland Dupré Library, University of Louisiana at Lafayette, Lafayette, Louisiana (hereafter cited as ULL).

2. Vandiver, ed., "A Collection of Louisiana Confederate Letters," 7.

3. Horace Maynard, quoted in Wesley, *The Politics of Faith during the Civil War,* 126–27.

4. Taylor, "Discontent in Confederate Louisiana," 411.

5. Bragg, *Louisiana in the Confederacy*, 58.

6. John T. Jeter letter to William, April 18, 1861, in the Annie Jeter Carmouche Papers and Reminiscences, UNC.

7. Sheehan-Dean, *The Calculus of Violence*, 50. Over two million men served in the Union army and about nine hundred thousand in the Confederate army.

8. Escott, *Military Necessity*, 2-3. Escott notes that historians have linked the South's military tradition with several regional aspects: rural landscape, familiarity with the outdoors and handling firearms, ideals of chivalry, and the presence of slavery, which required constant discipline and the use of violence to regulate and maintain. Ward notes that "unequal households," referring to the South's variant social classes, could (at least at first) unite in a military crusade against the Union, especially when placed in a social context of "racial and social equality." See Ward, *Garden of Ruins*, 29.

9. Albert Batchelor quoted in Glatthaar, *General Lee's Army*, 33.

10. Dixon quoted in Hyde, *Pistols and Politics*, 107.

11. Escott, *Military Necessity*, 168. For the impact the household had on soldier motivation, see Frank and Whites, *Household War*, 3-4. Civilian attitudes toward the conflict varied, but the hype over politics and reasons for fighting were usually trumped by their concerns for "the fate of their soldier kin and the viability of their households." See LeeAnn Whites, "Written on the Heart," in Frank and Whites, *Household War*, 119. Sheehan-Dean notes that the destruction caused by Union forces in Virginia kept resources out of the hands of Confederate armies; however, it also fueled "Confederate hatred of the North." Protecting their families motivated soldiers to continue the struggle. See Sheehan-Dean, *Why Confederates Fought*, 5, 65-66. Glatthaar explains that family ties with Confederate soldiers usually led to military support, even if Southerners did not initially favor secession. See Glatthaar, *General Lee's Army*, 24.

12. Beauregard quoted in Williams, *P. G. T. Beauregard*, 46.

13. Culpepper, "The Life, Letters, and Legacy of Dr. Bartholomew Egan," 76. Some classes resumed "for the benefit of those students who were too young to serve in the war," but the conflict eventually forced the university's closing in 1863, as Mount Lebanon's facilities became a hospital. See ibid., 77, 83.

14. Andrew McCollam letter to Mother, January 20, 1861, Folder 13, Andrew McCollam Papers, Series 1.2, 1861, #449, UNC.

15. Andrew McCollam letter to Father, April 18, 1861, Folder 13, Andrew McCollam Papers, UNC.

16. Andrew McCollam letter to Father, May 1, 1861, Folder 13, Andrew McCollam Papers, UNC.

17. Statement of Louisiana Students at the University of North Carolina, [no month or day] 1861, Folder 1, Thomas Benjamin Davidson Papers, 1857-1866, #1922-Z, UNC.

18. "Battalion Mounted Men," *Pointe Coupee Democrat*, September 28, 1861; "[Communicated] Parish of Pointe Coupee," *Pointe Coupee Democrat*, September 28, 1861.

19. "They Are Gone," unnamed newspaper, no date, Folder 1, Scrapbook pages 7-8, Carmen Breazeale Collection, NSU.

20. "Miss Sallie Seogin's Address," *The South-Western* (Shreveport), September 18, 1861.

21. "Presentation of the Flag to the Lecomte Guards," and "Miss Lecomte's Address," unnamed newspaper, no date, Folder 1, Scrapbook, pages 3-4, Carmen Breazeale Collection, NSU.

The newspaper clipping describes the flag as "a rich and beautiful one, made of silk red, white and blue stripes, the corner being red, with a single star in the centre. It was presented by Miss Eliza Lecomte daughter of the gentleman who has given name to the Guards."

22. Handerson, *Yankee in Gray,* ed. Clyde Lottridge Cummer, 88.

23. Stone, *Brokenburn,* ed., Anderson, 13.

24. Ellis Diary, entry titled "A Retrospect," p. 17, LSU.

25. Cutrer and Parrish, eds., *Brothers in Gray,* 38.

26. *Special Report of the Military Board to the Legislature of the State of Louisiana* (Baton Rouge: J. M. Taylor, State Printer, 1861), 3–4.

27. Alex de Clouet letter to Paul, October 17, 1861, UAAMC-COLL-22, Box 1, Folder 17, DeClouet Family Papers, ULL. Governor Moore hoped the state's militia reorganization would be "so clear, stringent and comprehensive that evasion would be impossible." See Glatthaar, *General Lee's Army,* 12.

28. Alex de Clouet letter to Paul, May 9, 1861. UAAMC-COLL-22, Box 1, Folder 17, De-Clouet Family Papers, ULL. Led by "Mr. Alcibiade," likely refers to Alcibiade DeBlanc. This company became part of the 8th Louisiana Infantry.

29. Savas, "A Death at Mansfield: Col. James Hamilton Beard and the Consolidated Crescent Regiment," in *The Louisiana Purchase Bicentennial Series in Louisiana History, Volume V,* ed. Bergeron, 469.

30. Alfred Flournoy Sr. letter to Alfred Flournoy Jr. June 16, 1861. Folder 28, Mildred McCoy Collection, NSU.

31. Stone, *Brokenburn,* ed., Anderson, 17.

32. Schreckengost, *The First Louisiana Special Battalion,* 36.

33. Moriarty, *A Fine Body of Men,* 21.

34. Hughes, *The Pride of the Confederate Artillery,* 1, 10–11.

35. Stalling, *Louisianians in the Western Confederacy,* 6. The Zouave uniform was associated with elite troops in the French military, which began in 1830 after France conquered Algiers. See Schreckengost, *The First Louisiana Special Battalion,* 33–34.

36. Frank Richardson letter to Father, September 4, 1861, Folder 2, Frank Liddell Richardson Papers, UNC.

37. Jones, *Lee's Tigers,* 16.

38. "New German Company," *Daily Picayune,* May 3, 1861.

39. Rosen, *Jewish Confederates,* 28–29, 35, 37.

40. Bielski, *Sons of the White Eagle in the American Civil War,* 30–31, 52.

41. Ibid., 66–71.

42. Haynes, *A Thrilling Narrative,* ed., Bergeron, 17.

43. Many Acadians were "the *petits habitants*" who simply wanted to be left alone but were eventually conscripted. Brasseaux, *Acadian to Cajun,* 58–59, 63. Brasseaux notes a distinction between many of the river Acadians, who were more inclined to support the Confederacy, and the prairie Acadians, usually lower on the social ladder, who saw the conflict as an elitist affair. See ibid., 62, 73.

44. B. W. Blakewood quoted in Ibid., 62.

45. Taylor, *Destruction and Reconstruction,* 49.

46. Stalling, *Louisianians in the Western Confederacy,* 6–7.

47. Wallace, "Coppens' Louisiana Zouaves," 270.

48. Bielski, *Sons of the White Eagle,* 103–4.

49. Moriarty, *A Fine Body of Men,* 20.

50. Winters, *The Civil War in Louisiana,* 31–33. Irish immigrants were often found do-ing antebellum society's lowest-paying and dangerous work—even performing tasks, such as digging canals and working on steamboat engines, that slaves were not allowed to do. See Schreckengost, *The First Louisiana Special Battalion,* 36. One Louisiana regiment, the 6th Louisiana Infantry, had numerous Irishmen in its ranks, as James P. Gannon claimed the unit's roster contained "16 Murphys, nine Murrays, eight Sullivans, seven O'Neills, seven Ryans, a half-dozen each of the Fitzgeralds and the Collins,' and at least 54 'Micks,' . . . from McCauley and McCormick to McGee and McMahon." New Orleans had more Irish immigrants than any other Southern city. See Gannon, *Irish Rebels, Confederate Tigers,* iii. The drop-off in trade in New Orleans after war broke out affected more than the wealthy planters. Widespread layoffs for urban workers often encouraged enlistments. See Pierson, *Mutiny at Fort Jackson,* 38.

51. Hewitt uses Company K, 14th Louisiana Regiment, as an example, noting the presump-tion that most foreign-born soldiers were among the lower class. He only uses volunteers in his analysis, since conscript statistics show that draftees "were more likely to desert than were the volunteers." Hewitt and Bergeron, eds., *Louisianians in the Civil War,* 6, 137–39.

52. Kelley, *The Irish in New Orleans,* 58. Kelley also notes how some New Orleans Irish, though many were poor, "also viewed the abolition of slavery as detrimental to their economic and social standing in the South." Emancipation could mean "increased competition for jobs and a fear that an over-supplied labor market would lower wages." See ibid.

53. Wallace, "Coppens' Louisiana Zouaves," 270–71.

54. Sheehan-Dean, *Why Confederates Fought,* 9.

55. "The Free Colored Natives of Louisiana." *New Orleans Daily Delta,* December 28, 1860. For examples and information on Louisiana's Black slaveowners' antebellum experience, see Schweninger, "Antebellum Free Persons of Color in Postbellum Louisiana," 348–52.

56. Hollandsworth, *The Louisiana Native Guards,* 3, 5–6.

57. Ibid., 2, 4.

58. "(From Plaquemines) Parish of Plaquemines, May 15, 1861," *Carrollton Sun,* May 22, 1861; Winters, *The Civil War in Louisiana,* 34.

59. Ripley, *Slaves and Freedmen in Civil War Louisiana,* 102–3.

60. "Augustin Guards," *Natchitoches Union,* December 26, 1861; Mills, *The Forgotten People,* 233–35. Mills's work covers the early foundation of the *gens de couleur libre* (free people of color) in Natchitoches's Cane River region. By the time of the Civil War, these individuals had obtained wealth, land, and slaves and "publicly favored the Confederacy throughout the conflict. They deprived themselves and their families to help maintain Confederate forces. They volunteered their services for whatever uses the Confederacy had for them. . . . Their role in the war, in fact, differed only slightly from that of white Creole planters." See ibid., 229–30. For an overview of the Free Black experience in southwestern Louisiana, see Brasseaux, Fontenot, and Oubre, *Creoles of Color in the Bayou Country.* By the time of the Civil War, these "Creoles of Color" in southwest Louisiana had become a "separate class, distinct from the dominant whites as well as from the slaves." The Creoles of Color sought to maintain their unique social status—

especially those who became slaveholders—and their Civil War experience provide examples of both support and resistance to the Confederacy. See ibid., 50, 71, 85–87, 104.

61. Schweninger, "Antebellum Free Persons of Color in Postbellum Louisiana," 353. However, once the Union's victory became apparent, most Free Blacks "quickly changed their stance." See ibid., 353–54.

62. Hewitt and Bergeron, eds., *Louisianians in the Civil War,* 100–119.

63. Hirsch and Logsdon, eds., *Creole New Orleans,* 73; Hall, *Africans in Colonial Louisiana,* 134, 173–74.

64. Hirsch and Logsdon, eds., *Creole New Orleans,* 76–77.

65. Dawdy, *Building the Devil's Empire,* 178; Haarman, "The Spanish Conquest of British West Florida, 1779–1781," 107–8; Robinson, "Sustaining the Glory," 5–6; Holmes, "Alabama's Bloodiest Day of the American Revolution," 210.

66. Hirsch and Logsdon, eds., *Creole New Orleans,* 55; Hall, *Africans in Colonial Louisiana,* 323–24.

67. Remini, *The Battle of New Orleans,* 37–38.

68. Likely the report referred mostly to the descendants of New Orleans's earlier defenders as most veterans would have been too old for service by the time of the Civil War. *Special Report of the Military Board,* 5.

69. Mills, *The Forgotten People,* 235–36.

70. Bell, *Creole New Orleans in the Revolutionary Atlantic 1775–1877,* 182; Ward, *Garden of Ruins,* 41. Michael P. Johnson and James L. Roark note how the Ellisons, a South Carolina Free Black family, offered their allegiance to their state—even claiming and acknowledging their White ancestry, which linked them to "White South Carolina nativity." Reinforcing their loyalty to their state, the Ellisons also complied with all wartime demands that South Carolina's Confederate government issued, which helped protect their unique social standing and property. See Johnson and Roark, *Black Masters,* 301–6.

71. Hollandsworth, *The Louisiana Native Guards,* 11, 21–22. Pierson notes the Confederacy's lack of military manpower could have been supplemented by these Free Black volunteers, but they were "snubbed" as "potential recruits who lay within its grasp"—along with the "refusal to arm the people it held as slaves (40 percent of its population)." See Pierson, *Mutiny at Fort Jackson,* 190. Bergeron examines the role of Louisiana's Free Men of Color who enlisted as soldiers in the Confederate ranks. Though mostly limited to militia service, a small number of Louisiana Free Blacks did enlist in the Confederate ranks and actually served as combat soldiers. See Hewitt and Bergeron, eds., *Louisianians in the Civil War,* 100–19. And some Louisiana Free Blacks remained in the state's militia or home guard units. For example, one Louisiana Unionist recalled visiting a Free Black man in late 1863, who had a son in a local home guard unit. See Haynes, *A Thrilling Narrative,* ed. Bergeron, 28.

72. Roland, *Louisiana Sugar Plantations,* 25–26.

73. Winters, *The Civil War in Louisiana,* 36–37.

74. Alfred Flournoy Sr. letter to Alfred Flournoy Jr. June 16, 1861, Folder 28, Mildred McCoy Collection, NSU. As many of the state's parish police juries stepped up to support the war effort, not all jurors followed through with their original commitments. See "A Journal of Camp Life as a Private Soldier" by W. H. King, entry for June 14, 1862, original journal at Texas State

Archives, Austin, Texas, xerox copy in W. N. King Collection, Folder 1, NSU (hereafter cited as W. H. King Journal, NSU).

75. New Orleans Crescent, June 17, 1861, quoted in Casey, ed., *Life at Camp Moore Among the Volunteers*, 33–37.

76. Owen, *In Camp and Battle with the Washington Artillery of New Orleans*, 8–9.

77. Alex de Clouet letter to Paul, May 9, 1861. UAAMC-COLL-22, Box 1, Folder 17, De-Clouet Family Papers, ULL.

78. Mingus, *The Louisiana Tigers in the Gettysburg Campaign*, 65. But not all regimental flags later in the war were from home. William Miller Owen recalled that, by the fall of 1861, "the army received the new battle-flags,—a blue St. Andrew cross upon a field of red.... Every regiment had now its own flag." See Owen, *In Camp and Battle with the Washington Artillery*, 60; Henry M. King letter to John F. Stephens, August 15, 1864, Folder 1861–1864 (4 items), #882, John F. Stephens Correspondence, LSU.

79. W. H. King Journal, entry for June 3, 1862, in W. N. King Collection, Folder 1, NSU. Parting soldiers were not the only ones who obtained homemade Confederate flags from female civilians. After the sugar cane harvest, one planter's wife in Terrebonne Parish presented her slaves with a flag "& told them they must not let the Yankees get a'hold of it." See Bond, *A Maryland Bride in the Deep South*, ed. Harrison, 212.

80. Winters, *The Civil War in Louisiana*, 38–39; Ward, *Garden of Ruins*, 31; "Programe of the Tableaux Vivants sold for the Benefit of the Louisiana Soldiers, 5th January 1865," January 5, 1865, Folder 1, Scrapbook pages 49–50, Scrapbook pages 69–70, unnamed newspaper with clipping "Grand Concert For the benefit of our Sick and Wounded Volunteers," Folder 2, Loose items from the scrapbook in Folder 1, "Grand Amateur Concert" program, "Grand Vocal and Instrumental Concert . . . For The Benefit Of The Gallant 18th Louisiana Volunteers" program, all scrapbooks in Carmen Breazeale Collection, NSU.

81. Moriarty, *A Fine Body of Men*, 17; Bond, *A Maryland Bride in the Deep South*, ed. Harrison, 201.

82. Draft, sewing society, to make and forward clothing to soldiers in the Confederate Army (original document), no date, Folder 4, W. P. Harris Collection, NSU.

83. Docie letter to My dear husband (Alfred Flournoy Jr.). July 22, 1861, Folder 28, Mildred McCoy Collection, NSU.

84. John A. Morgan letter to Sister, July 26, 1861, Box 1, Folder 2, May–December 1861, John A. Morgan Papers, LSU.

85. Confederate Civil War Solider Letter addressed to Opelousas, Louisiana, no date, UAAMC-COLL-Manuscript 251, Folder 1, Confederate Civil War Soldier Letter, ULL.

86. Ellen Louise Power Diary, January 1, 1862–September 28, 1863 (typed transcription), 57, Folder 2, in the Ellen Louise Power Diary, 1862–1863, #1459-Z, UNC (hereafter cited as Power Diary, UNC).

87. Bragg, *Louisiana in the Confederacy*, 92–93. Glymph, *Out of the House of Bondage*, 113. Glymph notes that Southern White women's wartime contributions have been praised; however, Southern Black women's contributions "went largely unnoticed by the nation whose citizens they fought to become." And their (often coerced) contributions to the Confederacy have also gone unnoticed. See ibid., 133.

3. CONSCRIPTION

1. H. A. Snyder Diary, January–August, November–December 1862, entry for January 2, 1862. 1 Volume, Box 1 of 1, Mss. 2198, LSU (hereafter cited as H. A. Snyder Diary, LSU).

2. Unnamed and undated newspaper, clipping of "Prudhomme Guards," Folder 1, Scrapbook pages 71–72, Carmen Breazeale Collection, NSU.

3. Alfred Flournoy Sr. letter to Alfred Flournoy Jr. March 16, 1862, Folder 28, Mildred McCoy Collection, NSU.

4. H. A. Snyder Diary, entries for January 8, 27, 1862, LSU.

5. Dufour, *The Night the War Was Lost*, 174.

6. Pierson, *Mutiny at Fort Jackson*, 63.

7. Odom, "The Political Career of Thomas Overton Moore," 24; Hollandsworth, *The Louisiana Native Guards*, 8.

8. Sheehan-Dean, *Why Confederates Fought*, 48–50.

9. Andrew McCollam letter to Father, May 1, 1861, Folder 13, Andrew McCollam Papers, UNC.

10. 2nd Louisiana Cavalry Regiment Notebook, 1863–1865 (typescript), entry for October 31, 1864, p. 22. Confederate States Army Collection, Mss. 585, LSU.

11. Oates, *Confederate Cavalry West of the River*, 45.

12. Edmonds, *Yankee Autumn in Acadiana*, 43. The 2nd Louisiana Cavalry was not the only unit to recruit young boys. See "Diary of H. N. Connor" by H. N. Connor (transcribed), no date, quote taken from "Notes" section of diary, which Connor added in from late 1865–66. UAAMC-COLL-Manuscript 402, Box 1, Folder 2, ULL (hereafter cited as H. N. Connor Diary, ULL). Partisan and guerrilla units had their share of young enthusiasts, as many "parents have infinite trouble in preventing" young recruits from enlisting. See Hélène Dupuy quoted in Michot, "'War Is Still Raging in This Part of the Country,'" 158.

13. Frazier, *Fire in the Cane Field*, 233.

14. The draft brought nearly two hundred thousand men into the Southern ranks. Noe, *Reluctant Rebels*, 108.

15. Jimerson, *The Private Civil War*, 188, 192–93, 214; Moore, *Conscription and Conflict in the Confederacy*, 144–45.

16. Noe, *Reluctant Rebels*, 6–7, 121.

17. Sacher, *Confederate Conscription and the Struggle for Southern Soldiers*, 4–7, 16–18, 22; Sacher, "A Very Disagreeable Business," 142–44.

18. Winters, *The Civil War in Louisiana*, 72.

19. Odom, "The Political Career of Thomas Overton Moore," 36–37.

20. H. A. Snyder Diary, entry for February 14, 1862, LSU.

21. Moore, *Conscription and Conflict in the Confederacy*, 1. Moore points out that Jefferson Davis pressed the Confederate government to adopt conscription measures for several reasons: it would force men to stay in the ranks for longer periods, not the short-term enlistments granted at the war's commencement; it would provide central control in creating and maintaining the Confederate war machine; and it would provide a level of fairness to force all Southerners to help bear the war's burden. See ibid., 13–14.

22. Faust, *Mothers of Invention*, 30. Adjutant General of Louisiana Forces Thomas Courtland Manning notified sixty-eight-year-old Dr. Bartholomew Egan that he was to become the state's surgeon general with the rank of colonel. Egan's duties were more administrative but still required physical stamina and dedication to aid the state's war effort. His service only lasted less than a year as he was appointed to help establish Louisiana's Northern State Laboratory to "superintend the preparation of indigenous medicines." See Culpepper, "The Life, Letters, and Legacy of Dr. Bartholomew Egan," 84–86, 90–91.

23. John A. Morgan letter to Sister, April 18, 1862, Box 1, Folder 3, February–August 1862, John A. Morgan Papers, LSU.

24. W. H. King Journal, entry for May 10, 1862, NSU.

25. Taylor, "Discontent in Confederate Louisiana," 414.

26. Moore, *Conscription and Conflict in the Confederacy*, 22–23.

27. Taylor, "Discontent in Confederate Louisiana," 414.

28. Thomas B. Davidson letter to Sister, July 24, 1862, Folder 1, Thomas Benjamin Davidson Papers, UNC.

29. W. H. King Journal, entry for June 8, 1862, NSU.

30. Sacher, "A Very Disagreeable Business," 144–45.

31. W. H. King Journal, entry for May 23, 1862, NSU. Earlier in the war, a group of "armed parties" composed of Louisiana soldiers who resembled naval press gangs of earlier conflicts had wandered "through the city and carried off by force men indiscriminately to the Camp or temporary barracks threatening them with violence unless they enlisted." Their deeds upset the British consul, as many British subjects were being "illegally mustered into the service." See Dufour, *The Night the War Was Lost*, 38–39.

32. Glatthaar, *General Lee's Army*, 404.

33. W. H. King Journal, entries for June 14, 1862, and September 29, 1862, NSU.

34. Ibid., entries for January 1, 1864, January 17, 1863, and September 26, 1863, NSU.

35. Sacher, "A Very Disagreeable Business," 145–46.

36. John Coleman Sibley letter to wife, September 3, 1862, Civil War Diary and Letters of 2nd Lt. John Coleman Sibley, 2nd Louisiana Cavalry, Company E, Confederate States of America, June 1862 to June 1865, transcribed by Carl Coleman Smith, 2006, edited and indexed by Donald Ray Parker, PhD, 2009, Box 1, John Coleman Sibley Collection, p. 70, NSU (hereafter cited as Civil War Diary and Letters of John Coleman Sibley, NSU).

37. P. L. Prudhomme letter to Lestan Prudhomme, August 26, 1862, Folder 270 (typed, translated Prudhomme Civil War letters—originals at LSU), Robert DeBlieux Collection, NSU.

38. Escott, *Military Necessity*, 74; Special Order No. 161 from Lieut. Genl. Taylor, June 9, 1864, Folder 27, George W. Logan Papers, UNC; Special Order No. 238 from Maj. Genl. Buckner, August 26, 1864, Folder 31, George W. Logan Papers, UNC; conscript exemption certificate (typescript), February 3, 1863, and C.S. Tax Act statement (typescript), August 22, 1864, UAAMC-COLL-65, Box 1, Folder 4, Gebert-Ray-Lee Families Papers, ULL.

39. Hd. Qr. Camp Pratt by Lt. Col. R. S. Burke, September 10, 1862, Avery Family Papers of Louisiana, 1796–1951 (microfilm), #M-3289, UNC.

40. *The War of the Rebellion: A Compilation of the Official Records of the Union and Confederate Armies*, ser. I, vol. 53, 812 (hereafter cited *OR*); Special Orders No. 40[?], By order of Brig. Genl. Blanchard and W. L. Riddich, March 12, 1863, Folder 5, George W. Logan Papers, UNC.

41. Taylor, "Discontent in Confederate Louisiana," 416; Brasseaux, *Acadian to Cajun*, 65–73. Brasseaux notes that by 1864 many Acadian deserters made their way back to the service without repercussions thanks to President Davis's 1863 pardon. See ibid., 71.

42. Haynes, *A Thrilling Narrative*, ed. Bergeron, 10–12. For individual accounts of brutal conscript officers, see ibid., 82–85.

43. Wadley Journal (typed transcription), p. 51, Folder 8a, Volume 3, UNC.

44. Pierson, *Mutiny at Fort Jackson*, 20, 29–30, 38.

45. Moore, *Conscription and Conflict in the Confederacy*, 115–17.

46. Dr. Bartholomew Egan quoted in Culpepper, "The Life, Letters, and Legacy of Dr. Bartholomew Egan," 86; W. H. King Journal, entry for May 14, 15, 1862, NSU.

47. John Coleman Sibley letter to wife, September 16, 1862, Civil War Diary and Letters of John Coleman Sibley, p. 75, NSU.

48. Brasseaux, *Acadian to Cajun*, 70.

49. Pierson, *Mutiny at Fort Jackson*, 82.

50. John M. Sacher, "Our Interest and Destiny Are the Same," 277. Sacher also notes that Moore continuously petitioned for more troops and also requested that conscription laws allow troops raised in Louisiana "to remain west of the Mississippi River" and that any soldiers that could be spared from other regions should be sent to help defend Louisiana. See ibid., 278.

51. By December 1862, Governor Moore pleaded with Jefferson Davis for the return of Louisiana troops. He claimed, "Unless something is done very soon you will learn from events how well-founded are my apprehensions." See *OR*, ser. I, vol. 53, 836–37. Louisiana officers and soldiers stationed in Virginia and Tennessee also echoed Governor Moore's concerns about their state's manpower shortage. For examples, see Gache, *A Frenchman, a Chaplain, a Rebel*, 121–22; W. Ezra Denson letter to John F. Stephens. October 10, 1861, Folder 1861–1864 (4 items), John F. Stephens Correspondence, LSU; E. S. Stephens letter to sister, October 31, 1861, Box 1, Folder 2, Stephens Collection, NSU. Stephens even attempted to use family connections to obtain a transfer from Governor Moore to return to Louisiana. See E. L. Stephens letter to parents, January 9, 1862, Box 1, Folder 3, Stephens Collection, NSU; E. L. Stephens letter to sister, August 15, 1862, Box 1, Folder 4, Stephens Collection, NSU; Louis Stagg letter to wife, Laure (transcribed), October 29, 1863, UAAMC-COLL-Manuscript 7, Folder 1, Louis Stagg Letters, 1855–1863, ULL. However, some soldiers, such as P. L. Prudhomme, realized the impossibility of fulfilling the requests of Louisiana soldiers hoping to return home. He acknowledged, "As to the idea of recalling her sons it is a bad principle to inaugurate and would be a very bad precedent as every other (state) (almost) in the Confederacy would claim her sons on the same ground." And returning soldiers from other states home for local defense would make "the Government powerless in the prosecution of our common fight." See P. L. Prudhomme letter to Lestan Prudhomme. November 28, 1862, Folder 270, Robert DeBlieux Collection, NSU.

52. Jefferson Davis to Lucius Dupré, October 11, 1862, Laurent Dupre Papers, 1862–1866 (microfilm), #1987, UNC. Though Louisiana's infantrymen remained in Virginia, several artillerymen of the 12th Louisiana Heavy Artillery, who originally hailed from southern Louisiana, obtained a transfer from Richmond to Port Hudson as the Confederate Secretary of War G. W. Randolph felt these men were "less likely to suffer the heat stroke and tropical illnesses that had caused problems for other Union and Confederate troops in Louisiana." See Thrasher, *Miserable Little Conglomeration*, 34–35.

53. H. A. Snyder Diary, entry for May 1, 1862, LSU. Pierson argues that Snyder's diary "documents the lukewarm attitude many Confederate militiamen had toward frill and military service" and "provides vital evidence that there were far more mutinies in Confederate ranks than just the one in Fort Jackson." Pierson notes that Snyder's future actions placed him further away from military pursuits as well as from Confederate loyalty, which might have originally been a front to hide his true Unionist sympathies. See Pierson, *Mutiny at Fort Jackson,* 98–104.

54. Noe, *Reluctant Rebels,* 8–9.

55. B. de Clouet letter to pape, November 1, 1862, UAAMC-COLL-22, Box 1, Folder 18, DeClouet Family Papers, ULL.

56. Sacher, "A Very Disagreeable Business," 152–54.

57. Laver and Whitney, "Where Duty Shall Call," 360–61.

58. In the summer of 1862, P. L. Prudhomme, a Louisiana soldier stationed in Mississippi, wrote to his father about the latest wartime news, noting the Northern draft's unpopularity, hoping it would "swell our ranks from the border states. . . . The emancipation bill having caused many to change notion." See P. L. Prudhomme letter to Lestan Prudhomme, August 18, 1862, Folder 270, Robert DeBlieux Collection, NSU. Weeks later, Prudhomme's brother, who served with the 2nd Louisiana Cavalry, also addressed the issue of Union conscription, albeit with inaccurate information. See F. A. Prudhomme letter to Lestan Prudhomme, October 11, 1862, Folder 270, Robert DeBlieux Collection, NSU. In March 1863, Louisiana soldier W. H. King highlighted the Union's draft—along with the ability for individuals with money to hire a "substitute or pay the Gov't $300.00. So it turns out that they are hard pressed for men or money." See W. H. King Journal, entry for March 14, 1863, NSU. For the Confederacy, a substitute was "an ineligible man" exempt from the draft, often someone "outside the draft's age range, but more frequently in Louisiana, foreigners living within Confederate lines." See Sacher, "A Very Disagreeable Business," 156–58.

59. Michot, "'War Is Still Raging in This Part of the Country,'" 166.

60. Dupuy, quoted in Michot, "'War Is Still Raging in This Part of the Country,'" 168–69. Unionist slaveholders also contributed slave laborers to the Union cause, albeit reluctantly. See Edward J. Gay certificate, August 20, 1864, Edward J. Gay and Family Papers, Mss. 1295, LSU (Louisiana Digital Library). For a further look at Union conscription in Louisiana, see Michot, "'War Is Still Raging in This Part of the Country,'" 167–68. Though many slaves ran away to Union lines expecting freedom, the Union army under General Nathaniel Banks called for Black enlistments, as Yankee officials "armed with lists in hand, went from plantation to plantation conscripting them, often at the point of a bayonet." See ibid.

61. Odom, "The Political Career of Thomas Overton Moore," 63; Sacher, "A Very Disagreeable Business," 146–147.

62. Melissa letter to "Dearest" (C. C. Dunn), March 8, 1863, Folder 1, Juanita Henry Collection, NSU.

63. Faust, *Mothers of Invention,* 30–31.

64. Glymph, *The Women's Fight,* 23; Glymph, *Out of the House of Bondage,* 24–25, 31, 45.

65. Edwards, *Scarlett Doesn't Live Here Anymore,* 2–3.

66. Rebecca Fletcher interview, August 21, 1940, Folder 19 (Folklore—Ex-slave tales & interviews), Federal Writers Project Collection, NSU.

67. Frazier, *Fire in the Cane Field,* 72.

68. Odom, "The Political Career of Thomas Overton Moore," 56. By 1864, Washington Parish had become a haven for not only local Confederate deserters but also attracted "deserter bands" from neighboring Mississippi, as these men were "claiming to have a government of their own." See Weitz, *More Damning than Slaughter*, 207.

69. Hewitt and Bergeron, eds., *Louisianians in the Civil War*, 40.

70. Glymph, *The Women's Fight*, 42–43.

71. Brother letter to sister Mary, August 10, 1863, Folder 32, in the Brashear-Lawrence Family Papers, Series 1.3, Correspondence, 1863, #3355, UNC.

72. Jeremiah Tucker letter to Tucker [wife], May 10, 1862, quoted in Richard and Richard, *The Defense of Vicksburg*, 31.

73. Louis Stagg letter to wife, Laure (transcribed), October 15, 1861, and October 29, 1863, UAAMC-COLL-Manuscript 7, Folder 1, Louis Stagg Letters, ULL; Isaac Hall letter to Mary Hall, no date, quoted in Richard and Richard, *The Defense of Vicksburg*, 29.

74. L. G. Causey letter to Husband (R. J. Causey), October 14, 1863. Folder Misc.: C, September–November 1863, Mss. 2133, R. J. Causey Correspondence, LSU.

75. M. M. Owen letter to husband, November 27, 1864, Folder 37, George W. Logan Papers, UNC.

76. Joseph Welsh Texada letter to Margaret Texada, September 5, 1864, Box 1, Folder 23, Mss. 5119, Texada Family Papers, LSU.

77. Hal letter to wife, November 27, 1861, Folder 13, Slack Family Papers, UNC.

78. Unnamed (wife, Dosie) letter to "My dear husband" (Alfred Flournoy Jr.), August 4, 1861, Folder 28, Mildred McCoy Collection, NSU.

79. Moore, *Conscription and Conflict in the Confederacy*, 144–45.

80. Glymph, *The Women's Fight*, 56–60. For an example of family strife over substitution, which was not deemed disloyal to the Confederacy, see R. J. Causey letter to Wife, October 8, 1863, Folder Misc.: C, R. J. Causey Correspondence, LSU; L. G. Causey letter to Husband (R. J. Causey), November 19, 1863, Folder Misc.: C, R. J. Causey Correspondence, LSU; Ural, *Don't Hurry Me Down to Hades*, 154.

81. Winters, *The Civil War in Louisiana*, 72.

82. Faust, *Mothers of Invention*, 55–56. But not all Louisianians saw the law as such. Governor Moore's Order 191 mirrored the "Twenty-Negro Law" by allowing one White male on plantations. Some men from Madison Parish reflected the growing animosity between the upper and lower classes, claiming "a rich man's son's too good to fight the battles of the rich." See Winters, *The Civil War in Louisiana*, 72–73. Sacher also notes that the "twenty-negro" law should have been "termed the 'overseer' law," arguing that the Confederate government realized the severity of class friction within the Confederacy and "in response to criticisms, twice altered the law to mitigate social conflict." The laws were geared toward "experienced overseers," not necessarily for the planters or their sons. See Sacher, "'Twenty-Negro,' or Overseer Law," 269–70.

83. *Southern Sentinel* quoted in Bragg, *Louisiana in the Confederacy*, 62. Not all historians conclude that the men of slaveholding families were uncommitted to pulling their weight in military service. Though some soldiers spoke out about the planter class's lack of commitment in the field, Noe argues that by 1862 the number of soldiers from slaveholding families reflected similar percentages "to the regional average." See Noe, *Reluctant Rebels*, 10, 16. Sheehan-Dean's example of Virginia soldiers notes, "The more wealth a community held, the more likely that it

would send high numbers of men to the army. Rich men fought this war." See Sheehan-Dean, *Why Confederates Fought,* 36. Glatthaar also provides evidence of the large contributions of slaveowners (or relatives of slaveowners) who served in the Army of Northern Virginia. See Glatthaar, *General Lee's Army,* 20, 30.

84. H. A. Snyder Diary, entry for March 11, 1862, LSU.

85. Glymph, "Noncombatant Military Laborers in the Civil War," 26. See also Woodward, "Marching Masters," 259–97. Woodward gives a detailed examination of the important role enslaved laborers made to the Confederate war effort.

86. Thrasher, *Miserable Little Conglomeration,* 28.

87. Caturget[?] letter to Lt. Col. G. W. Logan, March 7, 1863, Folder 5, George W. Logan Papers, UNC.

88. F. A. Prudhomme letter to Lestan Prudhomme. November 12, 1862. Folder 270, Robert DeBlieux Collection, NSU.

89. Williams and Wooster, "Camp Life in Civil War Louisiana," 190.

90. Williams, *P. G. T. Beauregard,* 70; O'Donovan, *Becoming Free in the Cotton South,* 77.

91. [Horby] Franklin letter to Margaret Texada, May 29, 1861, Box 1, Folder 16, Texada Family Papers, LSU.

92. Glymph, "Noncombatant Military Laborers in the Civil War," 25–26, 28. Though African American agency shaped Civil War events, some historians note that their participation, whether as laborers or soldiers, did not necessarily guarantee a Union victory. See Gallagher, *The Union War,* 88, 89. For insight on how Black agency related to Union wartime policies, see Lang, *In the Wake of War,* 43–44. Union soldiers had mixed feelings about African American participation, but as the war continued, one Federal soldier bluntly noted Black contributions to the Union, claiming, "This army would be like a one handed man without niggers." See Edmonds, *The Guns of Port Hudson, Volume Two,* 124; Sheehan-Dean, *The Calculus of Violence,* 53. For examples of Union soldier attitudes toward slaves who made it into their lines, see Sally P. Power, "A Vermont-er's Account of the Red River Campaign," 363; Laver and Whitney, "Where Duty Shall Call," 339–40; Hewitt and Bergeron, eds., *Louisianians in the Civil War,* 15–16. Union encroachment into Confederate territory and the Emancipation Proclamation helped unravel the South's social order. See Roland, *Louisiana Sugar Plantations,* 92. However, economics sometimes trumped Union policies regarding runaway slaves, especially when valuable, unharvested crops remained in the field. Even General Butler knew that total confiscation of slave property would wreck the economy, along with the army's inability to care for all runaways who made it to Union lines. Lack of provisions and illnesses became a common sight in the slave refugee camps, which highlighted the fact that their future remained uncertain. See Ripley, *Slaves and Freedmen in Civil War Louisiana,* 26–27, 157. For an excellent study on slave refugee camps, see Taylor, *Embattled Freedom.* Many Confederate Louisianians detested Butler's actions as one officer wrote that Butler's "name is loathed by every decant man, woman, [?] child in Christendom." See Hal letter to wife, October 6, 1862, Folder 14, Slack Family Papers, UNC.

93. Though (in)famous for his stern treatment of New Orleans women, Butler's actions and policies did not always favor escaped slaves who sought asylum within Union lines. See Pritchard, "Moving Toward Freedom?" 37–52.

94. Odom, "The Political Career of Thomas Overton Moore," 53–55; Brig. Gen. Albert Blanchard letter to Capt. R. L.[?] Robertson, December 28, 1862, Folder 1b, George W. Logan

Papers, UNC. Though this scenario might bring a planter's loyalty into question, the following month the Catahoula Police Jury aimed to cooperate with the planters and return their slaves. Apparently levee maintenance on the Tensas, Black, Little, and Ouachita Rivers, which protected plantation production—and a planter's property—trumped military work. See Wm. M. Few[?], Copy of Catahoula Parish Police Jury Resolution, January 27, 1863, Folder 2, George W. Logan Papers, UNC.

95. Gen. John Pemberton offered planters the rate of "$1.25 per day" for a slave's labor. Glymph, "Noncombatant Military Laborers in the Civil War," 29.

96. Ripley, *Slaves and Freedmen in Civil War Louisiana*, 11–12. W. H. King also notes attitudes toward the South conscripting Black laborers, see W. H. King Journal, entry for March 22, 1864, NSU.

97. Lowe, *Walker's Texas Division*, 167.

98. Ibid., 167.

99. Glymph, "Noncombatant Military Laborers in the Civil War," 28; A. Lazare letter to Col. G. W. Logan, June 13, 1863, Folder 12, George W. Logan Papers, UNC.

100. Wm. M. Few[?], Copy of Catahoula Parish Police Jury Resolution, January 27, 1863, Folder 2, George W. Logan Papers, UNC.

101. Ripley, *Slaves and Freedmen in Civil War Louisiana*, 13. But not all Black laborers were enslaved. At least one incident near Natchitoches involved a Free Black man who found himself in a Confederate labor camp. Though free, he explained to his wife, "We are in a way slaves." He continued, "The negroes [slaves] are treated better than we are. We are obliged to do the hardest kind of work and the negro looks on." Perhaps this laborer's predicament explains why some Free Blacks opted for Louisiana militia service. See Hewitt and Bergeron, eds., *Louisianians in the Civil War*, 118. As the war dragged on, many Free Blacks in Southwest Louisiana resisted Confederate conscription, becoming active in Jayhawker bands. See Brasseaux, Fontenot, and Oubre, *Creoles of Color in the Bayou Country*, 85–86.

102. O'Donovan, *Becoming Free in the Cotton South*, 72, 82–85.

103. Memorial, Petition & Resolutions from the Planters of Morehouse Parish to Lt. Col. G. W. Logan, [no date given, but in petition the date March 2, 1863, appears], Folder 10, George W. Logan Papers, UNC.

104. Henry Ginder letter to Mary Ginder, June 12, 1863, quoted in Richard and Richard, *The Defense of Vicksburg*, 194–95.

105. "To The Planters of Louisiana," August 24, 1863, Folder 56, George W. Logan Papers, Confederate Army Orders Package 2, #1560, UNC. Some conscripted slaves had special protection from government officials if engaged in important wartime projects. See Gov. Henry Watkins Allen letter to Dr. B. Egan, August 10, 1864, Folder 109, Egan Collection, NSU. For a comparison of Georgia planters who resisted supplying Black laborers to the Confederacy, see O'Donovan, *Becoming Free in the Cotton South*, 78–82, 88.

106. Frazier, *Fire in the Cane Field*, 84. For an account of slave laborers attempting to escape from a Confederate fortification in north Louisiana, see 2nd Lt. D. Castleberry to Lieut. Col. G. W. Logan, February 2, 1863, Folder 3, George W. Logan Papers, UNC. For details on this episode, along with other accounts of enslaved individuals' agency, see Ward, *Garden of Ruins*, 214–16.

107. See Plater, *The Butlers of Iberville Parish, Louisiana*, 159; Odel Jackson interview,

May 31, 1940, Folder 19 (Folklore—Ex-slave tales & interviews), Federal Writers Project Collection, NSU; Henry Reed interview, June 1940, Folder 19 (Folklore—Ex-slave tales & interviews), Federal Writers Project Collection, NSU; Bayside Plantation Record Book, 1860–1868 (transcribed), entry for August 5, 1863, UAAMC-COLL 481, Box 1, ULL; H. N. Connor Diary," entry for July 1, 1863, ULL; Pritchard, "Moving Toward Freedom?" 56–62, 64–71, 74–76.

108. H. N. Connor Diary, no date, quote taken from "Notes" section of diary, which Connor added in from late 1865 to 1866, ULL.

109. See "Yankee Barbary," unnamed newspaper, no date, Folder 33, Cloutier Collection, NSU.

110. F. A. Prudhomme letter to Lestan Prudhomme, October 11, 1862, Folder 270, Robert DeBlieux Collection, NSU.

111. Frazier, *Fire in the Cane Field*, 224–25. Many Louisianians also harbored fears of possible slave revolts—even as early as 1861. See Blanche DeClouet letter to Paul (typescript), June 25, 1861, UAAMC-COLL-22, Box 3, Folder 4, DeClouet Family Papers, ULL. For an example of slave unrest in 1863 in southeastern Louisiana, see L. G. Causey letter to Husband (R. J. Causey). November 19, 1863, Folder Misc.: C, R. J. Causey Correspondence, LSU. Union occupation in some Louisiana towns served as a quarry for recruiting Black troops, see Power Diary, January 1, 1862–September 28, 1863 (typed transcription), pp. 97–98, Folder 2, UNC.

112. Ripley, *Slaves and Freedmen in Civil War Louisiana*, 22–24. By 1864 efforts to convert slave laborers into wage-earners were still pocked by numerous problems. For example, one planter refused to accept these new terms, telling a Union official that "he would never pay a nigger a d——d cent while he could find a Confederate to carry a gun." See ibid., 57. For a captured Confederate's experience witnessing Black celebrations over the Emancipation Proclamation, See John Coleman Sibley Diary, entry for June 11, 1864, Civil War Diary and Letters of John Coleman Sibley, p. 42, NSU. While slavery helped bring about the conflict, the Union's original war goals did not include abolishing the peculiar institution. Northerners had mixed feelings about emancipation and its effects on society as the "sweeping change would . . . create more instability and uncertainty." See Lang, *In the Wake of War*, 74. The Union's initial aim was to engage in a "political commitment to defeat the South without touching slavery," especially since it needed support from the border states; however, growing momentum for ending slavery as a war aim eventually took root. See Grimsley, *The Hard Hand of War*, 121–41.

113. W. H. King Journal, entry for April 16, 1863, and entry for December 5, 1863, NSU.

114. Ripley, *Slaves and Freedmen in Civil War Louisiana*, 42–43, 114–15.

115. J. Harvey Brown quoted in Thrasher, *Miserable Little Conglomeration*, 82.

116. Cyrus F. Boyd quoted in Winters, *The Civil War in Louisiana*, 175–76.

117. John Coleman Sibley letter to wife, June 15, 1863, Civil War Diary and Letters of John Coleman Sibley, p. 114, NSU.

118. "Deadly Affray with a Gang of Runaway Negroes." *New Orleans Daily Delta*, August 5, 1862.

119. W. H. King Journal, entries December 28, 29, 1863, NSU.

120. Ripley, *Slaves and Freedmen in Civil War Louisiana*, 28–29; Wiley, ed. "*This Infernal War*," 140.

121. Hewitt and Bergeron, eds., *Louisianians in the Civil War*, 14; Louis Stagg letter to wife,

Laure (transcribed), June 9, 1863, UAAMC-COLL-Manuscript 7, Folder 1, Louis Stagg Letters, ULL.

122. Gleeson, "The Rhetoric of Insurrection and Fear," 238–57.

123. Roland, *Louisiana Sugar Plantations*, 107–8.

124. Pritchard, "Moving Toward Freedom?" 10, 17–18. One young Southerner near Murfreesboro, Tennessee, noted that a slave, once making it to Union lines—and being put "to hard work"—decided his predicament was no better than slavery, and he "says he will never leave his master again." See Ash, *When the Yankees Came*, 33.

125. Ellis Diary, entry titled "A Retrospect," p. 4, LSU. One Louisiana officer noted, "Lincoln's infamous abolition proclamation have I believe been invaluable to our cause," as he felt "Every proclamation of Lincoln & his generals" usually led to disastrous consequences, as he listed examples from General Pope's proclamation for confiscating enemy property in Virginia to Butler's actions in Louisiana. But despite these personal opinions, the Emancipation Proclamation likely turned the tide of the conflict. See Hal letter to wife, October 6, 1862, Folder 14, Slack Family Papers, UNC.

4. CAMP LIFE

1. E. J. Ellis quoted in Wiley, *The Life of Johnny Reb*, 130.

2. Fred Taber letter to parents and sister, January 11, 1862, Box 1, folder 1861–1862, #412, A-57, Frederick R. Taber Papers, LSU.

3. William J. Walter letter to Paul, April 26, 1862, in Davis, ed. "A Louisiana Volunteer," 84.

4. Wiley discusses Confederate camp life in a variety of settings, most notably relating to a soldier's exposure to camp sins and his ordeal in winter quarters. See Wiley, *Life of Johnny Reb*, 36–67. Kathryn Shively Meier examines Civil War camps in Virginia through the lens of health care, noting how environmental factors often made camps undesirable places to inhabit. See Meier, *Nature's Civil War*, 1, 46, 128–32. Similarly, Faust notes how Civil War camps often resembled cesspools, which became breeding grounds for disease—and ultimately death. See Faust, *This Republic of Suffering*, 4, 63.

5. Durham, "Dear Rebecca," 170–71.

6. Vandiver, ed., "A Collection of Louisiana Confederate Letters," 23.

7. E. L. Stephens letter to Pa and Ma. July 10[?], 1861. Box 1, Folder 1, Stephens Collection, NSU.

8. Alfred Flournoy Sr. letter Charley, March 7, 1861, Folder 28, Mildred McCoy Collection, NSU.

9. Winters, *The Civil War in Louisiana*, 24.

10. Russell quoted in Stalling, *Louisianians in the Western Confederacy*, 6.

11. Ellis Diary, entry titled "A Retrospect," p. 6, LSU.

12. Dufour, *The Night the War Was Lost*, 117.

13. Russell quoted in Stalling, *Louisianians in the Western Confederacy*, 6. The problem of electing officers was not unique to Louisiana units. See Krick, "The Power of the Land: Leadership on the Battlefield," in *Struggle for a Vast Future*, ed., Sheehan-Dean, 65.

14. W. H. King Journal, entry for May 11, 1862, NSU. Escott notes how electing officers did

have some positive influences since the officers usually hailed from the same region or town as their men. See Escott, *Military Necessity,* 166–67.

15. Eugene Janin letter to Father, September 22, 1861, Folder 2, Eugene Janin Papers 1854–1866, #3194-Z, UNC.

16. Eugene Janin letter to Father, October 7, 1861, Folder 2, Eugene Janin Papers, UNC.

17. William J. Walter letter to Hattie, May 10, 1862, in Davis, ed., "A Louisiana Volunteer," 87. Walter wrote that one of their lieutenants became their captain "not by election, for had it depended upon that he would not have received *three votes,* but by a decision of the War Department." See ibid.

18. Bledsoe, *Citizen-Officers,* x, xii. For information on the influence of political ideology on Civil War armies, see Matsui, *The First Republican Army.* Lang also notes how the ideology of republicanism shaped Civil War armies, especially as early volunteers—who were all free men—saw their military service as "*temporary* . . . understanding that they would return quickly to private life at the completion of their service." Though now serving as soldiers under officers they chose—men whom they considered their social equals—these men expected their civil liberties and individualism to remain protected. See Lang, *In the Wake of War,* 4–5, 7.

19. "Your Brother Thomas" letter to Sister, February 8, 1862, Folder 1, Thomas Benjamin Davidson Papers, UNC.

20. John A. Morgan letter to Sister, July 26, 1861, Box 1, Folder 2, May–December 1861, John A. Morgan Papers, LSU.

21. Amos Anselm letter to Mrs. Eleanor Anselm (My dear Mother), September 2, 1861, printed in "Letters from Confederate Soldier to His Mother In St. Landry Parish Tell Gripping Story of War," 214. *Daily World* [magazine supplement], "Some History of St. Landry Parish from the 1690s," November 3, 1955, Powell A. Casey Collection, LSU (hereafter "Letters from Confederate Soldier," LSU). Anselm was wounded at Sharpsburg, Maryland, and did not survive the war. See ibid, 219.

22. Frank Richardson letter to Father, November 6, 1861, Folder 2, Frank Liddell Richardson Papers, UNC.

23. Frank Richardson letter to Father, September 4, 1861, Folder 2, Frank Liddell Richardson Papers, UNC. Ironically, Richardson did not stay a private long. He became an ordinance sergeant, and apparently liked his new position, which exempted him from many of the detested aspects of soldier life. See Frank Richardson letter to Father, December 1, 1861, Folder 2, Frank Liddell Richardson Papers, UNC.

24. Ellis Diary, entry titled "A Retrospect," p. 35, LSU.

25. Williams, *P. G. T. Beauregard,* 64.

26. W. H. King Journal, entry for May 12, 1862, NSU; Frank Richardson letter to Mother, September 18, 1861, Folder 2, Frank Liddell Richardson Papers, UNC; Wiley, *Life of Johnny Reb,* 109; Bond, *A Maryland Bride in the Deep South,* ed. Harrison, 253.

27. Louis Stagg letter to wife, Laure (transcribed), October 6, 1861, UAAMC-COLL-Manuscript 7, Folder 1, Louis Stagg Letters, ULL.

28. Durham, "Dear Rebecca," 169–70. An attempt by two English brothers to produce Enfield firearms in New Orleans to curve the weapon shortage never received the backing—nor capital—from the city's investors, which was needed to commence operations. See: Dufour, *The Night the War Was Lost,* 64.

29. John A. Morgan letter to Mother, June 2, 1861, Box 1, Folder 2, May–December 1861, John A. Morgan Papers, LSU.

30. Hewitt and Bergeron, eds., *Louisianians in the Civil War,* 51.

31. W. H. King Journal, entries for April 30, 1862, and May 23, 1862, NSU.

32. "Appeal for Small Arms," *South-Western,* (Shreveport) August 21, 1861. Though weapon shortages existed at the war's commencement, units were able to obtain needed guns as the war progressed, and these were not simply civilian donated firearms, but military arms of various models. For example, in an 1865 Arms Report for Co. A, 2nd Louisiana Cavalry, the list contained the names of 114 enlisted soldiers (including sergeants and corporals) and the types of arms each soldier possessed or was issued, which included 51 Enfield rifles, 7 Sharp rifles, 3 improved Sharp rifles, 3 Maynard rifles, 2 Springfield rifles, 2 Mississippi rifles, 1 Moss rifle, 6 Burnside rifles. Of this arms list, 35 soldiers had no type of firearm listed, 3 soldiers had their weapons listed as "lost," and 1 soldier "retd his guns to Ord dpt." See 2nd Louisiana Cavalry Regiment Notebook, 1863–1865 (typescript), Report of Arms of Co. A, pp. 47–51. Confederate States Army Collection, #585, LSU.

33. Thomas O. Moore to George W. Logan, February 14, 1862, Folder 1b, George W. Logan Papers, UNC.

34. William Nicholson letter to sister, October 4, 1861, Folder 1861, William Nicholson Letters, LSU.

35. Wiley, ed., *"This Infernal War,"* 33, 39.

36. John letter to brother, no date [1861?], Folder 13, Slack Family Papers, UNC. Confederate cavalrymen west of the Mississippi River, at least in the war's early years, were able to obtain many-bladed weapons. Two New Orleans companies (Thomas, Griswold & Co., and Dufilho's), along with contracted blacksmiths from Arkansas, helped provide the needed swords and sabers. See Oates, *Confederate Cavalry West of the River,* 69.

37. John Coleman Sibley Diary, entry for March 7, 1863, Civil War Diary and Letters of John Coleman Sibley, p. 12, NSU. Louisiana was not the only Confederate state to suffer from a lack of firearms. By 1862 the Confederate government eventually required new recruits to arm themselves when reporting for duty. After an inspecting officer evaluated the weapon, the soldier could either sell the firearm to the military or keep it and receive a monthly stipend of one dollar. See Oates, *Confederate Cavalry West of the River,* 66.

38. Hall, *The Story of the 26th Louisiana Infantry, in the Service of the Confederate States,* 32.

39. Frank Richardson letter to Father, September 23, 1861, Folder 2, Frank Liddell Richardson Papers, UNC.

40. *New Orleans Daily Crescent,* May 9, 1861, quoted in Casey, ed., *Life at Camp Moore,* 7.

41. *Baton Rouge Advocate,* May 24, 1861, quoted in Casey, *Life at Camp Moore,* 12–13; *New Orleans Bee,* May 31, 1861, quoted in Ibid., 21; Power Diary, January 1, 1862–September 28, 1863 (typed transcription), p. 49, Folder 2, UNC; Benjamin Smith letter to Mr. R. H. Carnae, August 23, 1861, Folder 1861 (1 item), #1676, Benjamin Smith Letter, LSU.

42. Owen, *In Camp and Battle with the Washington Artillery,* 14, 50 (illustration), 53.

43. Jones, *Lee's Tigers Revisited,* 47–48, 220, 435n. 17.

44. For the names of the numerous Civil War camps and installations found within Louisiana, see Casey, *Encyclopedia of Forts, Posts, Named Camps, and Other Military Installations in Louisiana.*

45. John S. Billiu letter to wife, May 14, 1861, Box 1, folder 1, John S. Billiu, Civil War Letters, LSU. Today the site is located in Tangipahoa Parish, which was later formed from portions of St. Helena, Livingston, Washington, and St. Tammany Parishes. During the war, Camp Moore was part of St. Helena Parish. See Casey, *The Story of Camp Moore*, 6.

46. John E. Hall letter to wife, April 2, 1862, Box 8, Folder 58, Larry Crain Collection, SLU.

47. Patrick, quoted in Stalling, *Louisianians in the Western Confederacy*, 12; John A. Morgan letter to Sister, May 16, 1861, Box 1, Folder 2, May–December 1861, John A. Morgan Papers, LSU. Manually obtaining water from a river or creek remained labor intensive; however, at least one Louisiana camp had access to a "steam pump . . . for the supply of the camp with water," which no doubt made life easier for at least some soldiers. See A. Parnell letter to P. F. Kendall, Esq., July 26, 1861, Misc. Box, 5, Folder 2, Rebel Archives Collection, Acc. 730, NSU.

48. *New Orleans Crescent*, May 17, 1861, quoted in Casey, ed., *Life at Camp Moore*, 8.

49. By 1864, Confederate leadership in north Louisiana issued orders to "prevent the abuse which is bathing daily indulged in by the men by constant bathing in the river, at all hours of the day." Time limits were set as the men would only "be permitted to bathe in the river between the hours of /8/ Eight A.M. and /4/ Four O'clock P.M." See Genl. Order No. 8 by Lt. Col. Geo. W. Logan, July 4, 1864, Folder 29, George W. Logan Papers, UNC.

50. *New Orleans Sunday Delta*, May 19, 1861, quoted in Casey, *Life at Camp Moore*, 9; John A. Morgan letter to Sister, May 16, 1861, Box 1, Folder 2, May–December 1861, John A. Morgan Papers, LSU.

51. Hewitt and Bergeron, eds., *Louisianians in the Civil War*, 52.

52. J. D. Garland letter to Pa, Ma, and Sister, November 7, 1863, J. D. Garland Papers, Mss. 153, LSU.

53. Miss Sydney Harding Diaries, 1863–1865, Diary for March 10–December 31, 1864, 29 (transcribed copy), Folder 4, Mss. 721, LSU.

54. John S. Billiu letter to wife, November 4, 1861. Box 1, folder 9, John S. Billiu, Civil War Letters, 1861–1862, Mss. 4941, LSU.

55. Silas T. White letter to father, November 8, 1861, Silas T. White Papers, 1861–1862, Mss. 368, LSU.

56. Cashin, *War Stuff*, 1–2; Wadley Journal (typed transcription), pp. 36–37, Folder 7b, Volume 2, UNC.

57. Reubin A. Pierson quoted in Casey, *Life at Camp Moore*, 40–41.

58. Genl. Order No. 8 by Lt. Col. Geo. W. Logan, July 4, 1864, Folder 29, George W. Logan Papers, UNC.

59. W. H. King Journal, entry for June 25, 1862, NSU.

60. Ibid., entry for June 26, 1862, NSU. Soldiers manning the forts on the Mississippi River had similar experiences. After the capture of Fort Jackson, one Union soldier commented on the unsanitary conditions he saw within the compound, which included "stagnant water" and large amounts of "filth was everywhere to be seen." See Pierson, *Mutiny at Fort Jackson*, 24.

61. Gallagher notes that the Confederacy "mobilized between 750,000 and 850,000 men. . . . At least 258,000 of them perished during the war (94,000 on the battlefield and 164,000 from disease)." See Gallagher, *The Confederate War*, 28–29.

62. Faust, *This Republic of Suffering*, 4, 138.

63. Hal letter to wife, November 27, 1861, Folder 13, Slack Family Papers, UNC.

64. Mary W. Milling letter to husband, January 16, 1863, Folder 8, James S. Milling Papers 1863, #3583-Z, UNC.

65. Frank Richardson letter to Father, September 11, 1861, Folder 2, Frank Liddell Richardson Papers, UNC.

66. Wiley, ed., *"This Infernal War,"* 75.

67. John Coleman Sibley Diary, entry for December 17, 1863, Civil War Diary and Letters of John Coleman Sibley, p. 33, NSU.

68. Patrick, *Reluctant Rebel,* ed. Taylor, 88.

69. Vandiver, ed., "A Collection of Louisiana Confederate Letters," 17, 20; E. L. Stephens letter to Ma and Pa, June 25, 1861, Box 1, Folder 1, Stephens Collection, NSU; Louis Stagg letter to wife, Laure (transcribed), October 6, 1861, UAAMC-COLL-Manuscript 7, Folder 1, Louis Stagg Letters, ULL; Charles Cosby letter to "Ma and Sister," August 24, 1864, Box 1, Folder 3, Charles V. Cosby to Margaret Texada Correspondence, 1864–1865, Texada Family Papers, LSU; Hal letter to wife, January[?] 28, 1862, Folder 14, Slack Family Papers, UNC; Joseph Renwick letter to Margaret, August 23, 1864, Box 1, Folder 1, 1863–1865, Mss. 626, Renwick (W. P. and Joseph) Papers, 1863–1884, LSU; W. H. King Journal, entry for October 1–3, 1862, NSU.

70. Meier, *Nature's Civil War,* 1–3.

71. Smith, "The Letters of John Achilles Harris," 10, 13.

72. Cutrer and Parrish, eds., *Brothers in Gray,* 238.

73. Louis Stagg letter to wife, Laure (transcribed), October 6, 1861. UAAMC-COLL-Manuscript 7, Folder 1, Louis Stagg Letters, ULL.

74. Bever, *At War with King Alcohol,* 2–9.

75. Ibid., 14–17, 45.

76. Thrasher, *Miserable Little Conglomeration,* 51–52.

77. Wiley, *Life of Johnny Reb,* 40–43; Jones, *Lee's Tigers Revisited,* 19, 56–57.

78. Cutrer and Parrish, eds., *Brothers in Gray,* 6.

79. Culpepper, "The Life, Letters, and Legacy of Dr. Bartholomew Egan," 91–93.

80. Bever, *At War with King Alcohol,* 48.

81. Cutrer and Parrish, eds., *Brothers in Gray,* 72.

82. Thrasher, *Miserable Little Conglomeration,* 70.

83. Bennett, *A Narrative of the Great Revival,* 36.

84. Bever, *At War with King Alcohol,* 168.

85. Hewitt and Bergeron, eds., *Louisianians in the Civil War,* 67; Williams and Wooster, "Camp Life in Civil War Louisiana," 189, 196; Bearss, ed., *A Louisiana Confederate,* 129; John A. Morgan letter to Sister, July 20, 1861, Box 1, Folder 2, May–December 1861, John A. Morgan Papers, LSU; W. H. King Journal, entry for May 8, 1862, NSU; John Hall letter to Effie Hall, July 1, 1862; and Granville Alspaugh to Amelia Alspaugh quoted in Richard and Richard, *The Defense of Vicksburg,* 55, 103; Lowe, *Walker's Texas Division,* 86; Edmonds, *The Guns of Port Hudson,* 156.

86. Patrick, *Reluctant Rebel,* ed. Taylor, 82; Estaville, *Confederate Neckties,* 42.

87. Posey quoted in Aubrecht, *The Civil War in Spotsylvania County,* 78.

88. Cunningham, *Doctors in Gray,* 197.

89. Cutrer and Parrish, eds., *Brothers in Gray*, 159; Wiley, ed., *"This Infernal War,"* 193.

90. Geo. W. Logan to Brig. Genl. Blanchard, February 2, 1863, Folder 51, George W. Logan Papers, Letter Book volume 1—January 20, 1863–May 19, 1863, #1560, UNC.

91. H. A. Snyder Diary, entries for March 12, 14, 16, 1862, LSU.

92. Owen, *In Camp and Battle with the Washington Artillery*, 203–4.

93. Frank Richardson letter to Father, September 23, 1861, Folder 2, Frank Liddell Richardson Papers, UNC.

94. Russell quoted in Casey, *Life at Camp Moore*, 14.

95. Owen, *In Camp and Battle with the Washington Artillery*, 14.

96. Glatthaar, *General Lee's Army*, 81.

97. Mitchell, *Civil War Soldiers*, 58; Wiley, ed., *"This Infernal War,"* 285–86.

98. Amos Anselm letter to Mrs. Eleanor Anselm (My dear Mother), September 2, 1861, p "Letters from Confederate Soldier," LSU.

99. Dufour, *The Night the War Was Lost*, 35.

100. W. H. King Journal, entry for November 5, 1862, NSU.

101. Williams and Wooster, "Camp Life in Civil War Louisiana," 197.

102. E. S. Stephens letter to William W. Upshaw, November 22, 1861, Box 1, Folder 2, Stephens Collection, NSU.

103. Wiley, ed., *"This Infernal War,"* 30.

104. Mingus, *The Louisiana Tigers in the Gettysburg Campaign*, 10.

105. Wiley, ed., *"This Infernal War,"* 32.

106. Porter quoted in Pierson, *Mutiny at Fort Jackson*, 117.

107. H. W. Howe quoted in ibid., 117.

108. Eugene Janin letter to Father, November 25, 1861, Folder 2, Eugene Janin Papers, UNC.

109. W. H. King Journal, entry for May 19, 1862, NSU.

110. Hall, *The Story of the 26th Louisiana Infantry*, 27. This view of the subordination of Louisianians of French-Catholic heritage (specifically the Acadians) is at odds with other accounts that cast doubt on their commitment to the Confederacy. See Bergeron, "Prison Life at Camp Pratt," 388–89, and Brasseaux, *Acadian to Cajun*, 58–73.

111. William J. Walter letter to Henrietta, August 8, 1861, in Davis, ed. "A Louisiana Volunteer," 82.

112. H. A. Snyder Diary, entry for April 7, 1862, LSU.

113. Thomas A. Benton letter to Lt. Col. G. W. Logan, February 27, 1863, Folder 4, George W. Logan Papers, UNC; Lowe, *Walker's Texas Division*, 115; William Kennedy letter to wife (?), May 1863, Box 4, Folder 46, Larry Crain Collection, SLU; W. H. King Journal, entry for May 21, 1862, NSU.

114. For information and a comparison of discipline in the Union army, see Ramold, *Baring the Iron Hand*.

115. William Kennedy letter to wife, April 23, 1863, Box 4, Folder 46, Larry Crain Collection, SLU.

116. "Proceedings of a Batt. Court Martial," August 5, 1864, Folder 31, George W. Logan Papers, 1864–August, #1560, UNC.

117. Levi Nathan Dunham Diary (transcribed copy), entry for July 6, 1864, p. 4, Levi Nathan

Dunham Diary and Cashbook, 1854, 1856, June–August 1864, Volume 1, Folder Misc.: D, Mss.# 4393, LSU.

118. "General Orders No. 4," Natchitoches, January 11, 1865, Folder 56, George W. Logan Papers, Confederate Army Orders Package 2, #1560, UNC.

119. Bergeron, "Prison Life at Camp Pratt," 388–89.

120. W. H. King Journal, entry for December 11, 1863, NSU.

121. Ibid., entries for December 27, 30, 1863, NSU.

122. Ibid., entry for October 31, 1864, NSU.

123. T. J. Shaffer letter to Andrew, January 20, 1862 [1863], Folder 14, Andrew McCollam Papers, Series 1.2, 1862–1863, UNC.

124. Seymour, *The Civil War Memoirs of Captain William J. Seymour*, ed., Jones, 101.

125. John Coleman Sibley letter to wife, January 1, 1863, Civil War Diary and Letters of John Coleman Sibley, p. 90, NSU.

126. Brasseaux, *Acadian to Cajun*, 72. Mark A. Weitz notes that several Confederate commanders, including Robert E. Lee, believed that "leniency breeds contempt, and without the death sentence there is little hope of deterring men from deserting." See Weitz, *More Damning than Slaughter*, 7.

127. Wiley, ed., *"This Infernal War,"* 61.

128. Frank Richardson letter to Mother & Father, August 17 [11?], 1862, Folder 3, Frank Liddell Richardson Papers, UNC.

129. Weitz, *More Damning than Slaughter*, 13, 26, 44–45, 87.

130. Ellis Diary, entry titled "A Retrospect," p. 24, LSU.

131. Maj. Genl. Taylor to Lt. Col. G. W. Logan, March 10, 1863, Folder 5, George W. Logan Papers, UNC.

132. General Order No. 2, signed S. S. Anderson, A.A. Genl., January 6, 1863, Folder 2, George W. Logan Papers, UNC.

133. Bielski, *Sons of the White Eagle*, 219. Southern civilians, too, also remained under the watchful eyes of their community, which caused many to think twice about how to respond to—and comply with—enemy occupation. See Ash, *When the Yankees Came*, 45.

134. Weitz, *More Damning than Slaughter*, 150–51, 242–44. Weitz claims that Louisiana's highest desertion rates were in the summer of 1864 and that "over the course of the war only 535 men deserted to the enemy. . . . Based on the *Official Records*, Louisiana had the third-lowest total of deserters of the war, behind only Florida and South Carolina." See ibid., 257.

135. Pierson, *Mutiny at Fort Jackson*, 130. Pierson noted that many Louisianians who joined the Union army were largely immigrants or from the north (he cites Benjamin Butler reporting over a thousand Louisianians had joined the Union army by September 1862), but that native Southerners were also part of the fold—"This was not really a war of 'North against South,' . . . It was a war between the United States of America and the Confederate States of America." However, Pierson later states that Butler also hired "2,000 men" to clean the New Orleans and the fact that U.S. loyalty provided employment. Union loyalty, whether military service or government employment, equated to earning money. See ibid., 149. Georgena Duncan provides an Arkansas case study on Southerners who joined Union regiments (some of whom had previous Confederate service), arguing that many local men had a mixed bag of reasons for supporting

both sides, which blurred the ideas—and definitions—of unionism, patriotism, and survival. See Duncan, "Uncertain Loyalties: Dual Enlistment in the Third and Fourth Arkansas Cavalry, USV," 305–32.

136. W. H. King Journal, entry for October 31, 1864, NSU.

137. Lt. Col. Geo. W. Logan letter to Maj. S. Surget, July 1, 1864, Folder 28, 1864—Lists, Ordinances, Reports, Muster Rolls, George W. Logan Papers, UNC. Glatthaar examines the roles and experiences of body servants in the Army of Northern Virginia. See Glatthaar, *General Lee's Army*, 309–14.

138. John Coleman Sibley letter to wife, August 23, 1862, Civil War Diary and Letters of John Coleman Sibley, p. 67, NSU.

139. Winters, *The Civil War in Louisiana*, 35.

140. Taylor, *Destruction and Reconstruction*, 69.

141. Williams, *P. G. T. Beauregard*, 52.

142. Frank Richardson letter to Mother & Father, August 17 [11?], 1862, Folder 3, Frank Liddell Richardson Papers, UNC.

143. Smith, "The Letters of John Achilles Harris," 12.

144. Fred Taber letter to sister and mother, October 19, 1861, Box 1, folder 1861–1862, Frederick R. Taber Papers, LSU.

145. Buck, "A Louisiana Prisoner-of-War on Johnson's Island, 1863–65," 234.

146. Hal letter to wife, February 2, 1862, Folder 14, Slack Family Papers, UNC.

147. Frank Richardson letter to Father, September 1, 1861, Folder 2, Frank Liddell Richardson Papers, UNC.

148. Frank Richardson letter to Father, September 23, 1861, Folder 2, Frank Liddell Richardson Papers, UNC. Body servants who earned money sometimes sent it back home to their families via furloughed soldiers. See Wiley, ed., *"This Infernal War,"* 65.

149. Frank Richardson letter to Father, November 6, 1861, and Frank Richardson letter to Mother, December 14, 1861, Folder 2, Frank Liddell Richardson Papers, UNC.

150. Frank Richardson letter to Father, June 13, 1862, Folder 3, Frank Liddell Richardson Papers, UNC.

151. Wiley, ed., *"This Infernal War,"* 37.

152. Owen, *In Camp and Battle with the Washington Artillery*, 21–22. Owen also mentions that two of the body servants "Jim Ingraham and Dick Kenner, who served the fourth company officers' mess" later became Louisiana politicians during Reconstruction. See ibid, 22.

153. John Coleman Sibley letter to wife, January 24 ,1863, Civil War Diary and Letters of John Coleman Sibley, p. 98, NSU.

154. John Hall letter to Effie Hall, April 2, 1862, quoted in Richard and Richard, *The Defense of Vicksburg*, 17.

155. Wiley, ed., *"This Infernal War,"* 5.

156. Lowe, *Walker's Texas Division*, 93–94.

157. John Coleman Sibley Diary, entry for April 17, 1863, Civil War Diary and Letters of John Coleman Sibley, p. 16, NSU.

158. Frank Richardson letter to Father, April 10, 1862, Folder 3, Frank Liddell Richardson Papers, UNC.

159. Carmichael, *The War for the Common Soldier*, 42–43.

160. W. Ezra Denson letter to John F. Stephens, October 10, 1861, Folder 1861–1864, John F. Stephens Correspondence, LSU.

161. Alfred Flournoy Jr. letter to wife, May 22, 1861, Folder 28, Mildred McCoy Collection, NSU; Eugene Janin to Father, October 7, 1861, Folder 2, Eugene Janin Papers, UNC.

5. PHYSICAL INTERACTIONS

1. Ellis Diary, entry titled "A Retrospect," p. 24, LSU.

2. *New Orleans Sunday Delta,* June 2, 1861, quoted in Casey, *Life at Camp Moore,* 19.

3. William Nicholson letter to sister, September 28, 1861, Folder 1861, William Nicholson Letters, LSU.

4. Frank Richardson to Father, November 6, 1861, Folder 2, Frank Liddell Richardson Papers, UNC.

5. Charles Cosby letter to Madam (Margaret Texada), March 1, 1864, Box 1, Folder 2, Charles V. Cosby to Margaret Texada Correspondence, 1863–1864, Texada Family Papers, LSU. Even as Louisiana troops marched through Pennsylvania during the Gettysburg campaign, their dancing and merrymaking caught the attention of the local Northerners. See Mingus, *The Louisiana Tigers in the Gettysburg Campaign,* 66. French-speaking Acadian soldiers serving in the Army of Northern Virginia were no strangers to a good time; however, not all Confederate commanders and fellow soldiers were as impressed with their music and dancing skills. See Parrish, *Richard Taylor,* 159–60; Taylor, *Destruction and Reconstruction,* 49.

6. Louisiana Confederate Felix Poché noted an opportunity to attend a "grand Indian ball game (Raquette)," but remained unimpressed with the other spectacles mimicking an Indian dance, which "The singing absurd, and the dance insipid, nothing like the real Indian dance." See Bearss, ed., *A Louisiana Confederate,* 47, 117.

7. Isaac Hall letter to Mary Hall and Children, March 23, 1862, quoted in Richard and Richard, *The Defense of Vicksburg,* 12, 16, 50.

8. Williams and Wooster, "Camp Life in Civil War Louisiana," 190–91.

9. Owen, *In Camp and Battle with the Washington Artillery,* 50.

10. Bielski, *Sons of the White Eagle,* 101–3. The unit's colonel, Valery Sulakowski, had prior military experience in Austria as a staff officer and knew the value of discipline. See Kajencki, "The Louisiana Tiger," 49–51.

11. Wallace, "Coppens' Louisiana Zouaves," 273–75.

12. Gache, *A Frenchman, a Chaplain, a Rebel,* 43.

13. Jones, "Going Back into the Union at Last," 56.

14. Mingus, *The Louisiana Tigers in the Gettysburg Campaign,* 76.

15. "Your Brother TBJ" to Sister, May 18, 1861, Folder 1, Thomas Benjamin Davidson Papers, UNC.

16. Cutrer and Parrish, eds., *Brothers in Gray,* 31–32.

17. Bearss, ed., *A Louisiana Confederate,* 81–82.

18. Frank Richardson to Mother, October 8, 1862, Folder 3, Frank Liddell Richardson Papers, UNC.

19. W. H. King Journal, entry for May 10, 1862, NSU.

20. Wiley, ed., *Fourteen Hundred and 91 Days in the Confederate Army,* 211.

21. Brasseaux, *Acadian to Cajun,* 73.

22. Durham, "Dear Rebecca," 181.

23. Thrasher, *Miserable Little Conglomeration,* 49, 97.

24. W. H. King Journal, entry for November 4, 1862, NSU.

25. Owen, *In Camp and Battle with the Washington Artillery,* 21.

26. "An Act For The Enlistment Of Cooks In The Army," November 3, 1862, Folder 56, George W. Logan Papers, Confederate Army Orders Package 2, #1560, UNC.

27. John Coleman Sibley letter to wife, March 22, 1863, Civil War Diary and Letters of John Coleman Sibley, p. 110, NSU.

28. For example, in southeastern Louisiana, Hyde notes that since many men were in the Confederate service, "inadequate resources remained to sustain the prewar legal structure." In some cases, this placed the burden of law enforcement on Confederate commanders. Later in the war, the 1st Louisiana Cavalry operated in southeastern Louisiana, which "occasioned great rejoicing among the men of the command and inspired a new confidence among the long-suffering resident." See Hyde, *Pistols and Politics,* 118, 132. For an example of soldiers assisting traveling women, see Bearss, ed., *A Louisiana Confederate,* 160.

29. W. W. [?] to Major E. Lurget[?], July 1, 1864, Folder 29, George W. Logan Papers, UNC.

30. W. H. King Journal, entry for December 22, 1863, NSU.

31. Owen, *In Camp and Battle with the Washington Artillery,* 70–71.

32. Bearss, ed., *A Louisiana Confederate,* 4–5.

33. Robert Newell letter to Sarah, March 1863, Box 1, folder 2b, Robert A. Newell Papers, LSU.

34. Frazier, *Fire in the Cane Field,* 99.

35. Wadley Journal (typed transcription), 79, 88, Folder 7b, Volume 2, UNC.

36. William Nicholson letter to sister, September 27, 1861, Folder 1861, William Nicholson Letters, LSU.

37. William Nicholson letter to sister, October 4, 1861, Folder 1861, William Nicholson Letters, LSU.

38. Frazier, *Fire in the Cane Field,* 113.

39. Scriber and Arnold-Scriber, *The Fourth Louisiana Battalion in the Civil War,* 177.

40. Power Diary, January 1, 1862–September 28, 1863 (typed transcription), p. 80, Folder 2, UNC.

41. Sheeran, *Confederate Chaplain,* ed., Durkin, 55.

42. Bearss, ed., *A Louisiana Confederate,* 13.

43. Ellis Diary, entry titled "A Retrospect," pp. 26–27, LSU.

44. Wesley, *The Politics of Faith during the Civil War,* 131.

45. W. H. King Journal, entry for November 29, 1863, NSU.

46. Smith, "The Letters of John Achilles Harris," 7.

47. John Coleman Sibley Diary, entry for December 6, 1863, Civil War Diary and Letters of John Coleman Sibley, p. 33, NSU.

48. Sheeran, *Confederate Chaplain,* 55.

49. Shattuck, *A Shield and a Hiding Place,* 43–45.

50. Antebellum preachers had a prominent role in both Northern and Southern society

before the war, influencing the religious, public, and political realm. See Wesley, *The Politics of Faith during the Civil War, 3.* For information on camp revivals, see Woodworth, *While God is Marching On;* Romero, *Religion in the Rebel Ranks;* Faust, "Christian Soldiers," 63–90; Jones, *Christ in the Camp;* Shattuck, *A Shield and a Hiding Place.*

51. John E. Hall letter to Julia, April 13, 1862, Box 8, Folder 58, Larry Crain Collection, SLU.

52. Hal letter to wife, January[?] 28, 1862, Folder 14, Slack Family Papers, UNC.

53. R. J. Causey letter to Wife, September 25, 1863, Folder Misc.: C, R. J. Causey Correspondence, LSU.

54. Jacob Alison Frierson letter to Ma, June 23, 1864, Box 1, Folder 1, Frierson, Jacob Alison Correspondence and Minutes, 1864–1865, LSU.

55. John Bond Diary, entry for November 2, 1862, quoted in Richard and Richard, *The Defense of Vicksburg,* 87.

56. Amos Anselm letter to Mrs. Eleanor Anselm (My dear Mother), July 24, 1861, "Letters from Confederate Soldier," LSU.

57. John Coleman Sibley letter to wife, December 7, 1863, Civil War Diary and Letters of John Coleman Sibley, p. 137, NSU. Though some army chaplains and civilian preachers did abandon the cause, many remained in the ranks despite the hardships of soldiering. For more information on the religious experiences of Confederate soldiers and chaplains, see Norton, *Rebel Religion;* Pitts, *Chaplains in Gray;* Romero, *Religion in the Rebel Ranks;* Romero, "Louisiana Clergy and the Confederate Army," 277–300; and Hieronymus, "For Now and Forever."

58. Lowe, *Walker's Texas Division,* 77.

59. "Your Brother TBJ" to Sister, May 18, 1861, Folder 1, Thomas Benjamin Davidson Papers, UNC.

60. Dawson, *A Confederate Girl's Diary,* ed. Robertson, 27.

61. J. D. Garland letter to My dear parents, February 18, 1864, J. D. Garland Papers, LSU.

62. T.B. quoted in Casey, *Life at Camp Moore,* 69, 72.

63. Owen, *In Camp and Battle with the Washington Artillery,* 295.

64. Marvel, *Lee's Last Retreat,* 12–13, 36.

65. Miss Sydney Harding Diaries, 1863–1865, Diary for July 20, 1863–January 20, 1864 (transcribed copy), entry for July 26, 1863, Folder 2, LSU.

66. John Coleman Sibley letter to wife, September 7, 1862, Civil War Diary and Letters of John Coleman Sibley, p. 72, NSU.

67. W. H. King Journal, entry for May 27, 1862, NSU. At least one Union camp near Baton Rouge also fostered ungentlemanly conduct in the presence of female visitors. John H. Crowder, a young Black lieutenant stationed near Baton Rouge, related to his mother an anecdote of two fellow officers who were "the most pucillanamous dirty Low life men that I ever seen . . . they seem to think that there is not a woman that they cannot sleep with, every woman seems to be a 'common woman' with them . . . a married Lady with a young girl came to camp to see us . . . one of the privates; made signs at the married lady of the most disrespectful kind." When the lady pointed the soldier out to some of the officers in camp, he insulted them and "then left." See John H. Crowder letter to Mother, April 27, 1863, Folder 1, in the John H. Crowder Letters (photocopied), #5276-Z, UNC.

68. Wiley, ed., *"This Infernal War,"* 208.

69. Wadley Journal (typed transcription), pp. 17-19, Folder 8a, Volume 3, UNC.

70. Miss Sydney Harding Diaries, 1863-1865, Diary for July 20, 1863-January 20, 1864 (transcribed copy), entries for July 26 and November 4, 1863, Folder 2, LSU.

71. Miss Sydney Harding Diaries, 1863-1865, Diary for March 10, 1864-December 31, 1864 (transcribed copy), p. 16, Folder 4, LSU.

72. Power Diary, January 1, 1862-September 28, 1863 (typed transcription), p. 49, Folder 2, UNC.

73. Thrasher, *Miserable Little Conglomeration,* 51.

74. Jimmie letter to John Coleman Sibley, May 28, 1865, Civil War Diary and Letters of John Coleman Sibley, p. 197, NSU.

75. Louis Stagg letter to wife, Laure (transcribed), October 6, 1861, UAAMC-COLL-Manuscript 7, Folder 1, Louis Stagg Letters, ULL.

76. Lowe, *Walker's Texas Division,* 119.

77. W. H. King Journal, entry for December 8, 1863, NSU.

78. Faust, *Mothers of Invention,* 10.

79. Ibid., 17. In an earlier work, Faust notes the central role Southern women played in the Civil War—and the South's defeat. See Drew Gilpin Faust, "Altars of Sacrifice," 1201-3.

80. Ward, *Garden of Ruins,* 134-35.

81. Dawson, *A Confederate Girl's Diary,* ed. Robertson, 24.

82. Wiley, ed., *"This Infernal War,"* 326-27.

83. Lizzie Fitzgerald letter to Delia Singleton, April 27, 1862, Archive #241 MSS Microfilm of John David Phillips, Jr. of Boyce, Louisiana, Sixteen letters of Lizzie Fitzgerald, Lake Providence, La., to Miss Delia Singleton, Bayou Chicot, La.., 1858-1866, NSU (hereafter Letters of Fitzgerald to Singleton, NSU).

84. Lizzie Fitzgerald letter to Delia Singleton, August 15, 1862, Letters of Fitzgerald to Singleton, NSU.

85. Cater, *As It Was,* xix.

86. W. H. King Journal, entry for May 22, 1862, NSU.

87. Cutrer and Parrish, eds., *Brothers in Gray,* 51.

88. John Coleman Sibley Diary, entry for November 20, 1864, Civil War Diary and Letters of John Coleman Sibley, p. 48, NSU.

89. William H. Tamplin letter to Tincia[?], February 20, 1864, Folder 1862-1865, n.d., #3015, William H. Tamplin Letters, LSU.

90. Hal letter to wife, February 2, 1862, Folder 14, Slack Family Papers, UNC.

91. Geo. W. Peyton, H. T. Jones, W. H. Gordan, and Robert Stothart to Maj. Samuel McCutcheon [all separate requests], August 23-24, 1864, Folder 31, George W. Logan Papers, 1864—August, #1560, UNC.

92. Pos. R. Garcia to Miss Maggie, January 12, 1864, Folder 1, Marguerite E. Williams Papers, 1858-1864, #3102-Z, UNC.

93. Power Diary, January 1, 1862-September 28, 1863 (typed transcription), p. 51, Folder 2, UNC.

94. E. J. Ellis quoted in Wiley, *Life of Johnny Reb,* 130-31.

95. W. H. King Journal, entry for June 13, 1862, NSU.

96. Ibid., entry for June 19, 1862, NSU.

97. Ash, *When the Yankees Came,* 77–107.

98. Patrick, *Reluctant Rebel,* ed. Taylor, 133.

99. Bond, *A Maryland Bride in the Deep South,* ed. Harrison, 241.

100. Amelia Faulkner letter to Henrietta Lauzin, May 24, 1864, Mss. 5, Gras-Lauzin Papers, LSU (Louisiana Digital Library).

101. W. H. King Journal, entry for May 29, 1862, NSU.

102. H. N. Connor Diary, no date, quote taken from "Notes" section of diary, which Connor added in late 1865–66, ULL.

103. Owen, *In Camp and Battle with the Washington Artillery,* 21.

104. William H. Tamplin letter to sister, August 11, 1863, Folder 1862–1865, William H. Tamplin Letters, LSU.

105. Frank Richardson letter to Mother & Father, August 17 [11?], 1862, Folder 3, Frank Liddell Richardson Papers, UNC.

106. Isaac Erwin Diary, entries for July 30, 31, 1862, and August 6, 10, 24, 1862, Folder 1210, Melrose Collection, NSU; Wiley, ed., *"This Infernal War,"* 307.

107. Wadley Journal (typed transcription), p. 17, Folder 8a, Volume 3, UNC.

108. John Coleman Sibley letter to wife, February 6, 1863, Civil War Diary and Letters of John Coleman Sibley, p. 99, NSU.

109. Wadley Journal (typed transcription), p. 96, Folder 7b, Volume 2, UNC.

110. One sick Louisiana soldier stationed in Mississippi wrote his sister that he "came to where an old free negro lived, so I put up with him and was treated very well." See Cutrer and Parrish, eds., *Brothers in Gray,* 150. Some Free Blacks did support the Confederacy; one, who was a New Orleans real estate agent, gave "$500 to aid the Confederate army." See Winters, *The Civil War in Louisiana,* 39. In 1864, a group of Confederates tasked with a scouting mission in south Louisiana aimed to capture Union pickets stationed nearby. The soldiers "ran across a negro that had been through the lines and knew where the sentinels were posted and agreed to put us to the place that night." With the African American's help, the Confederates made it to the picket lines, but fearing capture they decided to abort the mission of taking Yankee prisoners, but not without taking a Federal horse as a prize. See Confederate Soldier Manuscript Scouting Trip to Louisiana, letter, no date, UAAMC-COLL-Manuscript 252, Folder 1, ULL.

111. Gleeson, "The Rhetoric of Insurrection and Fear," 261.

112. This was no small operation. Louisiana Unionist Dennis Haynes recalled being held captive by a planter who was moving to Texas, and his transport included a wagon train that stretched "over a mile" long. Haynes noted that the planter had "along all his stock, cattle, and sheep, about twenty wagons, about a dozen carriages, and three hundred negroes." See Haynes, *A Thrilling Narrative,* ed., Bergeron, 14–15.

113. Hewitt and Bergeron, eds., *Louisianians in the Civil War,* 32. The war took its toll on many plantations and their ability to provide enough food for themselves—and for wartime refugees. One Louisianian expressed her concerns to her husband about the influx of refugees arriving in the Florida Parishes, claiming that "there was nothing to eat . . . and these that come bring nothing with them, they will be sure to starve." See Hyde, *Pistols and Politics,* 123.

114. Isaac Erwin Diary, entry for August 10, 1862, Folder 1210, Melrose Collection, NSU.

115. J. D. Garland letter to My dear parents, February 18, 1864, J. D. Garland Papers, LSU. For information about African American experiences in Union occupied Louisiana, see Ward, *Garden of Ruins,* 146–50, 163–95.

116. Isaac Erwin Diary, entries for February 23, 1863, and May 9, 1863, Folder 1210, Melrose Collection, NSU.

117. Bayside Plantation Record Book 1860–1868 (transcribed), entry for April 20, 1863, UAAMC-COLL 481, Box 1, ULL.

118. John Coleman Sibley Diary, entry for December 30, 1863, Civil War Diary and Letters of John Coleman Sibley, p. 34, NSU.

119. Charles D. Moore letter to wife, March 4, 1863, Charles D. Moore letters to wife Kate, March 20, 1862–April 6, 1864, Mss. 5231, LSU. Moore also stated a few days later that Union soldiers were also running away, claiming dissatisfaction with army life. See Charles D. Moore letter to wife, March 18, 1863. Some Louisiana residents also saw and interacted with Union deserters, sometimes offering them shelter. See Power Diary, January 1, 1862–September 28, 1863 (typed transcription), p. 97, Folder 2, UNC.

120. Lizzie Fitzgerald letter to Delia Singleton, August 15, 1862, Letters of Fitzgerald to Singleton, NSU.

121. W. H. King Journal, entry for April 17, 1863, NSU.

122. Wadley Journal (typed transcription), p. 197–98, Folder 8b, Volume 4, UNC.

123. Bayside Plantation Record Book 1860–1868 (transcribed), entry for January 8, 1864, UAAMC-COLL 481, Box 1, ULL.

124. Isaac Erwin Diary, entries for May 10, 31, 1863, and June 6, 1863, Folder 1210, Melrose Collection, NSU.

125. Miss Sydney Harding Diaries, 1863–1865, Diary for March 10, 1864–December 31, 1864 (transcribed copy), p. 43, Folder 4, LSU.

126. Blanche DeClouet letter to Paul (typescript), June 25, 1861, UAAMC-COLL-22, Box 3, Folder 4, DeClouet Family Papers, ULL.

127. Glatthaar, *General Lee's Army,* 307.

128. Ripley, *Slaves and Freedmen in Civil War Louisiana,* 9.

129. L. G. Causey letter to Husband (R. J. Causey), November 19, 1863, Folder Misc.: C, R. J. Causey Correspondence, LSU.

130. John M. Sacher, "'Twenty-Negro,' or Overseer Law," 269–72.

131. O'Donovan, *Becoming Free in the Cotton South,* 86–87.

132. Sheehan-Dean, *The Calculus of Violence,* 56–57.

133. Power Diary, January 1, 1862–September 28, 1863 (typed transcription), pp. 97–98, Folder 2, UNC.

134. Ripley, *Slaves and Freedmen in Civil War Louisiana,* 42–43, 114–15.

135. Hewitt and Bergeron, eds., *Louisianians in the Civil War,* 14; Louis Stagg letter to wife, Laure (transcribed), June 9, 1863, UAAMC-COLL-Manuscript 7, Folder 1, Louis Stagg Letters, ULL.

136. *New Orleans Daily Crescent,* August 28, 1861, quoted in Casey, *Life at Camp Moore,* 53–54.

137. T.B. quoted in Casey, *Life at Camp Moore,* 73–74.

138. Bearss, ed., *A Louisiana Confederate,* 8.

139. Bragg, *Louisiana in the Confederacy,* 36; Brasseaux, Fontenot, and Oubre, *Creoles of Color in the Bayou Country,* 75–78. After the Civil War, many of these Free Black property owners—like many of their White neighbors—"found themselves impoverished." See ibid., 87.

140. T.B. quoted in Casey, *Life at Camp Moore,* 76.

6. SOLDIER PROVISIONS AND TRADE

1. *OR,* ser, I, vol. 53, 616–17. For a study on the Trans-Mississippi theater's strategic importance and logistics, see Hess, *Civil War Supply and Strategy,* 266–90.

2. Gienapp, *Abraham Lincoln and Civil War America,* 137–38.

3. Sacher, "'Our Interest and Destiny Are the Same,'" 270. The commander at the time of Moore's missive to Davis was "the ill, seventy-one-year-old Gen. David Twiggs . . . barely able to walk." Mansfield Lovell replaced Twiggs. See ibid., 270–71.

4. For examples of the importance of the "household" to soldiers, see Whites, "Written on the Heart," in Frank and Whites, *Household War;* Whites, "Forty Shirts and a Wagonload of Wheat." For a discussion on Confederate women's involvement in wartime trade, see Ruminski, "'Tradyville,'" 524–27. Earl J. Hess claims that weak Confederate supply "support systems" always kept them tethered to the South, hindering long-term offensive operations. Living off the land—often at the local population's mercy—proved a weak link in Confederate war strategy. See Hess, *Civil War Supply and Strategy,* 12–13.

5. Johnson, "Trading with the Union," 308–9.

6. Ibid., 316.

7. Ash, *When the Yankees Came,* 80–81.

8. W. H. King Journal, entry for May 7, 1862, NSU.

9. Roland, *Louisiana Sugar Plantations,* 30.

10. P. L. Prudhomme letter to Lestan Prudhomme, November 28, 1862, Folder 270, Robert DeBlieux Collection, NSU.

11. Hyde, *Pistols and Politics,* 114. Hyde notes that many of these farmers feared the lack of a protection force, which they felt "is due to so loyal a population," and would only encourage attacks from "an enemy greedy for destruction."

12. Lowe, *Walker's Texas Division,* 114.

13. Vandiver, ed., "A Collection of Louisiana Confederate Letters," 6–7.

14. Smith, "The Letters of John Achilles Harris," 10.

15. Fred Taber letter to sister, September 12, 1861, Box 1, Folder 1861–1862, Frederick R. Taber Papers, LSU.

16. Silas T. White letter to father, January 17, 1862, Silas T. White Papers, LSU.

17. Vandiver, ed., "A Collection of Louisiana Confederate Letters," 23, 27.

18. William Nicholson letter to sister. 27 September 1861. Folder 1861, William Nicholson Letters, LSU.

19. Williams and Wooster, "Camp Life in Civil War Louisiana," 192.

20. John Coleman Sibley letter to wife, September 3, 1862, Civil War Diary and Letters of John Coleman Sibley, p. 70, NSU.

21. John Coleman Sibley letter to wife, September 25, 1864, Civil War Diary and Letters of John Coleman Sibley, p. 157, NSU.

22. Frank Richardson to Father, September 1, 1861, Folder 2, Frank Liddell Richardson Papers, UNC.

23. Louis Stagg letter to wife, Laure (transcribed), October 15, 1861, and November 26, 1861, UAAMC-COLL-Manuscript 7, Folder 1, Louis Stagg Letters, ULL.

24. John E. Hall letter to wife, April 2, 1862, Box 8, Folder 58, Larry Crain Collection, SLU.

25. Isaac Hall letter to Mary Hall and Children, May 26, 1862, quoted in Richard and Richard, *The Defense of Vicksburg,* 39.

26. T. J. Shaffer to Andrew, January 20, 1862 [1863], Folder 14, Andrew McCollam Papers, UNC.

27. John Coleman Sibley letter to wife, December 8, 1862, Civil War Diary and Letters of John Coleman Sibley, p. 86, NSU.

28. Phelps quoted in Jones, *Lee's Tigers,* 34.

29. W. H. King Journal, entry for May 8, 1862, NSU. Campaigning soldiers often foraged while marching; however, the army provided a few days' worth of rations (when available) for the men on the move. But not all soldiers took food conservation seriously. One soldier claimed his comrade would eat his allotted rations in one sitting "then starve or steal until next draw day." See Mingus, *The Louisiana Tigers in the Gettysburg Campaign,* 18.

30. Isaac Erwin Diary, entry for September 13, 1863, Folder 1210, Melrose Collection, NSU.

31. For example, Confederate cake, which substituted cornmeal for flour, became common among Louisiana residents. See Bond, *A Maryland Bride in the Deep South,* ed. Harrison, 325. Many Louisianians found substitutes for the ever-scarce coffee, which included using dried, parched, and ground okra seeds or rye, along with another recipe that used sweet potatoes or "a weed known as Indian or wild coffee." See Dufour, *The Night the War Was Lost,* 63.

32. John Coleman Sibley letter to wife, November 14, 1862, Civil War Diary and Letters of John Coleman Sibley, p. 84, NSU.

33. Power Diary, January 1, 1862–September 28, 1863 (typed transcription), pp. 82–88, Folder 2, UNC. While serving in Tennessee, Edwin Fay noted the hospitality of local civilians— and their willingness to share what they had. See Wiley, ed., *"This Infernal War,"* 72.

34. John Coleman Sibley letter to wife, November 5, 1862, Civil War Diary and Letters of John Coleman Sibley, p. 82, NSU; Edmonds, *The Guns of Port Hudson, Volume Two,* 295.

35. Vandiver, ed., "A Collection of Louisiana Confederate Letters," 39–40; J. D. Garland letter to Pa and Mother, January 20, 1864, J. D. Garland Papers, LSU. For information on the struggle to feed the Army of Northern Virginia, see Hess, *Civil War Supply and Strategy,* 328–56.

36. T.B. quoted in Casey, *Life at Camp Moore,* 69.

37. Jones, *Lee's Tigers,* 13.

38. Durham, "Dear Rebecca," 173.

39. Patrick, *Reluctant Rebel,* ed. Taylor, 91.

40. Alexander Pierre Allain Diary, trans. Raymond E. Allain Sr., entry for April 11, 1864, Private Collection of Raymond E. Allain Sr. (hereafter cited as Allain Diary, APC). Transcriber Raymond E. Allain Sr. notes the inconsistencies with the diary's entry dates as each notebook page has a printed date and some of the entries have a handwritten date by the author. Because of this, the author's handwritten date will be used when provided, but in its absence the printed date on the page will be used.

41. For example, Georgia soldier R. H. Brooks, who served in Virginia, wrote that "we all

have suffered very much ever since for something to eat. . . . but we all stand it and is as harty as bucks. we spend all we can get for something to eat to keep from perishing." R. H. Brooks letter to wife, July 25, 1863, Archive #245, Mansfield Museum MSS Microfilm Reel 6 of 6, NSU. For an in-depth study of the challenges of supplying Civil War soldiers, see Hess, *Civil War Supply and Strategy*.

42. *Port Hudson: Its History*, 13.

43. John A. Morgan letter to Sister, March 24, 1863, Box 1, Folder 4, January–May 1863, 1864, John A. Morgan Papers, LSU.

44. Power Diary, January 1, 1862–September 28, 1863 (typed transcription), p. 96, Folder 2, UNC. Like soldiers, military animals, especially calvary horses, also suffered from a lack of provisions. See Williams and Wooster, "Camp Life in Civil War Louisiana," 194.

45. "The Siege and Fall of Port Hudson," *Daily Dispatch* (Richmond), July 23, 1863. The soldiers at Vicksburg, who were also short on rations, resorted to eating mules, but whether they actually ate rats is questionable. One response to the idea that rats were eaten might have referred to muskrats. See Richard and Richard, *The Defense of Vicksburg*, 218–19.

46. W. H. King Journal, entry for September 21, 1864, NSU.

47. Owen, *In Camp and Battle with the Washington Artillery*, 76.

48. Food shortages were not the only thing Confederate soldiers contended with. A lack of equipment also made apparent the Confederacy's failure to keep their men supplied. Officials kept soldiers accountable for their issued items; however, some soldiers felt their lack of prepa-rations remained an individual concern. See W. H. King Journal, entry for December 21, 1863, NSU; Frank Richardson letter to Father, September 23, 1861, Folder 2, Frank Liddell Richardson Papers, UNC. Battlefield recovery and capturing Yankee supplies sometimes brought an intermis-sion to provisional deficiencies, and an alternative to illicit trade—or confiscation, especially after a rebel victory. See John Coleman Sibley Diary, entry for June 22–23, 1863, Civil War Diary and Letters of John Coleman Sibley, p. 22, NSU; Meiners, "Hamilton P. Bee in the Red River Cam-paign of 1864," 27; James T. Wallace Diary, p. 60, entry for April 9, 1864, Folder 1, James T. Wallace Diary 1862–1865, #3059-Z, UNC; Mingus, *The Louisiana Tigers in the Gettysburg Campaign*, 55; Julien Rachal letter to sister, April 12, 1864, Folder 23, Mildred McCoy Collection, NSU.

49. Alfred Flournoy Sr. to Alfred Flournoy Jr., June 16, 1861, Folder 28, Mildred McCoy Collection, NSU.

50. Alex de Clouet letter to Paul, October 17, 1861, UAAMC-COLL-22, Box 1, Folder 17, DeClouet Family Papers, ULL.

51. H. A. Snyder Diary, entry for January 2, 1862, LSU.

52. Andrew McCollam Jr. to Father, March 20, 1863, Folder 14, Andrew McCollam Papers, UNC. The Union blockade, which perhaps testifies to its effectiveness, had some positive health benefits for many Louisianians as it kept yellow fever at bay. See Hearn, *The Capture of New Orleans, 1862*, 65.

53. J. D. Garland letter to Pa, Ma, and Sister, November 7, 1863, J. D. Garland Papers, LSU.

54. Williams and Wooster, "Camp Life in Civil War Louisiana," 193. As a price comparison, one Louisiana planter noted that his son purchased a sack of flour in 1863 that "cost 130$." See Isaac Erwin Diary, entry for April 25, 1863, Folder 1210, Melrose Collection, NSU.

55. William Nicholson letter to sister, September 27, 1861, Folder 1861, William Nicholson Letters, LSU.

56. Dufour, *The Night the War Was Lost,* 112; John Coleman Sibley Diary, entry for November 20, 1864, Civil War Diary and Letters of John Coleman Sibley, p. 48, NSU.

57. W. Ezra Denson letter to John F. Stephens, November 16, 1861, Folder 1861–1864, John F. Stephens Correspondence, LSU. However, some soldiers remained able to get supplies, For example, one group of Louisianians in Mississippi enjoyed their commanding officer's culinary feats, such as "a most delicious chicken pie. . . . He occasionally regales us with Gumbo." See P. L. Prudhomme letter to Lestan Prudhomme, February 28, 1863, Folder 270, Robert De-Blieux Collection, NSU.

58. J. Ray letter to Lucinda (typescript), July 16, 1862, UAAMC-COLL-65, Box 1, Folder 4, Gerbert-Ray-Lee Families Papers, ULL. Confederate officials under Henry Watkins Allen's direction also took the initiative, establishing drug and medicinal laboratories to manufacture turpentine, opium, castor oil, and medicinal whiskey to benefit the sick and wounded. Success, with mixed results, depended on both military and civilian cooperation. See Gov. Henry W. Allen to the Enrolling Officer of St. Martin Parish, February 18, 1865, Folder 3, Annie Blackwell Thorne Correspondence, UNC; Culpepper, "The Life, Letters, and Legacy of Dr. Bartholomew Egan," 90–91.

59. P. L. Prudhomme letter to Lestan Prudhomme, November 28, 1862, Folder 270, Robert DeBlieux Collection, NSU.

60. Melissa letter to "Dearest" (C. C. Dunn), March 8, 1863, Folder 1, Juanita Henry Collection, NSU; L. G. Causey letter to Husband (R. J. Causey), October 14, 1863, Folder Misc.: C, R. J. Causey Correspondence, LSU.

61. [No Name] letter to Sallie, December 21, 1861, Box 1, Folder 2, May–December 1861, John A. Morgan Papers, LSU.

62. Roland, *Louisiana Sugar Plantations,* 43.

63. See Brasseaux and Fontenot, *Steamboats on Louisiana's Bayous,* 79–109; Grimsley, "Remorseless, Revolutionary Struggle: A People's War," in *Struggle for a Vast Future,* ed. Sheehan-Dean, 100–101. Though Louisiana's railroad infrastructure paled in comparison with other regions, it did have an important route that connected New Orleans with Northern cities. During the war, military transportation took precedence. See Estaville, *Confederate Neckties,* 19, 24. For discussions on the growing competition between steamboats and railroads, see Gudmestad, *Steamboats and the Rise of the Cotton Kingdom,* 165–68. For discussions on the railroad's wartime contribution (and destruction) in Louisiana, see Estaville, "A Small Contribution," 95–96, 101, 103; Bacon, *Among the Cotton Thieves,* 88–89.

64. John A. Morgan letter to Sister, November 12, 1861, Box 1, Folder 2, May–December 1861, John A. Morgan Papers, LSU. For insight into soldiers' (often miserable) experiences on trains, see William Dixon Diary, entry for May 2, 1862, quoted in Richard and Richard, *The Defense of Vicksburg,* 26. For examples of civilians using railroads to visit their soldiers in camp, see John Bond Diary, entry for February 3, 1863, quoted in Richard and Richard, *The Defense of Vicksburg,* 115; Ellis Diary, entry titled "A Retrospect," p. 29, LSU.

65. Hess, *Civil War Supply and Strategy,* 335.

66. John Coleman Sibley letter to wife, May 2, 1863, Civil War Diary and Letters of John Coleman Sibley, p. 113, NSU. Numerous farm animals often fell victim in the wake of warring armies, along with other barnyard structures. See George H. Hepworth quoted in Wade, "'I Would Rather Be among the Comanches,'" 48.

67. Joseph Welsh Texada letter to Margaret Texada, September 5, 1864, Box 1, Folder 23, Texada Family Papers, LSU.

68. Joseph Welsh Texada letter to Margaret Texada, September 17, 1864, Box 1, Folder 24, Texada Family Papers, LSU.

69. Col. Louis Bush letter to Mr. Benj. DeBlieux, June 13, 1864, Folder 35, Robert DeBlieux Collection, NSU; Request for return of 2 saddles to Mrs. Kleinpeter, December 29, 1862, Box 1, Folder 18, Kleinpeter Collection, SLU.

70. Bearss, ed., *A Louisiana Confederate*, 187.

71. Sacher, "Our Interest and Destiny Are the Same," 272–74. For more on Governor Moore's appeal to Southern soldiers to avenge Southern women under Union occupation in New Orleans, see Frank, *The Civilian War*, 30. For a recent study on Butler, which shifts his image away from illicit trade dealings to his role in promoting freedom and rights for African Americans, see Leonard, *Benjamin Franklin Butler*. For an analysis of Butler's actions in relation to Louisiana's Civil War households and Union occupation, see Ward, *Garden of Ruins*, 45–76.

72. Plater, *The Butlers of Iberville Parish, Louisiana*, 153.

73. *OR*, ser. I, vol. 53, 892–94.

74. Brother to sister Mary, August 10, 1863, Folder 32, Brashear-Lawrence Family Papers, UNC.

75. Taylor, "Discontent in Confederate Louisiana," 416–17.

76. W. H. King Journal, entry for May 9, 1862, NSU.

77. Lowe, *Walker's Texas Division*, 114.

78. Sacher, "Our Interest and Destiny Are the Same," 275–76.

79. Roland, *Louisiana Sugar Plantations*, 70–71.

80. Taylor, "Discontent in Confederate Louisiana," 424.

81. James T. Wallace Diary, entry for April 3, 1864, p. 59, Folder 1, UNC.

82. John Coleman Sibley letter to wife, January 16, 1863, Civil War Diary and Letters of John Coleman Sibley, p. 94, NSU.

83. Jones, *Lee's Tigers*, 33.

84. Lowe, *Walker's Texas Division*, 133.

85. Roland, *Louisiana Sugar Plantations*, 55. One Northern tutor who remained in Louisiana during the war saw the destruction firsthand. Her sympathies for the South were so strong that she wrote, "I informed my fiancée [a Federal officer] that I would return home, but after seeing the horror Federal soldiers have wreaked upon the South I could not marry him unless he resigned." See Hyde, *Pistols and Politics*, 115.

86. Sacher, "Our Interest and Destiny Are the Same," 274–75.

87. Bragg, *Louisiana in the Confederacy*, 261.

88. Frazier, *Fire in the Cane Field*, 74–75.

89. Bragg, *Louisiana in the Confederacy*, 259. Bragg discusses two men who are mentioned as returning to the Union: John K. Elgee, who had served on the 1861 Secession Convention flag committee, and Lewis Texada, who had run for lieutenant governor in 1856.

90. Brasseaux, *Acadian to Cajun*, 72–73. While Louisiana residents' sincerity toward Union occupation remained doubtful, Ward notes that "these friendly relationships with southern household members proved beneficial to occupier and occupied alike," which centered on the (complex) idea of mutualism "between state and people." See Ward, *Garden of Ruins*, 80–81.

91. L. G. Causey letter to Husband (R. J. Causey), October 14, 1863, Folder Misc.: C, R. J. Causey Correspondence, LSU.

92. Ibid. Southerners across the Confederacy suffered from the increasing taxes and impressment put on them by their states and Confederate authorities, and often it was the poorer civilians who suffered most. See Escott, *Military Necessity,* 76–79.

93. Brother to sister Mary, August 10, 1863, Folder 32, Brashear-Lawrence Family Papers, UNC.

94. Mary W. Milling to husband, April 4, 1862, Folder 7, James S. Milling Papers, UNC.

95. John E. Hall letter to wife, April 26, 1862, Box 8, Folder 58, Larry Crain Collection, SLU.

96. The Confederacy's cotton diplomacy, which officials hoped would end hostilities by bringing on European intervention and Northern dissension, failed. See Owsley, "The Confederacy and King Cotton," 371–97. However, cotton diplomacy's ideology had merit, as cotton was an important commodity for both Britain and France. Its shortage during the Civil War did affect the two nations—even causing some social unrest in France. See Sainlaude, *France and the American Civil War,* 141–42.

97. Taylor, "Discontent in Confederate Louisiana," 417–18; Odom, "The Political Career of Thomas Overton Moore," 63. Though hampered by politics, cotton trading—both "authorized and unauthorized . . . flourished" by 1864. See Hewitt and Bergeron, eds., *Louisianians in the Civil War,* 79.

98. Winters, *The Civil War in Louisiana,* 103. Some fortunate residents received compensation for their destroyed cotton. See Receipt for cotton seized and burned by Confederate Capt. W. B. Krump of the 1st Regiment Louisiana Rangers during the Civil War. 4 July 1862, Box 1, Folder 17, Kleinpeter Collection, SLU. For an eyewitness to the destruction, see H. A. Snyder Diary, entry for April 25, 1862, titled "Gloomy Friday," LSU.

99. P. L. Prudhomme to Lestan Prudhomme, November 28, 1862, Folder 270, Robert De-Blieux Collection, NSU.

100. Stone, *Brokenburn,* 100–101.

101. Dawson, *A Confederate Girl's Diary,* ed. Robertson, 16–17.

102. Leigh, *Trading with the Enemy,* 18–19. For more on the complexities between Confederate authorities and civilians, see Ward, *Garden of Ruins,* 208–11.

103. Anonymous letter to Cousin William, May 6, 1863, Folder Misc.: A, May 6, 1863, Mss. #3674, Anonymous Civil War Letter, LSU. According to this letter, Federal confiscation of property also included slaves, much to the dismay of many planters.

104. Sutherland, *A Savage Conflict,* 215.

105. Sacher, "Our Interest and Destiny Are the Same," 274. Under Louisiana's Union occupation, Federal authorities also dealt with similar domestic issues, often working with local law enforcement to protect private property and discourage violence with mixed results. See Ward, *Garden of Ruins,* 106–7.

106. Bearss, ed., *A Louisiana Confederate,* 195.

107. Poché claimed he and his men "found and captured 10 bales of Cotton enroute to the enemy . . . The cotton being still within our lines, we did not bother it and put it under a $20,000 bond, to be held subject to the orders of the government." Poché's squad also captured three smugglers and proceeded to conduct a raid. Unable to capture the Provost Marshall, the

Confederates captured his clerk, a Union captain, and "another soldier from the 38th Iowa." See Bearss, ed., *A Louisiana Confederate,* 229–30.

108. Hyde, *Pistols and Politics,* 124.

109. Taylor, "Discontent in Confederate Louisiana," 419.

110. Brasseaux, Fontenot, and Oubre, *Creoles of Color in the Bayou Country,* 50–52.

111. Jacob Thompson quoted in Ruminski, "'Tradyville,'" 511–12. Ruminski explores the wartime illegal trade in Mississippi, Confederate nationalism, and the questions of loyalty as he argues that "trading with the Union did not necessarily indicate disloyalty to the Confederacy." See ibid., 514.

112. Surdam, "Traders of Traitors," 302–3. Johnson notes that by purchasing Southern cotton, the Union could (among other things) disrupt the Confederacy's foreign trade, along with providing a boon to Northern textile mills. See Johnson, "Contraband Trade During the Last Year of the Civil War," 636–37. Later in the war, the Massachusetts governor encouraged Federal cotton confiscation, especially as textile mills starved for cotton. See Anders, *Disaster in Damp Sand,* 9.

113. Lauriston Bullard quoted in Leigh, *Trading with the Enemy,* 1–2.

114. Bacon, *Among the Cotton Thieves,* 82; Lang, *In the Wake of War,* 100–101. See also Hess, *The Civil War in the West,* 70–74.

115. Banks quoted in Taylor, "Discontent in Confederate Louisiana," 419. Union Gen. David Hunter claimed it was the corruption caused by "Cotton and politics, instead of the war," which caused the Federal defeat during the Red River Campaign. Adm. David Porter also blamed Banks's failure on cotton speculation, testifying, "The whole affair was a cotton speculation." Porter argued, "Cotton killed that expedition. . . . The army should not have gone into that business at all." See Smith, "For the Love of Cotton," 18–19.

116. Power, "A Vermonter's Account of the Red River Campaign," 356–60.

117. J. D. Garland letter to Mother, January 10, 1864, J. D. Garland Papers, LSU.

118. For examples of Confederate attacks on Union river vessels, see Lowe, *Walker's Texas Division,* 153.

119. Joseph Welsh Texada letter to Margaret Texada, September 15, 1864, Box 1, Folder 24, Texada Family Papers, LSU.

120. Johnson, "Contraband Trade During the Last Year of the Civil War," 637–39.

121. Ruminski, "'Tradyville,'" 512.

122. Bearss, ed., *A Louisiana Confederate,* 89.

123. W. H. King Journal, entry for February 13, 1864, NSU.

124. Ibid., entry for March 10, 1864, NSU.

125. Lowe, *Walker's Texas Division,* 163.

126. William H. Tamplin letter to Tincia[?], February 20, 1864, Folder 1862–1865, William H. Tamplin Letters, LSU.

127. Ruminski, "'Tradyville,'" 511.

128. Bearss, ed., *A Louisiana Confederate,* 89.

129. Petty quoted in Lowe, *Walker's Texas Division,* 162–63.

130. "Port Hudson: Its History," 10.

131. Rosen's excellent study on Jewish Confederates examines the Jewish experience in the

Old South, and he argues Southern society was not as restrictive, compared with what transpired in the late nineteenth and twentieth centuries. See Rosen, *Jewish Confederates*. For examples of anti-Semitism on the Union side, especially associated with illicit trading, see ibid., 275. During the Vicksburg campaign, Gen. Ulysses Grant feared that Jewish peddlers engaged in espionage and issued an order for their removal. Lincoln rescinded Grant's order, especially since some Jewish soldiers served in the Federal army. See Oates, *With Malice Toward None*, 345.

132. W. H. King Journal, entry for June 3, 1862, NSU.

133. John E. Hall letter to wife, April 2, 1862, Box 8, Folder 58, Larry Crain Collection, SLU.

134. John Coleman Sibley letter to wife, December 14, 1862, Civil War Diary and Letters of John Coleman Sibley, p. 89, NSU.

135. Bearss, ed., *A Louisiana Confederate*, 8. One Louisiana officer, P. L. Prudhomme, notes the complex attitudes of the "French population" near Natchitoches. While simultaneously believing foreign nationals did not pull their weight in supporting the war, he also notes how some French citizens suffered at the hands of Union soldiers. See P. L. Prudhomme letter to Lestan Prudhomme, November 28, 1862, Folder 270, Robert DeBlieux Collection, NSU; Michot, "War Is Still Raging in This Part of the Country," 169–70.

136. Lowe, *Walker's Texas Division*, 164.

137. Ibid., 161–62.

138. F. A. Prudhomme letter to Mrs. Lestan Prudhomme, November 19, 1862, Folder 270, Robert DeBlieux Collection, NSU.

139. "Your Most Obt. Sr. Arendanbros[?]" to Sam. T. Thorne, January 30, 1864, Folder 3, Annie Blackwell Thorne Correspondence, 1860–1869, Series 1, #4521, UNC.

140. Ruminski, "'Tradyville,'" 524–26.

141. Ash, *When the Yankees Came*, 46–47.

142. See Patrick, *Reluctant Rebel*, ed. Taylor, 132–33.

143. L. G. Causey letter to Husband (R. J. Causey), October 14, 1863, Folder Misc.: C, R. J. Causey Correspondence, LSU.

144. Isaac Hall letter to Mary Hall and Children, May 26, 1862, quoted in Richard and Richard, *The Defense of Vicksburg*, 39.

145. Johnson, "Contraband Trade During the Last Year of the Civil War," 652. Ash notes that while some Union officers allowed trade with Southern civilians, sometimes strict regulations existed "about what the sellers took away . . . for fear that it would find its way to the Confederacy or to guerrillas." See Ash, *When the Yankees Came*, 102.

7. WARTIME COMMUNICATIONS

1. Dosie letter to "My dear husband" (Alfred Flournoy Jr.), July 31, 1861, Folder 28, Mildred McCoy Collection, NSU.

2. John Coleman Sibley letter to wife, March 29, 1863, Civil War Diary and Letters of John Coleman Sibley, p. 111, NSU.

3. Wiley, ed., *"This Infernal War,"* 121.

4. John Hall letter to Effie Hall, May 15, 1862, quoted in Richard and Richard, *The Defense of Vicksburg*, 35.

5. J. D. Garland letter to Pa, Mother, and all, October 4, 1863, and October 27, 1863, J. D.

Garland Papers, LSU; F. A Prudhomme to Lestan Prudhomme, November 12, 1862, Folder 270, Robert DeBlieux Collection, NSU; T. J. Shaffer to Andrew, January 23, 1863, Folder 14, Andrew McCollam Papers, UNC. Carmichael notes the importance of letters as valuable sources for studying Civil War history, as they encompass "jarring contradictions . . . and the ugly realities of daily life." Careful not to cast preconceived judgments on historical actors, perhaps expressing self-righteousness in the process (especially with the issue of slaveholding), Carmichael encourages modern readers to "acknowledge the great distance that separates us from people in the past. If we refuse to do so, we risk losing touch with valuable historical sources." See Davis and Bell, eds., *The Whartons' War*, ix.

6. Woods, *Emotional and Sectional Conflict in the Antebellum United States*, 3.

7. John A. Morgan letter to Sister, May 16, 1861, Box 1, Folder 2, May–December 1861, John A. Morgan Papers, LSU.

8. Williams and Wooster, "Camp Life in Civil War Louisiana," 190.

9. E. L. Stephens letter to parents, June 14, 1862, Box 1, Folder 4, Stephens Collection, NSU.

10. Alfred Flournoy Jr. letter to wife, September 22, 1861, Folder 28, Mildred McCoy Collection, NSU.

11. Louis Stagg letter to wife, Laure (transcribed), October 6, 1861, UAAMC-COLL-Manuscript 7, Folder 1, Louis Stagg Letters, ULL.

12. J. Y. Sanders letter to friend, January 23, 1863, UAAMC-COLL-Manuscript 145, Folder 1, Jared Young Sanders Civil War Letters, 1862–1865, ULL.

13. Frank Richardson to Mother, September 18, 1861, Folder 2, Frank Liddell Richardson Papers, UNC.

14. Isaac Hall letter to Mary Hall and Children, April 1, 1862, quoted in Richard and Richard, *The Defense of Vicksburg*, 15.

15. Alfred Flournoy Sr. letter to My dear son, August 18, 1861, Folder 28, Mildred McCoy Collection, NSU.

16. William J. Walter letter to Paul, December 5, 1861, in Davis, ed., "More Letters of a Louisiana Volunteer," 299.

17. John McCormick to Miss Maggie E. Williams, March 22, 1864, Folder 1, Marguerite E. Williams Papers, UNC.

18. Edmond Vige letter to Catherine Vige, July 13, 1862, Folder Misc.: V, 1862 (2 items), Edmond Vige Letters, Mss.# 3819, LSU.

19. Alexander Declouet letter to Paul (typescript), September 28, 1861, UAAMC-COLL-22, Box 3, Folder 4, DeClouet Family Papers, ULL.

20. L. M. Orton letter to R. D. Orton, May 25, 1862, Folder 6, Aimer Collection, NSU.

21. A. L. Grow letter to Mrs. Mary I. McLean, December 13, 1863, Folder 20, Henry Machen Collection, NSU.

22. Jno S. Dea to Miss Maggie, October 7, 1862, Folder 1, Marguerite E. Williams Papers, UNC.

23. F. A. Prudhomme letter to Mrs. Lestan Prudhomme, November 19, 1862, Folder 270, Robert DeBlieux Collection, NSU.

24. A. L. Grow letter to Mrs. McLane, July 21, 1863, Folder 19, Henry Machen Collection, NSU.

25. W. Ezra Denson letter to John F. Stephens, October 10, 1861, Folder 1861–1864, John F. Stephens Correspondence, LSU.

26. William J. Walter to Paul, December 5, 1861, in Davis, ed., "More Letters of a Louisiana Volunteer," 297.

27. Sheehan-Dean, *Why Confederates Fought*, 68.

28. Carmichael, *The War for the Common Soldier*, 43–44.

29. Alfred Flournoy Jr. letter to "My sweet Docy." July 8, 1861, Folder 28, Mildred McCoy Collection, NSU.

30. Dosie letter to My dear husband (Alfred Flournoy Jr.), July 31, 1861, Folder 28, Mildred McCoy Collection, NSU.

31. Glymph, *Out of the House of Bondage*, 100–101, 104–5.

32. John E. Hall letter to wife, April 26, 1862, Box 8, Folder 58, Larry Crain Collection, SLU.

33. R. J. Causey letter to Wife, October 8, 1863, Folder Misc.: C, R. J. Causey Correspondence, LSU.

34. John Coleman Sibley letter to wife, February 18, 1863, Civil War Diary and Letters of John Coleman Sibley, p. 102, NSU.

35. Hunton Love interview, January 8, 1940, Folder 19 (Folklore—Ex-slave tales & interviews), Federal Writers Project Collection, NSU.

36. Wiley, ed., *"This Infernal War,"* 5–6, 217, 279–80.

37. For example, Gallagher argues that in 1863, just the units constituting the Union's Army of the Potomac could have possibly mailed over a million letters in only a one-month time frame. By compounding all the units in both the Union and Confederacy, many millions of letters would have been circulating at any given moment during the conflict. See Gallagher, *The Union War*, 57–58.

38. Bearss, ed., *A Louisiana Confederate*, 21; H. E. Lawrence to wife, November 29, 1861[?], Folder 31, in the Brashear-Lawrence Family Papers, UNC. Throughout the war, both Union and Confederate soldiers remained anxious for mail, as one historian notes, "Soldiers would endure much for their country, but being cut off from word of family and friends seemed unbearable." See Rable, "Hearth, Home, and Family in the Fredericksburg Campaign," in Cashin, ed., *The War Was You and Me*, 88–89. For an example of soldiers sending money home (for both family use and to repay debts), see Louis Stagg letter to wife, Laure (transcribed), June 9, 1863, UAAMC-COLL-Manuscript 7, Folder 1, Louis Stagg Letters, ULL.

39. L. G. Causey letter to Husband (R. J. Causey), October 14, 1863, Folder Misc.: C, R. J. Causey Correspondence, LSU.

40. Eugenia Murphy letter to brother (A. E. Murphy), August 16, 1864, Folder 4, Frances Bonnette Collection, NSU.

41. L. G. Causey letter to Husband (R. J. Causey), October 14, 1863, Folder Misc.: C, R. J. Causey Correspondence, LSU.

42. L. G. Causey letter to Husband (R. J. Causey), November 19, 1863, Folder Misc.: C, R. J. Causey Correspondence, LSU.

43. Nelson, "Writing during Wartime," 58. Nelson also goes into detail about both the "wartext" (wartime writings) of both men and women during the Civil War and how these writings sometimes mirrored—or shifted from—the time period's social norms. See ibid., 45–49.

44. Whites, "Written on the Heart," in Frank and Whites, *Household War*, 118–19.

45. Frank Richardson to Father, November 6, 1861, Folder 2, Frank Liddell Richardson Papers, UNC.

46. Frank Richardson to Mother & Father, April 22, 1862, Folder 3, Frank Liddell Richardson Papers, UNC.

47. John F. Cooney letter to Mother, June 4, 1862, Misc: C folder, 1862, Mss. #4314, John F. Cooney Letter (photocopy), LSU.

48. Hughes, *The Pride of the Confederate Artillery*, 191.

49. Eugene Janin to Father, October 29, 1861, Folder 2, Eugene Janin Papers, UNC.

50. W. H. King Journal, entry for June 27, 1862, NSU.

51. P. L. Prudhomme letter to Lestan Prudhomme, August 26, 1862, Folder 270, Robert DeBlieux Collection, NSU.

52. Frank Richardson to Mother, December 14, 1861, Folder 2, Frank Liddell Richardson Papers, UNC.

53. Whites, "Written on the Heart," 126.

54. John A. Morgan letter to Sister, September 21, 1861, Box 1, Folder 2, May–December 1861, John A. Morgan Papers, LSU.

55. Lizzie Fitzgerald letter to Delia Singleton, August 15, 1862, Letters of Fitzgerald to Singleton, NSU.

56. John E. Hall letter to wife, April 26, 1862, Box 8, Folder 58, Larry Crain Collection, SLU.

57. Frank Richardson to Father, September 9, 1862, Folder 3, Frank Liddell Richardson Papers, UNC. Richardson's intelligence about Baton Rouge being retaken was false. Though Confederates attempted to retake the city, it remained in Union hands.

58. A. L. Grow letter to Mrs. Mary I. McLean, December 13, 1863, Folder 20, Henry Machen Collection, NSU.

59. William H. Tamplin letter to Tincia[?], March 10, 1864, Folder 1862–1865, William H. Tamplin Letters, LSU.

60. P. L. Prudhomme letter to Lestan Prudhomme, no date, Folder 270, Robert DeBlieux Collection, folder 270, NSU.

61. Jones, *Lee's Tigers Revisited*, 313.

62. Fred Taber letter to sister and mother, October 19, 1861, Box 1, folder 1861–1862, Frederick R. Taber Papers, LSU. Newspapers not only provided entertainment, but also at times were heavily relied upon by the commanders of both armies to gather news, monitor troop movements, etc., which was useful for campaign planning. See Feis, "That Great Essential of Success," in *Struggle for a Vast Future*, ed., Sheehan-Dean, 143.

63. Silas T. White letter to father, November 8, 1861, Silas T. White Papers, LSU.

64. Frank Richardson to Mother, December 14, 1861, Folder 2, Frank Liddell Richardson Papers, UNC.

65. [?] Levron to Mae, no date, Folder 14, Andrew McCollam Papers, UNC.

66. Williams and Wooster, "Camp Life in Civil War Louisiana," 197, 200.

67. E. L. Stephens letter to brother, August 3, 1862, Box 1, Folder 4, Stephens Collection, NSU.

68. G. B. Crain letter to R. D. Orton, August 24, 1863, Folder 6, Aimer Collection, NSU.

69. Wiley, ed., *"This Infernal War,"* 29.

70. A. L. Grow letter to Mrs. Mary I. McLean, December 4 [1863], Folder 20, Henry Machen Collection, NSU.

71. W. H. King Journal, entry for May 13, 1862, NSU.

72. John Bond Diary, entry for December 20, 1862, quoted in Richard and Richard, *The Defense of Vicksburg,* 101.

73. L. G. Causey letter to Husband (R. J. Causey), October 14, 1863, Folder Misc.: C, R. J. Causey Correspondence, LSU.

74. Alfred Flournoy Sr. letter to Alfred Flournoy Jr., June 16, 1861, Folder 28, Mildred McCoy Collection, NSU.

75. Dawson, *A Confederate Girl's Diary,* ed. Robertson, 114, 399.

76. Emile to "Dearest Love," January 3, 1864, Annie Jeter Carmouche Papers and Reminiscences, UNC.

77. Anonymous letter to Isa, April 18, 1863, Folder Misc.: A, April 18, 1863, Mss. 2824, Anonymous Civil War Letter, LSU.

78. Bearss, ed., *A Louisiana Confederate,* 140.

79. F. A. Prudhomme letter to Lestan Prudhomme, November 12, 1862, Folder 270, Robert DeBlieux Collection, NSU.

80. W. H. King Journal, entry for May 29, 1862, NSU.

81. O. V. Metoyer letter to Ben, September 7, 1864, Folder 33, Cloutier Collection, NSU.

82. P. L. Prudhomme letter to Lestan Prudhomme, September 25, 1862, Folder 270, Robert DeBlieux Collection, NSU.

83. Joseph Welsh Texada letter to Margaret Texada, October 14, 1864, Box 1, Folder 24, Texada Family Papers, LSU.

84. Cater, *As It Was,* xvii. Not all Southerners held back criticisms of General Lee. See Gallagher, *The Confederate War,* 129–31.

85. Henry Ginder letter to Mary Ginder, June 28, 1863, quoted in Richard and Richard, *The Defense of Vicksburg,* 216. Despite this soldier's keen observation, Lee's gambles could have paid heavy dividends if successful. Another consideration for the Army of Northern Virginia's treks into Northern territory was, as in the case of the Antietam Campaign, to bring relief to Virginia's farmers, who not only dealt with providing for Confederate needs, but also for those of the enemy, which was operating in the same vicinities. See Sheehan-Dean, *Why Confederates Fought,* 90. For other examples of soldiers criticizing Lee's generalship, see Glatthaar, *General Lee's Army,* 287.

86. Fred Taber letter to mother, November 15, 1861, Box 1, folder 1861–1862, Frederick R. Taber Papers, LSU.

87. Alfred Flournoy Jr. letter to wife, May 22, 1861, Folder 28, Mildred McCoy Collection, NSU.

88. White, "The Soldier's Dream of Home," in Frank and Whites, *Household War,* 77–78, 92. For a full study on dreaming in the Civil War, see also White, *Midnight in America.*

89. Jno S. Dea letter to Miss Maggie, October 7, 1862, Folder 1, Marguerite E. Williams Papers, UNC.

90. Wiley, ed., *"This Infernal War,"* 281.

91. Hal letter to wife, November 27, 1861, Folder 13, Slack Family Papers, UNC.

92. John Coleman Sibley Diary, entry for September 25, 1863, Civil War Diary and Letters of John Coleman Sibley, p. 3, NSU.

93. Ellis Diary, entry titled "A Retrospect," p. 1, LSU.

94. Unpublished "J. A. Boyd Book," Listed poems written in January and March 1863, Box

4, Folder 46, Larry Crain Collection, SLU. Boyd served in Co. A, 1st Mississippi Infantry and was killed at Port Hudson on June 14, 1863.

95. Joseph Welsh Texada letter to Margaret Texada, June 24, 1864, Box 1, Folder 23, Texada Family Papers, LSU.

96. John Coleman Sibley letter to wife, December 8, 1862, Civil War Diary and Letters of John Coleman Sibley, p. 87, NSU.

97. John Coleman Sibley letter to wife, September 12, 1864, Civil War Diary and Letters of John Coleman Sibley, p. 156, NSU.

98. William J. Walter to Caddy, April 28, 1864, in Davis, ed., "More Letters of a Louisiana Volunteer," 300.

99. William J. Walter to Henrietta, August 8, 1861, in Davis, ed. "A Louisiana Volunteer: Letters of William J. Walter, 1861–1862," 81. Civilians, too, often reminisced about the prewar years. Home, what many soldiers claimed they fought for, dominated their wartime thoughts and emotions. As one historian claims, soldiers and civilians "could look back on domestic life in an idealized way and at the same time feel a great sadness over what had been sacrificed and what more might still be lost." Rable, "Hearth, Home, and Family in the Fredericksburg Campaign," in Cashin, ed., *The War Was You and Me*, 104.

100. Isaac Hall letter to wife, March 15, 1862, quoted in Richard and Richard, *The Defense of Vicksburg*, 10.

101. Isaac Walker letter to Holly Walker, November 30, 1862, quoted in Richard and Richard, *The Defense of Vicksburg*, 95.

102. Edwin Leet letter to Sarah A. Leet, October 18, 1864, Folder Misc.: L, 1864–1865, Mss. #1353, Edwin Leet Letters, LSU.

103. Edwin Leet letter to Sarah A. Leet, February 24, 1865, Folder Misc.: L, Edwin Leet Letters, LSU.

104. Sheehan-Dean, *Why Confederates Fought*, 133–35.

105. Louis Stagg letter to wife, Laure (transcribed), June 9, 1863, UAAMC-COLL-Manuscript 7, Folder 1, Louis Stagg Letters, ULL.

106. Joseph Welsh Texada letter to Margaret Texada, April 23, 1864, Box 1, Folder 23, Texada Family Papers, LSU.

107. Melissa letter to "Dearest" (C. C. Dunn), March 8, 1863, Folder 1, Juanita Henry Collection, NSU.

108. Power Diary, January 1, 1862–September 28, 1863 (typed transcription), p. 85, Folder 2, UNC.

109. Docie letter to My dear husband (Alfred Flournoy Jr.), July 22, 1861, Folder 28, Mildred McCoy Collection, NSU.

110. Frank Richardson to Father, December 10, 1861, Folder 2, Frank Liddell Richardson Papers, UNC.

111. "Marriages in the Army—A Caution." *Daily Dispatch* (Richmond), March 21, 1863.

112. Taylor, *Destruction and Reconstruction*, 64. Translation: "Madame! I never arrive too late."

113. John Coleman Sibley Diary, entry for May 17–25, 1863, Civil War Diary and Letters of John Coleman Sibley, pp. 18–19, NSU.

114. Ibid., entry for December 4, 1864, p. 49; John Coleman Sibley letter to wife, September 8, 1862, Civil War Diary and Letters of John Coleman Sibley, p. 73, NSU.

115. Hal letter to wife, February 5, 1862 [written on same letter dated February 2, 1862], Folder 14, Slack Family Papers, UNC.

116. John Coleman Sibley Diary, entry for December 14, 1862, Civil War Diary and Letters of John Coleman Sibley, p. 10, NSU.

117. J. T. Hardesty letter to sister, July 9, 1863, quoted in Richard and Richard, *The Defense of Vicksburg,* 237.

118. John Coleman Sibley Diary, entry for July 24, 1864, Civil War Diary and Letters of John Coleman Sibley, p. 43, NSU.

119. Wiley, ed., *"This Infernal War,"* 144–45.

8. SOLDIERS AND CIVILIANS AT WAR

1. Emile to "Dearest Love," January 20, 1864, Annie Jeter Carmouche Papers and Reminiscences, UNC.

2. John Coleman Sibley Diary, entry for June 21, 1863, Civil War Diary and Letters of John Coleman Sibley, p. 20, NSU.

3. William H. Tamplin letter to Mrs. R. A. Tamplin, May 15, 1864, Folder 1862–1865, William H. Tamplin Letters, LSU.

4. Lucien Flournoy letter to Uncle (Dr. Alfred Flournoy Sr.), April 26, 27, 1864, Folder 28, Mildred McCoy Collection, NSU.

5. W. H. King Journal, entry for September 22, 1864, NSU.

6. Isaac Erwin Diary, entry for July 21 and 24, 1861, NSU.

7. For example, Erwin's diary entries for early April 1861, have him noting details about the Fort Sumter crisis. Though his plantation activities take center stage in his writing, he kept up with wartime events far from home. See Isaac Erwin Diary, entry for April 12 and 14, 1861, NSU.

8. McPherson, *For Cause and Comrades,* 35, 131–47.

9. See Sheehan-Dean, *The Calculus of Violence,* 2; Royster, *The Destructive War;* and Frank, *The Civilian War,* 4–18.

10. Ash, *When the Yankees Came,* 38.

11. Ash, *Middle Tennessee Society Transformed, 1860–1870,* 172.

12. "The Fourth Regiment L.S.V." *Sugar Planter,* August 17, 1861.

13. "Your devoted friend" letter to Rachel, August 11, 1861, Box 8, Folder 60, Larry Crain Collection, SLU.

14. John A. Morgan letter to Sister, August 11, 1861, Box 1, Folder 2, May–December 1861, John A. Morgan Papers, LSU.

15. John A. Morgan letter to Sister, April 10, 1862, and John A. Morgan letter to Sister, May 19, 1862, Box 1, Folder 3, February–August 1862, John A. Morgan Papers, LSU.

16. "Your Brother Thomas" letter to Sister, February 8, 1862, Folder 1, Thomas Benjamin Davidson Papers, UNC.

17. Granville Alspaugh letter to Amelia Alspaugh, July 2, 1862, quoted in Richard and Richard, *The Defense of Vicksburg,* 57.

18. Amos Anselm to Mrs. Eleanor Anselm (My dear Mother), September 2, 1861, "Letters from Confederate Soldier," LSU.

19. Eugene Janin to Father, August 2, 1861, Folder 2, Eugene Janin Papers, UNC.

20. Benjamin Smith letter to Mr. R. H. Carnae, August 23, 1861, Folder 1861 (1 item), #1676, Benjamin Smith Letter, LSU.

21. Dufour, *Gentle Tiger,* 5. One New Orleans resident and Louisiana militia member mentioned attending a funeral for a Louisianian killed in a duel while serving in Virginia, which "This serious affair originated all about (the price of) a candle [one]." See H. A. Snyder Diary, entry for January 6, 1862, LSU.

22. Dufour, *Gentle Tiger,* 5–6.

23. Mingus, *The Louisiana Tigers in the Gettysburg Campaign,* 3.

24. Cutrer and Parrish, eds., *Brothers in Gray,* 190.

25. Unnamed newspaper clipping with printed letter from Paul Bossier to Henry Hertzog, Esq., August 13, 1861, Scrapbook of Odalie Prudhomme Lambre concerning the Civil War, pp. 1, 2, Folder 1, Carmen Breazeale Collection, NSU.

26. Unnamed newspaper clipping with printed letter from Fulbert Cloutier to father, August 14, 1861, Scrapbook of Odalie Prudhomme Lambre concerning the Civil War, pp. 1, 2. Folder 1, Carmen Breazeale Collection, NSU. Though often overshadowed by the Eastern theater's large-scale battles, Thomas W. Cutrer notes that the Trans-Mississippi's participants "operated efficiently under peculiar difficulties unknown east of the Mississippi" and displayed the same soldier qualities of "courage, their perseverance, and their self-sacrifice" as their eastern comrades. See Thomas W. Cutrer, *Theater of a Separate War: The Civil War West of the Mississippi River 1861–1865,* rev. ed. (Chapel Hill: University of North Carolina Press, 2023), 7.

27. Vandiver, ed., "A Collection of Louisiana Confederate Letters,"11.

28. Hal letter to wife, July 15, 1862, Folder 14, Slack Family Papers, UNC.

29. There were two Camp Lovells in Louisiana during the Civil War. One was located above Fort St. Philip on the Mississippi River, and the other, which is mentioned above, was in St. Mary Parish on the Atchafalaya River. See Casey, *Encyclopedia of Forts, Posts, Named Camps, and Other Military Installations in Louisiana,* 110.

30. Hall, *The Story of the 26th Louisiana Infantry,* 139–41. Seventy-nine soldiers signed the letter sent to Winchester Hall, requesting him to lead them. Hall promised to do what he could to get them into action, but he also explained to his men that they "were under orders, and could not move without them." See ibid., 4–5.

31. Arceneaux, *Acadian General,* 36, 52. The 4th Louisiana Infantry also served at Shiloh and, like the 18th Louisiana, suffered heavy casualties. Both regiments had men from the Lafourche region, which was where many men from Company I, 26th Louisiana Infantry, were from. Peña, *Touched by War,* 64. Over a decade after the Civil War ended, Alfred Roman, who had served as an officer in the 18th Louisiana Infantry, recorded his personal account of Shiloh, which indicated that heavy casualties were also linked to things such as poor discipline, lack of food, and exhaustion. See: Unpublished account "Autograph of Col. Alfred Roman," August 20, 1878, UAAMC-COLL-Manuscript 73, Folder 1, Alfred Roman Civil War Memoirs, 1878, ULL.

32. Edmond Livaudais quoted in Daniel, *Shiloh,* 240.

33. Frank Richardson to Father, April 10, 1862, Folder 3, Frank Liddell Richardson Papers, UNC. Even President Lincoln suffered a loss from Shiloh, as Mary Todd Lincoln's half-brother Samuel Todd, who had joined the Crescent Regiment in New Orleans, was mortally wounded and died in an ambulance wagon en route to a hospital. See Ural, *Don't Hurry Me Down to Hades,* 71.

34. Frank Richardson to Father, May 8, 1862, Folder 3, Frank Liddell Richardson Papers, UNC.

35. McPherson, *For Cause and Comrades*, 37.

36. Ellis Diary, entry titled "A Retrospect," p. 18, LSU.

37. For a detailed look at the Battle of Shiloh, see Daniel, *Shiloh;* Cunningham, *Shiloh and the Western Campaign of 1862.* Hess notes that the war in the West was no less bloody than in the East, although the Eastern battles were bigger. He points out that "the loss ratio was actually higher in Western engagements than in the Eastern battles. The loss ratios in the East and the West were 8.4 percent and 10.3 percent respectively." See Hess, *The Civil War in the West*, 314.

38. Louis Stagg letter to wife, Laure (transcribed), October 6, 1861, UAAMC-COLL-Manuscript 7, Folder 1, Louis Stagg Letters, ULL.

39. Vandiver, ed., "A Collection of Louisiana Confederate Letters," 19, 26.

40. Dosie letter to My darling husband (Alfred Flournoy Jr.), July 11, 1861, Folder 28, Mildred McCoy Collection, NSU. Though defenses were lacking, Confederate leaders also doubted New Orleans residents' loyalties—because of its "large, heterogeneous population"—as these people were "difficult to govern." General Lovell declared martial law in New Orleans in March 1862. See Hess, *The Civil War in the West*, 77–79.

41. John E. Hall letter to wife, April 2, 1862, Box 8, Folder 58, Larry Crain Collection, SLU. Though the horrors of war had not physically reached Louisiana until the conflict's second year, some residents saw their first glimpse of uniformed Yankee soldiers in the fall of 1861, as Union POWs captured at Manassas arrived in New Orleans. See William Nicholson letter to sister, October 4, 1861, Folder 1861, William Nicholson Letters, LSU; Dufour, *The Night the War Was Lost*, 68–69; Scriber and Arnold-Scriber, *The Fourth Louisiana Battalion in the Civil War*, 17.

42. Albert Patterson interview, May 22, 1940, Folder 19 (Folklore—Ex-slave tales & interviews), Federal Writers Project Collection, NSU. General Lovell quickly realized holding the city against the Union gunboats was futile and ordered the removal of men and supplies to avoid capture. See Peña, *Touched by War*, 65. For more on the engagement at Fort Jackson, see Pierson, *Mutiny at Fort Jackson*.

43. Stone, *Brokenburn*, 100.

44. John E. Hall letter to wife, April 26, 1862. Box 8, Folder 58, Larry Crain Collection, SLU. Despite the city's loss, some Confederate soldiers remained hopeful for a turn of events. See William J. Walter to Hattie, May 10, 1862, in Davis, ed. "A Louisiana Volunteer: Letters of William J. Walter, 1861–1862," 86. Some Confederate leaders did not sulk in defeat after the city's capture but actually formulated a plan (which never transpired) to retake control of the city. See Brig. Gen. Daniel Ruggles letter to Gen. Samuel Cooper, September 11, 1862, Williams Research Center, Historic New Orleans Collection, Accession Number 81-86-L, Mss. 254 (Louisiana Digital Library). Even if Ruggles's plan warranted serious merit, numerous contingencies remained in play that could have doomed success. See Prushankin, "They Came to Butcher Our People: The Civil War in the West," in *Struggle for a Vast Future*, ed. Sheehan-Dean, 143. Even as late as 1864, Henry Watkins Allen, Louisiana's second Confederate governor, appealed to sympathetic New Orleanians to remain loyal; however, Allen's appeal came to naught, as Union forces never relinquished control of the occupied city. See *OR*, ser. I, vol. 53, 960.

45. P. L. Prudhomme letter to Lestan Prudhomme, November 28, 1862, Folder 270, Robert DeBlieux Collection, NSU. Historians have emphasized the importance of New Orleans's loss.

See Hearn, *The Capture of New Orleans;* Dufour, *The Night the War Was Lost,* 9–10, 334–35, 339–41.

46. Mansfield Lovell letter to Van, March 9, 1862, Folder Misc.: L, 1862, Mss. #2687, Mansfield Lovell Letter, LSU; Sacher, "Our Interest and Destiny Are the Same," 263, 277.

47. Peña, *Touched by War,* 70.

48. Adjutant Generals Office letter from Headquarters Louisiana Army, District North Louisiana to General, May 29, 1863, Folder Misc.: L, May 29, 1863, Mss. 2142, Louisiana Militia Document, LSU; Cutrer, *Theater of a Separate War,* 186. Though serving in neighboring Mississippi, Lt. P. L. Prudhomme wrote home to Natchitoches, claiming that the militia forces near his vicinity were "not only useless but detrimental to the cause," especially as they consumed precious provisions that "are getting scarce and that at a great expense. . . . What necessity is there for the Militia when the Confederate Army is here." See P. L. Prudhomme letter to Lestan Prudhomme, March 10, 1863, Folder 270, Robert DeBlieux Collection, NSU. The Union army also had its share of rivalries between the regular troops and volunteers. See Bacon, *Among the Cotton Thieves,* 13.

49. Frazier, "'Out of Stinking Distance': The Guerrilla War in Louisiana," in *Guerrillas, Unionists, and Violence on the Confederate Home Front,* ed. Sutherland, 158. Frazier also notes the frustrations of Confederate authorities as sometimes militiamen evaded service when called to active duty. See Ibid., 160.

50. Bielski, *Sons of the White Eagle,* 70–71. Despite the various issues and opinions surrounding the use of militia forces, Confederate authorities called upon them throughout the war and, in some instances (usually under the wing of active Confederate forces) could perform. See Frazier, *Fire in the Cane Field,* 75–79, 114–22. Gen. Richard Taylor favored disbanding militia units, which were usually unreliable, as he felt strongly against "employing troops in the vicinity of their own homes." See ibid., 143; Cutrer, *Theater of a Separate War,* 202.

51. Joseph Blessington quoted in Richard and Richard, *The Defense of Vicksburg,* 263.

52. Joseph Welsh Texada letter to Margaret Texada, June 24, 1864, Box 1, Folder 23, Texada Family Papers, LSU.

53. Sacher, "Our Interest and Destiny Are the Same," 278–79.

54. Sutherland, *A Savage Conflict,* 28–29, 70–74, 138–41. Sutherland notes that the Partisan Ranger Act, which appealed to many Southerners who remained at home, combined with the unpopularity of conscription, proved counterproductive, as both measures kept many men out of the conventional ranks. See ibid., 100–101; and Fellman, *Inside War,* 98. For more on guerrilla violence (and scalping), see Beilein, *Bushwhackers,* 104, 120, 154, 162–63, 166–67, 182–83; Fellman, *Inside War,* 23, 176–77, 188–89.

55. Sheehan-Dean, *The Calculus of Violence,* 73; Hyde, "Bushwhacking and Barn Burnings," 180–82. Sutherland argues that guerrilla warfare, which appealed to many Southerners, remained controversial in part because of the Confederacy's authorities "knew not how to make them part of some broader plan." It was this indecisiveness that led to much of the "independent and ungovernable" guerrilla conduct. See Sutherland, *A Savage Conflict,* ix, x.

56. Beilein, *Bushwhackers,* 2–6, 10; Fellman, *Inside War,* xvii.

57. Ash, *When the Yankees Came,* 49.

58. Haynes, *A Thrilling Narrative,* ed. Bergeron, 65, 81–86.

59. Phillips, "The Hard-Line War: The Ideological Basis of Irregular Warfare in the Western

Border States," in *The Civil War Guerrilla,* ed. Beilein and Hulbert, 23–25. For more on the Leiber Code and Professor Leiber's ideology and terminology, see Sutherland, *A Savage Conflict,* 126–28.

60. Fellman, *Inside War,* 82–83.

61. See Hyde, *Pistols and Politics,* 134. Through mid-May and early June 1862, Louisiana's Adjutant and Inspector General Grivot authorized "certain persons to organize bands of partisan rangers" in several parishes. The authorization also proclaimed that men enrolled in such units would be exempt from conscription when actively fulfilling their ranger service. See *OR,* ser. I, vol. 53, 814–15. Moore justified irregular force formations since Louisiana's defense troops remained inadequate. However, complaints about these irregular soldiers arose, mainly over discipline issues and because partisan actions usually led to "brutal reprisals from Union troops," which affected civilians. See Sacher, "Our Interest and Destiny Are the Same," 279–80. For examples of Union reprisals or threats of them, see Winters, *The Civil War in Louisiana,* 104; Sheehan-Dean, *The Calculus of Violence,* 97; K. B. Lowry "notice" copy, October 7, 1862, Folder Misc.: L, 1862, Mss. #753, K. B. Lowry Notice, LSU. But not all irregular forces disrupted civilian tranquility, and their actions aided the Confederate war effort—even causing some Union soldiers to fear them. See Bond, *A Maryland Bride in the Deep South,* ed. Harrison, 236.

62. Hyde, "Bushwhacking and Barn Burnings," 174–77; Hyde, *Pistols and Politics,* 129. One Union officer, Frank Twitchell, noted the violent actions of Louisiana's guerrilla forces in 1864, which included the capturing and burning of a transport "with 15 officers and a few soldiers" on board, who were never seen or heard from again. Hanging bodies and skeletons were sometimes the only remnants found of Union soldiers who ventured from the confines and safety of their camps. Lang, *In the Wake of War,* 109.

63. Hyde, Jr., "Bushwhacking and Barn Burnings," 180–82. For a discussion of the use of the "black flag" among guerrilla forces, see Beilein and Hulbert, eds. *The Civil War Guerrilla,* 2. For an overview of the guerrilla war in Louisiana, see Frazier, "Out of Stinking Distance," in *Guerrillas, Unionists, and Violence on the Confederate Home Front,* ed. Sutherland, 151–70.

64. Fellman, *Inside War,* 97.

65. Beilein, *Bushwhackers,* 16, 43–44; Michot, "'War Is Still Raging in This Part of the Country,'" 158–59; Sutherland, *A Savage Conflict,* 201–2. For more information on civilian interaction with guerrilla forces, see Whites, "Written on the Heart," in *Household War,* ed. Frank and Whites and Whites, "Forty Shirts and a Wagonload of Wheat." Ward argues that "guerrilla war was culture war," which often highlighted the localness and communal ties that existed between these operators and civilians. See Ward, *Garden of Ruins,* 108–9. For more on women and guerrillas, see Fellman, *Inside War,* 193–230.

66. Beilein, *Bushwhackers,* 73; Fellman, *Inside War,* xix; Sutherland, *A Savage Conflict,* 217–18.

67. Lang, *In the Wake of War,* 105–6; Keith quoted in ibid., 115. Union forces also resorted to taking local hostages to combat guerrilla operations. See Ash, *When the Yankees Came,* 66.

68. Fialka, "Controlled Chaos: Spatiotemporal Patterns within Missouri's Irregular Civil War," in *The Civil War Guerrilla,* ed. Beilein and Hulbert, 45.

69. Sutherland, *A Savage Conflict,* 46–47.

70. Thrasher, *Miserable Little Conglomeration,* 77.

71. The Louisiana Native Guards' transition into the Union army, which now heavily re-cruited ex-slaves (not the Free People of Color who originally constituted the unit), proved a turning point in the Civil War, as these troops were the first African Americans to experience combat. Hewitt claims that the Native Guards' assault on Port Hudson did more to assure the Confederacy's defeat than Confederate losses at Gettysburg and Vicksburg. See Hewitt and Bergeron, eds., *Louisianians in the Civil War*, 152. But not all Native Guardsmen joined of their free will. See Laver and Whitney, "Where Duty Shall Call," 351.

72. Joseph Welsh Texada letter to Margaret Texada, September 5, 1864, Box 1, Folder 23, Texada Family Papers, LSU.

73. Watson quoted in Ural, *Don't Hurry Me Down to Hades*, 159.

74. By early 1865, some Confederate officials, including General Lee, favored enlisting slaves as soldiers to make up for the South's manpower shortage. Lee also noted that an emancipation plan must accompany any bondsman's service. See Moore, *Conscription and Conflict in the Confederacy*, 346–47. For more on the debate about using slaves as soldiers, see Rosen, *Jewish Confederates*, 48; Bond, *A Maryland Bride in the Deep South*, ed. Harrison, 317; Richard Lance-lot Maury quoted in Sheehan-Dean, *Why Confederates Fought*, 185; Owen, *In Camp and Battle with the Washington Artillery*, 366; Ellis Diary, entry titled "A Retrospect," p. 4, LSU. Gallagher frames the debate about arming the enslaved in the lens of Confederate nationalism, arguing that the Confederates who supported this idea "undoubtedly believed the plan would apply to only a small part of the southern slave population; they sought independence with slavery largely intact." Gallagher claims, "A majority of Confederate soldiers probably supported the idea of arming slaves . . . because they considered it a necessary condition to win independence." Gal-lagher, *The Confederate War*, 81–85. Glatthaar also discusses this issue, along with the various Confederate opinions that existed. See Glatthaar, *General Lee's Army*, 304–14.

75. Samuel Boyer Davis to Lt. Col. G. W. Logan, June 25, 1863, Folder 13, George W. Logan Papers, UNC.

76. Bond, *A Maryland Bride in the Deep South*, ed. Harrison, 320–22. For more on the com-plexities surrounding Louisiana's guerrilla forces and Jayhawkers, see Ward, *Garden of Ruins*, 220–26; and Weitz, *More Damning than Slaughter*, 223–25. When Confederate forces retreated from New Orleans, city leadership called "on a local defense unit, the European Brigade" for assistance putting down "rioting and looting" from the city's lower-class Whites. See Ash, *When the Yankees Came*, 23.

77. Sutherland, *A Savage Conflict*, 216. For a contrasting view of Louisiana Jayhawkers, see Haynes, *A Thrilling Narrative*, ed. Bergeron.

78. Unknown author letter to Arthemase, April or May 1864, Box 22, Folder 8A, J. H. Wil-liams Collection, NSU.

79. *OR*, ser. I, vol. 53, 842, 843. However, not all residents felt better off with rebel troops stationed nearby—especially when they were responsible for atrocities. See Patrick, *Reluctant Rebel*, ed. Taylor, 132, 141.

80. Lizzie Fitzgerald letter to Delia Singleton, April 1, 1865. Letters of Fitzgerald to Single-ton, NSU.

81. Dawson, *A Confederate Girl's Diary*, ed. Robertson, 50, 51; Power Diary, January 1, 1862–September 28, 1863 (typed transcription), pp. 92–93, Folder 2, UNC; Julia Hunt to Fanny, Oc-

tober 20, 1864 [typescript copy], Folder 33, Brashear-Lawrence Family Papers, UNC; "Yankee Barbary," unnamed newspaper, no date, Folder 33, Cloutier Collection, NSU; "Alexandria, ... June 22, 1864." *The Louisiana Democrat,* June 22, 1864, Folder 33, Cloutier Collection, NSU; Edmonds, *Yankee Autumn in Acadiana,* 293; Statement written by Gov. Henry Watkins Allen, unnamed newspaper, no date, Folder 33, Cloutier Collection, NSU.

82. William J. Walter to Caddy, April 28, 1864, in Davis, ed., "More Letters of a Louisiana Volunteer," 300. In southeastern Louisiana, Hyde provides examples of Union brutality toward civilians, including rape and murder. See Hyde, *Pistols and Politics,* 130–31. For other wild tales of Union destruction, see copy of Brown, ed., *A Soldier's Life: The Civil War Experiences of Ben C. Johnson,* 99–100, Larry Crain Collection, Box 8, Folder 59, SLU.

83. Haynes, *A Thrilling Narrative,* ed. Bergeron, 8–10.

84. P. L. Prudhomme letter to Lestan Prudhomme, September 25, 1862, Folder 270, Robert DeBlieux Collection, NSU.

85. Wadley Journal (typed transcription), p, 19, Folder 8a, Volume 3, UNC.

86. Gache, *A Frenchman, a Chaplain, a Rebel,* 173. One casualty Gache specifically mentioned in his letter was Gen. Francis R. T. Nicholls (who later became a Louisiana governor). Nicholls's remained dedicated to his soldiers and command, despite having lost a foot and an arm in separate battles. For other examples of high Louisiana casualties or steadfastness to the cause, see Glatthaar, *General Lee's Army,* 254; Foster, *Vicksburg: Southern City Under Siege,* 52; Scriber and Arnold-Scriber, *The Fourth Louisiana Battalion in the Civil War,* 113, 174–75.

87. Hughes, *The Pride of the Confederate Artillery,* 47–48.

88. Seymour, *The Civil War Memoirs of Captain William J. Seymour,* ed. Jones, 77.

89. Ellis Diary, entry titled "A Retrospect," pp. 33–34, LSU.

90. John Coleman Sibley Diary, entry for April 12–14, 1863, Civil War Diary and Letters of John Coleman Sibley, pp. 14–15, NSU.

91. Pos. R. Garcia to "Dear Friend" [Miss Maggie E. Williams], October 1, 1863, Folder 1, Marguerite E. Williams Papers, UNC. Several other Confederates experienced similar battlefield experiences and loss. For another example, see R. H. Brooks letter to wife. Date [? too faded], written from Camp Near Culpepper Court House, Virginia, Archive #245, Mansfield Museum MSS Microfilm Reel 6 of 6, NSU.

92. Edmonds, *The Guns of Port Hudson, Volume Two,* 138–39.

93. William Dixon Diary, entry for June 28, 1862, quoted in Richard and Richard, *The Defense of Vicksburg,* 53–54.

94. Thrasher, *Miserable Little Conglomeration,* 127.

95. George W. Guess quoted in Gallagher, *The Confederate War,* 162. But despite the widespread soldier and civilian participation in warfighting, there was still a large number of individuals who escaped much of the suffering. For example, a group of men from Trinity, Louisiana, petitioned the Confederate commander not to engage with Federal forces "in . . . or near the town." See "We the undersigned citizens of the Town of Trinity" Petition, July 16, 1863, Folder 15, George W. Logan Papers, UNC.

96. Welman F. Pugh Diary, 1862–1863, entry titled "On the death of Francis Welman Pugh (dated 10th of August 1863)," Mss.# 2113, Col. W. W. Pugh and Family Papers, LSU.

97. Cutrer and Parrish, eds., *Brothers in Gray,* 109.

98. Allain Diary, entry for May 28, 1864, APC.

99. [?] Ezra Denson letter to Mr & Mrs Stephens, June 21, 1864, Box 1, Folder 8, Stephens Collection, NSU.

100. Henry M. King letter to John F. Stephens, August 15, 1864, Folder 1861–1864, John F. Stephens Correspondence, LSU.

101. Scriber and Arnold-Scriber, *The Fourth Louisiana Battalion in the Civil War*, 175.

102. Cuthbert H. Slocomb quoted in Hughes, *The Pride of the Confederate Artillery*, 206.

103. Louisiana officer quoted in Miller, *Empty Sleeves*, 76.

104. Miss Sydney Harding Diaries, 1863–1865, Diary for March 10, 1864–December 31, 1864 (transcribed copy), page 17, Folder 4, LSU.

105. Foster, *Vicksburg: Southern City Under Siege*, 48.

106. John A. Morgan letter to Sister, August 19, 1862, Box 1, Folder 3, February–August 1862, John A. Morgan Papers, LSU.

107. Mingus, *The Louisiana Tigers in the Gettysburg Campaign*, 194.

108. Julien Rachal letter to sister, April 12, 1864, Folder 23, Mildred McCoy Collection, NSU.

109. Joseph Welsh Texada letter to Margaret Texada, April 23, 1864, Box 1, Folder 23, Texada Family Papers, LSU.

110. Miller, *Empty Sleeves*, 20–21, 116–40. Miller's work covers the "darker side of the conflict," highlighting the physical and psychological suffering Civil War soldiers, surgeons, and nurses experienced, arguing that "freedom and reunion came at a heavy price." See ibid., 1–16.

111. Stone, *Brokenburn*, ed. Anderson, 258, 277.

112. Lowe, *Walker's Texas Division*, 96.

113. Owen, *In Camp and Battle with the Washington Artillery*, 45.

114. Miller, *Empty Sleeves*, 21.

115. "After the Battle of Yellow Bayou," p. 34, Bound Volume 5, Melrose Collection, NSU.

116. John A. Morgan letter to Sister, August 19, 1862, Box 1, Folder 3, February–August 1862, John A. Morgan Papers, LSU.

117. W. H. King Journal, entry for November 4, 1864, NSU.

118. While in college, years after the war, the Union officer's daughter befriended the daughter of a Louisiana Confederate veteran who knew the mortally wounded soldier, telling her that the soldier's daughters were alive and lived about twenty miles from his home. Mingus, *The Louisiana Tigers in the Gettysburg Campaign*, 200–201.

119. G. B. Crain letter to R. D. Orton, August 24, 1863, Folder 6, Aimer Collection, NSU.

120. Charles Cosby letter to "Ma and darling Sister," December 15, 1864, Box 1, Folder 2, Charles V. Cosby to Margaret Texada Correspondence, 1863–1864, Texada Family Papers, LSU.

121. John McCormick to Miss Maggie E. Williams, March 22, 1864, Folder 1, Marguerite E. Williams Papers, UNC.

122. T. J. Shaffer to Andrew, March 4, 1865, Folder 17, Andrew McCollam Papers, UNC.

123. Patrick, *Reluctant Rebel*, ed. Taylor, 201–2.

124. F[?] B. Harris to Dick, May 23, 1863[4], Folder 6, Aimer Collection, NSU. According to the letter's transcriber, it is believed that Harris served in the 4th Texas Cavalry.

125. H. N. Connor Diary, entry for September 17, 1863, ULL.

EPILOGUE

1. John Coleman Sibley Diary, entry for March 19, 1865, Civil War Diary and Letters of John Coleman Sibley, p. 57, NSU.

2. Wadley Journal (typed transcription), p. 333, Folder 8b, Volume 4, UNC.

3. Joseph Renwick letter to Wife, April 14, 1865. Box 1, Folder 1, Renwick (W. P. and Joseph) Papers, 1863–1884, LSU.

4. Cutrer, *Theater of a Separate War,* 423.

5. Marvel, *Lee's Last Retreat,* 4, 11, 40.

6. Dawson, *A Confederate Girl's Diary,* ed. Robertson, 435.

7. Cutrer, *Theater of a Separate War,* 423.

8. Ellis Diary, entry titled "The Month of April 1865," pp. 2–3, LSU.

9. Marvel, *Lee's Last Retreat,* 182–84.

10. Clampitt, *Lost Causes,* 32, 50. For an example of hopes for peace, see Isaac Erwin Diary, entry for April 18, 1865, Folder 1210, Melrose Collection, NSU.

11. Isaac Erwin Diary, entry for April 19, 1865, Folder 1210, Melrose Collection, NSU.

12. Ellis Diary, entry titled "The Month of April 1865," p. 5, LSU.

13. Bond, *A Maryland Bride in the Deep South,* ed. Harrison, 336.

14. Marvel, *Lee's Last Retreat,* 202–6.

15. Bragg, *Louisiana in the Confederacy,* 308.

16. Clampitt, *Lost Causes,* 133.

17. Bragg, *Louisiana in the Confederacy,* 308.

18. Faust, *Mothers of Invention,* 238.

19. Winters, *The Civil War in Louisiana,* 429.

20. H. Lawrence to children, June 8, 1865, Folder 34, Brashear-Lawrence Family Papers, UNC.

21. Roland, *Louisiana Sugar Plantations,* 138. Roland notes an example of land "in normal times would have brought $150,000 sold for scarcely more than $30,000." Ibid., 138. Though flawed, sharecropping provided a means of survival for all parties involved. Individuals who participated in the sharecropping system, both planter and worker alike, were bound by a contract. Early after the war, US government authorities oversaw and approved these binding contracts, which were signed by all involved, including witnesses. See Widow François Richard fils Freedmen labor contract, August 16 ,1865, UAAMC-COLL-Manuscript 164, Box 1, Folder 3, Richard, François Papers, 1832–1899, ULL. In St. Martin Parish, planter Alexander DeClouet fell in line with the South's new labor structure. According to his contract, he agreed to pay his "Laborers the rates of monthly wages," but also withheld "One twentieth of the monthly wages of such Laborers to be retained in the hands of the employer for the purpose of supporting Schools for the education of the children of Freedmen." A Freedmen's Bureau agent, "or other Agent of the U.S. Government, properly authorized to receive it," would oversee that the collected portion of the sharecropper's earnings would be spent accordingly; and land on the plantation had to be set aside for a freedmen's school. See Agreement with Freedmen, August 11, 1866, UAAMC-COLL-22, Box 2, Folder 1, DeClouet Family Papers, ULL.

22. William Stewart quoted in Ward, *Garden of Ruins,* 227.

23. The war-weary Trans-Mississippi Confederates also dealt with continuous poor logisti-

cal support throughout the war, so further resistance would have led to increased (and, for many men, unnecessary) suffering. See Hess, *Civil War Supply and Strategy,* 289–90.

24. John Coleman Sibley Diary, entries for May 13, 16, 1865, Civil War Diary and Letters of John Coleman Sibley, p. 59, NSU.

25. Bond, *A Maryland Bride in the Deep South,* ed. Harrison, 337.

26. Henry Rightor to A. McCollam, May 7, 1865, Folder 17, Andrew McCollam Papers, UNC.

27. White, "Demobilization of Louisiana Confederate Forces, April–July 1865," in *The Louisiana Purchase Bicentennial Series in Louisiana History, Volume V,* ed. Bergeron, 564. For more details on surrendered and paroled Confederates, see Janney, "Free to Go Where We Liked," 4–28. Janney claims that the Army of Northern Virginia's soldiers "dispersed from Appomattox more like soldiers than vanquished rebels" and that many "Confederate civilians continued to support them even in defeat." See ibid., 4.

28. Scriber and Arnold-Scriber, *The Fourth Louisiana Battalion in the Civil War,* 239.

29. "Farewell Address of Gov. H. W. Allen. To the People of Louisiana. Executive Office, Shreveport, La. June 2, 1865," unnamed newspaper, Scrapbook of Odalie Prudhomme Lambre concerning the Civil War, pp. 49, 50, Folder 1, Carmen Breazeale Collection, NSU.

30. White, "Demobilization of Louisiana Confederate Forces, April–July 1865," 566–68.

31. Owen, *In Camp and Battle with the Washington Artillery,* 393.

32. Catherine Cornelius interview, no date, Folder 19 (Folklore—Ex-slave tales & interviews), Federal Writers Project Collection, NSU.

33. Amnesty Oath for A. D. Boudreaux, November 2, 1865, UAAMC-COLL-Manuscript 116, Folder 1, Boudreaux, Aurelien Drouzin Legal Papers, 1837–1894, ULL. For some high-ranking Confederate officers, fears of what was to become of them set in as many questions lingered about how to go about this process of granting pardons and reestablishing loyalty. Gen. P. G. T. Beauregard, for instance, sought direction from Gen. Robert E. Lee on what course of action to take as he wrote, "It is hard to ask pardon of an adversary you despise." Both Lee and Gen. Joseph E. Johnston advised Beauregard to submit to the old flag, which he did. See Williams, *P. G. T. Beauregard,* 257–58.

34. Williams, *P. G. T. Beauregard,* 262. The animosity and violence between Louisiana's Confederates and Unionists, which had been a bloody affair, did not disappear with the war's end. See "The Reconstruction of States. By Captain D. E. Haynes, of Louisiana." Washington, DC, December 30, 1865 (3 pp.), Box 1, Folder 15, Dennis E. Haynes, "The Reconstruction of States" 1865, Texada Family Papers, LSU.

35. Wadley Journal (typed transcription), 276, Folder 8b, Volume 7, UNC.

36. William J. Walter letter to Hattie, October 1, 1864, in Davis, ed., "More Letters of a Louisiana Volunteer," 302.

37. Hyde, *Pistols and Politics,* 138.

38. Miller, *Empty Sleeves,* 132–33. However, Miller also cites examples of how an empty sleeve benefited Louisiana veterans who ran for political office. See ibid., 129–30.

39. Jones, *Lee's Tigers Revisited,* 385–91; for newspaper quotation, see 389.

40. Ibid., 389; "Maj. DeClouet Enthused Over Peace Jubilee," unknown newspaper, exact date unknown, 1917, UAAMC-COLL-22, Box 2, Folder 9, DeClouet Family Papers, ULL. For an example of battlefield memory and the creation of a national park at Shiloh battlefield, espe-

cially on postwar consensus and interaction with veterans and civilians, see Smith, *This Great Battlefield of Shiloh*, 73–105. Smith notes that many of Shiloh Park's monument dedication ceremonies highlighted "reconciliation and harmony" between the aging veterans, "not constitutional correctness or Lost Cause mentality." See ibid., 90–92.

41. Rosen, *Jewish Confederates*, 102–3. On one of Hart's visits, the woman's relatives were upset that no ham had been served at their meal. Respectful of Hart's Jewish faith, the lady replied, "No, there shall be no ham on my table when my 'Jewish son' is here." See ibid.

42. Emile E. Delseries to "Miss" [Maggie E. Williams], May 6, 1865, Emile E. Delseries to "Kind Friend" [Maggie E. Williams], June 26, 1865, Emile E. Delseries to "Kind Friend" [Maggie E. Williams], August 29, 1865, Folder 2, Marguerite E. Williams Papers, UNC.

43. Wm. L Pasent to "Most Esteemed Friend" [Maggie E. Williams], December 3, 1865, Folder 2, Marguerite E. Williams Papers, UNC.

44. Hughes, *The Pride of the Confederate Artillery*, 278–81.

45. Rasmussen, "The Monetary Crisis of the Fall of New Orleans," 1–3.

46. Civil War Diary and Letters of John Coleman Sibley, p. 200, NSU.

47. Buck, "A Louisiana Prisoner-of-War on Johnson's Island, 1863–65," 234–235, 242.

48. Joiner, "No Pardons to Ask nor Apologies to Make," 30–34.

49. Frank L. Richardson, "War As I Saw It: 1861–1865," *Louisiana Historical Quarterly* 6 (1923): 86–89. Online copy, HathiTrust.

BIBLIOGRAPHY

PRIMARY SOURCES

Manuscripts

Allain, Raymond E., Sr. Private Collection (Jeanerette, Louisiana)
    Alexander Pierre Allain Diary. Transcribed by Raymond E. Allain Sr.
Southeast Louisiana Studies and Archives, Southeastern Louisiana University
    (Hammond, Louisiana)
    Larry Crain Collection
    Kleinpeter Collection
Southern Historical Collection, Louis Round Wilson Special Collections Library,
    University of North Carolina at Chapel Hill
    Avery Family Papers of Louisiana, 1796–1951
    Brashear-Lawrence Family Papers
    Annie Jeter Carmouche Papers and Reminiscences, 1853–1915
    John H. Crowder Letters
    Thomas Benjamin Davidson Papers, 1857–1866
    Laurent Dupré Papers, 1862–1866
    Louis Hébert Autobiography, 1894
    Andrew McCollam Papers
    James S. Milling Papers
    Eugene Janin Papers, 1854–1866
    George W. Logan Papers
    Ellen Louise Power Diary, 1862–1863
    Frank Liddell Richardson Papers, 1851–1869
    Slack Family Papers
    Annie B. Thorne Papers
    Sarah Lois Wadley Journal

James T. Wallace Diary, 1862–1865

Marguerite E. Williams Papers, 1858–1864

Special Collections, Lower Mississippi Valley Collection, Hill Memorial Library,
    Louisiana State University (Baton Rouge, Louisiana) and Louisiana Digital
    Library (LDL)

Anonymous Civil War Letter, April 18, 1863

Anonymous Civil War Letter, May 6, 1863

John S. Billiu Civil War Letters, 1861–1862

Sarah Ker Butler Papers (LDL) R. J. Causey Correspondence, 1863

Confederate States Army Collection, 2nd Louisiana Cavalry Regiment Notebook,
    1863–1865

John F. Cooney Letter, 1862

Levi Nathan Dunham Diary and Cashbook, 1854, 1856, 1864 E. John Ellis Diary,
    1862–1865

Jacob Alison Frierson Papers

Foster (James and Family) Correspondence, 1861–1866 J. D. Garland Papers

Edward J. Gay Papers. (LDL)

Gras-Lauzin Papers

Edwin Leet Letters

John H. Guild Letters, 1862–1864

John W. Gurley Papers. (LDL)

Miss Sydney Harding Diaries, 1863–1865

Mansfield Lovell Letter, 1862 K. B. Lowry Notice, 1862

Louisiana Militia Document, 1863

Donald Mackay Letter. (LDL)

Charles D. Moore Papers

Thomas O. Moore Inaugural Address, January 23, 1860

John A. Morgan Papers

Robert A. Newell Papers

William Nicholson Letters

Prudhomme Family Papers

Col. W. W. Pugh and Family Papers

Renwick (W. P. and Joseph) Papers, 1863–1884

Benjamin Smith Letter, 1861

Alonzo Snyder Papers (LDL) H. A. Snyder Diary, 1862

John F. Stephens Correspondence

Frederick R. Taber Papers

William H. Tamplin Letters

Texada Family Papers

Edmond Vige Letters, 1862
Silas T. White Papers, 1861–1862
University Archives and Acadiana Manuscripts Collection, Edith Garland Dupré
    Library, University of Louisiana at Lafayette (Lafayette, Louisiana)
Aurelien Drouzin Boudreaux Legal Papers
Bayside Plantation Record Book
Confederate Civil War Soldier, Letter, no date
Confederate Soldier Manuscript Scouting Trip to Louisiana, Letter, no date
DeClouet Family Papers
Gerbert-Ray-Lee Families Papers
François Richard Papers
Alfred Roman Civil War Memoirs, 1878
Jared Young Sanders Civil War Letters, 1862–1865
Louis Stagg Letters, 1855–1863
Watson Memorial Library, Cammie G. Henry Research Center, Northwestern State
    University (Natchitoches, Louisiana)
Aimer Collection
Frances Bonnette Collection
Carmen Breazeale Collection
Cloutier Collection
Robert DeBlieux Collection
Egan Collection
Federal Writers Project Collection W. P. Harris Collection
Juanita Henry Collection W. N. King Collection
Henry Machen Collection
Mansfield Museum Microfilm Collection
Mildred McCoy Collection
Melrose Collection
John David Phillips, Jr. Microfilm Collection
Rebel Archives Collection
Safford Collection
John Coleman Sibley Collection
Stephens Collection J. H. Williams Collection
Williams Research Center, Historic New Orleans Collection (New Orleans,
    Louisiana) and Louisiana Digital Library (LDL)
Daniel Ruggles Letter 1862 (LDL)
F. S. Twitchell Letter 1862 (LDL)

Newspapers

Carrollton Sun	*Morning Advocate*
Daily Dispatch	*Natchitoches Union*
Daily Picayune	*New Orleans Daily Delta*
Daily World (St. Landry Parish)	*Pointe Coupee Democrat*
Galveston Weekly News	*Shreveport South-Western*
Harper's Weekly	*Sugar Planter*

Government Sources

Special Report of the Military Board, to the Legislature of the State of Louisiana. J. M. Taylor, State Printer, 1861.

US War Department. *The War of the Rebellion: A Compilation of the Official Records of the Union and Confederate Armies.* 128 vols., index. Washington, DC: Government Printing Office, 1886. Reprint, National Historical Society, 1971.

US Federal Census, 1860.

Published Primary Sources

Bacon, Edward. *Among the Cotton Thieves.* The Everett Companies Publishing Division, 1989.

Bearss, Edwin C., ed. *A Louisiana Confederate: Diary of Felix Pierre Poché.* Translation from the French by Eugenie Watson Somdal. Louisiana Studies Institute, Northwestern State University, 1972.

Bennett, William W. *A Narrative of The Great Revival Which Prevailed in the Southern Armies During the Late Civil War Between the States of the Federal Union.* Sprinkle Publications, 1989.

Bond, Priscilla. *A Maryland Bride in the Deep South: The Civil War Diary of Priscilla Bond.* Edited by Kimberly Harrison. Louisiana State University Press, 2006.

Casey, Powell A., ed. *Life at Camp Moore among the Volunteers: As Told in Letters, Diaries and Newspaper Accounts.* FPHC, Inc., 1985.

Cater, Douglas John. *As It Was: Reminiscences of a Soldier of the Third Texas Cavalry and the Nineteenth Louisiana Infantry.* State House Press, 1990.

Cutrer, Thomas W. and T. Michael Parish, eds. *Brothers in Gray: The Civil War Letters of the Pierson Family.* Louisiana State University Press, 1997.

Davis, Edwin A., ed. "A Louisiana Volunteer: Letters of William J. Walter, 1861–62." *Southwest Review* 19, no. 1 (October 1933): 78–87.

——, ed. "More Letters of a Louisiana Volunteer." *Southwest Review* 20, no. 3 (April 1935): 292–302.

Dawson, Sarah Morgan. *A Confederate Girl's Diary.* Edited by James I. Robertson Jr. Indiana University Press, 1960.

Gache, Pere Louis-Hippolyte, S.J. *A Frenchman, a Chaplain, a Rebel: The War Letters of Pere Louis-Hippolyte Gache, S.J.* Translated by Cornelius M. Buckley, S.J. Loyola University Press, 1981.

Hall, Winchester. *The Story of the 26th Louisiana Infantry, in the Service of the Confederate States.* Butternut Press, 1984.

Handerson, Henry E. *Yankee in Gray: The Civil War Memoirs of Henry E. Handerson with a Selection of His Wartime Letters.* Edited by Clyde Lottridge Cummer. Press of Western Reserve University, 1962.

Haynes, Captain Dennis E. *A Thrilling Narrative: The Memoir of a Southern Unionist.* Edited by Arthur W. Bergeron Jr. University of Arkansas Press, 2006.

Joiner, Gary D., Marilyn S. Joiner, and Clifton D. Cardin, eds. *No Pardons to Ask, nor Apologies to Make: The Journal of William Henry King, Gray's 28th Louisiana Infantry Regiment.* University of Tennessee Press, 2006.

Jones, John William. *Christ in the Camp: Or Religion in Lee's Army.* B. F. Johnson and Company, 1887.

Owen, William Miller. *In Camp and Battle with the Washington Artillery of New Orleans.* Introduction by Nathaniel Cheairs Hughes Jr. Louisiana State University Press, 1999.

Patrick, Robert. *Reluctant Rebel: The Secret Diary of Robert Patrick 1861–1865.* Edited by F. Jay Taylor. Louisiana State University Press, 1959, 1987, 1996.

Port Hudson: Its History from an Interior Point of View as Sketched from the Diary of an Officer St. Francisville Democrat Lieut. Howard C. Wright 1863, Reprint, Committee for the Preservation of the Port Hudson Battlefield, 1963.

Richardson, Frank L. "War as I Saw It: 1861–1865." *Louisiana Historical Quarterly* 6 (1923): 86–106. Online at HathiTrust.

Seymour, William J. *The Civil War Memoirs of Captain William J. Seymour.* Edited by Terry L. Jones. Louisiana State University Press, 1991.

Sheeran, Rev. James B. *Confederate Chaplain: A War Journal of Rev. James B. Sheeran, c.ss.r. 14th Louisiana, C.S.A.* Edited by Joseph T. Durkin, S. J. Bruce Publishing Company, 1960.

Stone, Kate. *Brokenburn: The Journal of Kate Stone, 1861–1868.* Edited by John Q. Anderson. Louisiana State University Press, 1955.

Taylor, Richard. *Destruction and Reconstruction: Personal Experiences of the Late War.* Edited by Richard B. Harwell. Longmans, Green, 1955.

Urquhart, Kenneth Trist, ed. *Vicksburg: Southern City Under Siege: William Lovelace Foster's Letter Describing the Defense and Surrender of the Confederate Fortress on the Mississippi.* Historic New Orleans Collection, 1980.

Vandiver, Frank E., ed. "A Collection of Louisiana Confederate Letters." Reprinted from *Louisiana Historical Quarterly* 26, no. 4 (October 1943): 3–40.

Wiley, Bell Irvin, ed. *Fourteen Hundred and 91 Days in the Confederate Army: A Journal Kept by W. W. Heartstill for Four Years, One Month and One Day or Camp Life; Day by Day of the W. P. Lone Rangers from April 19, 1861 to May 20, 1865.* McCowart-Mercer Press, 1953.

———, ed. With the Assistance of Lucy E. Fay. *"This Infernal War:" The Confederate Letters of Sgt. Edwin H. Fay.* University of Texas Press, 1958.

SECONDARY SOURCES

Books

Anders, Curt. *Disaster in Damp Sand: The Red River Expedition.* Guild Press of Indiana, 1997.

Arceneaux, William. *Acadian General: Alfred Mouton and the Civil War.* Center for Louisiana Studies University of Southwestern Louisiana, 1981.

Ash, Stephen V. *Middle Tennessee Society Transformed, 1860–1870: War and Peace in the Upper South.* University of Tennessee Press, 2006.

———. *When the Yankees Came: Conflict and Chaos in the Occupied South, 1861–1865.* University of North Carolina Press, 1995.

Aubrecht, Michael. *The Civil War in Spotsylvania County: Confederate Campfires at the Crossroads.* History Press, 2009.

Beilein, Joseph M., Jr. *Bushwhackers: Guerrilla Warfare, Manhood, and the Household in Civil War Missouri.* Kent State University Press, 2016.

Beilein, Joseph M., Jr., and Matthew C. Hulbert. *The Civil War Guerrilla: Unfolding the Black Flag in History, Memory, and Myth.* University Press of Kentucky, 2015.

Bell, Caryn Cossé. *Creole New Orleans in the Revolutionary Atlantic 1775–1877.* Louisiana State University Press, 2023.

Bergeron, Arthur W., Jr. *Guide to Louisiana Confederate Military Units 1861–1865.* Louisiana State University Press, 1989.

———. *The Louisiana Purchase Bicentennial Series in Louisiana History, Volume V, The Civil War in Louisiana, Part A: Military Activity.* Center for Louisiana Studies, University of Louisiana at Lafayette, 2002.

Bever, Megan L. *At War with King Alcohol: Debating Drinking and Masculinity in the Civil War.* University of North Carolina Press, 2022.

Bielski, Mark F. *Sons of the White Eagle in the American Civil War: Divided Poles in a Divided Nation.* Casemate Publishers, 2016.

Bledsoe, Andrew S. *Citizen-Officers: The Union and Confederate Volunteer Junior Officer Corps in the American Civil War.* Louisiana State University Press, 2015.

Booth, Andrew B., comp. *Records of Louisiana Confederate Soldiers and Louisiana Confederate Commands, 3 volumes.* 1920. Reprint Company, 1984.

Bragg, Jefferson Davis. *Louisiana in the Confederacy.* Louisiana State University Press, 1941, 1969, 1997.

Brasseaux, Carl A. *Acadian to Cajun: Transformation of a People, 1803–1877.* University Press of Mississippi, 1992.

Brasseaux, Carl A., and Keith P. Fontenot. *Steamboats on Louisiana's Bayous: A History and Directory.* Louisiana State University Press, 2004.

Brasseaux, Carl A., Keith P. Fontenot, and Claude F. Oubre. *Creoles of Color in the Bayou Country.* University Press of Mississippi, 1994.

Carmichael, Peter S. *The War for the Common Soldier: How Men Thought, Fought, and Survived in Civil War Armies.* University of North Carolina Press, 2018.

Casey, Powell A. *Encyclopedia of Forts, Posts, Named Camps, and Other Military Installations in Louisiana, 1700–1981.* Claitor's Publishing Division, 1983.

Cashin, Joan. *War Stuff: The Struggle for Human and Environmental Resources in the American Civil War.* Cambridge University Press, 2018.

———, ed. *The War Was You and Me: Civilians in the American Civil War.* Princeton University Press, 2002.

Caskey, Willie Malvin. *Secession and Restoration of Louisiana.* Louisiana State University Press, 1938.

Clampitt, Bradley R. *Lost Causes: Confederate Demobilization & the Making of Veteran Identity.* Louisiana State University Press, 2022.

Cunningham, H. H. *Doctors in Gray: The Confederate Medical Service.* Louisiana State University Press, 1958, Reprint, 1986.

Cunningham, O. Edward. *Shiloh and the Western Campaign of 1862. Edited by Gary D. Joiner and Timothy B. Smith.* Savas Beatie, 2007.

Cutrer, Thomas W. *Theater of a Separate War: The Civil War West of the Mississippi River 1861–1865.* Revised Edition. University of North Carolina Press, 2023.

Daniel, Larry J. *Shiloh: The Battle That Changed the Civil War.* Touchstone, 1997.

Davis, William C., and Sue Heth Bell, eds. *The Whartons' War: The Civil War Correspondence of General Gabriel C. Wharton & Anne Radford Wharton, 1863–1865.* University of North Carolina Press, 2002.

Dawdy, Shannon Lee. *Building the Devil's Empire: French Colonial New Orleans.* University of Chicago Press, 2008.

Downs, Gregory P. *After Appomattox: Military Occupation and the Ends of War.* Harvard University Press, 2015.

Dufour, Charles L. *Gentle Tiger: The Gallant Life of Roberdeau Wheat.* Louisiana State University Press, 1957, 1985, 1999.

———. *The Night the War Was Lost.* Doubleday, 1960.

Edmonds, David C. *The Guns of Port Hudson: The Investment, Siege and Reduction, Volume Two.* Acadian Press, 1984.

——. *Yankee Autumn in Acadiana: A Narrative of the Great Texas Overland Expedition through Southwestern Louisiana October–December 1863*. Center for Louisiana Studies, 2005.

Edwards, Laura F. *Scarlett Doesn't Live Here Anymore: Southern Women in the Civil War Era*. University of Illinois Press, 2000.

Escott, Paul D. *Military Necessity: Civil-Military Relations in the Confederacy*. Praeger Security International, 2006.

Estaville, Lawrence E., Jr. *Confederate Neckties: Louisiana Railroads in the Civil War*. McGinty Publications, 1989.

Faust, Drew Gilpin. *Mothers of Invention: Women of the Slaveholding South in the American Civil War*. Vintage Books, 1997.

——. *This Republic of Suffering: Death and the American Civil War*. Vintage Books, 2008.

Fellman, Michael. *Inside War: The Guerrilla Conflict in Missouri During the American Civil War*. Oxford University Press, 1989.

Frank, Lisa Tendrich. *The Civilian War: Confederate Women and Union Soldiers during Sherman's March*. Louisiana State University Press, 2015.

Frank, Lisa Tendrich, and LeeAnn Whites, eds. *Household War: How Americans Lived and Fought the Civil War*. University of Georgia Press, 2020.

Frazier, Donald S. *Fire in the Cane Field: The Federal Invasion of Louisiana and Texas, January 1861–January 1863*. State House Press, 2009.

Freehling, William H. *The Road to Disunion, Volume II: Secessionists Triumphant, 1854–1861*. Oxford University Press, 2007.

Gallagher, Gary. *The Confederate War*. Harvard University Press, 1997.

——. *The Union War*. Harvard University Press, 2011.

Gannon, James P. *Irish Rebels, Confederate Tigers: The 6th Louisiana Volunteers, 1861–1865*. Savas Publishing, 1998.

Gienapp, William E. *Abraham Lincoln and Civil War America: A Biography*. Oxford University Press, 2002.

Glatthaar, Joseph T. *General Lee's Army: From Victory to Collapse*. Free Press, 2008.

Glymph, Thavolia. *Out of the House of Bondage: The Transformation of the Plantation Household*. Cambridge University Press, 2008.

——. *The Women's Fight: The Civil War's Battles for Home, Freedom, and Nation*. University of North Carolina Press, 2020.

Grimsley, Mark. *The Hard Hand of War: Union Military Policy Toward Southern Civilians, 1861–1865*. Cambridge University Press, 1995, Reprint, 1996.

Gudmestad, Robert. *Steamboats and the Rise of the Cotton Kingdom*. Louisiana State University Press, 2011.

Hall, Gwendolyn Midlo. *Africans in Colonial Louisiana: The Development of Afro-Creole Culture in the Eighteenth Century.* Louisiana State University Press, 1992.

Hearn, Chester G. *The Capture of New Orleans, 1862.* Louisiana State University Press, 1995.

Hess, Earl J. *The Civil War in the West: Victory and Defeat from the Appalachians to the Mississippi.* University of North Carolina Press, 2012.

———. *Civil War Supply and Strategy: Feeding Men and Moving Armies.* Louisiana State University Press, 2020.

Hewitt, Lawrence Lee, and Arthur W. Bergeron Jr., eds. *Louisianians in the Civil War.* University of Missouri Press, 2002.

Hirsch, Arnold R., and Joseph Logsdon, eds. *Creole New Orleans: Race and Americanization.* Louisiana State University Press, 1992.

Hollandsworth, James G., Jr. *The Louisiana Native Guards: The Black Military Experience During the Civil War.* Louisiana State University Press, 1995.

Horn, Jonathan. *The Man Who Would Not Be Washington: Robert E. Lee's Civil War and His Decision That Changed American History.* Scribner, 2015.

Hughes, Nathaniel Cheairs, Jr. *The Pride of the Confederate Artillery: The Washington Artillery in the Army of Tennessee.* Louisiana State University Press, 1997.

———. *Pistols and Politics: Feuds, Factions, and the Struggle for Order in Louisiana's Florida Parishes, 1810–1935.* Louisiana State University Press, 2018.

Hyde, Samuel C., Jr., ed. *The Enigmatic South: Toward Civil War and Its Legacies.* Louisiana State University Press, 2014.

Jimerson, Randall C. *The Private Civil War: Popular Thought During the Sectional Conflict.* Louisiana State University Press, 1988.

Johnson, Michael P., and James L. Roark. *Black Masters: A Free Family of Color in the Old South.* Norton, 1984.

Jones, Terry L. *Louisiana in the Civil War: Essays for the Sesquicentennial.* CreateSpace, 2015.

———. *Lee's Tigers: The Louisiana Infantry in the Army of Northern Virginia.* Louisiana State University Press, 1987, 2002.

———. *Lee's Tigers Revisited: The Louisiana Infantry in the Army of Northern Virginia.* Louisiana State University Press, 2017.

Kelley, Laura D. *The Irish in New Orleans.* University of Louisiana at Lafayette Press, 2014.

Lang, Andrew F. *In the Wake of War: Military Occupation, Emancipation, and Civil War America.* Louisiana State University Press, 2017.

Leigh, Philip. *Trading with the Enemy: The Covert Economy During the American Civil War.* Westholme Publishing, 2014.

Leonard, Elizabeth D. *Benjamin Franklin Butler: A Noisy, Fearless Life.* University of North Carolina Press, 2022.

Lowe, Richard. *Walker's Texas Division C.S.A. Greyhounds of the Trans-Mississippi.* Louisiana State University Press, 2004.

Marvel, William. *Lee's Last Retreat: The Fight to Appomattox.* University of North Carolina Press, 2002.

Matsui, John H. *The First Republican Army: The Army of Virginia and the Radicalization of the Civil War.* University of Virginia Press, 2016.

Meier, Kathryn Shively. *Nature's Civil War: Common Soldiers and the Environment in 1862 Virginia.* University of North Carolina Press, 2013.

McCurry, Stephanie. *Confederate Reckoning: Power and Politics in the Civil War South.* Harvard University Press, 2010.

McPherson, James M. *For Cause and Comrades: Why Men Fought in the Civil War.* Oxford University Press, 1997.

Miller, Brian Craig. *Empty Sleeves: Amputation in the Civil War South.* University of Georgia Press, 2015.

Mills, Gary B. *The Forgotten People: Cane River's Creoles of Color.* Louisiana State University Press, 1977.

Mingus, Scott L., Sr. The Louisiana Tigers in the Gettysburg Campaign: June–July 1863. Louisiana State University Press, 2009.

Mitchell, Reid. *Civil War Soldiers: Their Expectations and Their Experiences.* Viking Penguin, 1988.

Moore, Albert Burton. *Conscription and Conflict in the Confederacy.* Macmillan, 1924.

Moriarty, Donald Peter, II. *A Fine Body of Men: The Orleans Light Horse, Louisiana Cavalry, 1861–1865.* Historic New Orleans Collection, 2014.

Nelson, Scott, and Carol Sheriff. *A People at War: Civilians and Soldiers in America's Civil War, 1854–1877.* Oxford University Press, 2008.

Noe, Kenneth W. *Reluctant Rebels: The Confederates Who Joined the Army after 1861.* University of North Carolina Press, 2010.

Norton, Herman. *Rebel Religion: The Story of the Confederate Chaplains.* Bethany Press, 1961.

Oates, Stephen B. *Confederate Cavalry West of the River.* University of Texas Press, 1961.

———. *With Malice Toward None: A Biography of Abraham Lincoln.* Harper Perennial, 1994. Reprint, 2011.

O'Donovan, Susan Eva. *Becoming Free in the Cotton South.* Harvard University Press, 2007.

Parrish, T. Michael. *Richard Taylor: Soldier Prince of Dixie.* University of North Carolina Press, 1992.

Peña, Christopher G. *Touched By War: Battles Fought in the Lafourche District.* C.G.P. Press, 1998.

Pierson, Michael D. *Mutiny at Fort Jackson: The Untold Story of the Fall of New Orleans.* University of North Carolina Press, 2008.

Pitts, Charles F. *Chaplains in Gray: The Confederate Chaplains' Story.* Broadman Press, 1957. Reprint, R.M.J.C. Publications, 2003.

Plater, David D. *The Butlers of Iberville Parish, Louisiana.* Louisiana State University Press, 2015.

Ramold, Steven J. *Baring the Iron Hand: Discipline in the Union Army.* Northern Illinois University Press, 2010.

Remini, Robert V. *The Battle of New Orleans: Andrew Jackson and America's First Military Victory.* Penguin Books, 1999.

Richard, Allan C., Jr., and Mary Margaret Higginbotham Richard. *The Defense of Vicksburg: A Louisiana Chronicle.* Texas A&M University Press, 2004.

Ripley, C. Peter. *Slaves and Freedmen in Civil War Louisiana.* Louisiana State University Press, 1976.

Roland, Charles P. *Louisiana Sugar Planters During the Civil War.* Louisiana State University Press, 1957. Reprint, 1997.

Romero, Sidney J. *Religion in the Rebel Ranks.* University Press of America, 1983.

Rosen, Robert N. *The Jewish Confederates.* University of South Carolina Press, 2000.

Royster, Charles. *The Destructive War: William Tecumseh Sherman, Stonewall Jackson, and the Americans.* Knopf, 1991.

Sacher, John M. *Confederate Conscription and the Struggle for Southern Soldiers.* Louisiana State University Press, 2021.

———. *A Perfect War of Politics: Parties, Politicians, and Democracy in Louisiana, 1824–1861.* Louisiana State University Press, 2003.

Sainlaude, Stève. *France and the American Civil War: A Diplomatic History.* Translated by Jessica Edwards. University of North Carolina Press, 2019.

Schreckengost, Gary. *The First Louisiana Special Battalion: Wheat's Tigers in the Civil War.* McFarland, 2008.

Scriber, Terry G., and Theresa Arnold-Scriber. *The Fourth Louisiana Battalion in the Civil War: A History and Roster.* McFarland, 2008.

Shattuck, Gardiner H., Jr. *A Shield and Hiding Place: The Religious Life of the Civil War Armies.* Mercer University Press, 1987.

Sheehan-Dean, Aaron. *The Calculus of Violence: How Americans Fought the Civil War.* Harvard University Press, 2018.

———. *Why Confederates Fought: Family and Nation in Civil War Virginia.* University of North Carolina Press, 2007.

———, ed. *Struggle for a Vast Future.* Osprey, 2006.

Smith, Timothy B. *This Great Battlefield of Shiloh: History, Memory, and the Establishment of a Civil War National Military Park.* University of Tennessee Press, 2004.

Stalling, Stuart. *Louisianians in the Western Confederacy: The Adams-Gibson Brigade in the Civil War.* McFarland, Publishers, 2010.

Sutherland, Daniel E. *A Savage Conflict: The Decisive Role of Guerrillas in the American Civil War.* The University of North Carolina Press, 2009.

———, ed. *Guerrillas, Unionists, and Violence on the Confederate Home Front.* The University of Arkansas Press, 1999.

Taylor, Amy Murrell. *Embattled Freedom: Journeys through the Civil War's Slave Refugee Camps.* University of North Carolina Press, 2018.

Thrasher, Christopher. *Miserable Little Conglomeration: A Social History of the Port Hudson Campaign.* University of Tennessee Press, 2023.

Ural, Susannah J. *Don't Hurry Me Down to Hades: The Civil War in the Words of Those Who Lived It.* Osprey, 2013.

Ward, J. Matthew. *Garden of Ruins: Occupied Louisiana in the Civil War.* Louisiana State University Press, 2024.

Weitz, Mark A. *More Damning than Slaughter: Desertion in the Confederate Army.* University of Nebraska Press, 2005.

Wesley, Timothy L. *The Politics of Faith During the Civil War.* Louisiana State University Press, 2013.

White, Jonathan W. *Midnight in America: Darkness, Sleep, and Dreams during the Civil War.* University of North Carolina Press, 2017.

Whites, LeeAnn, and Alicia P. Long, eds. *Occupied Women: Gender, Military Occupation, and the American Civil War.* Louisiana State University Press, 2012.

Wiley, Bell Irvin. *The Life of Billy Yank: The Common Soldier of the Union.* Louisiana State University Press, 1952, Reprinted 1981.

———. *The Life of Johnny Reb: The Common Soldier of the Confederacy.* Louisiana State University Press, 1943. Reprint, 1999.

Williams, T. Harry. *P. G. T. Beauregard: Napoleon in Gray.* Louisiana State University Press, 1955. Reprint, 1995.

Winters, John D. *The Civil War in Louisiana.* Louisiana State University Press, 1963. Reprint, 1991.

Woods, Michael E. *Emotional and Sectional Conflict in the Antebellum United States.* Cambridge University Press, 2014.

Woodworth, Steven E. *While God is Marching On: The Religious World of Civil War Soldiers.* University Press of Kansas, 2001.

Articles

Bergeron, Arthur W., Jr. "Prison Life at Camp Pratt." *Louisiana History: The Journal of the Louisiana Historical Association* 14, no. 4 (Autumn 1973): 386–91.

Buck, Martina. "A Louisiana Prisoner-of-War on Johnson's Island, 1863–65." *Louisiana History: The Journal of the Louisiana Historical Association* 4, no. 3 (Summer 1963): 233–42.

Dew, Charles B. "The Long Lost Returns: The Candidates and Their Totals in Louisiana's Secession Election." *Louisiana History: The Journal of the Louisiana Historical Association* 10, no. 4 (Autumn 1969): 353–69.

———. "Who Won the Secession Election in Louisiana?" *Journal of Southern History* 36, no. 1 (February 1970): 18–32.

Duncan, Georgena. "Uncertain Loyalties: Dual Enlistment in the Third and Fourth Arkansas Cavalry, USV." *Arkansas Historical Quarterly* 72, no. 4 (Winter 2013): 305–32.

Durham, Ken. "'Dear Rebecca': The Civil War Letters of William Edwards Paxton, 1861–1863." *Louisiana History: The Journal of the Louisiana Historical Association* 20, no. 2 (Spring 1979): 169–196.

Estaville, Lawrence E., Jr. "A Small Contribution: Louisiana's Short Rural Railroads in the Civil War." *Louisiana History: The Journal of the Louisiana Historical Association* 18, no. 1 (Winter, 1977): 87–103.

Faust, Drew Gilpin. "Altars of Sacrifice: Confederate Women and the Narratives of War." *Journal of American History* 76, no. 4 (March 1990): 1200–1228.

———. "Christian Soldiers: The Meaning of Revivalism in the Confederate Army." *Journal of Southern History,* 53, no. 1 (February 1987): 63–90.

Gleeson, David T. "The Rhetoric of Insurrection and Fear: The Politics of Slave Management in Confederate Georgia." *Journal of Southern History* 89, no. 2 (May 2023): 237–66.

Glymph, Thavolia. "Noncombatant Military Laborers in the Civil War." *OAH Magazine of History* 26, no. 2, Civil War at 150: Mobilizing for War (April 2012): 25–29.

Haarman, Albert W. "The Spanish Conquest of British West Florida, 1779–1781." *Florida Historical Quarterly* 30, no. 2 (October 1960): 107–34.

Holmes, Jack D. L. "Alabama's Bloodiest Day of the American Revolution: Counterattack at the Village, January 7, 1781." *Alabama Review* 29, no. 3 (1976): 208–19.

Hyde, Samuel C., Jr. "Bushwhacking and Barn Burning: Civil War Operations and the Florida Parishes' Tradition of Violence." *Louisiana History: The Journal of the Louisiana Historical Association* 36, no. 2 (Spring 1995): 171–86.

Janney, Caroline E. "Free to Go Where We Liked: The Army of Northern Virginia after Appomattox." *Journal of the Civil War Era* 9, no. 1 (March 2019): 4–28.

Johnson, Ludwell H. "Contraband Trade During the Last Year of the Civil War." *Mississippi Valley Historical Review* 49, no. 4 (March 1963): 635–52.

———. "Trading with the Union: The Evolution of Confederate Policy." *Virginia Magazine of History and Biography* 78, no. 3 (July 1970): 308–325.

Joiner, Gary D. "'No Pardons to Ask nor Apologies to Make': The Journal of William Henry King." *Louisiana History: The Journal of the Louisiana Historical Association* 53, no. 1 (Winter 2012): 30–50.

Jones, Terry L. "Going Back into the Union at Last." *Civil War Times Illustrated* 29, no. 6 (1991): 12–17.

Kajencki, Colonel Francis C. "The Louisiana Tiger." *Louisiana History: The Journal of the Louisiana Historical Association* 15, no. 1 (Winter 1974): 49–58.

Laver, Tara Zachary, and William H. Whitney. "'Where Duty Shall Call:' The Baton Rouge Civil War Letters of William H. Whitney." *Louisiana History: The Journal of the Louisiana Historical Association* 46, no. 3 (Summer 2005): 333–70.

Meiners, Fredericka. "Hamilton P. Bee in the Red River Campaign of 1864." *Southwestern Historical Quarterly* 78, no. 1 (July 1974): 21–44.

Michot, Stephen S. "'War Is Still Raging in This Part of the Country': Oath-Taking, Conscription, and Guerrilla War in Louisiana's Lafourche Region." *Louisiana History: The Journal of the Louisiana Historical Association* 38, no. 2 (Spring 1997): 157–84.

Nelson, Michael C. "Writing during Wartime: Gender and Literacy in the American Civil War." *Journal of American Studies* 31, no. 1 (April 1997): 43–68.

Odom, Van D. "The Political Career of Thomas Overton Moore, Secession Governor of Louisiana." *Louisiana Historical Quarterly* 26, no. 4 (October 1943): 3–82.

Owsley, Frank Lawrence. "The Confederacy and King Cotton: A Study in Economic Coercion." *North Carolina Historical Review* 6, no. 4 (October 1929): 371–97.

Power, Sally P. "A Vermonter's Account of the Red River Campaign." *Louisiana History: The Journal of the Louisiana History Association* 40, no. 3 (Summer 1999): 355–64.

Rasmussen, Hans. "The Monetary Crisis of the Fall of New Orleans." *Civil War Book Review* 24, issue >2 (2022): 1–5.

Robinson, King S. "Sustaining the Glory: Spain's Melting Pot Army in the Lower Mississippi Valley, 1779–1781." *Southeast Louisiana Review* 1 (Fall 2008): 5–23.

Roland, Charles P. "Louisiana and Secession." *Louisiana History: The Journal of the Louisiana Historical Association* 19, no. 4 (Autumn 1978): 389–99.

Romero, Sidney J. "Louisiana Clergy and the Confederate Army." *Louisiana History: Journal of the Louisiana Historical Association,* 2, no. 3 (Summer 1961): 277–300.

Ruminski, Jarret. "'Tradyville': The Contraband Trade and the Problem of Loyalty in Civil War Mississippi." *Journal of the Civil War Era* 2, no. 4 (December 2012): 511–37.

Sacher, John M. "'Our Interest and Destiny Are the Same:' Gov. Thomas Overton Moore and Confederate Loyalty." *Louisiana History: The Journal of the Louisiana Historical Association* 49, no. 3 (Summer 2008): 261–86.

———. "'Twenty-Negro,' or Overseer Law: A Reconsideration." *Journal of the Civil War Era* 7, no. 2 (June 2017): 269–92.

Sacher, John M. "'A Very Disagreeable Business': Confederate Conscription in Louisiana." *Civil War History* 53, no. 2 (June 2007): 141–69.

Schweninger, Loren. "Antebellum Free Persons of Color in Postbellum Louisiana." *Louisiana History: The Journal of the Louisiana Historical Association* 30, no. 4 (Autumn 1989): 345–64.

Shugg, Roger Wallace. "A Suppressed Co-Operationist Protest Against Secession." *Louisiana Historical Quarterly* 19, no. 1 (January 1936): 3–7.

Smith, Kathleen T. "The Letters of John Achilles Harris, Confederate Soldier, To His Wife, Rebecca Stringfellow Harris 1861–1864." *North Louisiana History* 6, no. 1/2 (Winter/Spring 2015): 169–96.

Smith, Michael Thomas. "'For Love of Cotton': Nathaniel Banks, Union Strategy, and the Red River Campaign." *Louisiana History: The Journal of the Louisiana Historical Association* 51, no. 1 (Winter 2010): 5–26.

Surdam, David G. "Traders or Traitors: Northern Cotton Trading During the Civil War." *Business and Economic History* 28, no. 2 (Winter 1999): 301–12.

Taylor, Ethel. "Discontent in Confederate Louisiana." *Louisiana History: The Journal of the Louisiana Historical Association* 2, no. 4 (Autumn, 1961): 410–28.

Wade, Michael G. "'I Would Rather Be among the Comanches': The Military Occupation of Southwest Louisiana, 1865." *Louisiana History: The Journal of the Louisiana Historical Association* 39, no. 1 (Winter 1998): 45–64.

Wallace, Lee A., Jr. "Coppens' Louisiana Zouaves." *Civil War History* 8, Issue 3 (September 1962): 269–82.

Whites, LeeAnn. "Forty Shirts and a Wagonload of Wheat: Women, the Domestic Supply Line, and the Civil War on the Western Border." *Journal of the Civil War Era,* 1, no. 1 (March 2011): 56–78.

Williams, Robert W., Jr., and Ralph A. Wooster. "Camp Life in Civil War Louisiana: The Letters of Private Isaac Dunbar Affleck." *Louisiana History: The Journal of the Louisiana Historical Association* 5, no. 2 (Spring 1964): 187–201.

Unpublished Dissertations and Theses

Culpepper, Scott. "The Life, Letters, and Legacy of Dr. Bartholomew Egan." Master's thesis, Northwestern State University of Louisiana, 2000.

Hieronymus, Frank L. "For Now and Forever: The Chaplains of the Confederate
    States Army." PhD diss., University of California, Los Angeles, 1964. ProQuest/
    UMI.
Pritchard, William Ryan. "Moving Toward Freedom? African-American Mobility and
    the Perils of Emancipation in Civil-War Era Louisiana, 1862–1867." PhD diss.,
    University at Buffalo, State University of New York, 2016.
Woodward, Colin Edward. "Marching Masters: Slavery, Race, and the Confederate
    Army, 1861–1865." PhD diss., Louisiana State University, 2005.

INDEX